BOOKNOTES

Booknotes

America's Finest Authors on Reading, Writing, and the Power of Ideas

Brian Lamb

TIMES BOOKS

RANDOM HOUSE

*This book is dedicated to those who taught me in
the early years in Lafayette, Indiana:*

*To my high school broadcasting teacher, William S. Fraser,
who taught me the basics of interviewing.*

*To C. J. Hopkins, my high school journalism teacher,
who taught me to ask who, what, why, where, when, and how?*

*To Henry Rosenthal, who gave me my first job in radio
and who let me do everything for $1 an hour.*

*And to Richard F. Shively, who gave me my first job in television
and told me if you program a commercial television station
for only your taste, you'll go broke.*

Study has been for me the sovereign remedy against all the disappointments of life. I have never known any trouble that an hour's reading would not dissipate.

—*Montesquieu*
(1689–1755)

I know there are good books and bad books. It can be fiction or nonfiction. It can be philosophy. It can be history. Really, when it comes to books, it is its value, its depth. You make an acquaintance with a book as you do with a person. After ten or fifteen pages, you know with whom you have to deal. When you have a good book, you really have something of importance. Books are as important as friends and maybe more so. Because all of us are living in very limited circles, books enable us to run away from them.

—*Remarks by former Israeli Prime Minister Shimon Peres,*
to C-SPAN's Susan Swain on the Washington Journal.
The interview was televised on July 4, 1996,
from Independence Hall in Philadelphia, where
Mr. Peres was awarded the Liberty Medal.

Acknowledgments

As many *Booknotes* authors have mentioned on the show, an idea becomes a book with the help of many. I would like to thank Christopher Ogden, who planted the seed for the possibility of a book on *Booknotes,* and author Richard Norton Smith for suggesting I contact literary agent Raphael Sagalyn to see if the proposal would interest any publishers. The support and informal guidance of author David Halberstam have also been an inspiration to me throughout the project.

I would also like to thank Peter Osnos, former publisher of Times Books at Random House, who believed in the idea enough to acquire the book. Peter played a pivotal role in making this project happen. When he came to visit C-SPAN in the early stages of this book, he advised me that there would be at least one major crisis over the course of the project. Peter's foresight came true in the spring of 1996, when Jeanne Daley, who had done most of the initial research and draft outlines for the book, decided to leave C-SPAN and return to practicing law at a federal government agency.

The researcher position was quickly filled by Robin Scullin, who fortunately had a publishing background and the tenacity to jump right into the manuscript. Her understanding of authors (particularly this one) and her editorial contributions helped me complete a work that lets the *Booknotes* writers speak for themselves. Robin's enthusiasm and dedication made all the difference in making this train get out of the station and run on time.

Also at C-SPAN, Susan Swain, our executive vice president, helped me focus the book on author stories about writing. Her editing skills shaped the direction of this work from start to finish. C-SPAN's other executive vice president, Rob Kennedy, also had a hand in reviewing the manuscript, and provided important counsel on the business aspects of this book as well.

This book was fine-tuned with the red pencil of Geoff Shandler, our dedicated editor then at Times Books. Geoff line-edited the manuscript not once but several times. While numerous authors on *Booknotes* have said that their editors were sometimes too busy to attend to the details of their actual book, I know that Geoff has reviewed every sentence that is printed here.

Other C-SPAN employees made important contributions, including Barkley Kern, Kat Yakatis, Lea Anne Long, Christine Cupaiuolo, Nick Aretakis, Hope Landy, Ruth Kane, Marge Amey, Paul Hanulya, Deborah Lamb, Amanda Adams, Kevin Leonard, and Bruce Collins. In addition, special thanks to the *Booknotes* production team for their work on the program over the years, especially Greg Barker, Eileen Quinn, Barry Katz, Peter Slen, Sarah Trahern, Connie Brod, and Bret Betsill.

The following C-SPAN Summer 1996 Interns helped us review 400 transcripts for possible author photos: Shannon Claiborne, Susan Ihrke (now a member of the C-SPAN Viewer Services staff), Michael Tetuan, Marc Knightdale, and Sarita Venkat.

A special thanks to Dr. John Splaine, a University of Maryland professor and C-SPAN consultant, for his encouragement.

This book would not have happened without the contributions of the authors and all of the writers who have dedicated a full hour of their time to telling *Booknotes* viewers about the who, what, why, where, when, and how they write.

This book and the series it chronicles are a reflection of the C-SPAN network. Therefore, in closing, it's most appropriate to thank a group of people who have made C-SPAN a reality—our network's board of directors. C-SPAN was founded by and continues to get its major funding from the cable television industry. Since 1978, 107 cable executives have served on our board, contributing their time and energy to C-SPAN's development. Tom Baxter, former president of Comcast Cable and C-SPAN's chairman for the past two years, is a regular *Booknotes* watcher and has lent his enthusiastic support to the creation of this book.

Contents

REPORTERS

PUBLIC FIGURES

Contents / xiii

Introduction

"Where do you write?" "Do you use a computer?" "How did you research this?" "What first got you interested in writing about this?" "How did you get a publisher's attention?" "Why are these folks in your dedication?"

THESE ARE THE KINDS of questions asked each week on *Booknotes,* an author-interview program on our cable network, C-SPAN. After nine years and nearly 470 author interviews, these basic questions still yield interesting, sometimes surprising answers. Forrest McDonald writes history on his rural Alabama porch—naked. Richard Ben Cramer interviewed 1,000 people for his landmark 1992 political biography, *What It Takes: The Way to the White House.* Clare Brandt explored Lake Champlain and the Hudson River in small boats for her biography of Benedict Arnold. Robert Caro read through 650,000 pages from the LBJ Library for the second book in his Lyndon Johnson series. Cheryl Wudunn dedicated the book she and her husband, Nicholas Kristof, coauthored on China to the sister she lost in the KAL airliner downing.

Shelby Foote, the historian who became familiar to television audiences through his appearances in Ken Burns's television series *The Civil War,* has developed a routine for his writing. Virtually a hermit when in the middle of a book, he writes and sleeps in the same room, committing himself to writing 500 to 600 words a day—all with a "dip pen." It took him twenty years to complete his 1.5-million-word trilogy on the Civil War, so long that he moved two times during the writing, penning the books in three different locations in Memphis.

Stories like these, known to regular viewers of C-SPAN's *Booknotes* series, illustrate that the *how* of a book is almost always as interesting as the *what* of a book.

THIS BOOK ASSEMBLES in one place some of the best of *Booknotes*'s weekly author interviews, with an emphasis on the process of writing and publishing. It is intended for people who love books and writing. Here you'll read 120 authors' tales about how and why they write, where they work, and what happens if they get writer's block. We also see how book editors, literary agents, spouses, and other family members play essential roles in the process of making a book. After a while, you begin to get a sense of just how challenging it is to write for a living.

We're all familiar with best-sellers. They are widely bought, read, and talked about. But they are hardly the whole picture of the publishing industry. Fifty to seventy thousand new titles are published each year; only a few hundred make the best-seller lists. Nor do the big money, celebrity book contracts reflect the experiences of most authors. Although he'd published several books, when he switched his venue to poetry, former President Jimmy Carter couldn't get a publisher interested. For years, after each rejection, he'd wait awhile and then resubmit his work. Journalist Robert Timberg had to take out a home equity loan to finish his book about five Vietnam-era figures. These are the kinds of stories—the devotion to the craft, the willingness to take risks—that you'll find in the pages of this book.

Booknotes viewers and other readers drawn to this book are not likely to be average book consumers. One of the things I've learned since getting involved with books and authors is that there are book buyers and there are book lovers. The book business is growing at an enviable rate—some 8 percent annually; however, 40 percent of all books bought in the United States are bought in the fourth quarter—the holiday season—and half of the books bought *are never read.* By contrast, *Booknotes* viewers are readers. We know because we hear from them often with their suggestions for our program.

The roots of this book are long, much longer than the nine-year history of *Booknotes.* A longtime consumer of television, I was one of those people who for years watched in frustration as the commercial networks' morning shows served up five-minute author interviews. Surmising the dedication these authors had put into their subjects, I was nearly always left wanting more than these quick bites. Still, it took more than nine years after I helped the cable industry launch C-SPAN for books to become an integral part of our network's public affairs menu.

·   ·   ·

A BOOK ABOUT VIETNAM paved the way for C-SPAN's love affair with the written word.

In 1988, Random House published Neil Sheehan's long-awaited treatment of the Vietnam War, *A Bright Shining Lie.* Assigned to cover the war first for UPI and later for *The New York Times,* Neil Sheehan filed reports that filled the front pages of America's newspapers during the war years. Later, it was he who got the famous Pentagon Papers story from the antiwar activist Daniel Ellsberg. Mr. Sheehan's book on Vietnam, sixteen years in the making, was anticipated to be one of the definitive works on that chapter of our country's history.

Vietnam was an important topic for C-SPAN. It had shaped an American generation. And, two decades after the fall of Saigon, the echoes of Vietnam continued to be heard in debates in the halls of Congress— C-SPAN's bread-and-butter programming fare. Vietnam was also part of my personal history: I spent two of the war years in the Navy, working the media relations desk at the Pentagon. All these reasons contributed to C-SPAN's invitation to Neil Sheehan: would he come to our studio and tape for two and a half hours, telling his story?

Neil Sheehan said yes. Our resulting special series—which aired in five half-hour segments during September and October of 1988—gave birth to *Booknotes.* That experience, and the response to it (in the final installment we opened our phone lines so viewers could participate) made it clear there was an audience for a long-form author interview program.

Booknotes launched officially on Sunday, April 2, 1989. We chose Sunday nights at 8 P.M. Eastern and Pacific times, because we knew it would be nearly impossible to have that time slot preempted by live coverage of the House of Representatives, C-SPAN's core programming commitment. (Sunday sessions of the House, while not unimaginable, are extremely rare.) Also, we hoped to capitalize on the Sunday night public affairs audience CBS had long established with *60 Minutes.*

After nine years we're still not sure how many people watch *Booknotes.* C-SPAN, which was founded in 1979 by the cable industry, is carried by its affiliates as a public service. They don't ask us to measure ratings, so we've never had them taken. Anecdotally, however, *Booknotes* seems to have attracted something of a following.

In 1994, we celebrated the fifth anniversary of *Booknotes* with a two-hour special that told the series' history. During the program's two breaks we ran a thirty-second spot telling viewers that the first 500 people who wrote us with a self-addressed, stamped envelope would receive a small commemorative brass bookmark.

Two days later, on Tuesday, a call came into the network's executive suite. Would we please come down to the mailroom, quickly? Zubair Hussain, our administrative assistant, and Angie Hunter, then our manager of viewer services, stood there, surrounded by gray canvas bags from the postal service. Hundreds of envelopes, many arriving by express mail services, sat in stacks around the room. It was quickly determined that additional help would be needed to process the requests. In all, 10,000 *Booknotes* viewers wrote in.

Oh, yes. Despite our caveat that only the first 500 responses would be honored, all 10,000 got their *Booknotes* bookmark. How can you turn away friends?

These days whenever I travel I seem to find friends of *Booknotes*, although they invariably call it "Book Beat" or "Bookends"—almost anything but *Booknotes*. What is enjoyable is that our conversations are never about *me*. Invariably, people want to tell me about a favorite author or about a writer who's enraged them.

That's how it should be. The focus on *Booknotes*—as in this book—is always on the authors. If you watch the program, you'll see one of the simplest sets on television: two chairs, a coffee table we purchased at a local discount store, and a black backdrop. Our only music is the classical piece that has opened and closed the program since the beginning—Tomaso Albinoni's Concerto No. 5. The message is, nothing should distract from the author and his or her story.

My questions are also intentionally simple. Again, my goal is for viewers to hear the author, not the interviewer. And, it's always an hour interview, straight through, no breaks; authors who can't commit the time don't get on.

Booknotes books are always hardback; always nonfiction; always history, politics, or public policy—the kinds of topics that extend the public affairs programming we do regularly on C-SPAN; and they're widely available, so that viewers anywhere in the country can find them.

One other *Booknotes* peculiarity: authors can only appear once on the program, no matter how many other books they publish. That's a concept borrowed from *Broadcasting* magazine, the granddaddy of television trade publications. Each week, *Broadcasting* publishes a profile of an industry leader. But it happens only once in your career, no matter what else you go on to accomplish.

That "one-time" rule is what led us, in 1996, to launch our second book series. This program, dubbed *About Books,* covers book and author events—lectures, book signings, readings, printing plant tours, book club discussions, and the like. This series allows C-SPAN2 viewers to see the behind-the-scenes activities that go into making books and to hear how books are being discussed in different venues across the country.

If you're not familiar with C-SPAN and C-SPAN2, *Booknotes* or *About Books* can provide you with a good introduction to our programming concept. We're a private, nonprofit company that got its start with the simple idea of using television to give Americans a front row seat at national institutions. C-SPAN has as its core daily telecasts of sessions of the U.S. House of Representatives; C-SPAN2 carries U.S. Senate proceedings live. Beyond that, you'll find seminars, press conferences, congressional hearings, election coverage—the kinds of things that reflect the ongoing national dialogue about issues. Books, which often either affect or record our national debate, are an important adjunct to our other public affairs programming. You'll find all this—the Congress, the book events, the seminars, everything—offered in long form and without commentary. And, since our affiliates offer C-SPAN as a public service, there are no commercials.

If you tune in to either of our book series, you'll soon note that authors from two publishing houses, Simon & Schuster and Random House, are frequently featured; with nearly one quarter of all sales of nonfiction hardbacks in the United States, these two publishers dominate the business. However, we regularly reach out to the works of smaller publishers, like those specializing in African-American authors or conservative writers, and to some of the 114 university presses throughout the country.

BUT MORE ABOUT THIS BOOK. In its pages, you'll find some former presidents. Richard Nixon came to our studio in Washington, D.C., accompanied only by a former state trooper who drove him from his New Jersey home. Mr. Nixon had agreed to tape two hours about his book *Seize the Moment.* Seventy-nine when he wrote the book, Mr. Nixon requested a break for a nap between the two hour-long tapings. He returned from his hotel wearing a fresh shirt and new tie for the second session.

You'll also read about notable authors like David Halberstam. Before the taping on his book *The Fifties,* he told me he was a regular *Booknotes* watcher, and his goal was to "best" the interview he'd seen with the Truman biographer David McCullough. After the hour, I asked him how he thought he'd done. "Did it," he declared—he'd achieved his goal of telling as much as he could about the labor of writing. In his chapter, you will read more about his longstanding friendly rivalry with Mr. McCullough.

Because so much of the book focuses on how writers write, the accompanying photographs attempt to capture those stories. I couldn't have guessed it when we started this project, but taking the authors' photos—I took most of them myself—made for some unforgettable experiences. Armed with two "point-and-shoot" cameras, I traveled to the authors' homes or offices, or other places where they researched or wrote their books. David Halberstam agreed to return to the New York Society Library; Albert Murray invited me into the apartment on West 132nd Street in Harlem where he's lived for the past sixty-two years. He wrote all nine of his books there, surrounded by his collections of art and jazz recordings, with a view of the George Washington Bridge outside his window. Neil Sheehan and I revisited his and John Paul Vann's papers at the Library of Congress. And David Herbert Donald showed me his impressive personal library—at his home on Lincoln Road in Lincoln, Massachusetts, a fitting address for one of Lincoln's best-known biographers. After a tour of his extensive book collection, he made lunch for me and historian Doris Kearns Goodwin.

In Concord, Massachusetts, a town near Lincoln, Ms. Goodwin creates an environment in her home office that evokes the period she's writing about. Her photograph shows some of her memorabilia—posters, art, books. To really get in the spirit, she also plays the music of the era while she writes.

George Will, I decided, just had to be captured in his home office in Washington, at work with his yellow pad and a Montblanc fountain pen— a scene he vividly described in our *Booknotes* interview. However, when I arrived at his Georgetown office, there was a laptop computer at his desk. "What gives?" I wanted to know.

It turns out that on February 5, 1995, as George left ABC's Washington studios after taping *This Week,* he fell on an icy sidewalk. His right arm was broken. John Kasich (R-OH), the House Budget Committee Chairman who was a guest on the program, drove George to the hospital, where his arm was set in a cast. When he returned home, his writing arm out of commission for at least six weeks, he pointed to his wife's computer and asked, "How do you turn that thing on?" In short order, the man who described himself on *Booknotes* as "happiest when he is writing" was hooked. "I turned out twelve columns in fifteen days," he explained—faster than he ever could write by hand. "Haven't filled my fountain pen since."

· · ·

WITH ALL THIS DISCUSSION of how books come to be, I ought to tell you a little about how this particular book was published. As it became clear that our authors had interesting stories to tell about the craft of writing, the idea of collecting them into a book gathered steam. To explore the possibility, we turned to two people whose names kept coming up in many *Booknotes* interviews—the literary agent Rafe Sagalyn in Washington and Peter Osnos, the former publisher of Times Books at Random House in New York. Rafe, who is himself an author, has represented many D.C. writers, including David Maraniss, who appears in this book. Peter Osnos, a former *Washington Post* reporter, was in his twelfth year as publisher of Times Books when we began talks about the idea of telling some of the *Booknotes* author stories in book form.

Rafe and Peter were both familiar with *Booknotes,* and we soon had an agreement. Times Books assigned Geoff Shandler to be our editor. Then, as all our *Booknotes* authors will attest, came the hard part. Ironically, although this is a book about writing, there wasn't a lot of writing to be done—the authors' words speak for themselves. Instead, there was an enormous amount of sifting through four hundred interview transcripts to decide which stories to include and—harder still—which to set aside.

Each essay contains the author's story in his or her own words from the *Booknotes* transcript. We have omitted my questions and edited the interviews for length and clarity. An extra space in the text indicates a move to a new section of the original interview. In the editing process, we were very careful to maintain our authors' original meanings. Our goal is to allow you to "hear" the voices of these authors, not only when they described their subject matters, but when they spoke of the writing process—the who, what, why, where, when, and how of putting a book together. If you would like to read any of the *Booknotes* transcripts in their entirety, you'll find them all on C-SPAN's Web page.

For those who saw an interview when it originally aired, these selections will be a chance for you to revisit some wonderful moments. And for those of you who may have missed our programs, this book offers a chance for you to get to know some of America's greatest contemporary writers.

Storytellers

৩৩

I'm one of those people that believes you should start writing before you think you're ready. I think that among my scholarly friends there's a library of unwritten books based on mounds of research that have been done, and I think you can err in both directions.

—Joseph Ellis

David McCullough

David McCullough appeared on Booknotes *on July 19, 1992 for a conversation on* Truman: A Life and Times. *Nearly 1,000 pages long, the book won the Pulitzer Prize for biography in 1993.*

I NEVER MET PRESIDENT TRUMAN, but I saw him once when I was just a youngster on my first job in New York. I was very starry eyed. I had gotten a job on a new magazine called *Sports Illustrated.* I was coming home from work one night. We lived over in Brooklyn. I came out of the subway stop at the old St. George Hotel, and a big car pulled up. There was a small crowd waiting. I stood with the crowd and the big car pulled up and Gov. [Averell] Harriman stepped out. I'd never seen a governor before, so I was quite excited about that. Then out stepped former President Truman. I was just astonished. I remember thinking, "My God, he's in color," because we only had black-and-white television, black-and-white newspapers at the time. I think the fact that he had very high color—he radiated good health—made him seem not just vital, but a person. He certainly didn't seem like a little man to me. To me, at that moment, he was six feet eight. But I never spoke to him. I never met him. I've often thought, wouldn't it be interesting if you could go back in time and I could be able to reach out and touch him on the shoulder in 1956 that fall night and say, "Mr. President, I'm going to write your biography some day"?

[AT YALE UNIVERSITY], I was an English major and a minor in fine arts. I was torn about whether I wanted to be a writer or a painter. I never imagined that I would wind up writing history and biography. I feel in my work that I'm following in a tradition or a school of other writers who have not been trained academically as historians, but who are writers who work in the past the way a foreign correspondent might work in another country—people like Barbara Tuchman, Bruce Catton, Paul Horgan, Wallace Stegner, Robert Caro, lots of them. I suppose we're lapsed journalists.

I stayed at Time-Life for almost five and a half years, and then when John Kennedy was elected, I came down to Washington to be part of the New

Frontier, a very lowly member. I worked at the U.S. Information Agency when Ed Murrow was running it, which was very exciting and wonderful.

But after the president was killed and after Murrow was ill and leaving his post, I went back to New York to work as an editor and writer at *American Heritage* magazine. My major effort there was the picture history of World War II, which is still in print, lo these many years. At that point, I started writing my first book, at night and on weekends, which was *The Johnstown Flood*, published in 1968.

I started this book [*Truman: A Life and Times*] ten years ago, in 1982. I was looking for a subject. I'd started working on a book about Pablo Picasso. I quit that book. I stopped after a few months because I found I disliked him so. He was, to me, a repellent human being, and he didn't really have a story of the kind that interested me. He was instantly successful. He never really went very far or had any adventures, so to speak. He was an immensely important painter. He was the Krakatoa of modern art. But I found he wasn't somebody I wanted to spend five years with as a roommate, so to speak.

My editor at Simon & Schuster suggested that I think about doing Franklin Roosevelt because at that time there was not a good one-volume biography of Franklin Roosevelt. Just on impulse, just in a visceral way, I said, "No. If I were going to do a twentieth-century president, it wouldn't be Franklin Roosevelt. It would be Harry Truman." And he said, "Well, why not Harry Truman?" I looked into it, and I found that there was not a good biography of Harry Truman. There isn't a complete life and times. The last chapter in my book—that part of his life has never been written about. It comprises the last twenty years of his life, a very important part of his life. Beyond that, there was this immense collection of letters and diaries. He poured himself out on paper all of his life. He left a written, personal, very revealing record, unlike that of any president that I know of, and I'm sure we're never going to have another president that leaves anything like that. We don't write letters much anymore, and we don't keep diaries much anymore. He did both his whole life, long before he ever realized that he was going to be a figure in history. To give you an example, in one month in 1947 when he was president and when his wife, Bess, was back in Independence [Missouri] looking after her mother, Harry Truman, the president of the United States, wrote to her thirty-seven times. These weren't just simple, "How are you? The weather is turning cool," or whatever. These were real letters.

As far as I'm concerned, what makes this book a success is that it reaches readers. It's already a best-seller. It became rapidly a best-seller within a matter of weeks. For a 922-page serious biography to go right to the top of the best-seller list in the summertime—I won't say it's unprecedented, but it's certainly rare. I think that is in part because Truman still has a very high standing, great appeal among all of us. But I think, too, that in a political year he represents something that the country, more than in other years perhaps, wants to reach out for—an authenticity, a clarity, a lack of artifice in his personal and his presidential manner. Truman stood for something. He always stood for something. You might not have agreed with his position, but you knew where he stood.

It's hard to just do this without sounding very self-serving, but I know many people who have told me and written to me that they've read [my book] two or three times. Much more common—and, of course, it pleases me enormously—is they say, "I forgot that it was 1,000 pages long." I have almost no proof that people have not read it. I'm sure there are some. It may be one of those books people buy and don't read. That may have been true of books that I've written and others have written that are only 200 pages long, too. I don't know.

WE HAVE FIVE CHILDREN, and they all helped in one way or another, some extensively. One son drove me all through France to follow the whole war, Harry Truman's part in World War I. That same young fellow took the photograph on the back of the book. That's Bill McCullough. And Jeffrey McCullough, who is another son, helped with research on Capitol Hill at the Library of Congress. Others helped with either research or sustaining their father through difficult times.

The book is dedicated to our youngest daughter, Dorrie McCullough, who did very valuable work helping with the research on the restoration of the White House, but more than that, who was with us, my wife and me, all the time through those ten years. We moved to Washington to do the Smithsonian series when I was fifty years old, which is exactly the time that Truman came to Washington as a senator. We came with one daughter, who was a teenager, just as Margaret [Truman] was then. We lived in a very small apartment and were making all the adjustments one does living in Washington, so I felt a certain empathy, when writing about Truman in his senatorial years, from firsthand experience. I think it was very valuable for me in writing the book to have been here. The paleontologists, in order to better understand the fossil record, study the living form. Well, in studying the historical record about the Senate and the White House and the whole way that the bureaucracy works and the press works, everything about

Washington, it helped to study the living form as well as the historical record.

I'VE NEVER READ ANY OF THE RUSSIANS. I've read some of Tolstoy's short stories, but I've never read any of the major Russian works. I've never read *Moby Dick.* I've never read a lot of the poetry of the nineteenth century. And I've never—this is the age of confessional television, isn't it?—I've never read Herodotus. I've never read Thucydides. But Bruce Catton's *A Stillness at Appomattox,* James Agee's *A Death in the Family,* [William] Styron's *Lie Down in Darkness*—those books just changed my life. I just think of those right away. I don't even have to search. The book that I could honestly say probably changed my life, though I didn't know it then—I see it now—was Catton's *A Stillness at Appomattox,* which my aunt gave me as a graduation present from college. I aspired to write fiction, novels, maybe plays. When I went to college, everybody was going to be a writer, and I never dared talk about that. I never dared mention that. It seemed very presumptuous. But I secretly wanted to do that—to be that. When I saw the Catton book, I realized that history could be written about life. It could be written about human beings. It could be written about the feeling of places. It had all the narrative quality and the art of the written word about something that really happened. That was a revelation for me.

I love to write. Lately, it seems all I've been writing is commencement speeches, but I like the tactile part of it. It is a difficult art form—very difficult. I work on a manual typewriter because I like the feeling of making something with my hands. I like paper. I like to see the key come up and hit that paper.

I feel that each project I've undertaken has been a huge adventure, a lesson in a world, a subject, a territory I knew nothing about. People will sometimes say to me, "Well, what's your theme?" as I start on the new book. "I haven't the faintest idea. That's one of the reasons I'm writing the book." "Well, you don't know much about that subject." "That's exactly right. I don't know anything about the subject—or very little. And, again, that's why I'm writing the book." I think if I knew all about it and I knew exactly what I was going to say, I probably wouldn't want to write the book, because there would be no search, there would be no exploration of a country I've never been to—that's the way one should feel.

Shelby Foote

Shelby Foote has written 1.5 million words on the Civil War. For his September 1994 appearance on Booknotes, *he was scheduled to discuss a Modern Library edition that focuses on one three-day Civil War battle fought in 1863,* Stars in Their Courses: The Gettysburg Campaign. *Earlier in his career, Mr. Foote wrote several novels that he also described in the interview.*

I HAVE A STRONG BELIEF that novelists have a great deal to teach historians about plotting, about character drawing, about other things, especially the concern about learning to be a good writer, which many historians don't bother to do.

I write about the Mississippi Delta. All those novels are concerned with that. It's my homeland. It's what I know. It's all in my experience. I enjoy very much doing the research and getting to know these people well enough. I felt no different working with facts that I got out of documents than I did with facts, so-called, that I got out of my head. They're both facts. You have to be true to them. A good novelist is as true to his facts as a historian is to his. It's true you can't give Lincoln the color eyes you want to. They were gray blue, but there they are. They're gray blue and you deal with them.

What I do is I work at development. I don't stop the story to tell you who somebody was. I release things about his life as the story goes along. I've got a long way to go, you see. I've got a million and a half words there, and I take my time. You don't find where Lee courted his wife until the Battle of Fredericksburg. He's looking through his binoculars across the Rappahannock at an oak tree in the yard of a house over there, and that's where he courted his wife. It picks these pieces up as you go along until finally, I hope, you get to know these people the way you do get to know people in real life, finding out little by little about them instead of just three pages of biography.

I suspect I like to think of myself as a novelist because that's what I was for most of my life and that's the way I thought of myself, and I haven't changed. It pleases me when someone tells me what they like best is my novels. But I've faced the fact that I probably am more apt to be known for writing this three-volume history on the Civil War than for anything else.

I began [my three-volume history] in 1954 under a contract with Bennett Cerf at Random House for a short history of the Civil War, and I sat down to outline this short history and saw that I would be simply writing a summary and wouldn't be interested in doing it. So I wrote and told them at Random House that I'd be willing to go whole hog, spread eagle on the thing, three volumes. There was some hesitation, I presume, but in about a week I got word to go ahead, and I went ahead for the next twenty years. I finished it in '74. I began it in the spring of '54 and finished in the spring of '74. I did not do anything else, during that whole time, of any import. I didn't write a novel; I didn't do any of those things. Just worked on the war.

I'm not sure how I got interested in writing. That's always hard for a writer to say. I'm sure my interest began as an interest in reading, which then was translated into an interest in writing. I often wondered, "How did this fellow do this?" I can remember a Sunday school prize or something when I was about eleven years old; I won a copy of *David Copperfield*. Up to that time I'd read the Bobbsey Twins and then Tom Swift and the Rover Boys and Tarzan, but since I got this as a prize, I decided I should read it.

I found a world that was realer than the world I lived in, unlike these Tarzan and other books. I knew David Copperfield better than anybody I knew in the real world, including myself. I said, "My God," to myself, "this is a whole world." I didn't then read all of Dickens or start becoming a serious reader until three or four years later, but I remember vividly having that reaction to that book *David Copperfield*. I think most writers probably have that experience.

I first got interested in the Civil War as a boy. Any Deep South boy, and probably all Southern boys, have been familiar with the Civil War as a sort of thing in their conscience going back. I honestly believe that it's in all our subconsciouses. This country was into its adolescence at the time of the Civil War. It really was; it hadn't formulated itself really as an adult nation, and the Civil War did that. Like all traumatic experiences that you might have had in your adolescence, it stays with you the rest of your life, certainly in your subconscious, most likely in your conscience, too.

I think that the Civil War had the nature of that kind of experience for the country. Anybody who's looked into it at all realizes that it truly is *the* outstanding event in American history, insofar as making us what we are. The kind of country we are emerged from the Civil War, not from the Revolution. The Revolution provided us with a constitution; it broke us loose from England; it made us free. But the Civil War really defined us. It said what we were going to be, and it said what we're not going to be. It drifted away from the Southern, mostly Virginian, influence up into the New

England and Middle Western influence, and we became that kind of nation instead of another kind of nation.

When I started really thinking about writing [the series] I was thirty-seven or so. I had been to a lot of Civil War sites. It was a sort of hobby of mine. I was going back and forth to New York three or four times a year, driving in those days up U.S. 11 through the Shenandoah Valley and all that, and I would stop at battlefields all along the way and go out of my way to go to them just to see what they felt like.

In visiting battlefields, it's very important that you go at the same time of year, if possible on the very anniversary of the battle, because the place is so different other times of year. To understand the Battle of Shiloh, if you went there when it was fought, in early April, you could see what it was like. If you went there in February or later on in July, it would be a different field, and you wouldn't understand the way the new growth of leaves choked everything in, so nobody knew what direction north, south, east, or west was. So you get that thing and you get the weather, you get the soil and you get the coloration of things; get the true feel of it.

I wrote the first volume on the exact western city limits of Memphis because it was on the bluff overlooking the Mississippi River. The second volume was written on the eastern limits of Memphis, which Yates Road was then. And the third volume was written where I live now, right in the geographical center of Memphis. All three volumes were written, every line of them, there in Memphis.

I've always worked in the room where I usually sleep, so that I sleep near my desk, and the typewriter's over here. There's something about it. When I go somewhere else, like in the summer I'll go down on the coast or something, I can't work away from home. I'd have to stay there for two weeks before I could start writing. I'm not like, say, D. H. Lawrence, who could write anywhere and, in fact, never had a home. But to me it's a very deliberate thing. Five or six hundred words is a good day for me.

I write with a "dip pen," which causes all kinds of problems—everything from finding blotters to pen points—but it makes me take my time, and it gives me a real feeling of satisfaction. I'm getting where I'm going. A dip pen is the kind you used to see in post offices all the time when you were a boy. I would love to find one of those inkwells they had in post offices. They had a spring in them. When you pressed down, it would wet the pen point, and then when you lifted it out, it would close it again so the ink didn't evaporate. I can't find one. I'm absolutely certain that right here in Washington there are 5 million of them in a warehouse somewhere, but I can't find one. But a dip pen, you have to dip it in the ink and write three or four words and dip it again. It has a real influence on the way I write, so different not only from a typewriter but from using a pencil or a fountain pen.

Mostly I keep all the facts and figures in my head. Particular quotations that I want to be sure to keep up with I'll write on a piece of paper and stick on a piece of beaverboard that's in front of my desk so I won't forget to get it, but mostly I carry this in my head. But by way of preparation for this, I did something that I think anybody would find useful. I got large cardboard posters and drew columns down [them], and then put the year, '61, '62, '63, '64, '65, and I had "diplomacy," "military," "political," and other things so that at a glance I could tell what was going on at that particular time, and that's where the plotting came in, so that you weave the diplomatic situation and the political situation and the military situation all into a narrative.

I don't allow anybody around while I'm writing. My wife manages to live with me, and my son and our dog, but I like to be let alone when I'm working. I see these Hollywood movies where the man gets up in the middle of the night and dashes off a few thousand words, and his little wife comes in to make sure he's comfortable and everything. That's all foolishness. It would never be anything like that. In fact, I'm privately convinced that most of the really bad writing the world's ever seen has been done under the influence of what's called inspiration.

After it's written, the 500 words every day, I set it aside to dry; then copy it off on a typewriter, make a typewritten copy of it, and then recopy on that until finally the day is over and I'm all the way satisfied with it, and I put it on the stack—make a clean copy and put it on the stack. That way I don't have to engage in something that to me is a particular form of heartbreak, which is revision. I don't do that. My best friend in life for sixty years was Walker Percy. And he felt exactly the opposite way about how to write. He said, "If I knew what was going to happen next, I wouldn't be able to write. I wouldn't be interested in writing if I knew what was going to happen." I'm just not that way.

My editor at Random House for thirty-five years now has been Bob Loomis. He's a good editor, and our arrangement is that he will encourage me, he will do everything in the world to make me feel that I'm doing well and this and that and the other, but he doesn't mess with the text.

William Faulkner had [this kind of arrangement]. I've seen a Faulkner proof. Somebody presumed to read the galley proofs and make a correction of something, and Faulkner scratched it out. The next time he got to one, he saw another correction mark, and he wrote, "Goddamn it, leave it alone!" That's the way I felt about it, too.

Forrest McDonald

Forrest McDonald is the Distinguished Research Professor of History at the University of Alabama, and the author of fifteen books. He came in May 1994 to Booknotes *to discuss* The American Presidency: An Intellectual History, *published by the University Press of Kansas.*

I GREW UP IN TEXAS, went to school at the University of Texas, got all my degrees there. I was an English major as an undergraduate because I wanted to write the great American novel. I wrote a very bad novel—I mean, it rots! I still have it. But I learned as I went along that I like to write. It's hard work for me to write, and it's more fun to have written than to write, but I found that I could do it in history, so I've been in history ever since.

I WRITE IN THE NUDE most of the time. We live in total isolation out in the country. They don't even read the electric meter because the electric man can't find it. We have to read our own meter. And it's warm most of the year in Alabama, so why wear clothes? I mean, they're just a bother. You'd see me sitting on the porch. We have a house that's mainly glass and otherwise screen.

I write it out by hand. My wife, who is a very fine harpsichordist and has become a fantastic typist, then transcribes. I do a lot of editing before I turn it over to her and then she edits with her fingers as she goes along. So we're really at a third or fourth draft by the time we get a first typed draft. We never use word processors. Then we'll let it sit and edit it some more, and I'll keep on writing.

The key to turning out good stuff is rewriting. The key to grinding it out is consistency. It sounds silly, but if you write four pages a day, you've written 1,200 pages in a year—or 1,400, whatever it is. You accumulate the stuff. So what I normally do is give myself quotas. They'll vary depending on the depth and complexity of the subject, but somewhere between three and five pages—that's my day's writing. I've got to do it every day. I can't go out and work on my farm until I've done my day's writing, and working on my farm is so pleasurable. So that's incentive; I hold myself hostage, so to speak, and it gets done.

The book began with a political controversy which I wanted to understand, but didn't want to get involved in—that was the shift in positions of attitudes of liberals and Democrats on one side and Republicans and conservatives on the other, attitudes toward the presidency, the tremendous growth of presidential power. I wanted to understand that. I got into the thing because I've spent most of my adult life in the eighteenth century. So I had that background, and I started exploring. What I learned was that people wanted me to write a polemic from one side or the other—are you for it, or against it? Well, I could see good in it, and I could see bad in it; I can see danger in it, and I can see wonderful, good things in it. I didn't find it difficult at all to remain detached about the whole thing.

A lot of stuff is available on microfilm, but the archival collections are not open anymore because of vandalism, because of people stealing manuscripts and all this kind of stuff. When I first worked at the National Archives, they just turned me loose in the stacks. Now you've got to go in, and you've got to tell them what volume you want or document you want, and you sit down in a waiting room and they will bring the stuff down for you, and that's that. You can't work that way; you can't get things done.

I talked with Nixon because Nixon invited me. He heard about something I had written and wanted to meet me, and through mutual friends I went up and had dinner with him in New Jersey. It was unreal being there. I'm sitting there talking to this very, very bright, knowledgeable, articulate guy and every once in a while it would hit me: This is Richard M. Nixon. When I drove up to his apartment, he's standing there with the door open, big greeting and stuff like that. There was a large unreality quotient involved.

I don't write with a popular audience in mind, specifically. And I certainly don't write just for historians, the way most historians do. I write for anybody who is intelligent and who is interested in the subject. I think they can read it, but this is something I'm absolutely not good at . . . knowing what kind of market there will be for things. I'm just not oriented that way. The predecessor of this book was *Novus Ordo Seclorum*—now who's going to buy a book on the intellectual origins of the Constitution? I didn't even bother to go over to my agent because I thought, this is not a commercial book. So I went to [the University Press of] Kansas. They published it, as they published this one—and there's something like 55,000 or 60,000 copies of that thing around. That one, I thought, was terribly esoteric. Whether this is going to be a popular book, or sort of some in, groupie book, I don't know. There is an awful lot of interest in the presidency right now, but that doesn't necessarily sell books.

I've got lots more books in me. I was discussing this last night and the one that I proposed to somebody, my wife dumped all over. And we're absolute partners in this venture, so unless she wants to play, we won't do it.

James Reston, Jr.

James Reston, Jr., formerly a professor of creative writing at the University of North Carolina and now a full-time writer, came to the program to discuss his seventh book, titled The Lone Star: The Life of John Connally. *Prior to this biography, Mr. Reston had written four works of nonfiction and two novels. This interview aired on December 17, 1989, and was our fortieth* Booknotes.

W HEN I WAS GROWING UP, I realized I wanted to be a writer. My whole upbringing was formed by that wonderful experience for a youngster, to have that sense of men and women of words around you.

When you have a reasonably well-known father, people tend to view you as a clone. That is a real mistake on their part because it is very rarely that sons are clones of their fathers. Many assumptions are made that you have an intensely political sensibility. My father, James Barrett Reston, is a political writer and columnist. They assume that I know everything about politics, when, in fact, affairs of the heart have been much more of interest to me throughout my whole career.

But the great benefit of it is that, of course, you have been around people who have been in the word business all your life. If you grow up in a newspaper household, the virtue of skepticism—especially skepticism towards authority—is very deeply ingrained from the early years. I think that is the most essentially important virtue for a good writer.

THE SUBJECT OF JOHN CONNALLY was really picked for me. That is the truthful answer in the whole thing. I had another subject in mind, and that just didn't work out for other reasons. We waited around for two to three months—this was back in October of 1986. That was when the stories appeared of John Connally falling from grace with his horrendous bankruptcy difficulties. That seemed to have this sort of Shakespearean or Grecian quality to it—a man who had been so big and high in American powerful circles had fallen so far, so fast. A biographer always looks for this kind of dimension in a subject.

There is always a dialogue that goes on between a publisher and an author. We had essentially agreed to do another subject, which, I will confess to you, was Jesse Helms, because I had taught at the University of North Carolina for ten years. So Helms made sense. It then turned out that there was a book on Helms coming out, so we had to search around. John Connally is probably not pleased to know that he is a substitute for Jesse Helms in this case.

Mr. Connally did not offer his cooperation on this book. Absolutely none at all, zero. In terms of what he will think of this book, you see, people never look at themselves the way that others look at them. Here is a man who was really larger than life: who had extraordinary achievements; who came just so close—a hair's breadth—to being president of the United States, and who never seemed to have a loss of confidence in himself. Obviously he had a very grand view of himself. This is a book which presents all of those achievements and gives full scope to them, but also lays out his faults which, in many cases, are rather large.

One of the things that sustained me—as Connally would put these blocks in my way—was simply the form of biography because of these elements that it has, that go across the elements of other forms: of drama, of fiction, of journalism, of scholarship. For someone with a novelist's sensibility, but also with a concern for the exactitude of a historian, this brought together the best qualities that I have to offer as a writer.

I think any solid, self-respecting biography has to start at the great libraries that have materials in [them]. I suppose most important to me in this whole book was the LBJ Library in Austin, Texas. But I also spent time at the JFK Library [in Boston] because of the assassination, of course. The Nixon Project, here in Alexandria, Virginia, was terribly important because of Connally's time with Nixon; and lastly, the National Archives, because Connally had this extraordinary bribery trial and all of those documents are in the National Archives. Once I got the solid primary research under my belt, then I started to move out and talk to people. But if you are trying to tell, in effect, forty years of American political history through the life of one man—especially the earlier history—people's memories by this time start to fade a bit. So one has to be very careful in the interviewing process.

This was an independent biography, not the so-called authorized biography or the unauthorized biography. I mean, it is unauthorized, but we always tend to think of the unauthorized biography as something that sets out to gut, slash, and trash the figure. The Kitty Kelley book on Frank Sinatra is always the one that is sort of used as an example. This is not that kind of book. Nevertheless, I was quite sure that there would be attempts—probably by Connally intimates and perhaps by Connally himself—to attack the book, to attack the research in the book, and try to undermine it. For that reason, I spent a great deal of time on the biographer's notes, which ended up being 100 pages or so in typescript.

Connally's papers were delivered to the LBJ Library right in the same time frame as his bankruptcy. I came to believe that he had only donated these papers to the LBJ Library because he wanted to protect them—because they are valuable—from his creditors. Out of that ensuing struggle came a rather novel legal problem. Never before had a major gift of personal papers been made to a presidential library in connection with a bankruptcy, when all the creditors are out there looking for every single thing of value in the bankrupt person's possession, and these papers were estimated to be worth three or four million dollars. So Connally—I like to think of it in the dead of the night—threw all of these papers off onto the dock of the LBJ Library. Then, when the gift was given to the LBJ Library, he put a five-year restriction on access to it, which I always came to refer to as the "Jim Reston Restriction." He was giving the history but preventing the only historian working on him [from] having access to it.

There is this well-known biography of Lyndon Johnson by Robert Caro. And the same debate amongst the Lyndon Johnson coterie existed toward Caro that has existed for me in the Connally coterie with this book: "Should I talk to Reston or shouldn't I talk to him? You know, he is a serious writer and he seems to be doing a good job." But Caro, some would say, went against some of his confidences, and so on. So it is a touchy argument in a way.

I WENT TO COLLEGE at the University of North Carolina and studied philosophy. I ended up teaching creative writing there. I stopped teaching in 1981. That was a classic thing, you know. I think one grows out of teaching writing after a while. Many of us writers do teach it, particularly in the early part of our career, because we have to make a living. I was well served by being in Chapel Hill for ten years where there was a wonderful literary community, mainly fiction writers. But I was ready to leave it and I wanted to see if I could just write. People often say to me, "What are you doing, just writing now?" And I have been "just writing." I wanted to see whether I could made a living doing that exclusively.

I have always been comfortable in being a writer, even if my family did not have anything to eat. There were never any doubts that books would be the center of my existence. I have this wonderful home now at Harper &

Row [now HarperCollins] which is not so easily accomplished in today's publishing world. I was very, very keen to get cracking on another book and be well into the research by the time this one came out. The publication process has always paralyzed me. You wait for two to three months before the book comes out. You can't do anything. Then when the book comes out, you wait for the reviews, and you wait for the television people to attack you. You see, the destiny and the fate of the book really is not in for six to eight months. So if you give yourself over to this kind of paralysis, it can be really quite a large block of time.

° *Edmund Morris*

While Edmund Morris has yet to appear on Booknotes, *he made an appearance on a new C-SPAN program* About Books *in July of 1996. During the
interview, Mr. Morris discussed his latest book, a biography of former President Ronald Reagan, published by Random House. Mr. Morris continues his
work on a three-volume biography of Theodore Roosevelt. He won a Pulitzer
Prize for the first volume in 1981.*

I WRITE BY LONGHAND. I like to see the words coming out of the pen.
And once they distribute themselves, one has the stylistic struggle to try
and turn that clumsy sentence on the page into something lucid. That can
take a long time. I remember once spending seven hours on one sentence—seven hours. And I looked at it the next morning, it was a pretty
banal sentence. That's writing. Writing is a reduction to essentials, elimina-
tion, and that takes time.

At the moment, I'm writing with an Eversharp fountain pen from the
mid-1930s, a nice green marbled fountain pen. For my Theodore Roosevelt
biography, I wrote on very special paper. I came across a ream of it. It was
called "certificate bond," 11 inches by 17—huge, big sheets. It had a beautiful white marble texture to it, so it was sensuously pleasurable to write on.
I colored it with handwriting. I figured out that one of these large sheets of
handwriting was equivalent to one page of book. So when I had 700 sheets
of it, I knew I had a book of approximately 700 pages. However, I no
longer write on that paper. For the Reagan biography, I just write on a normal 8½-by-11 paper, rough-lined paper. After I've bashed out the fair copy, I
then type it into the computer and get a more objective look at it.

It's not possible to count how often I make changes to the drafts. I tried
once to figure out how many times one writes the average sentence, but
what can I say? I would think that the manuscript of a book of the kind
that I'm writing, every sentence would be done at least seven times.

When I finish, I'd like the book to be 777 pages long. The reason being
that the figure of seventy-seven runs through Reagan's life. In particular, he
saved seventy-seven lives as a young lifeguard. He worked seven summers,

saved seventy-seven lives. He was in his seventy-seventh year when he left the White House. And, anyway, I liked the idea of a book about 777 pages. That's about the size Random House could handle, but they don't want it to be any longer or bigger than that.

The writer's perennial problem, from the very first page, is: how do you get the reader's attention? And one does it, I guess, by presenting one's own take on the subject. I think that I see Ronald Reagan differently from the next man, simply because I am different from the next man. He is a large person. And like most large persons, [he] can be described from many angles and many takes, as we say. I think my view of him in print is going to be quite challenging, simply because I see him from a literary point of view, whereas most people see him from a political point of view.

In examining the lives of other people, one examines one's own. A biographer is, in a sense, a doppelgänger, a double goer; he becomes the shadow of his character. And an identity develops between the two, which may be loving, may be hypocritical. I think both these extremes are dangerous. If you love your subject, you end up writing soppy stuff. And if you hate your subject, it becomes unreadable for obvious reasons. So I think the best relationship that a biographer can have with his subject is one of mild affection. The interest must be there. One has to spend many years with this person, so you'd better make sure, up front, that it's going to be a congenial relationship.

Writers have blocks. Sure, I had a block. I've had blocks. One has many blocks. On a Tuesday morning, you cannot write. On Wednesday, it comes back. But my block with Reagan was not so much a writer's block as a necessary period of puzzling him out. He was overfamiliar. He was the recently departed president of the United States, amply covered in many books—I think something like seventy books came out of the Reagan administration within a year or two of his departure. And my problem as a writer was to be able to deal with him on the page in a way that would make him different and interesting. Plus, he was a mysterious person, very hard to figure out and, for that reason, very hard to write about.

I will tell you that by going to Tampico [Illinois], I learned more about Ronald Reagan than I could have learned in a year of studying books—just from the physical environment he was born in. I walked out into the corn. It's a one-horse town. It's a one-block town in the middle of the middle of America. There's nothing there except one main street where he was born and then corn stretching in all directions—flat, circular horizon, this great blue sky, a windmill or two lazily rotating.

And I stood in the corn thinking, "This is the environment that little Dutch Reagan was born into." His first consciousness developed here, even

though [his family] moved away quite soon. But the rest of the world, even now, is a million miles away. And you think, in 1911, '12, '13, '14, [there was] no radio, no television, and no telephone. The remoteness of the rest of the world and the sense of peace and stability and silence and absolute solidity, rock-solid, Midwestern, American security is palpable. When I looked around me, I sensed the birth of this unshakably solid personality.

My next book will be volume two on Theodore Roosevelt. I had to put it aside when I took on Reagan. And the last volume, which will describe his postpresidential life, is still unwritten except for the last line, which I already have done. And I won't tell you what it is. But it's that final palm tree on the edge of the desert to which you are flogging your camel as glossy palm leaves wave in the distance. I don't think one could negotiate the whole sandy stretch of desert unless one had the prospect of that final palm tree to rest and relax under. So I'm keeping it to myself.

I remember with my last editor, on the Roosevelt book, sitting down with him at the end, when I had my huge manuscript of basic text, typescript, and he wanted the odd sentence out. And he had a little jar of Wite-Out. He'd be sitting there with my manuscript, slop, slop, with this obscuring fluid. And I remember him saying to me, "Don't you just love Wite-Out?" I could see he was an editor in action here. They love to obliterate. I said, "That's my words you're obliterating, fellow."

A writer makes a living the same way a porcupine makes love: very carefully. I was well paid for the Reagan book, which is why we are temporarily unafraid of our landlord. But insecurity always threatens a writer. We've had bad years. We may have more bad years, but at the moment, the mortgage gets paid. My wife [Sylvia Morris] is also a writer, and we live on her advance as well as mine.

THE VIEW OF THE CAPITOL really does something to me whenever I see it, because I remember as a small boy, I used to hang out in the United States Information Service Library in Nairobi and take out books on America. I remember that icon there, the shape of the Capitol floating above the trees. It always attracted me, even as a kid in Africa. I was very much drawn to America and wanted to come here. So when I see it now, when I sit at my desk looking at it, I feel very content.

I think writers should write, and talkers should talk. I don't much like talking, although I know I'm garrulous, because the luxury of being a writer is you can edit, you can go back. When I talk, I'm constantly wanting to take that sentence back and change its shape. With a writer, you can

do that—with writing, you can do that. When you're talking, the fugitive sentence has flown; you can't get it back.

I think all my really deep influences have been people I've not known, the people that I studied and identified with as an adolescent. I've always been very drawn to music, so musical figures like Franz Liszt, who has an overwhelming personality, and Beethoven, and my literary heroes, Charles Dickens and Evelyn Waugh, and historians like [William Hickling] Prescott. These are the people I think have influenced me. I certainly try to approach within striking distance of stylists like Evelyn Waugh. I would like to be as good a person as Franz Liszt was. I'd sure like to be able to play the piano like he did.

[In writing these two biographies], I've certainly learned the difference between the sedentary intellectual, which is what I am, and the political man of action, which is what Reagan and Theodore Roosevelt both were. Even though Theodore Roosevelt himself was an intellectual, he was by no means sedentary, and early in life eschewed the life of an academic intellectual because he wanted to go out in the world and change things, the usual motivation for a politician: "I want to change things." Guys like me do not want to change things in the physical sense, though we are very happy if our books influence the world around us in some way or other. But for me to sit, following these men through their active lives, is extremely fascinating and makes me understand how necessary politicians are, men of action, to counterbalance the inactivity of us scholarly types.

Doris Kearns Goodwin

Doris Kearns Goodwin came to C-SPAN from her home in Concord, Massachusetts, to describe her experiences writing No Ordinary Time: Franklin and Eleanor Roosevelt: The Home Front in World War II. *Her Booknotes interview aired on New Year's Day, 1995.*

*U*SUALLY, I START WRITING early in the morning. My husband and I both get up really early. For some reason, he awakens, like, at five-thirty or six o'clock in the morning, so he gets me up to go have breakfast with him, and sometimes we work out, if we're in one of those moods, which we're not always in. Then we both start working pretty early, even sometimes before the kids go to school at seven o'clock, and work until, like, the middle of the afternoon, and then we can go play tennis or go do errands. I mean, that's the fun about having a husband who's in the same line of business. You can take your breaks together.

I fear I write in longhand. I am so primitive, still. I cannot think on the typewriter. I've never been able to. So I write it all out in longhand, and then the worst stage is I then copy it all over, so that a typist can read the writing. And that's when I edit, when I copy it all over. Then I give it to a typist, who types it up on a computer and gives it back to me. I don't really look at it all until the whole first draft is done. Finally, at the very end, when I have to really edit the thing, we put it all on my husband's computer. He taught me how to actually work on the computer to edit. I'm still not sure I can write on it originally, because I don't think I can think on it. But at least I've learned how to edit on the computer, so I feel very proud.

I wrote the book mostly at home. I have a study right on the second floor of my house. We live right on the main street in Concord, so it's wonderful. You can walk right into the town. And I filled the study with pictures of Franklin and Eleanor, with pictures of the war, Rosie the Riveter, and pictures of the women going to work in the factories, so that the ambience felt like World War II. I got all the books I could find on this era. I wanted them with me this time. I love libraries, and usually you use libraries a lot, but in this case, I wanted to be able to have the books as much present, so I went to every used bookstore, and so the whole room was filled with Roosevelt and World War II books. It was a great place to work.

I would guess, of the six years I spent on this book, probably four of them were research and two of them were writing. Even in the last two years of writing, I still needed to do more research. You'd come upon something and you wouldn't know the answer to it, so you'd have to go back to Hyde Park. I was probably at the library there within weeks of finishing the book.

I HAVE WRITTEN TWO BOOKS before this one. The first one was *Lyndon Johnson and the American Dream,* and that came out of the experience, that I will forever treasure, of having been twenty-three and twenty-four years old, and working for President Johnson in the White House, and then helping him with his memoirs. I still keep thinking Johnson is still around. I keep thinking he's thinking, "This book on the Roosevelts is 700 pages. The one on me was only 350 pages. How can you do that?" So that was the first book, and it was a great experience to try and understand that giant of a man, who I found so sad in his retirement, while he was at the ranch, that it was almost like he had nothing else left in his life once politics was taken from him. That whole experience, I think, seared into my mind forever, and made up that first book.

The second book was called *The Fitzgeralds and the Kennedys.* It was a three-generation history of the Kennedy family. In fact, it partly was made possible by the fact that I was given access to Rose and Joe Kennedy's private papers that had been in the attic for over fifty years, because my husband had originally been on the White House staff with John Kennedy. So we knew the Kennedy family. I think one of the reasons why this book on the Roosevelts means so much is that it's really the first time I've had to slog it through as an ordinary historian, without the advantage of knowing Lyndon Johnson or knowing the Kennedy family.

FOR ALL THE THOUSANDS OF BOOKS that have been written about World War II, there have been very few that focus on what happened here at home, and most of those have been essay kind of books, like a chapter on civil rights, a chapter on the Japanese incarceration camps, or on women in the factories, but there has been very little evidence of trying to understand Roosevelt's leadership, how he mobilized this democracy. In some ways, I think, that's his greatest contribution to the war, even more than the strategy of the war itself—how he got our country to produce the weapons for the war. That's what won the war, in lots of ways. And turning around a peace economy, an isolationist economy, an economy that was still in the midst of a depression, and somehow making it so productive is a great story.

The White House ushers' diaries were one of my most incredible tools. Anybody can come see them. They're in the Roosevelt Library, and they're on microfiche. What happened is, at the end of the day, there would be a White House usher who would record everything that happened during the day: Roosevelt awakens at seven, has a massage at seven-fifteen, goes to breakfast, and then they'd record who he had lunch with, who he had dinner with; and then you could use that as a foundation to go. For example, suppose he had lunch with Henry Stimson [secretary of war], or [Harold] Ickes [secretary of the interior], or [Henry] Morgenthau [secretary of the treasury], I knew that they all had diaries, so I could go to their diaries to find out what he talked about at lunch. Or they'd record that Eleanor was with Joe Lash [the official Roosevelt biographer], and I knew that he had a diary. So, in some ways it was like the detective's tool. They're public, but they hadn't been used before.

As far as [FDR's] paralysis goes, what astonished me was that the majority of the people thought, as I did, that he was simply lame, and the reason they were allowed to feel that way was that not a single newsreel ever showed him in his wheelchair, on his braces, being crippled. There was almost like an unspoken code of honor, on the part of the press, that the president wasn't to be seen that way. Sometimes reporters would see him being actually carried from a car into a building like a child, and yet they never took a picture. If a young guy came along and tried to do that, an older guy would knock the camera to the ground. As a result, there was a kind of dignity to the office of the presidency then that I think is really missing right now, on both the side of the press and the president. Roosevelt understood the importance of holding his private life secure. He would never have thought about talking about his mother's domineeringness or his feelings about Lucy Mercer. I mean, there was a reserve that I suspect served us better, at that time.

I did get emotional while writing this book. I mean, you live with these characters for six years. It took me longer to work on this book, I'm afraid, than the war to be fought. That was what was pretty embarrassing. I would find myself talking to Franklin and Eleanor; talking to Harry Hopkins and Lorena Hickok; to Anna [Roosevelt], as if they were still alive. You really feel their presence—and when bad things happen to them, when one of them hurts another, you feel it. That's the only way you can do it, when you get so absorbed in all of this.

It seems to me that the challenge is not to do what's so prevalent today in biography—to expose and to label and to stereotype. What I really wanted to try and do was to extend empathy; to understand why they needed all these [extramarital] relationships, and not to judge them harshly because of their own human needs.

I think my favorite thing in the book is the discovery that Eleanor and Franklin still loved each other during this period of time. The conventional wisdom among historians was that, after the affair with Lucy Mercer in 1918, their marriage had become a pure political partnership. I was so happy to discover, even though it meant discovering that they could still hurt each other during this period, that there were still alive emotions. There were yearnings. They kept missing each other. I almost felt like I wanted to push them together because I could feel that love between them. But I was very glad to find that out.

Albert Murray

Albert Murray came to the studio on June 16, 1996, to talk about his latest book, Blue Devils of Nada: A Contemporary American Approach to Aesthetic Statement. *Mr. Murray has taught literature at Colgate University, the University of Massachusetts, and the University of Missouri.*

THE FACT THAT THOMAS JEFFERSON HAD SLAVES is something you could be very, very self-righteous about. But what is most significant about Thomas Jefferson is that he wrote the Declaration of Independence. We're talking about "all men are created equal," and "the consent of the governed," all those things. So the basis for rejecting or struggling against slavery has been laid in the social contract by Thomas Jefferson. There was no such basis in Africa or any other place. So you're not talking about people who were free. They were owned by chiefs and they were property to be sold in Africa.

There was no Underground Railroad in Africa, there was no abolitionist movement in Africa, but there was in the United States because [the country] had bought that aspect of the human proposition underlying the social contract upon which America's based. So it was in violation of what was promised of a conception of human possibility that the whole nation was predicated upon. And they didn't get it straight until after the Civil War. So you have the Declaration of Independence, where the philosophy really is expressed. It's "consent of the governed" and all that. You've got the Preamble to the Constitution, you've got the Bill of Rights, right? Then you have the Emancipation Proclamation, which says, "If you're enslaved and you want to be free, that's not a crime." All this is coming out of the original social contract.

Then you get the Gettysburg Address, which put it on a postage stamp, as Faulkner would say—put the whole thing on a postage stamp. Then you got the Thirteenth, Fourteenth, and Fifteenth Amendments. All of this comes from Thomas Jefferson, really, as an extension, an aberration or refinement of a point of view about human beings that was put out there and became our heritage because of Thomas Jefferson. Without that, you can't have a civil rights movement, you couldn't have anything. You wouldn't have had the Civil War, you wouldn't have had any of that without this assumption. Now, you don't find that in the Bible. You don't find that promise. Even the aristocrats after the Magna Carta, after the French Revolution, which, incidentally, came after the American Revolution—you don't find any of those promises guaranteed to citizens.

Those back-to-Africa movements, if you've studied American history, they're not going to go over there to reestablish tribal life, they wanted to establish the United States of Africa. In fact, most people of African descent, when they think about it, even if they're Afrocentric, they really are thinking of Africa as a United States. All these different countries they think are states.

Thomas Jefferson gives you the basis for the struggle for your humanity and for human dignity, [though] he had some contradictions in his life. But somebody was calling me the other day, and they were talking about how many slaves Jefferson had or didn't have, and how he treated his slaves or whatnot. And then somebody's now run a survey on how many slaves were held by black slave owners in the United States. And they never get criticized either because any number of people got into that when it was legal, and it became illegal. The important thing was that the basis for it becoming illegal had already been established by Thomas Jefferson.

I HAVE LIVED IN NEW YORK since I retired from the air force in 1962, so that's thirty-some years. I came to Manhattan because I was a writer, because I had already begun writing and I thought I'd do it. I didn't really come to New York to be in Harlem. I came to New York to be near the Strand Book Store, the Gotham Book Mart, Greenwich Village, the writers, Random House, all of that.

I live in Harlem because that was where I'd found a place when I came in 1962. But if I had had the money, I probably would have lived in Greenwich Village to be closer to writers. But I would have lived on Park Avenue, Fifth Avenue if I could afford it. I have no particular reason to live in Harlem except it's the best real estate buy I've come across.

I WRITE AT HOME. I have a little wing off my living room, which was really designed as a breakfast nook, that leads out to the terrace. I have a desk there that I designed. And then in the corner, I have the sound equipment for my McIntosh CD player and a Bang & Olafson record player and a real good sound system, and the speakers are out there, part of the room. I have books on those shelves and books along the other shelves. It's like a studio. And I'm looking downtown in my library because I'm between Lenox, which is Sixth Avenue uptown, and Fifth, so I'm right in the center of Manhattan. So I'm right back up in "the spyglass tree," which is the title of my second novel, where you have that perspective on Manhattan, and I try to make the most of it.

MY HOMETOWN IS MOBILE, ALABAMA. I came up on the outskirts of Mobile in a section rife with juke joints, but not too far away was a very good county training school also. So I'm a product of a sort of cross section of American experience. I was born in 1916, during World War I. I left Mobile when I went to college in 1935.

Growing up in Mobile was a matter of discovering what the world was like, and Mobile is a fascinating place; it was an exotic place. It had been under five flags. It had been French, Spanish, Confederate, American, whatnot. It was a seaport town. There were people from all over the world. You grew up knowing people, hearing foreign languages, and things like that.

When I got to the third grade, that's when I discovered the earth because I had my first geography book. I started reading about people in various parts of the world and climbing up in the chinaberry tree in the front yard of our house—the shotgun house that we lived in, you could look across the railroad, you could look across Mobile River, you could look through the canebrakes. I would go up and play at boxing the compass, thinking about the world. When I got to the third grade, I had a map of the world. In the third grade room, there was a globe spinning on its axis, and the whole world was mine, and I feel it's been my oyster ever since. It's whatever I can make of it and make of myself in it.

THE TITLE OF THE NEW BOOK is *The Blue Devils of Nada,* and "nada" is nothingness, or entropy. The whole business of the blues is that the blues represents entropy. What we do when we play the blues is precisely that: we play with the blues, we stomp the blues. We get rid of the blues. So that blues music is good-time music because it dispels the menacing elements in the environment, or at least it holds them at bay, so we can get on with the human proposition.

The book is about the creative process. It's really about what we could call the vernacular imperative for American aesthetics—how to process raw

American experience into aesthetic statement or into a work of art using native devices. So it's a big thing, the interaction in the United States of the learned tradition imported by certain immigrants to a frontier situation in a context of free enterprise—not economic free enterprise but free to be enterprising, freedom to be enterprising, experimental frontier exploration. How do you process that into aesthetic statement and give an image of American character and a basis for American identity? That's what this is really about.

Count Basie picked me to write his autobiography. I'll give you a little story. Willard Alexander, who was his promoter, wanted him to get around to doing a book. He'd been promising to write for a long time. So he got in touch with Alec Wilder, who was a composer and a big jazz fan and so forth, and Alec Wilder said, "No, I can't touch it because I wouldn't want Albert Murray to read what I was trying to write about Count Basie. But I would like to read a book that [Albert Murray] would help Count Basie write." So Willard Alexander, Basie's promoter and producer, got in touch with me and I said, "Well, Alec Wilder is a friend of mine, he's a fan. You can't trust him. You have to read something of mine yourself."

I sent [Willard Alexander] a copy of *Stomping the Blues.* . . . he read it and called me back and said, "Why don't you have lunch with Count Basie and see what happens?" Well, I had been involved with Count Basie as a fan . . . since the band first struck. When I was in college in 1936, his band came on the scene. I was aware of the whole thing. I would have done the book for nothing just out of sentimentality.

So Count Basie and I got together, and I started telling him about my approach to writing, which is based on organizing the material as the jazz musician organizes it. And it's based on trying to reach a language which swings like the music swings. You get to that in prose through Hemingway, so you've got that four-four, and that's going to echo Walt Whitman and everything else that's vernacular. So you're fulfilling the vernacular imperative—to deal with experience which is idiomatically American, but deal with it with a technique that would give it universal appeal and affect. And, of course, jazz is our most exportable aesthetic commodity.

DUKE ELLINGTON AND I became very close after a number of years. I became a guy he would call to ask things, to talk to about books of ideas and so forth. I did radio programs with him when he came down to Tuskegee and I just hung around with him for a long time. And Billy Strayhorn, who was his arranger and staff adviser on literary matters, used to read things that I would write in *The New Leader* and various other places to him. Duke would recite these things to me. He'd say, "That's pretty good. I like that." And so he became interested in me on that—as a literary person who was interested in jazz.

I DIDN'T KNOW LOUIS ARMSTRONG. But Louis Armstrong was what you grew up knowing when I was in high school. We knew all of the records note by note. We would play it. We had a band at Mobile County Training School. I used to go when the band was rehearsing. They were getting all the records. They would make the transcriptions of the records. Armstrong was just a part of everything, as much a part of my growing up as the books that I was reading. He was there before Hemingway, he was there before Thomas Mann, he was there before [André] Malraux. I would fold it all into that, which is why I write what I hope is the literary equivalent to jazz.

HEMINGWAY IS OMNI-AMERICAN. Hemingway created what you could call "the grand style" of our epoch. A grand style is not a big style—it doesn't mean grandiose. It means the style or the method of stylizing experience which seems most natural to a given culture at a given time. So people will talk about the long periods of Proust, the convolutions of Henry James. When you took a manuscript into any editor, he puts on his glasses, he edits it with Hemingway glasses. He cuts out the extra adjectives, back down to where it swings and where it's highly evocative. It's as if Count Basie and Hemingway were reading the same style sheet at *The Kansas City Star.* It's a most American thing. So if you're going to put the blues idiom onto something that's already literary, Hemingway would be the guy.

DUKE ELLINGTON and Count Basie and Louis Armstrong succeeded. I think they've succeeded in their fields of finding what Constance Rourke—who's a big touchstone with me—wrote in a book called *American Humor: A Study of the National Character.* The book speaks of something that's very, very basic to this whole approach that I represent. She speaks of providing emblems for pioneer people who require resilience as a prime trait. To me, that adds up to swinging, and that's equivalent to what a frontiersman does, what an explorer does. It is the basis of the open, experimental attitude that you get in American character and the inventiveness that we're noted for. No art form encapsulates or expresses that more comprehensively and more effectively and on a higher level of sophistication than jazz, which is the ultimate extension, elaboration, and refinement of the blues.

I LISTEN TO MUSIC A LOT, but generally it's in my head, and my books are geared to music. If you read a novel, I could play a soundtrack. I have a whole tape of soundtrack that goes with everything, you see. It's my Proustian madeleine. You know when Proust tastes the tea, sticks the madeleine, the cookie—the little thing—into the tea and tastes it, and it brings back all that "remembrance of things past" of such a lost time. When I play certain pieces of music, the people come alive and I can hear them talking, and I can do what I want to do with them, so I can get back to it.

Carlo D'Este

On January 28, 1996, Carlo D'Este appeared on Booknotes *to talk about his book* Patton: A Genius for War. *Mr. D'Este is a military historian who lives on Cape Cod, Massachusetts. His previous book,* Decision in Normandy, *was reprinted as a World War II fiftieth anniversary paperback edition in March 1994.*

I WAS A CAREER OFFICER. I served in the United States Army from 1958 to 1978. I never dreamed that I was going to become a writer after I retired. I was stationed in England and retired over there. I did some graduate work at the University of London, and I decided that the academic life probably wasn't really what I wanted to do. So I ended up writing a book about the Normandy Campaign, which was published in 1983. It was pretty well received and that kind of launched me. I haven't stopped writing since.

There have been a lot of books about [Gen. George S.] Patton. Most of them have been about Patton's battles and campaigns. No one had shown how Patton's early life had shaped his career, had shaped the man who later became a general, and I wanted to go back, I wanted to explore his antecedents. I wanted to look at what made him tick. One just doesn't become a general that quickly. This was a lifetime of preparation for Patton. He was sixty years old when he died. The last four of those years are the years that we know about. The other fifty-six years of his life were fascinating. He had so many different careers and achievements that, had he never entered World War II, had he been retired, for example, he would have been a success. He didn't think so, but he would have been.

The narrative itself is—I would hesitate to point out—about 824 pages. I didn't really know what I was getting into when I started this. I had no idea what sort of book I was going to write. But I found that this man had such an extraordinary life. It was filled with so many dramatic events that I just wrote it the best way I could in terms of letting the story tell itself, and that's basically the way it ended up. It was such a big life that perhaps I could argue that it would be very difficult to do it in much less.

I had a great deal of help from Patton's daughter Ruth Ellen. His daughter Bea died at a very young age—in fact, just a few years after his own death. But Ruth Ellen lived until two years ago. Like most of the Patton family, she had an extraordinary memory. In fact, she had a photographic mind. And she could recall events that took place when she was four or five years old. She could quote her father and she could quote verse; she could quote Kipling not by the minute but by the hour. She lived not too far from me—a couple of hours—in the old original Patton homestead, which he and his wife Beatrice bought in 1928, in Hamilton, Massachusetts, called Green Meadows. [Ruth Ellen] had read my earlier books, so she knew who I was. I had sort of been after her. I had written several letters saying, "Would you please let me come talk to you about your father? Because I really think I want to do a book on him." A letter came one day that said, "Come and see me." So I did. Suffice to say, it was one of the most memorable days of my life. I learned things just watching her, seeing in her elements of her father—this marvelous intellect, this ability to remember things that simply makes me green with envy. I can't remember things that happened last week.

She had written this five hundred-and-some-odd-page family memoir pretty much for family use. It was really about her mother. It was never published. She didn't intend to publish it. It was for the benefit of other generations of Pattons, so they would have some idea of what a marvelous intellectual, brilliant woman George S. Patton was married to. We know a lot about Patton, but we don't know too much about Beatrice. That's one of the things I try to do in this book, to show the vital importance of the role that Beatrice played in his life.

I probably began the research for this book some fifteen years ago, but I never really seriously considered writing his biography until about 1988. I felt I had to really pay my dues, if you will, by doing writing about the war and getting an understanding of him and the characters that were part of his life. So by 1988, I felt that a biography of him was necessary. So I started it in 1988. When I began the research, I was still finishing up another book. I began seriously to write it about 1990.

I spent the most time probably right here in Washington. Certainly a substantial part of what we now call the Patton papers—the Patton collection—is in the Manuscript Division of the Library of Congress. So there's something like 125 boxes. So I spent week after week here. I would come for a week or two at a time and go home, try to digest it all. It took me six months just to put it on my computer so I could figure out what it was. I spent a lot of time at the Military History Institute at Carlisle [Pennsylva-

nia] and in British archives looking for material about him—things that
the British said about him. There are various monographs, papers in the
Imperial War Museum, in various collections in London. I spent time at
West Point. There's a growing collection of Patton material at West Point.

And then there's just an inordinate number of obscure yet important
secondary sources out there that I had to track down. And I had to go to
lots of different places. People would send me things. I would go through
newspaper clippings. I would go to the main part of the Library of Congress, the Reading Room, to learn about dyslexia, for example. So it wasn't
just finding things out about Patton. I had to learn about dyslexia before I
could really write about this man's life, because dyslexia was one of the two
major things that drove him.

I believe it has been firmly established by my research that Patton was a
dyslexic. The problem was that George S. Patton never knew that he was a
dyslexic. He went through his entire life, in many instances, believing that
he was slow. When he was young, he believed he was stupid. Dyslexia was a
driving force in this man's life. I think it obsessed him or led to an obsession
that he was destined someday to become a general who would command the
greatest army ever assembled, and that it was his destiny to do this.

His dyslexia had been mentioned in one or two previous books, but it's
never been, in my opinion, really analyzed. I don't think it's been related in
importance to Patton himself. So this was an area that, [for] a biographer, it
was extremely important—that I learn about dyslexia before I could write
about Patton. David McCullough had the same experience with a book he
did about young Teddy Roosevelt. Teddy Roosevelt had asthma. I learned
this from McCullough at a lecture I attended years ago. And he was talking
about how he couldn't have written Roosevelt's biography without first
learning about asthma. So I took my cue, really, from him.

THIS IS THE FIFTH BOOK I'VE DONE. The first four were works of military history. I did one on Normandy. I did a book on the Sicily Campaign.
The most recent book was a book about Anzio and the war in Italy. Then I
did a smaller book a couple of years ago on the war in the Mediterranean.
The Mediterranean, in general, is an area that military historians have not
paid a great deal of attention to. The war in Europe has been far more
attractive. Normandy has sort of been the thing that lures historians and
storytellers, and the Battle of the Bulge in Arnhem. The war in Italy and
the war in Sicily, for example, were some of the most brutal and difficult
aspects of World War II.

With the image of Patton in the 1970 movie, starring George C. Scott as George Patton, I think the one thing Patton would comment on immediately is George C. Scott had this wonderful, deep, very military, manly voice. Patton, unfortunately, the thing he hated the most about himself was that he felt he was cursed with a fairly high-pitched, almost a squeaky voice. It used to bug him a great deal that he didn't have a deeper, more manly approach to things. This is one aspect.

The other thing is that the real Patton probably was a better actor in his own right than George C. Scott because there were really two Pattons. There was the Patton that portrayed himself to the world—the tough guy, the macho character, the profane general who was dressed inordinately, with ivory-handled pistols and so forth, and arrived with the sirens screaming and so forth—and then there was the real Patton, the Patton whom very few people saw, the intellectual Patton.

He often wrote poems during World War I and during the interwar period, quite a bit. His poetry, I think, is almost a mirror to his soul. Through his poetry, you can see the torment and you can begin to grasp a little bit what drove this man. One of the reasons that I have some examples of his poetry is to try to show the reader some of the depth of this man's character, some of the things that he felt. He always felt that men were the key to winning battles, that it was soldiers that won battles; it wasn't machinery, it wasn't fancy guns or weapons or anything like that. In fact, he wrote an essay in the 1930s specifically addressing this problem and saying, "We mustn't pay attention to the advent of modern armaments and everything, because it is the soldier who wins battles, and it is the leader who helps take those soldiers forward to do that."

I think George Patton was a hero. To whole generations of Americans, he represented some very old-fashioned virtues. It may sound corny, perhaps, in this day and age, but he seriously believed in the West Point creed of "Duty, honor, and country." Patriotism was one of the strongest words in his vocabulary. He believed that a citizen had a duty to serve his country in a time of crisis, in a time of war.

MY PARENTS HAD A TREMENDOUS IMPACT on my life. My father was a world-class musician who fought in World War I. He hated it. He didn't really want to be a soldier, but he was conscripted as a young officer into the Austrian army. He came over to the United States in the twenties on a musician's visa, and he was an oboist and an English horn player. He came from Trieste. He played for Arturo Toscanini and the NBC Symphony. He was a man who gave me a sense of the importance of being a gentleman. He was such a tremendous influence on my life. He died, unfortunately, at a very young age. I had just graduated from college, so I was about twenty-two, but he'd been ill for ten or twelve years.

My mother just died two years ago. She was ninety-five, and she showed me the kind of courage that I simply can't put into words. She was a double amputee; she'd lost both her legs. People thought it was diabetes, but she had arteriosclerosis, and gangrene set in on her feet. It was one of these things. They had to save her life, they had to cut her leg off. She was eighty-seven when she lost her first leg, and they said she'd never walk again, and she did. Then, a year and a half later, they took off her other leg, so she's now a double amputee. That woman lived on her own until three or four months before she died. I moved her next door to where I was, so I could help take care of her. She was legally blind on top of it. But she showed me—there's all sorts of courage in this world. There's the courage that people show on the battlefield, and then there's the kind of quiet courage that she showed me.

Simon Schama

Simon Schama was born in London and has taught history at Cambridge, Oxford, and Harvard universities. He is now the Old Dominion Foundation Professor of the Humanities at Columbia University. His fourth book, Citizens: A Chronicle of the French Revolution, *was a best-seller. Mr. Schama appeared on the program on July 14, 1989, the bicentennial of the storming of the Bastille.*

I HAD A PUBLISHER IN ENGLAND who said to me as I was finishing my last book on Holland, "How about writing a book on the French Revolution for the bicentennial year?" I said, "There are thousands of books on the French Revolution. The world does not need another book on the French Revolution." "Listen," he said to me, clever man. "Supposing you had an aunt who knew nothing about the French Revolution, knew nothing about the eighteenth century, and wanted a history as a great story, what would you give her?" I said, "You have a point." I had been going around preaching that historians ought to tell more stories and stop talking to other historians. So he said, "Why don't you stop talking about it and try to?" Once I started to do it, it all came tumbling out. I did a lot more research. It was a book that really kind of just came pouring out of me, for better or worse, and has the virtues and vices of a literary impulse.

It took nearly two years. It was finished in '88, so I wrote it between the end of '86 and the fall of '88. I wrote some of it in France; I wrote some of it overlooking Lake Tahoe, an improbable place, but I wrote quite a bit of it in France. I wrote a lot of it at home in Lexington, Massachusetts, a place important for another revolution where the British Empire started to come unglued. Harvard has a magnificent French Revolutionary collection, in fact, in the library. There was this wonderful person called Archibald Cary Coolidge, who was the university librarian at Harvard in the 1920s. He was a kind of intellectual robber baron. Harvard had lots of money then, not that it's completely broke now. He said, "Nineteen twenty-one will be Portugal year." He went off to Portugal and to the University of Coimbra and bought everything he could lay his hands on. Nineteen twenty-five, or thereabouts, was France year, and he bought a collection of 50,000 books, newspapers, documents, posters, letters, and that helped me a good deal to do some of the work, at least in research at Harvard.

James McPherson's wonderful book on the American Civil War, *Battle Cry of Freedom,* was a best-seller; Paul Kennedy's book was a best-seller; Barbara Tuchman absolutely, correctly, was an instant best-seller in almost everything she did. There is an enormous hunger, not only in America either, for good, well-written narrative history. Historians in universities for a long time have sneered at this, have turned their backs on it and said, "If you write well you must have something to hide." It's kind of an inferior level of discourse—journalism. There's a wonderful phrase in a very condescending review in *The New York Review of Books,* where my reviewer, who was extremely critical, said, "Schama stoops to low journalistic devices in order to arrest the attention of his readers." That was a very wicked thing to do. How dare I? I'm trying to wrest the attention of my readers—it's much better than if they fall asleep. There are a lot of people, contrary to popular impression, who actually write very well in university departments, but they just don't feel they're permitted to relax somewhat and write history as a story and as an account of human experiences.

Both in America and in Britain, I've been very kindly treated by the book reviewers, but there are two hostile lines. The one I really mind, I suppose, and which makes me feel depressed, is the line which says, "You can't have a narrative and make an argument. The two simply don't go together. If you want to make an argument in a book, you must adopt what's called analytical history. You begin with a phrase like 'More light will be shed on. . . .' Above all you must begin in this analytical mode with preferably a fairly long recitation on what other historians have thought before you. Buggins has thesis B; Juggins revised Buggins; I, Muggins, will revise both Juggins and Buggins." So it's terribly incestuous, to begin with, but that is the kind of required canonical model you're supposed to do it in.

There's a wonderful phrase that W. H. Auden, the English poet, said, that "History is breaking bread with the dead." I had this extraordinary sense of companionship with a lot of these people. In fact, when I finished the book, I actually felt an odd sense of bad faith, that I had been part of these people's lives. I was saying, "Fine, Knopf. Have the book, forget about the French Revolution, bye-bye. See you when you're published." I felt this extraordinary sense that I was leaving these people's lives behind. I finished the book deliberately not with what historians usually do, which is say, "Now we will survey what's happened." I try and do that, but I said, "OK, the historian's impersonal voice, that's enough of that. Let's just tell the story again. Let's revisit this human experience in places of stillness." I wanted to finish with this sense of what the human cost really had been. I didn't sleep very well when I wrote this book, but I lived by day very well indeed. It was a very nineteenth-century kind of writing.

I'M REALLY PHYSICALLY QUITE LAZY, as a matter of fact. But I did something which I had never done in my life [when I wrote this book]. I got up at five o'clock and sometimes earlier in the morning, which is extraordinary for an Englishman. It's less extraordinary in America. I wrote it in this absolutely wonderful time before my children get up at about eight o'clock. I wrote through the day as well. But there were three hours of the dawn coming up where a lot got written and then again quite late at night, actually. Some in the daytime too, but I have to say that it was a book that tumbled out. I really was writing at some speed, but most of all it was never a chore to write.

I like writing at home with my dog, Morgan, who sort of slept under my computer. When the Revolution was too much, I used to reach for his hopeless, silky hair. So it was very calming. I have to say it was a wonderfully sedative effect. He should have had a credit in the preface.

Joseph Ellis

Joseph Ellis was awarded a Guggenheim Foundation grant in 1988 "to do a book on late eighteenth century America and that was to be a study of a prominent person, an ordinary person in a community, and a study of the changes sweeping through late eighteenth century America." Mr. Ellis chose to write about the second president of the United States, John Adams. A professor at Mount Holyoke College, Mr. Ellis appeared on Booknotes *on September 5, 1993, to discuss his book on Adams,* Passionate Sage.

I STARTED WITH [JOHN] ADAMS, and I never got out of Adams. The Adams material, the Adams correspondence is 608 reels of microfilm. Stretched in a straight line, it would be about five miles. So the sheer volume was really daunting. But Adams was just a hoot. He was just much more interesting than I had imagined him to be. I remember thinking of a book—that for me still is the best biography I've ever read of an American—by Justin Kaplan, called *Mr. Clemens and Mark Twain*. It was published back in the '60s, and I remember thinking when I read Kaplan's book, he has it easy because Clemens's Twain is just so wonderfully quotable. I had the same feeling when I got inside the Adams papers, that this is a man whose words are just so memorable and so wonderful.

I have always had a certain interest in Adams. As a historian of this period, I have read books about Adams, and I've always thought that he is perhaps the most unappreciated great man in American history, that the gap between what Adams really represents and who he was and what we know of him is perhaps greater than for any other major figure. So, there's a sort of personal crusade here, on my part, to recover and bring into our late-twentieth-century world a fuller appreciation of who he was. I would teach him, I would teach classes at Mount Holyoke College, where I teach now, and I would ask the students to read the correspondence between Adams and Jefferson—great correspondence of their latter years. Most of the students would come into the class with a pretty clear appreciation of Jefferson. There's a monument right down here in Washington to him; he's a great figure, Monticello, etc. They knew very little about Adams. What would happen is they would fall in love with Adams and, in fact, begin to think that maybe of those two men Adams was a more impressive figure. So I began to think maybe it wasn't just me. Maybe it wasn't just Joe Ellis who is regarding Adams as highly.

The earlier edition of the Adams papers, which were published back in the nineteenth century, was a good edition indeed, ten volumes. They were edited by his grandson Charles Francis, who was one of the best historical editors of his day and who is also, unfortunately, a kind of archetypal Victorian. That means that he felt a need to censor out those things that would be embarrassing. Some of the most interesting stuff on Adams doesn't make it into that edition. Adams's vituperative comments on [Alexander] Hamilton and all his peers get censored out, and that's one of the reasons why getting into the real Adams papers gives you an understanding of how colorful he was, and this we had none of before.

This book attempts to assess the character and personality and thought of Adams as a whole, but it doesn't want to sort of begin at the beginning and end at the end. It begins with Adams as president, and it looks back at his early career; but its tightest focus is on his retirement years, when he's himself reliving his life and his years from 1800 to 1826 as the sage of Quincy [Massachusetts].

The job of a historian of the Revolutionary years is to get us to understand the way it was back then on its own terms, but if, in fact, we're not interested in trying to make some connections, then I don't think we're being historians. I think we're being antiquarians. There's got to be some sort of connection, it seems to me. That's the reason we read. That's the reason we study these people. That's the reason Adams is interesting. He speaks to us in some important ways. So I'll be the first to acknowledge that the late eighteenth century is a time when we need to appreciate its, if you will, differentness, separate culture out there. There's a kind of Grand Canyon between us and them.

John Adams read a lot. Even in his old age when his eyes were so bad, he had people read to him—and, you know, we think of Jefferson as a great reader, and he was. He was a great reader, and the Jefferson library was the foundation for the Library of Congress. Adams is perhaps the only member of the Revolutionary generation who was better read than Jefferson, and that's not just a special plea here. Jefferson himself said that.

The normal notion that you could look at a person's library and be able to tell by looking at the titles what the basic drift of this person's thinking and opinions were—you would be driven mad by Adams, because Adams liked to buy books that he disagreed with. He would then read these books, and in the margins he would write almost as much as was in the original text; and, by the way, many of these books are in Boston. They're in the Boston Public Library in the archival section, and you can go back there and read this marginalia. His marginalia is, in some ways, the most revealing statement of his political philosophy, because he will write things like, you know, in Rousseau, "Thou flea, thou vermin, thou wretch. Thou understandest not humankind."

[After some fellow historians reviewed the manuscript], I then picked some old friends who were not historians—one is what we refer to as a capitalist reptile (he plays the stock exchange on a regular basis), and the other is a businessman who read it to give us a perspective from outside the academy. I'm most interested, really, in bringing Adams to life for a general public. While I certainly want to have my *i*'s dotted and my *t*'s crossed, and I want this to be a critical success as a scholarly book, I'm most interested in getting it to a group of people who are not professional historians but read biography.

I made the decision to keep the book short—it's only 242 pages. My colleagues say I write with a quill pen. It's not a quill pen; it's a black pen. But I really think that some of these books that are coming out now that you can use as [doorstops], you can't sit them on your lap, and I think a book is something you should be able to read in a couple of sittings. And the length of this is the length that I thought it ought to be. I was under no pressure to cut it by any stretch.

I did an informal survey of the taverns and watering holes of western Massachusetts and there discovered that if you said the word "Adams" inside these places that they don't think of John. They think of Sam because of Samuel Adams Beer.

Blanche Wiesen Cook

The biographer Blanche Wiesen Cook, author of Eleanor Roosevelt: Volume 1, 1884–1933, *came to the program on April 11, 1993. Ms. Cook has edited 360 books for the Garland Reference Library of War and Peace. She is also the author of* The Declassified Eisenhower *and a book called* Crystal Eastman on Women and Revolution.

I THINK THERE IS NEW INFORMATION and I think there's a vastly different interpretation in this book. A lot of people have always portrayed Eleanor Roosevelt as really lonely and unhappy, without a private life of her own. I think the thing that is very controversial in my book is that I suggest that she had a very full life and a very full private life. I leave it up to the reader as to whether or not she had a full sexual affair with Lorena Hickok who, when she met her, was the highest-paid reporter for the Associated Press. I say over and over again that we don't know what people do in the privacy of their own private lives. The doors are closed, the drapes are drawn, and so on. But it does seem to me that the letters, and there are thousands of letters which they wrote to each other, reveal a very passionate friendship. We have both sides of that correspondence, although Lorena Hickok really destroyed much more of her own papers, so that there are many more letters from Eleanor Roosevelt to Lorena Hickok than Lorena Hickok to Eleanor Roosevelt.

I didn't start working on the first volume until 1981. I was not really interested in Eleanor Roosevelt. My own field is international relations, and I had just finished a book called *The Declassified Eisenhower,* which also took me ten years. I finished that and wrote in my journal, "I've now spent most of my vital youth with one dead general." I went around looking for something else to do. I discovered how important Eleanor Roosevelt was when this really lookist interpretation of her friendship with Lorena Hickok was published, this mean-spirited book that said these two unattractive women were so miserable and lonely that they became friends—and that they got it on. But they didn't really get it on because they were miserable and lonely. And Eleanor Roosevelt was a saint and a mermaid. So it was just a horrible book. I wrote a very nasty review of that book, and then people said, "Well, why don't you write a biography of Eleanor Roosevelt?" I thought, well, why? I mean, she's not really a hero. Then I went to look at her papers, and I discovered that we just didn't know, really, very much about her.

I wrote everything I've written, until Eleanor Roosevelt, literally longhand by fountain pen. One day I lost my fountain pen, and I could not find another decent fountain pen. Phyllis Wright has this wonderful store where I live in East Hampton [Long Island]—actually her store is in South Hampton—called East End Computers. She is a wonderful woman. I walked in there, and I said, "All right, it's time for me to change my life. I can't find a fountain pen in this town." She really not only taught me how to do it [use a computer], she helped me to do it. Every time I had a problem and I couldn't get my document up, I would call Phyllis Wright. She gave me her home phone number so I could call her day or night for that period of transition that drives writers crazy. Now I'm all plugged in. Now I have a computer everywhere and a laptop that I take everywhere. I still have a fountain pen. Someone bought me one, but the fountain pen era is over.

[This book] has just come out, and it's already in a second printing. People really like this book. I think it's an important book for women and men who want to imagine a more political and more decent future. It's a book also about self-esteem, about how you can look history in the face and say, "Well, I'm going to change my life. I'm going to make things better. I'm going to make things better not only for everybody who I identify with who needs to have things better, but I'm going to change my own life so that I'm going to be happy. I'm going to live fully." I think Eleanor Roosevelt's goal was to live fully. She wrote a wonderful book at the age of seventy-six in 1960. It's called *You Learn by Living,* in which she defines her own life as an adventurer and she says, "I have lived my life as an adventurer, and my goal was to taste things as fully and as deeply as I could and to learn from every experience because there is not a single experience that you can't learn something from."

Nicholas Basbanes

On October 15, 1995, Nicholas Basbanes appeared on Booknotes *to discuss his best-selling book,* A Gentle Madness: Bibliophiles, Bibliomanes, and the Eternal Passion for Books. *From 1978 to 1991, Mr. Basbanes was the book review editor at* The Sunday Telegram *in Worcester, Massachusetts.*

I COINED THE TITLE myself, actually. It was a description made of Isaiah Thomas, a great nineteenth-century American bibliophile and collector. When he died, his grandson Benjamin Franklin Thomas, said, "Grandfather was afflicted from the earliest age with the gentlest of infirmities: He was a bibliomaniac." And when I saw that description of him, I said, "There's my title."

On the cover of the book, it is, in fact, a woodcut—a very famous one. It's 500 years old. It was executed by Albrecht Dürer. It's called *The Book Fool,* and it was in . . . *Das Narrenschiff,* the original Ship of Fools. And the first fool of the whole navy, the fool at the helm, was the bibliomane, the book fool. And I've always loved that particular engraving, and I chose it for the dust jacket.

I'm just so proud of the job that [Henry] Holt did with this book. I don't know what it cost them to do that dust jacket. I'm sure it was expensive. They also didn't have to give me the end sheets inside, but they did that—you know, when you open the book and you see the end sheets. They did that to make it a better book. They didn't have to give me thirty-two pages of photographs, but they did. Sixteen would have sufficed. But they were committed to publishing this book, and doing it well. What they told me is they did it because they thought it was a book that deserved to be published, and they wanted to do the best job they could with it. And I'm very grateful to them for that.

If someone buys this book, they get a book, I hope, that they will keep and enjoy and pass on to others. They will have a record of the passion for collecting books—not only collecting books, but preserving knowledge over 2,500 years.

I am often asked if I'm a bibliomaniac myself, and my stark answer is, "I'm on the cusp." One review of my book recently suggested, "Well, Nick

Basbanes might not be a bibliomaniac, but he's at risk." I have been committed to books all my life. I'm a professional writer and journalist, and I was a book review editor in Massachusetts for thirteen years, and I've interviewed many, many authors. I've just always loved books, read them, and treasured them. So it was just a natural kind of a thing to want to write about this passion.

I was the book review editor at *The Sunday Telegram* in Worcester, Massachusetts, which is in central Mass. It's about forty-five miles from Boston. I grew up in Massachusetts. And I was book editor from 1978 to 1991. From the very beginning—I think this is pertinent—I always have interviewed authors, and I have always asked them to inscribe my books. I have perhaps 2,000 inscribed books. People wonder, "How does he have 2,000 books when he's only interviewed 1,000 authors?" Well, I cheated. If I were interviewing Joe Heller on *Good as Gold*, well, I might bring along a *Catch-22* and ask him to inscribe that. Or Arthur Miller, for instance if I was interviewing him on his autobiography *Timebends*, I would have *Death of a Salesman* there, which I sought out and found. So it became a collection, which I think is a unique collection, and that kind of explains, I guess, the passion for the subject.

Faulkner understood the value of his signed books. He actually went out of print in his lifetime and, thankfully, he came back. People rediscovered him. But for a period, he would sign limited editions of his books, and these accounted for some extra income.

One night, there was a dinner party at his editor's home, Bennett Cerf [one of the founders of Random House], and to their party was invited Alfred Knopf, who went up to Faulkner and said, "I scoured all these used book stores in the Lower East Side of Manhattan." He had about a half a dozen books, and he said he would appreciate it if Faulkner would sign some of them. Faulkner replied, "I can't sign any of these books." He said, "This is how I make my income." He said, "I only sign them for my friends." He is said to have had a few too many drinks that night, perhaps. But Cerf prevailed and said, "Can you at least sign one?" And he did.

I can date when I first started working on this book. It was in 1987, when I wrote a magazine piece about the American Antiquarian Society in Worcester, Massachusetts, which was established by Isaiah Thomas, the gentleman I mentioned earlier, and for whom the title of this book is more or less a salute, a little bow to my region. So I wrote this piece and it was very well received. And in the following year, I wrote another magazine piece about 1,200 years of book collecting in Boston, 1,200 years—350 at Harvard, 200 at the Massachusetts Historical Society, the Atheneum, and so on, until it adds up to about 1,200 years.

So this story on 1,200 years of book publishing in Boston was published and it had a very nice reception. And my wife suggested one day, "You know, there's your book, the book that you perhaps even were born to write." And you have that surge of energy—of the light flash and the cartoon character, and that's what spawned the idea for this book.

The toughest thing about writing this book was staying the course, I guess. It took eight years, but it was really not hard. I loved it.

WHAT I FOUND is that people collect [books] all over the United States, but the centers are, I think, obviously, in New York, because that's where the major auction houses are. That's where many of the great dealers are. But I have a chapter in the book I called "Continental Drift," which describes some of the great, great collecting activity that goes on in California. You find centers all over the country, and I think this is validated by the success of these antiquarian book fairs which you see traveling everywhere. Just recently, there was one in Washington, D.C. I was here signing copies of my book. I think they attracted 3,000 people. But at these little bazaars—they're traveling bazaars—you have perhaps as many as 120 entrepreneur book dealers from all over the United States. They'll bring their wares into one auditorium for a weekend, and people will come and have an opportunity to meet dealers from other parts of the country. These things go everywhere and have really brought book collecting to, literally, every region of the country.

In my book, I describe a postal employee who was a bachelor and lived out in Los Angeles. He just loved books. It is worth noting that he was a postal employee because that means he had a government job during the Depression—a steady job. He spent all of his income—everything—on books. He filled his house. He couldn't move. I mean, I think he finally had to sleep in the kitchen. When he died, he died among his books, alone. I think they found him two or three weeks afterwards. The books were dispersed by the county.

CHAPTER 13 IN THE BOOK revolves around Stephen Blumberg. Stephen is the individual who stole something on the order of 24,000 very rare books from 368 libraries in forty-five states, two Canadian provinces, and the District of Columbia. I thought he should be in the book because he stole these books not out of greed, not to sell them, as most other book thieves have done, but because he loved them and [loved] to collect them. He brought them together at a house in Ottumwa, Iowa, where he was finally arrested.

He was born in St. Paul. As you might have seen from some of those photographs, he looks sometimes like a homeless person. In one of the photos, he's in a Dumpster. The story behind it is that we were driving down to Ottumwa. He had this old 1969 Cadillac and he roared off the road. He saw a Dumpster; jumped in—and I mean headfirst—jumped in, and the thing was shaking back and forth. Refuse was flying out of the top, and I remember saying—I had my camera and I said, "Thank you." And when he popped up out of the Dumpster with a book, I shot a picture. He called that "rescuing treasures."

As we speak, we're into our third printing. The most recent number I've heard is, we're up to 35,000 copies, which is very gratifying to me—and I am gratified. I'm not really—at the risk of sounding immodest, I'm not really surprised. I am surprised at the response and the wonderful things people say about it, but my feeling, as a lifelong journalist, has always been, if you got a good story and you tell it well, people will want to read about it, and I was very confident from the beginning. The stories were wonderful. They haven't been told before, and I was confident in my ability to tell them well.

Ben Yagoda

Ben Yagoda lives in Swarthmore, Pennsylvania. He is a professor of journalism at the University of Delaware and a freelance journalist. Professor Yagoda appeared on Booknotes on September 25, 1994, to talk about his book Will Rogers: A Biography.

WHEN I WAS FIRST CONTEMPLATING writing the book, I took a trip out to Oklahoma to see what was there—and there was a notebook, and my eye spotted it. It said "Letters to Will Rogers from Famous People." I was flipping through it, and there were letters from Franklin D. Roosevelt, who was a friend of his, Calvin Coolidge, Bernard Baruch, people like that. There was a letter from Charles Lindbergh, who, it turned out, was also a friend of his. Will Rogers in the 1920s was the number-one proponent of aviation in the country. He was just an incredible enthusiast. When he died, ironically in an airplane crash, it was estimated he had logged more miles than any nonpilot in the country. Anyway, Lindbergh had written him this letter in 1929. He said, "Dear Will, I'm glad to see that you're riding the airlines. I hope you keep out of single-engine planes at night." Knowing how he had died, this just came as a shock. I had read other Rogers biographies. This quote was not in any of them. There's great material here, and the more I looked into him, the more fascinating he became to me.

I was surprised in the course of writing the book to discover—and I found this out fairly soon after starting—how incredibly famous and popular he was. It's a puzzling thing. . . . He was really at the height of his popularity when he died in 1935. But there was I, growing up in the sixties, seventies, never hearing hardly anything about him except when they came along in the movie theaters asking for donations [for the Will Rogers Foundation]. I still puzzle over that a little bit.

When I started off on Rogers, I didn't know anything about him, just these couple of quotations. As I got more and more into it, I was more and more fascinated. On the one hand, just because of all the things he did and represented, things about America, things about the media culture of the twentieth century, things about his background, having grown up in Indian Territory, a quarter-blood Cherokee, his father having fought for the Confederacy in the Civil War, as many Cherokee did. And then moving on through vaudeville, the Ziegfeld Follies, silent movies, the talking pictures, American humor—he just seemed to represent so much. So that was one of the things that excited me about the book. But another thing kept me going with it, and that was a bit of a deeper appeal—I need to quote a line to explain it: One of Rogers's best friends was the actor Joel McCrea, the movie actor who died actually about two or three years ago, who had said [in an interview], "There's a word for Will Rogers. That word is glory. He lent a little bit of glory to everything he touched."

I wouldn't say this book was easy but once I got the material, it was so good, and the structure, which I find usually the hardest thing of writing, the broader structure was there. It was the chronology of his life. If I had finished writing about 1912, I'd say, "Oh, God, what do I do now?" Well, 1913. It's right there. I try not to just do "and then this happened and then that happened," but the chronology was built in. So I would come up and I'd see where I stopped the day before, and I would try to advance the story a little bit, make it readable, and try to provide some insights about what was going on in the culture. But it was not like Red Smith said about writing—you know, "opening a vein and letting the blood out." It was more pleasant than that.

I have a few other subjects in mind for my next book. None have been crystallized. I feel that I found such a wonderful subject here, I haven't been able to find one that lives up to it. Then again, one of the reasons why it took me so long to find this, all the good subjects have been taken, it sometimes seems. It's been tough finding another one, but I'll be there.

Nathaniel Branden

Nathaniel Branden was one of the earlier and more memorable storytellers to appear as a guest on Booknotes. *Mr. Branden is a psychiatrist as well as an author. His appearance, which aired on July 2, 1989, was devoted to his book* Judgment Day: My Years with Ayn Rand.

I DECIDED TO WRITE THE MEMOIR only when I fell in love with the sheer drama of the story. I never had any interest in writing memoir or autobiography. I had written ten previous books in the field of psychology and philosophy. I had other motives, but the first motive, without which nothing would have happened, was I suddenly saw this incredible novel-like chain of developments, except that it all was true. To illustrate what I mean, a few simple facts: first, I'm fourteen years old and living in Toronto and I read *The Fountainhead* and fall in love with it. This becomes the chief companion of my rather lonely and alienated adolescence. At the age of eighteen, I meet the girl who will become my first wife. Why are we introduced? Because she is as enthusiastic about *The Fountainhead* as I am. That's the beginning of the plot integration.

Two years later, I write Ayn Rand a letter to ask her a number of rather challenging questions about her ideas. She's fascinated by my letter; it leads to a personal meeting. I stay talking philosophy till five-thirty in the morning. This is March of 1950, a month before I turn twenty, and she is forty-five years old. The next week, I bring Barbara [my wife] and we four—that is to say Ayn Rand, her husband Frank, Barbara, and I—become almost like a family. We become very, very close. We begin to read *Atlas Shrugged* in manuscript as it's being written, and we're having these intoxicating philosophical discussions, endlessly, endlessly, endlessly. Eighteen months later, after a long and agonizing process, Rand and I plunge into a love affair—with the knowledge and consent of Frank and Barbara.

Ayn Rand used to tell me that I should write novels, not just books on philosophy. I have a great love of theater. I had no outlet for that in my books on psychology. What excited me about telling [Ayn Rand's story] was when I saw it as a kind of nonfiction novel. That's what inspired me. So now the challenge was to take that story and to tell it, but to tell the difficulties—that was the excitement: (*a*) the difficulty of the sheer complexity of the story of the intertwining and intermingling of the philosophical, the sociological, the personal, the developmental; (*b*) the challenge to be almost terrifyingly honest, the challenge to almost terrifying self-confrontation. Because I did a lot of things I regretted very, very bitterly, and I had to go back and look at that. I am a man who is a professional psychologist—teaches other people to do it—and now, not only was I challenged to do it, but I was challenging myself to do it publicly. A lot of people have expressed shock that I was willing to be this self-disclosing in print. If the story was worth telling, it was worth telling truthfully.

[Ayn Rand] would be horrified [by this book], but she would be impressed by the quality of the writing. She always admired my writing, and literally this is far and away the best thing I've ever done. However, I think that the novelist in her and the writer in her would be in conflict with the woman in her.

Stephen Ambrose

To help mark the fiftieth anniversary of D-Day, the historian Stephen Ambrose appeared on Booknotes *on June 5, 1994, to discuss his seventeenth book,* D-Day, June 6, 1944: The Climactic Battle of World War II. *Mr. Ambrose, a professor of history at the University of New Orleans, has written numerous best-sellers, including biographies of Presidents Eisenhower and Nixon, and his 1996 work* Undaunted Courage: Meriwether Lewis, Thomas Jefferson and the Opening of the American West.

*Y*OU KNOW, D-DAY, you can't exaggerate it. You can't overstate it. It was the pivot point of the twentieth century. It was the day on which the decision was made as to who was going to rule in this world in the second half of the twentieth century. Is it going to be Nazism, is it going to be communism, or are the democracies going to prevail? If we would have failed on Omaha Beach and on the other beaches on the sixth of June in 1944, the struggle for Europe would have been a struggle between Hitler and Stalin, and we would have been out of it. If Stalin had won, the iron curtain would have been on the English Channel. This was Hitler's great chance to win the war—stop them in June of 1944 on the Atlantic coast; then he can move eleven Panzer divisions to the east. Eleven Panzer divisions might well have swung the balance on the eastern front, or they might have had another effect. They might have led Stalin to conclude, "Those blankety-blank capitalists. They're up to their old tricks. They're going to fight till the last Red Army soldier. To hell with that. I'm going to cut a deal with my friend Adolf again, just like we did in 1939. We'll divide Eastern Europe between us." That wouldn't have lasted. Sooner or later they would have clashed, but the democracies wouldn't have been in on it anymore.

On D-Day, I was in Whitewater, Wisconsin. My father was in the Pacific. I was ten years old, and I was doing what I could for the war effort. I had a victory garden; I collected tin cans. We used to save the tinfoil from the chewing gum and get great big balls of it, and we would turn it in. I'm not sure that it was anything more than a morale booster for the kids. I guess they made use of it. But we felt very much a part of the war effort.

I first got interested in military history and history in general as a sopho-more [at the University of Wisconsin]. I was a premed. I was going to fol-low in my father's footsteps. Then I went into a course in American history that the university required you to take. I wanted to take biology and anatomy and embryology, but they forced you to take a history course. So I just willy-nilly signed up for one. I walked in, and the professor—his name was William B. Hesseltine—had been talking about three minutes, and I wasn't a premed anymore. I was a history major. After that lecture I went up to him, and I said, "I want to do what you do for a living. How do I go about doing that?"

In my junior year in college at Christmas vacation time, I hitchhiked down to New Orleans with my roommate Dick Lamm, who later went on to great fame as governor of Colorado. When we left Madison [Wiscon-sin], it was forty degrees below zero. I'm not talking wind chill; I'm talking the real thing. We got down to New Orleans, and it was just gorgeous. I thought, gee, they let people live here? Plus, New Orleans is New Orleans, and I'm a small-town boy from the Midwest. You walk down Bourbon Street, and it makes an impression on you. So from the beginning I wanted to get a job in New Orleans. I had fallen in love with the city, and I'm still in love with it, hopelessly, lo these many years later.

I was a Civil War historian, and in 1964 I got a telephone call from Gen-eral Eisenhower, who asked if I would be interested in writing his biogra-phy. He had read a couple of my Civil War books. "Yes, sir," said I, and it got started there. I mean, you can't do Eisenhower's biography and not be interested in D-Day.

[Former President Eisenhower] was without any question the most impressive man I've ever met. Monty [Field Marshal Bernard Law Mont-gomery] once said of Eisenhower, "He has but to smile at you and you trust him at once," and I certainly had that experience of Eisenhower. Monty said, "He has the power of drawing the hearts of men toward him as the magnet attracts the bits of metal." He was wonderfully concerned; he was marvelously concentrated. I was just a kid. I was thirty years old when I was interviewing him. I'd walk in to interview him, and his eyes would lock on mine and I would be there for three hours and they never left my eyes. And he talked about what I wanted to talk about. There weren't any coughs and there wasn't any shifting of position and there wasn't any looking off to see what an aide over here or over there was doing. There wasn't any looking at the watch. It was straight on: "Let's talk about what you want to talk about. My time is valuable, your time is valuable, let's get at it." He was a man who had great concern for others. I was teaching at [Johns] Hopkins and going up two days a week to Gettysburg to work with him in his office, and he used to worry about where I would eat on the way home. He would warn me against certain restaurants, because he had made that drive so many times. Can you imagine?

Nixon had only been president for less than a year when Eisenhower died. Eisenhower was ambivalent about Nixon, as most people who knew Nixon were. He admired certain things about Nixon; he regretted quite a lot about Nixon. He found it amazing that Nixon could live a life without any personal friends. He used to shake his head at that: "I don't understand how he could do that." He used to say that Nixon spends too much time trying to look like a nice guy instead of just being one.

For myself, I began as a Nixon hater. I went to the University of Wisconsin. I was a liberal, and I thought Nixon was just the worst of the worst—a man without character, a man who everything he did was contrived. There was no spontaneity to the man, as far as I could see. Everything was done on the basis of, will this hurt or help Dick Nixon politically. So I was right up there with the Nixon haters until I began working on him.

I HAVE A CABIN in northernmost Wisconsin that I go to in the summers, where I do almost all of my writing. I've spent at least a part of every summer of my life there. My grandfather purchased it. It's twenty acres with a small lake. My grandfather was in the corps of engineers in 1938, so he had a salary. This place came up for sale for the back taxes, $161. He bought it, and he built this log cabin. Now it's become mine and it's where I go in the summer.

My wife [Moira] is indispensable to me when I work on these books. At the end of every day I want to hear how it came out. One of the things that drives me as a writer is curiosity, and I never can know what really happened until I sit down and have to write it up. After I've spent eight, ten hours at the typewriter, I'm dying to hear what I wrote. I don't want to just read it; I want to read it aloud and get a reaction and a response. So at the end of her day, she sits down with me, and if I've done ten pages that day or fifteen, she listens and then she jumps on me. She's always accusing me of triumphalism and making me cut back on that. I like to fly the flag high, and Moira wants to be a little more critical than that.

I get lovely letters from people from all over, and it just means the world to me. People say nice things to me about the books. They tell me that they've read them and they enjoy them, and that's the big, principal payoff. It most especially comes when veterans tell me that you've got it right. But

I don't like this taste of celebrityhood. I like being a writer, and I was a pretty well-known writer before this last month, but nobody knew my face. I wish it were back to that way, and it will be as soon as we get past June sixth [1994] [the D-Day fiftieth anniversary].

I'm right now into chapter 16 of a biography of Meriwether Lewis, which has been a dream of mine since 1976. We—Moira and I and our kids—wanted to do something special for the two hundredth birthday of the United States, something other than watching fireworks and getting drunk. We decided we were going to go to Lemhi Pass, which is on the Idaho-Montana border. It's the place where Meriwether Lewis became the first American to cross the Continental Divide. We camped up there that night, and we had the most gorgeous night, with the stars. You could reach up and touch them. We brought some booze along, and we had some students with us, and we got royally drunk and sang "God Bless America" and other patriotic songs, lying on our backs, looking at these stars.

I've wanted to write about Lewis for a long time, and for one reason or another—I was going to write about Lewis when I finished with Ike, and Alice Mayhew, my editor, said, "No, Steve, you've got to do Nixon next." I said, "Alice, I don't want to do Nixon. I don't like Nixon. You know, that's a big undertaking, to write a biography." She said, "You've got to do it." I said, "No, I'm not going to do it." Then she got me. She said, "Where else will you find such a challenge as this?" So I did the Nixon. That meant putting off the Meriwether Lewis. Then it was time to write the D-Day book, as I absolutely had long since planned to spend 1991 and 1992 and the first part of 1993 writing about D-Day. Well, I've got D-Day behind me, and now it's Meriwether Lewis.

I always think my last book is my best. So right now the D-Day book is my best, but this Meriwether Lewis book—wait until you see it. The best thing so far is Lewis's relationship with Thomas Jefferson. I love writing about Thomas Jefferson, and he had a very special relationship with Meriwether Lewis. They were neighbors. Lewis's father died when Lewis was very young, but he had been a friend of Jefferson's. Then Lewis was Jefferson's secretary for two years, living with him in the White House, just the two of them. You know, Jack Kennedy had that great line, when he had the Nobel Prize winners for dinner at the White House. He said, "There has never been such a gathering of brains and talent in this house since Thomas Jefferson dined alone." The only thing wrong with that line is, Thomas Jefferson never dined alone. He dined with Meriwether Lewis.

Martin Gilbert

The British historian Martin Gilbert appeared on our program in December 1991, and recounted some of the more remarkable moments he had during his twenty-five years as Sir Winston Churchill's official biographer. His book on the wartime prime minister of Great Britain is Churchill: A Life.

I'M CALLED THE OFFICIAL BIOGRAPHER, though, to the enormous credit of the Churchill family, they've never asked to see a single word of what I was writing until the books were printed and bound and ready for sale to the public. They never asked me to delete a word, or to skirt around a particular issue. So "official" is a misnomer if it's thought to mean a censored or restricted biographer. "Official biographer" means some poor sod had to be willing to give thirty years of his working life, give up his university teaching, give up his lecturing, give up the amenities of being, as it were, a clubbable don on an Oxford University high table, and be willing to sit in archives, which I enjoy. I don't complain about one moment. But basically it meant someone who would do it full-time, day after day for thirty years.

I wrote six of the eight volumes of the official narrative, and I produced eight volumes of documents—his letters and documents. In fact, I'm now doing his war documents. This is everything boiled down to one. It's a sort of, hopefully, delicious consommé of Churchill's life.

I never counted the words, but very much to my embarrassment, *The Guinness Book of World Records* did—and they put it in as the longest biography in the English language. It's about eight and a half million words. But you know, I started with fifteen tons of weight of his letters and papers, so it had to be constantly reduced and sifted through. I used to even read his laundry lists. People said, "What can you possibly learn from a laundry list? You certainly can't publish laundry lists." But on one occasion I found a laundry list from a Beirut hotel, and I thought to myself that I didn't know Churchill was in Beirut. From that laundry list—it had a date—I discovered a journey which was not, as it were, in the history books, which he had made to the Middle East—to Beirut, and then to Amman, and then to Jerusalem. Then I found British officials, young British officers at the time, who had been there at that year, 1934, and even they [had] acquired some historical documents about his views and thoughts during that visit. So, laundry lists have their uses, too.

THE WHOLE BIOGRAPHY, I wrote in pen and ink. In fact, this is the pen I wrote the eighth volume with—it's called a Pelikan. It's a serviceable ink pen. I think it may be French. Then I bought another pen to write this volume with, and my wife said, "Put it away. We have to become modern." So I acquired a computer. I wrote this on a computer, and I must say, I enjoyed it enormously.

I've always done all my own research. I was very lucky, indeed, but I always had one person to help me sort the files and go with me to the archives—if only because under the British system, one person can only call for three files, but two people can call for six. One of my assistants, Larry Arnn, is now running a policy study unit in Claremont, California. He was extremely good, but unfortunately he fell in love with my secretary, so he married her and she's also in California. Then I got another assistant who came—in 1971—and I fell in love with her, so she is now my wife. We sit together and we read every document together. I then write the chapter. She, then, reads it and says, "Wait a minute, you haven't properly interpreted that document," or "You haven't got the best out of it," or "You've exaggerated what it says." So it's been the two of us.

There is probably something new on every page. It was my ambition that you would open the book anywhere and read a page and say halfway down, "I never knew that. This is new." So, it's full of lovely new things and full of little aspects of history which perhaps have been neglected and forgotten. And also his humor and his all-aroundness. I mentioned his painting. He wasn't an obsessive man about politics. He was obsessive about right and wrong, but right and wrong in the wider sense.

I believe that about 35,000 copies sold. It came out on the first of November, so it's had almost a month's run—three or four weeks now—and the second reprint is out, and hopefully the third, fourth, fifth reprint, if your viewers will rush to buy it. Hopefully it will go on selling, because it is the sole one-volume work which contains his most personal stories, his most personal letters. Everybody said, "You'll never do it in one volume." There are many multivolumes, mostly incomplete, but many people have tried a multivolume, including myself. You know, the average man on the street can't carry around an eight-volume or even a three-volume set of his biography. We live in an age where, much as one would like to sit down and read books, you can't. So, here is Churchill in one volume. He fits. There's more to say, but there's so much there. It's a sort of fruitcake which has only fruit.

Winston Churchill read an enormous amount. He was almost the only person I've come across who, before he went to bed, would arrange for all the newspapers which were published in our country to arrive at about midnight. He didn't just read the London *Times*. He read the *Times* and the *Guardian*, and the *News Chronicle* and the popular papers, and the mass-circulation papers, and even the communist paper. He only cut out the communist paper when his wife said, "Darling, we must cut down on the papers. We haven't got enough money."

David Levering Lewis

David Levering Lewis is the Martin Luther King, Jr., Professor of History at Rutgers University in New Jersey. He joined us on January 2, 1994, to discuss W.E.B. DuBois: The Biography of a Race, 1868–1919, *which is the first of two volumes he is writing on DuBois. The first volume won the Pulitzer Prize for Biography in 1994.*

I WROTE THIS BOOK because it was one of the major missing American biographies. This is a large life that impinges upon so many issues, and there was no biography. There had been biographical attempts earlier— about twenty years earlier, and there's a very fine political biography that came out not so long ago. But none had access to the correspondence of DuBois, some 115,000 items deposited with the University of Massachusetts at Amherst. I was fortunate to have first access to them, so that meant it was simply a live option not to be sidestepped, the writing of the biography, because it could be done.

I wanted to use the life not simply to address and retrieve the multifaceted personality of DuBois, but to use it as a window onto much of the twentieth century. DuBois had said memorably in 1900, in England, addressing a conference, that the problem of the twentieth century was the problem of the color line. So I wanted to track that problem through his life on several continents in the first and second volumes.

Another reason for writing this biography is there were many people who have no knowledge of DuBois because he became a virtual un-person as a result of his political decisions in the last decade of his life—so much so that even people who had grown up admiring DuBois wanted to distance themselves from him. They felt genuinely that he was making mistakes; that communism was not only not the way, but that even if it had some redeeming features, it was too deadly a philosophy during the 1950s for African-Americans to espouse openly. So, for reasons of strategy and conviction, virtually everyone who had any profile or significance within Afro-America distanced himself from DuBois.

I was never bored by W.E.B. DuBois, and I don't dislike him. He's a hard guy to like. I admire him and am, at times, troubled by him.

It's hard to say what my favorite discovery was while writing the book. I found it amusing that he would agree to have a cigar named after him, provided it was a good cigar. I found that as an intellectual and as a formal man, he was also a great lover. Women found him simply irresistible. There will be more of that in volume 2.

bell hooks

On November 19, 1995, author bell hooks appeared on Booknotes *to discuss her eleventh book,* Killing Rage: Ending Racism. *Ms. hooks is Distinguished Professor of English at City College in New York City. Previously, she was an assistant professor at Yale University and a professor at Oberlin College.*

THE BOOK *Killing Rage* really came out of this experience I was having. I've always seen myself as a very nonviolent person. And I was on an airplane with a friend. We were both in first class and we both had seats. Then a white man wanted to come on at another stop and wanted a seat. He had the right boarding pass, which my friend didn't have. And we ended up in this enormous misunderstanding that became quickly very racialized.

After it all happened, my friend had been very humiliated in front of everyone and sent to coach and what have you. He sat down on her belongings and he said to me, "You know, I'm sorry. It wasn't my fault." And I felt such a sense of rage and powerlessness, but I really felt like I could murder him, and I was so stunned. It was as if all the pain of racism and white supremacy had just descended on me in that moment. I was struck by just how rage can also empower you. I felt very empowered and angry as I began to write the lead essay in the book. One of the things I keep saying in the book is that rage is healthy. None of us imagine that we can have a love relationship where we're never angry. The question becomes: What do you do with your anger? How do you utilize it?

I knew I had the ability to write from my church. My church used to encourage us to write, and I started to write. It was a southern black Baptist church, and I used to write. I used to say to my parents, "You know, I'm going to write when I grow up." I started off writing poetry and knew that I wanted to be a writer. Lately, I've been thinking about that a lot, especially when I teach students, that there seems to be a fundamental difference between somebody who knows what they want to do early in life. I mean, my whole life has been directed towards this goal. I remember saying when I was twelve years old, "I'm going to be a writer," and writing my little things and reading them to my sisters and brothers. And I now see in life that there is such a difference between people who know what they feel called to do and people who feel like they're still searching. It's amazing to me when I think about self-development and self-esteem, how different it is. I feel incredibly blessed in my life and part of that blessing is fulfilling the dreams that I had around being a writer.

THE NAME "bell hooks" is a pseudonym. It's my great-grandmother's name. My original name that I still use in daily life is Gloria Watkins. I came to my writing through the feminist movement and at that time, we were very concerned to critique the idea of stardom. The idea was that what was being said was more important than who said it. And many of us chose, in the early seventies, to use pseudonyms to write because we were trying to get away from the focus on the personality and the ego. And because I was involved with Eastern religion and Buddhism and other things, I was also trying to get away from that ego attachment that we have to a name. So the use of the small letters [on the title page] was a way to sort of say, first, it's not really me because I'm not just the book that I've written. I'm a holistic self. And it also really does work to make people think about a name. What makes a name important? Those small letters that are kind of equal. They don't have that kind of hierarchical look. That has an effect on people.

One of the figures that affected me early on was Emily Dickinson. I love her poems, and I often think of her as my Emily D. I thought my writing life would be like hers, that I'd be always reclusive somewhere, writing. The idea was you'd send these books away, and someone would accept them, and they'd publish them. We've become so much more sophisticated now around having authors go out and come on television—all of those things were not a part of how I imagined a writer's life when I was choosing this name to use and when I was seventeen years old. It has been interesting.

In terms of racism or sexism, often people develop an idea of you based on a name, or people will tell me that reading my books and the name, they have this idea that they're going to meet this, like. harsh or powerful kind of person. And then a lot of times people meet me, as one reporter from *The New York Times* said two days ago, he was shocked to find that I was so playful. And I think there are so many ways in our culture that we develop a stereotyped image of someone, and we hold to that image even though we have no basis for it. I think that takes us right back to assumptions we make about people based on skin color or sex or how they're dressed. We're just a culture obsessed with judgments, and I think that's been part of the difficulty of ending racism.

Remember, I wrote this book way before the O. J. Simpson case, the Million Man March, so it's not trying to capitalize on those events. Way before those events, like Andrew Hacker and other writers, I was trying to say: This country is still seething with racial tension. White supremacy is widespread. We've got polls telling us that many white people believe black people are genetically inferior, etc., etc. I thought this is a time of crisis that we, as a nation, need to be facing. Of course, as an individual, you can't force a collectivity to face it in the way that recent events have forced the issue of race and racism back onto the national agenda.

We live in a culture that is not full of literacy. I think that one of the great myths of our culture is that everybody can read and write and that, in fact, when it comes to selling books and writing books, most people have a sense of an audience out there that is a book-buying audience. And even though we've proven in the last few years that black people constitute a big book-buying audience, simply by shared numbers, we can never be the book-buying audience that white consumers constitute. I think as more people know that, it's easier to pitch a book towards a white audience in your thinking and how you write and the language that you use.

I was always fond of that commercial that said, "V.D. is for everybody." I wrote this book for everybody. What I think is odd about it is that a lot of the essays are very different. There are some repetitions in them because different essays might engage different people. I used four essays in the book that had been published elsewhere, and they were the essays that I had gotten the most mail back from white people, black people, other people of color, saying, "Oh, I didn't understand."

IN TERMS OF PHYSICAL ENVIRONMENT, I like to write in really tiny, enclosed spaces, and I don't know why this is. I like them to have a window, but I like them to be very small. I just bought an apartment in New York, and I have the teeniest little work space. It makes me laugh every time I enter it because it's so small.

I handwrite everything, and then I put it on computer. I think, for me, there's something about handwriting still that slows down the idea process. When you're working at the computer, I find you can just zoom ahead, and you don't have those moments of pause that you need. The physical experience of handwriting is your hand gets tired. There are things that will make you pause in a way that won't happen at the computer. You can stay at the computer forever.

I primarily write in the morning. I'm a meditator, so I get up to meditate and to have time for quiet spiritual contemplation. And then I like to write with fierce intensity for a few hours, and then I like to play for the rest of the day.

I grew up in Hopkinsville, Kentucky, where I just was last week. It was fabulous to be home with my parents. I had a book signing there. In keeping with the kind of community I grew up in, I saw my grade school teachers, those that haven't died and passed away, and my high school teachers. It was exciting because I grew up at an enormous time of turmoil in the fifties, where we were so racially segregated. We had the real hard-core South African apartheid.

I think that many people who don't live in the South forget that that history is still so recent. And I could sit there at this book signing with my high school white drama teacher, whom I fondly remember as one of the few white teachers that didn't look upon us as genetically inferior, who was caring towards us and who was very concerned with ending racial injustice. And I remember those years.

This is another thing that's a source of my tremendous hope about ending racism. I think those of us who really lived in apartheid know how far we've come as a nation. We know that things have changed, and we also know what hasn't changed. I wanted to evoke some of that in this book.

Monica Crowley

Monica Crowley was a foreign policy assistant to former President Richard Nixon from June 1990 to April 1994. She joined us to describe her experience writing Nixon Off the Record: His Candid Commentary on People and Politics, *on September 29, 1996.*

I WAS A JUNIOR at Colgate [University] and I was majoring in political science, and I was enrolled in a course on national security and foreign policy affairs. And that was taught by a very good, very conservative professor, and I consulted with this professor because I thought that I wanted to enter that area upon my graduation.

So as I prepared to leave campus between my junior and senior years, he gave me several books to read, one of which was Nixon's *1999: Victory Without War*. And that book had such a tremendous impact on my thinking about very crucial foreign policy issues that I sat down and I wrote Nixon a letter dealing with the issues that he raised in the book. And it was a substantive letter, which later he told me was the reason it caught his eye.

I mailed it, never expecting a response. About a month later I went to my mailbox, and I received a handwritten response from President Nixon, telling me how much he thought of my letter, how much he appreciated the fact that I'd actually read his book. He invited me to come to his office in New Jersey and discuss American foreign policy with him. So in October of my senior year—that was 1989—I traveled to his Bergen County office, in New Jersey, and he gave me two hours of his time. We talked about the state of the world. And what surprised me most about that initial meeting was that he was so generous with his most precious commodity, and that was his time.

I decided to do this book several months after Nixon passed away. Actually, Nixon gave me a lot of responsibilities and assignments on a daily basis, so I always carried a notepad with me whenever we spoke. So Nixon knew that I was taking some notes during the course of our conversations. He did not know the extent to which I was reconstructing those conversations, and he did not know about the diaries.

When I began taking these notes, I knew that I was granted a very rare and highly personal view into one of the most enduring and controversial presidents of the twentieth century and so I did not want to squander that opportunity. So I began taking these notes essentially from my own personal memory. I wanted to remember for myself what he did on a daily basis, who he was, what he said. And it was only after he passed away and I began to look through these diaries that I really realized the value and the totality of what I had. I met with William Safire of *The New York Times* in August of 1994, several months after Nixon had passed away, and, sort of off the cuff, mentioned to him that I had all of this material in diaries. And he really urged me to write the book. He said, "It must be written." This encouragement was fairly important because I felt that somebody of his stature and somebody who knew Nixon so well—if he thought that this wasn't a project that I should've pursued, then I wouldn't have done it.

When I first was preparing to meet him, for the very first time, I was prepared to encounter the public image of Richard Nixon, which really is very one-dimensional. It's sort of a dark, brooding, serious, mysterious character. And the Nixon I knew, that part of him was just a fraction of who he was. And what surprised me so much and delighted me was that Nixon was so much more than that.

The Nixon I knew was a brilliant man. He was a political mastermind, which even his detractors will concede. He was generous. He was thoughtful, thoughtful in the sense of compassionate. He was a warm person. He was a witty person. Nixon could be very funny at times, and that never, ever came across in his public image, and I think that's a shame. I tried to get some of that humanity across in this book. I hope I succeeded.

Let me tell you how I proceeded with the whole note-taking process. As I said, I always carried a notepad with me during our conversations. I would take some notes in shorthand, as he was talking, so that I had key words and phrases and so forth. And then I would go back to my desk immediately and reconstruct those conversations so I had them on paper while they were still fresh in my mind. Later that night I would go home and reconstruct them once again in my diaries so that I could put the conversation with a date and a time. Then a fourth stage occurred at the end of each week, when I would go back and review the week's conversations. And if I had forgotten something or if an insight had occurred to me, I'd jot those in as well. I think I was able to maintain and preserve the integrity of the dialogue doing it that way. But at the time, it didn't occur to me to write a book. I knew that I was being exposed to this incredible historic opportunity, so I was doing it for myself all along. Almost every day there was something that I thought, "My goodness, I have such a treasure here. What a great quote! What a great turn of phrase!" And I was glad that I was there to hear it.

This was not a hard book to do. It really wasn't, because I had the diaries, so I had all of the quotes there, and I had a lot of the insights that I had written in the diaries at the time. So the book pretty much wrote itself.

I had worked with Harry Evans at Random House on Nixon's last book, *Beyond Peace*. So I had somewhat of an association with [Mr. Evans]. And I let him know that I had several sample chapters done that Mr. Safire had read, and I had a simple outline for him, and would he be willing to read it? And he was, and he liked it, and so that's how it came to be.

I originally envisioned this book as a single volume. I thought it would take the shape of three major parts: Nixon and the world, which would deal with foreign policy—the end of the cold war, the Persian Gulf War, and so forth; Nixon and America, which would deal with a lot of his political views, which we see in this book; and Nixon on Nixon, more of Nixon on the personal side, what he thought about the deaths of Mrs. Nixon and [H. R.] Haldeman and John Connally and so forth. And then as I began writing, I realized that the story would be better told in two parts. I wanted to take the political material and publish it as a separate volume because I think it stood very powerfully on its own.

There is a great Hugh Sidey story in the book. Nixon was a very formal man, and he knew that he had been president of the United States; and with that came some responsibility to dignity, which is why he always wore a suit and tie every day of the week. Sidey arrived for his meeting with Nixon early, and Nixon did not want Sidey to see him before the appointed hour. I was standing with Nixon, and he ducked into the mail room. He called me over with a whisper and he said, "Talk to Sidey in my office. I'm going to go through the door and go home," because he was treating Sidey to lunch at his residence and Sidey had come to the office. So I went into Nixon's office, I sat down with Mr. Sidey and we had a very lovely, brief conversation, and Nixon exited the door, went home in the limousine and was ready to greet Mr. Sidey at the residence.

I thought it was an unbelievable episode—that this was a man that everybody in the world knows, and he is hiding out in the mail room. And I couldn't believe that I was actually a witness and a participant in it. But then I came to realize that, well, maybe there was something to this, that there was an image that Nixon had to protect. He wasn't a casual man. And he was simply being himself. That's who Nixon was. He wanted to preserve a measure of decorum in his conversations with people.

Shortly after the [1993] inaugural, [President] Clinton called Nixon and that began their surprisingly close relationship, surprisingly most of all to Richard Nixon, I think, because Nixon felt that they were of two different generations, two different political parties, and thought that Clinton would not call on him. And he thought that even if Clinton were inclined to call on him, that Mrs. Clinton, because of her Watergate experiences, would squash any inclination that Clinton might have. So he was surprised when he first got that telephone call, and Clinton invited him to the White House after one of their substantive discussions. And that's how it came about.

The second book will also be published by Random House. I haven't titled it yet, but it will deal with Nixon's foreign policy views and it will deal with Nixon's views on scandal more extensively: Whitewater, Watergate, the Clarence Thomas hearings, the Kennedys. It will deal with the legacy of Vietnam, what Nixon saw as the legacy of Vietnam for the United States, and the destruction of that entire era on American pop culture. And it will deal with Nixon on Nixon, his views on philosophy, on religion, on his family.

I would hope that the Nixon family would be pleased with the book. I think Nixon would have been pleased with it. This is an honest portrayal of who Nixon was in the last years of his life. And there's so much out there that's dishonest about Richard Nixon that honesty was really the only thing he ever wanted or expected out of profiles on him. So I think he would appreciate it. Also, I thought, when I was writing this book, I wanted this to be Richard Nixon's story. I did not want it to be Monica Crowley's story about Richard Nixon. And I thought that the best way for Nixon to influence history was to allow him to speak for himself.

Deborah Shapley

Journalist Deborah Shapley had over twenty private interviews with Robert McNamara for her book Promise and Power: The Life and Times of Robert McNamara. *She appeared on* Booknotes *on March 21, 1993.*

I CAME TO REALIZE that my whole generation, the baby-boomer generation, really was affected and scarred by Vietnam. There are 8.2 million people who served in the [U.S.] armed forces between 1961 and 1975, and all of those people have had some contact and some impact from the Vietnam tragedy in our experience. So actually, although I may have started out of professional interest and rather intellectual interest, as I went on, I got very pulled in by the need to try to understand this terrible riddle in our past. Even Bill Clinton, of course, has talked about Vietnam. And Bill Clinton is, I think, a year younger than I am. So, in a sense, I got drawn in on generational grounds.

I told him [Robert McNamara] that I was going to do the book [with or without his cooperation], because there was such a vast public record that a public policy writer, such as myself, could write a book even if he didn't cooperate. Many people told me he would never cooperate because his record was so complicated. I flew into it out of a sense of daring because people said it was impossible to do: jumping into all those fields and wars, getting into nuclear arms and systems analysis and international development and building motorcars. But that, of course, was part of the interest of doing a biography—because you can get involved in the subjects indirectly through such a personality.

Robert McNamara was secretary of defense under [Presidents] Kennedy and Johnson, as many, many Americans know. Before that, he had a long career at the Ford Motor Company, where he rose to become president in 1960. And then as many Americans did not realize, he was president of the World Bank for thirteen years, where he trooped around the world and did a lot of very important things, which Americans, being the way they are, tend to not hear about or have rather little curiosity about. McNamara is an extraordinary individual capable of great good who helped create the Vietnam tragedy. It's a very interesting pairing of success and failure in this man.

He tried to fight the war with a certain amount of frugality, not giving the military everything they asked for. That was an attitude stamped on him in childhood.

[HENRY] KISSINGER DIDN'T SEE his biographer for a while, but then he got drawn in and gave him a number of interviews. So it's sort of the same curiosity. That's how a public figure feels when they realize someone's on their trail and going to be interviewing all their old friends and reading all these documents. They sort of want to know. They want to get in on it, and they want to hear.

McNamara's very pleasant to deal with and very rigorous. He's actually a very good scholar for a guy who really had nothing to do with history and never wants to get into the past. One of McNamara's traits, as you see in the book, is a deep involvement with the present. "Let's march into the future. The past is behind." He's very American that way. I tried in the sessions to educate him by bringing in documents. In one session—I'll never forget—I brought in several different books, big books with footnotes with accounts of the Berlin crisis. I pointed out in my cover letter how none of these accounts agreed, and together they added up to a cruddy record. And he really got involved in this, and he said, "Look, this footnote doesn't agree with this sentence," and this and this. And he said, "How can you call any of this history?" So I was trying to show him a process, and McNamara's fascinated by process.

A great deal of what's in this book is told, to some extent, from his point of view, because if you're writing somebody's biography, you have to get in their skin. You have to imagine that you're them. Now, I don't think I have that much in common with him, but if you hear somebody talk about themselves at enough length, you can then start interpolating the motives beyond what they have even literally told you. It was a great help because I would get into situations where I had evidence and I didn't know what the answer was, and then I would have to say, "Well, now how would he respond to this? How was it most likely he looked at this?" With any luck, I'd run in and ask him. But after a while you get a feeling for somebody, for the way they're responding to a situation. So I felt I could proceed with greater confidence because of the sessions, even if they were formal.

He's trying in a sense to have it both ways. I think he agreed with me that it was terribly important for him to speak to my generation and to start coming forward. I mean, time is short and history is urgent at his back. But he's a very complicated man, and he doesn't want to open himself up to barrages of questions [about Vietnam] and [have] everybody after him about it. He's been attacked, he's been verbally insulted over it. I think he doesn't want to face it completely.

The most important revelation [in the book] is McNamara's development of his own position about why he stayed on and fought. If there was a valid military reason for continuing the fighting, that's something that many, many veterans and their families need to know.

I have gotten a little bit of feedback from people who were close to the Kennedy crowd, whom I won't name, that this book is too harsh on McNamara. [There is] a sentence about him being a pivotal figure in the decline of the American century whose virtues he embodies. But I think that's inevitable because the group of people who knew Kennedy and who were close to [McNamara] have a tremendous fondness for each other and they've been through a lot of pain. They've watched Kennedy's reputation be torn to shreds in book after book after book. I'm sure that in an ideal world they would love to see McNamara totally rehabilitated. I just can't do that with any credibility.

As I said to McNamara in a final meeting, "None of us sees ourselves the way our biographer would." I don't expect him to agree with this book, certainly not in its entirety. I've tried to be very fair.

Robert A. Caro

Robert A. Caro has been writing about President Lyndon B. Johnson since 1974. The first volume in his series, The Years of Lyndon Johnson, *was titled* The Path to Power *and received the National Book Critics Circle Award for Biography for 1982. The second volume in the Johnson biography,* Means of Ascent, *received the same award for 1990. Mr. Caro, who came to* Booknotes *in April 1990 to discuss the second volume, is currently at work on the third volume.*

I WAS A REPORTER at *Newsday,* and what I realized was not that I wanted to do biographies—I never conceived of writing books just on the lives of famous men. I really had no interest in that at all. What I wanted to do was explain how political power worked, because as a reporter I was covering politics and I felt that I wasn't really explaining what I had gone into the newspaper business to explain, which was how political power worked.

The first book I did for a tiny advance. I think it was a $2,500 advance. Nobody was really interested in the book and we were really just broke, pretty much, for seven years. I got a grant for one year, but I thought the book was only going to take one year. So at the end of the year—I was just a reporter, and we had no savings. We had a house on Long Island, so we sold that, but that was before the real estate boom. That gave us enough money, after the mortgage, for only fifteen more months. We moved into an apartment in Riverdale in New York and from time to time Ina, my wife, would go to work. But I also needed her to help me with the research on this. It was a continual struggle to do *The Power Broker.* For the first five years or so it was just a struggle from month to month to keep going. It was not a bestseller at first, but it almost immediately began to be used by hundreds of colleges in different courses. And I won the [1974] Pulitzer Prize and other prizes and was able to get a much better contract for Lyndon Johnson. Then the first volume of Johnson was a major best-seller, or whatever, and all the money problems have ceased. It's not even a consideration anymore.

· · ·

THE LBJ LIBRARY IS PART of the National Archives. All presidential libraries are part of the National Archives. But in Johnson's case, it's more complicated than that, because Johnson's papers were given to the federal government under a deed of gift, which was later incorporated in a will, and that deed of gift gives the library broad discretion as to what they can disclose. Anything that would harass or embarrass someone, they remove the document and replace it with a pink slip, and quite often, as you are going through these papers, as you're going toward an idea, you know, you're turning every page, going through the letters or the memos, as you're heading towards the crucial moment, you see a little line of pink slips sticking out—and it's often a crucial document. So what you really just try to do is keep going and looking in other boxes and all, trying to find out as much as you can.

I think I let the facts speak for themselves. I'm taking people through Lyndon Johnson's life as he lived it, chronologically. Nobody disputes that these are the things that he did. Nobody has challenged really, anything that I know of. As for [me] disliking him, that's not really true. The Johnson loyalists really dislike—as you can tell, even hate—my books. That, however, does not mean that I disliked Lyndon Johnson. I think that the story of his life, to me, is a very sad and poignant story. It's not a question of liking and disliking. I'm trying to understand and make people understand. More than trying to make people understand, I'm trying to learn how the political power worked, and how he used it, and I'm trying to portray that. Now, that's very unpleasant to some, as it appears in this volume. It's a very unpleasant story, but that doesn't mean it didn't happen.

Richard Reeves

Nationally syndicated columnist Richard Reeves talked about the making of his book President Kennedy: Profile of Power *on the December 12, 1993, program.*

*F*OR MY FIRST JOB, I worked in a factory in Phillipsburg, New Jersey, on the Delaware River. I was an engineer there. I hated it. I wasn't good at it, and I didn't like corporate life, either. I didn't like the complaints of my fellows. I found a guy in the town who wanted to start a newspaper. He had been in advertising, and we started a newspaper together. I did that at night, with no one knowing it, for about a year, until we got it off the ground. *The Phillipsburg Free Press* still exists out there.

By then I knew I was not born to be a manager, and the paper became successful, and we had employees. We had started with three people; then we had fifty. I was the general manager and the editor, and I just did not like being the boss. I'd see that people would think I was lying to them when I said there was no money—we were still paying off the debts we started with—and I didn't like it.

So, I went to *The Newark News* as a reporter. I got lucky on a couple of stories, and then I went to the [*New York*] *Herald Tribune*. They hired me in New York in 1965, and then the *Trib* folded in '66. *The New York Times* hired me next, and I stayed there through the early seventies and then went out on my own to write books. I also went in on the founding of *New York* magazine, which was old *Herald Tribune* people—Tom Wolfe and Jimmy Breslin and Clay Felker, Gail Sheehy, Gloria Steinem. All of us had had a connection with the *Trib* when we were kids.

My mother said she encouraged me to write. I always wanted to be a writer. I just happened to grow up in circumstances where that's all I wanted to do. I grew up in Jersey City. I had good marks in high school. But there was no such things as guidance in that world, and whatnot. If you went to college it was either [to] be a lawyer, a doctor, or an engineer. My father was a lawyer, and I didn't love what I saw him doing. I knew I could never be a doctor, so I thought I'd be an engineer. It was only in later life that I learned you could just sit and read books, and that was an education.

THE REAL PROBLEM of doing things like this on the Kennedys is that they run the library. They run the Kennedy Library, and it is less user-friendly and less research-friendly than the other presidential libraries I worked in on this book. A lot of the Kennedy stuff is from the LBJ Library. Both the Eisenhower and Johnson libraries are much more friendly, and you don't get the sense that they are trying to defend a position. Families should not have control of these libraries; this is the public's business. I have no great anger about it, but I think that I could have been saved a lot of time and a lot of other things if the Kennedy Library were, as it were, a nonconnected institution. Arthur Schlesinger, for instance, has been allowed to see things that no one else has ever been allowed to see because the family trusts him. That was a long time ago, but it helped him enormously. A lot of that stuff is not public at other places, but there is an obvious and visible attempt to control what information comes out [of the Kennedy Library].

In the case of this president, I think, there were many more tapes of things than anyone ever knew until now. These tapes were of the Oval Office and the Cabinet room and were recorded under Kennedy for the same reason that Nixon did it. Kennedy wanted to write his memoirs, and he wanted a record of what had happened. Many of his phone calls—in those days, phone calls were often monitored by secretaries who kept notes on them—but, in his case, they hadn't invented the tape recorder yet, really. There was a wire recorder controlled by his [personal] secretary, Evelyn Lincoln, and he would flick a switch on if he wanted a phone call recorded.

People who work for presidents or who deal with presidents are like athletes dying young. That is, the peak for most of them is so high that they write down everything and remember everything, so that in meeting after meeting or scene after scene, I was able to talk to six or eight people who were in a room of ten, and the rest of them had either notes on what they did or had talked about the scene in their own oral histories at the Kennedy Library. The oral histories at the Kennedy Library were done mainly in 1964, which was for me a tremendous help because many people in 1988 tell different stories, particularly about Vietnam, than what they were telling in 1964, so you've got a real reality check of what happened.

Probably the single thing that is most unbelievable that I was able to dig out because of Averell Harriman's papers and because he had recorded the conversations, is that Kennedy tried to get [then Soviet Premier Nikita] Khrushchev to consider a joint American-Soviet air strike at China to destroy their nuclear capability. It literally was lined up. It was going to be done like a firing squad; that is, neither the Russian crew nor the American crew would know that they had the real weapon. One weapon would be a dud; one weapon would be real, as they do on a firing squad so every man can think he didn't fire the fatal shot if he wanted to. Khrushchev turned him down.

I think the book is already a success for me because the reviews have talked about what I wanted to do, which is I wanted to show who John Kennedy was—he wasn't this sort of clown or Lothario figure. He did all those things, but that's not what he was about. When *The New York Times Book Review* came out and said, "This makes us for the first time look at what the presidency really is and what it means," that was enough for me. I was ready to go home and get a tan.

Paul Hendrickson

Booknotes *guest Paul Hendrickson is now a feature writer for* The Washington Post. *He joined us on October 27, 1996, to discuss his book* The Living and the Dead: Robert McNamara and Five Lives of a Lost War.

THIS IS A BOOK ABOUT ROBERT MCNAMARA, who is the archetypal figure of this war. I think when we say that name, it really does evoke a kind of knifepoint of memories for anybody who lived through that time. But it is not a conventional biography. It also brings into focus five other lives who were affected by Mr. McNamara's policies. And in a sense, they are like spokes to the hub of the wheel. If Mr. McNamara is the controlling force of the narrative, these lives come in, and these are ordinary people, ordinary Americans who lived extraordinary moments and who got caught up in the war, were traumatized by it, and were affected by the decisions of the policymakers.

This book has a long history, and you probably know some of it. I gave this book up because I couldn't do it. I felt abject failure about it. I went back to *The Washington Post* after working on it for nearly three years and feeling just total, total failure. I wrote another book in between. It was on a documentary photographer of the Depression named Marion Post Wolcott, and the book is called *Looking for the Light*. It is a book that I'm immensely proud of but much, much smaller in scope than this. About four years ago, my editor at Knopf said to me, "Paul, if you were going to mount the McNamara book again, if you were going to try again, what would you do?" And I said, "Jon, Jon"—his name is Jonathan Segal, and he's a wonderful man, a wonderful editor—"Don't even ask me. I can't face this." I had gotten into quite a dilemma over my inability to write this book. I was emotionally and financially broken. And I went back to the *Post,* not knowing—well, thinking for sure that my book career was over. Nobody would ever get me to write a book again because I had failed on this one high-visibility project, lots of money. I was unsure whether I could even do journalism again, my confidence was so shaken. I had found my own Vietnam the first time in trying to write this book the wrong way. I was trying to write a conventional biography of Robert McNamara. That's not my strength. I'm not a historian.

And Jon Segal said to me, "We've talked about this now and then, over and over. Just write me a letter about what you might do." So, over the next seventy-two hours, I wrote him a forty-five-page letter. It poured out of me. I think about seven or eight years, at that point, had already gone by—when this book was not being written, was being worked on full time, when another book had taken its place. But this book was always in me, always in my psyche, always either back-burnered or front-burnered, so that forty-five-page outpouring in seventy-two hours startled me, that there was so much pent up inside of me that wanted to get out and try to do this book.

The central thing I said to him in that letter was, "I wonder if I can do a book that would combine biography and history and narrative and novelistic detail, based in absolute fact, in which you make Mr. McNamara the controlling force of the narrative but you bring in these five other extraordinary lives. But I would make Mr. McNamara the center, and show how his policies and his deceptions terribly influenced the lives of these individuals." And I said, "Bring it all together and maybe, maybe that'll work as a book." And Jon's response was, "You got it, baby. You did it. You figured it out. Now all you have to do is go and do it."

THERE IS A STORY that functions as the prologue and the epilogue, the kind of bookend to the whole story. On a rainy Friday night in 1972, a twenty-seven-year-old artist in tennis shoes saw the icon of the Vietnam War standing just a few feet away: Robert McNamara. This was in the fluorescent-lit lunchroom of a ferryboat called the MV *Islander* that takes passengers from Woods Hole, Massachusetts, over to Martha's Vineyard island. It's seven miles of open water. And it can be quite choppy. This was a rainy Friday night.

This twenty-seven-year-old artist, who had avoided the war, whose two older brothers had served, who was regarded in some ways in his own family as "the shirker," stood there on the other side of the lunchroom and watched Mr. McNamara enjoying himself. Mr. McNamara had a companion and they were standing against the canteen bar of the lunchroom and they were having a high old time. You see a lot of celebrities going over to Martha's Vineyard. Celebrities are partly what Martha's Vineyard is about.

And a murderous rage began climbing up inside this man's throat. Almost unable to stop himself, he said [to me that] he was going to do something. And he told me he didn't even know what he was going to do.

He walked over to Mr. McNamara and he said, "Sir, you have a phone call. Please follow me." He was posing, in a sense, as a member of the crew. And Mr. McNamara—you know, one of the strange and in some ways wonderful things about Robert McNamara is there has been a lifelong quality of naïveté about him. He instantly put down his drink and followed the guy right out. So they walk out into the inky dark of the boat. They're out there alone in this narrow passageway, and wordlessly—the artist swears to me that he never said a damn thing—he just turned and got him by the shirt collar and the belt and he tried to hoist him over the side.

McNamara's glasses came off, according to the artist. McNamara's only words were "Oh, my God, no!" And there were about thirty-five or forty seconds of titanic struggle at the rail. And the way McNamara saved himself was by inserting his hands and holding on for dear life into the metal grillwork. And I feel that that kind of seesaw battle, which is forty-five seconds out of this artist's life and forty-five seconds out of McNamara's life, is the Vietnam War. It was the sixties struggle between what?—between immense authority on the one hand and [the] disenfranchised sixties, quote, "shirker." Rebellion and authority—that's what a lot of Vietnam and the sixties and all of these things we're dealing with now, in residue, are about.

When I set out to write the book, I had always heard of this incident. It was always a footnote somewhere. James Reston, Jr., in a book called *Sherman's March in Vietnam*, an odd but beautiful book about Vietnam, had it down in a couple of sentences; and actually, it was a little factually incorrect. But that intrigued me. I saw it in a book about Martha's Vineyard. I saw it as a paragraph in *Newsweek*. When you start researching a man's life, you come on all sorts of information. But nobody ever had the guy's name. Nobody ever had a full account of it.

So I set out to find him. And it took me a good while but finally, one day, a particular police officer in Vineyard Haven, Massachusetts—maybe this was the thirty-sixth call I had made in the last week—he said, "I know exactly who that is." I was very afraid to try to contact this man on the phone or write him a letter because I thought that he would just spook.

I went to Boston. I rented a car. I drove down to Woods Hole. I rode the ferry as a foot passenger over to Martha's Vineyard, and I had a taxicab take me to where I knew this artist's studio was because the policeman at Vineyard Haven had told me. There was a real tense moment there when I introduced myself. And I said, "I'm writing a book about Robert McNamara and I can't go on with this part unless you consent to talk to me."

He was smoking a pipe and he stood in the doorway and he just surveyed me. I felt like we were having our own thirty-five or forty seconds of extreme tension in an immediate context. And he just surveyed me. Then he said, "How do you know it was me?" And I told him what the police officer said, and by this time, I also had had some other corroboration. He said, "Come in." His stipulation was that I could not identify him by name. That was in 1985. A year later, I went back and got him to tell me, in extreme detail, the entire story over again. I was checking everything that was told to me the year before. And I also went back exactly a year later to see if I could convince him to change his mind [about using his name]. I had given him my solemn word; I wasn't about to break it. He said, "No. I still don't want it revealed."

That was in the middle eighties, which shows how long this book has taken. I have certainly been in touch with him very recently. And I was in touch with him on the production of this book. And it was still his will that his name not be revealed. And I was sworn to honor that.

I'm certainly not the only person who knows his identity. It's for years been folklore around Martha's Vineyard. I will say that a lot of people on Martha's Vineyard have it wrong. They think it's somebody else. But other people on Martha's Vineyard do know that he's the one. And he has to deal with that. But it will never ever be revealed by me as long as it continues to be his will. McNamara talked fleetingly to me about it, once, in no detail.

THE FIRST TIME I ever met Robert McNamara was in February of 1984. I am a staff writer at *The Washington Post,* and in November of 1983 there was a very famous television movie called *The Day After.* It was about a nuclear holocaust in Kansas City. It was very well publicized. It was the big event of that season—Jason Robard's movie. Afterward, in the studio audience, was a constellation of American heavyweights talking about the dilemmas of nuclear war—Elie Wiesel; Carl Sagan; Henry Kissinger; the secretary of state under Mr. Reagan, [George] Shultz, was there for a while—he had made an appearance earlier—and Robert McNamara. Of all these people talking in the studio after this two-hour television drama, McNamara was the one that spoke to me. He seemed to me the most humble, the most humane, the most intelligent; he spoke so movingly about the horrors of nuclear war. I wanted to interview him.

I went in instantly the next day and said to my editor at the Style section of *The Washington Post,* "Did you see that last night?" And she said, "I did." And I said, "Wow. I wonder if we could get McNamara?" She said, "I'm having the same thoughts." And she said, "But, you know, it's complicated because he's on the board of *The Washington Post.*" Among other things, he's a very good friend of Katharine Graham, then the chairman and the complete power of *The Washington Post.*

Mary Hadar, my editor, said, "Well, I'll ask Ben Bradlee [former executive editor of *The Washington Post*]." She asked Ben, and Ben said, "Go for it. Maybe you can get him. Maybe you can't." I sat down and wrote Mr. McNamara a letter. About five weeks later he called me on the phone early one morning, and he seemed right then in conflict with himself. "I have got your letter here, and I see you want an interview. Well, I don't think I'm interested in an interview and, by the way, the Style section? I don't read the Style section. And a feature article? No, I'm not interested in that. But, listen, maybe you want to come over next Thursday and I'll—you know, we'll just talk for a few minutes." There was, even then, a kind of left-hand-against-the-right-hand quality that I was picking up on the phone.

I boned up like a madman for the next four or five days just trying to understand everything I could about this man's life. And I must have passed the audition. I went to his office. I was very scared. Spent about an hour with him. And he invited me to come back. We then proceeded to have conversations over the next four months, and I ended up—that was in February, and I ended up, in May of 1984, writing a large three-part series about him in the *Post.*

Mr. McNamara withdrew his access, his cooperation with me completely after those articles were published. I would say those three pieces didn't turn out as he might have wished. I think also that once the book began, he was aware that anybody who closely and deeply went into his life would start acquiring the documents, the declassified documents. There the record and the pattern of the deception would be clear. And that's what happened to me.

I READ A REVIEW of my book this morning. There have been so many just lately, I can't even cite where this one was, and in a pretty far-off place, in Florida or Texas or somewhere. And the reviewer said, "What is it about Vietnam that allows the subject to take over its authors' lives?" And he cited Neil Sheehan spending sixteen years on *A Bright Shining Lie* and William Prochnau spending twelve years on *Once Upon a Distant War,* and here comes Hendrickson now with a clean decade at least in working on this. And really, it was twelve years. But it's important to say, in terms of honesty and accuracy, that I was not working on it at all times during those twelve years, but it's a continuum of twelve years that this book has lived with me.

So what is it? I don't know. I'm trying to answer that question by saying that the mountain is so large. Vietnam is such a contradictory subject.

In some ways, whatever power I have, whatever ability I have as a writer, depends on the human connection. I have to have that person in front of me. I have to sort of feel the emotion of that person in the room with me. Mr. McNamara removed himself. He became an abstract for me. I think it terrified me psychologically.

For me, the calling—and I'm sorry to use a word that might sound highfalutin—but for me, the calling, the vocation was to sit in that room and write that book when very few people knew that it was happening—my editor, my wife, my agent, my children, McNamara against his will—and to just do the best with it I could. That, to me, was when it was golden. Because I was doing the best I could and I was only responsible to the truth as I could find it. Now it's out there. The world has it, and the world can accept it or reject it.

Richard Norton Smith

Presidential historian and Republican speechwriter Richard Norton Smith appeared on Booknotes *on February 21, 1993, to talk about his book* Patriarch: George Washington and the New American Nation. *Mr. Smith has headed both the Hoover and Reagan presidential libraries and is currently director of Gerald Ford's library in Ann Arbor, Michigan, and President Ford's museum in Grand Rapids.*

THE BOOK IS THE LAST TEN YEARS of the life of George Washington, a period that really hasn't been covered in much detail before. It's a chance to really humanize Washington, at the same time depicting him as a political leader. It's hard to believe there is not a comprehensive one-volume account of Washington's presidency. But beyond that, everyone wants to know what George Washington was like, and it seemed to me it's this period of his life when he's most human because he is most vulnerable. He's an old man. His hearing is not very good, his memory is failing him. He was terribly sensitive about press criticism, of which there was an enormous amount during his presidency. He had a volcanic temper. His presidential secretary said that no sound on earth could compare with that of George Washington swearing a blue streak. He was convinced that the day he accepted the presidency would mean the decline of his reputation, which was very important to him, and that he would risk even the adulation that took the place of more conventional love in his life. Despite all that, at a time in life when most men would be happy with retirement, to sit on their laurels, Washington was willing to risk everything in what I think is a time of his greatest sacrifice and greatest service to the country. It's that last period of his life that in some ways made the biggest imprint on America, even today.

I don't know about other biographers, but with me, you get to a point where you've saturated yourself in primary source materials, in letters and diaries and contemporary accounts, and then, all of a sudden, you come to one story that jumps off the page and seemingly defines your character, who may have been very elusive until then. For me it was a story I found at Mount Vernon in a letter written by Washington's adopted granddaughter,

Nellie Custis, who recalled late in her own life how, during his presidency, at the end of a long day, Washington used to leave his office and walk into a room where children were playing. He was very fond of children. He was very sensitive about the fact that he did not have children of his own, and this apparently relaxed him. And the moment that the kids realized they were in the presence of the man called "Great Washington," they froze— even the children did. He had that impact on people, and eventually, very put out, he would turn around and walk out of the room.

What that said to me was, instead of looking at Washington, as we always do, as a very remote figure, we should try and go back two hundred years and ask how did he become such a remote figure that children would freeze when he walked into the room. I theorize, partly, that it was his own doing. He was a great actor. He understood that politics was theater, and he understood his symbolic significance to the republic, the only thing that held it together in many ways. But part of it was also imposed upon him by his countrymen who needed a symbol, a unifying symbol, and so they made him a demigod in his lifetime. They put him on a pedestal, and he paid a terrible price for his celebrity.

There is a wonderful thirty-seven-volume edition of Washington's writings that came out in the 1930s and '40s. The Mount Vernon Ladies Association, in conjunction with UVA [University of Virginia], is working on what will be [an edition of] more than a hundred volume[s], which will include all of the correspondence to Washington as well as from Washington. There is a wonderful fairly recently published six-volume edition of his diaries. I did some research in original materials in Philadelphia and Mount Vernon.

ONE OF THE QUALIFICATIONS that Washington insisted upon in hiring a staff—in fact, one of the chief qualifications—was excellent handwriting. He was very vain about his own penmanship, and if you stop and think, two hundred years ago there were no Xerox machines, there were no typewriters. Every presidential document had to be copied by hand, so it's not such a far-fetched requirement.

George Washington was six feet three inches tall, which was about a half-foot taller than his contemporaries. Contrary to popular imagery, he never wore a wig. He had reddish hair. I might point out, parenthetically, so did Jefferson and Hamilton and the Marquis de Lafayette, which means that Americans owe their liberties today to redheads, make of that what you will.

But, in addition to his physical attributes, he had this extraordinary natural dignity and, with it, a real sense of the theatrical. He knew how to use the theater of politics in ways that I think surprise Americans today. There is a wonderful, wonderful scene at the battlefield of Yorktown: the moment when everyone would be expected to crow in victory, when the Americans had, in effect, stumbled onto victory and defeated the British, and, needless to say, the Continentals were in a mood to rub it in; and Washington prohibited his men from cheering. As he put it—in a wonderful line—he says, "Posterity will huzzah for us." He was not only playing to the immediate crowd, he was playing to posterity.

JOHN ADAMS WAS HIS VICE PRESIDENT. It was not easy being George Washington's vice president. It's never been easy being vice president, particularly to be in the shadow of someone like Washington. Adams was a rather vain man, rather fussy, jealous, a little bit paranoid. He used to refer to Washington in moments of pique as "Old Muttonhead." Abigail Adams was even more resentful. Remarkable woman. She used to complain that there was a double standard. The press criticized the vice president for loyalist trappings, but, after all, it was the president who went to Federal Hall in a coach of state drawn by six white horses.

One of the real tragedies of Washington's life was his falling out with Jefferson. If it's any consolation, it was a falling out over principle and not personalities. I think Jefferson looked upon Washington as almost a surrogate father in some ways. Hamilton had something of the same relationship with Washington. You might even see their feud as sort of a sibling rivalry.

Sally Fairfax has been described as Washington's great love. That may or may not be true. We don't know. She was a young woman of dazzling virtuosity, who, I think, impressed a young man who was terribly self-conscious not only of his lack of formal education but his lack of polish. As a young man, Washington once sat down and copied out 110 rules of civility—the Emily Post of his day. He spent a lifetime, in effect, trying to escape his origins, and he comes to Sally Fairfax, who is related to Lord Fairfax. He met her in his twenties. He's terribly ambitious and a little bit bumptious, and he sees Sally Fairfax. I think Sally Fairfax's role, more than anything else, is that of a social tutor. She was an embodiment of not only womanhood but of the kind of aristocratic society that at that point Washington wanted very much to be a part of.

There is a wonderful letter that Washington wrote to her very near the end of his life, in which he laments the fact that the Revolution drove them apart. She and her husband left Virginia and went back to England. [The Washingtons] never saw them again. As an old man, [Washington] is looking back and rhapsodizing about what he said were some of the happiest days of his life. Historians have read something into this, I think a little more than is there, because attached to that letter was a letter by Martha. The two letters were sent together, and it strains credibility [to read his as a love letter]. They were sent together from Mount Vernon. In other words, George and Martha would write on the same piece of paper. Literally, they would send the same document, and it's a little bit hard to believe that Martha would sign her name . . . [if it was a] love letter.

There is no contemporary evidence that [Fairfax and Washington] were physically intimate. Who knows? What's fascinating about the Sally Fairfax story is the length to which modern Americans will go to not only humanize Washington but to try to make him one of us. The fact is, George Washington is not at home in the 1990s. What I've tried to do is to take the reader back to his own time, in his own terms, and to re-create, as much as possible, a sense of almost day-to-day life in the 1790s so you could understand Washington within his own context.

I WENT TO HARVARD. I graduated in '75 with a government degree, which, with all due respect to the government department, was more or less worthless. Then I kicked around for a couple of years as a freelance writer. I was also an intern at the White House in the summer of 1975. It was during the Ford administration, and I'm ashamed to say I wrote a piece about the experience, for *The Washington Post,* which later terminated the program. It was intended to be a humorous piece, but it was interpreted as something of an exposé.

I was in Washington for about nine years, writing speeches for a number of folks and writing books on the side. I came here in '79 to work for Bob Dole and stayed with Senator Dole really through the eighties. I also wrote for Mrs. Dole. I worked for Pete Wilson on the Hill for a while. He is now governor of California but was a senator. Since going out to West Branch [Iowa], I've been writing for other people. I've done some writing for former President Reagan and for Vice President and Mrs. Quayle.

I live in West Branch, Iowa. The real America. Population 1,907. West Branch is about ten miles from Iowa City. I went there because of my other job. I'm director at the Herbert Hoover Presidential Library [and Museum] there.

The library is in West Branch because Mr. Hoover was born there and because late in life he decided he would, in this if in nothing else, follow

Franklin Roosevelt's example and have a presidential library. It's interesting: the original building was about 6,000 square feet. Harry Truman was there on dedication day; they were very good friends. Truman walked around and he said, "Gosh, this building would fit in the basement of my library." I have visited every grave of every former president. I'm one of those rare Americans who can say that. It was a hobby as a child, a rather unusual hobby, admittedly, and sometimes an embarrassing hobby. I contracted heat stroke one day while visiting James K. Polk on the grounds of the Tennessee state capitol in the middle of August. I would not advise viewers to do this. I almost got arrested one night about seven o'clock at night trying to find Grover Cleveland in a cemetery in Princeton, New Jersey.

George Washington is buried at Mount Vernon. He was buried, originally, in a brick vault near the house and then thirty-two years later was moved to a larger vault down near the river. In between, there was a plan adopted by Congress to have him buried under the rotunda of the Capitol. It was a secret plan. Mrs. Washington gave her assent on condition that she could be buried along with the general. But that never happened. But if you go to the Capitol today, you will see the room where Washington was to have been buried, and that's where they store the catafalque, which is used in national mourning.

Washington the man is so much more complicated, nuanced, subtle, shrewd than the image we've been given. On the personal level, the thing that surprised me over and over again was his loneliness. I think he is a very poignant figure, even more than . . . a typically aging man dealing with his own mortality. In Washington's case it's the classic maxim "Beware what you wish for lest you get it."

Clare Brandt

Biographer Clare Brandt wrote The Man in the Mirror: A Life of Benedict Arnold. *When she appeared on* Booknotes *on March 20, 1994, Ms. Brandt described the travels she undertook to research this biography.*

I DON'T EVEN KNOW where I got started. I started reading some other biographies [of Benedict Arnold] that had been written in the past, and then as all good historians do, I strip-mined their bibliographies, which is one way to start. I started asking around. I went to libraries where I'd worked before: the New York Public Library and New-York Historical [Society] Library. One thing leads to another, leads to another, leads to another, and you find yourself just following your nose. I ended up going to England, to the public records office, to read all the British stuff about him and about the battles that he'd fought when he was a British officer. And, of course, I went to Philadelphia where he was commandant. I also went to all the places where he fought battles and went up the Kennebec River—not every square inch of it, but a lot of it I went up. I went to Quebec in January just to see how cold it was—it's cold! That's very important to me. I think it's important to know what it feels like to be in that place, as close as you can get to it. So, I tried to go to the place, and I tried to go [in] the right season of the year.

The reason I wrote this book and didn't let the other books deter me from writing it was that, to my satisfaction, nobody had really explained why he [committed treason]. I had to know more about this man and how he could encompass all these contradictions in his character. I wanted to know what tipped him over. Everybody says, "Oh, he did it for the money," which indeed he did. Everybody says, "Oh, he did it because he was badly mistreated by Congress," which indeed he was. Everybody says he was very discouraged because civilian support for the war was waning rapidly, which indeed it was. But every other officer in the Continental Army was in exactly the same situation and felt exactly the same way—the same angers, the same frustrations—but he's the only one who turned his coat and I wanted to know what it was. The minute I began to do the research I said, "There's something really personal about this man. He did this for a very personal reason, and I want to try to figure out what [it was]." So that's what I did.

THERE IS A WONDERFUL REPOSITORY of American documents at Ann Arbor, at the Clements Library at the University of Michigan. Sir Henry Clinton was the British commander in chief in New York at the time of Arnold's treason. They heard—I think this is the story they told me—that his trunk that he took around with him was for sale at an auction in London. And they bought it, sight unseen, shipped it back to Ann Arbor, opened the trunk, and inside it was all the correspondence between Arnold on the one hand, and [Henry] Clinton and Major [William] André on the other hand. Up until that time, nobody had seen any of this; and, up until that time, nobody had known that his wife Peggy was involved. But clearly, from the documents, she is. This is his second wife, Peggy Shippen.

GOING OUT ON A BOAT on Lake Champlain was just wonderful because you could understand how that battle went. So much of it depended on the wind and on the maneuverability of the ships. I got out there in a sailing boat . . . and realized the minute I got out there, this was incredibly difficult, because it's surrounded by mountains and the sailing is very, very tricky. These are wonderful visual things. I was there in October [, the month in which] he fought the Battle of Valcour Island. Little mists appear that make all the islands seem to float, and things like that. I don't think you can get all that kind of thing until you actually go.

The Library of Congress is wonderful to work at. The National Archives is very helpful. Research libraries all over the country—in New York, of course; the Historical Society of Philadelphia; the New Haven Colony—they're terrific. It's fun to go places because you can always find somebody there who's interested in what you're doing, and if you can't find it in the card catalog, they'll say "Oh, I think I know something you'd be interested in," and they lead you down a little corridor into a dusty stack and show you some wonderful treasure. They're dying to have people come and work there, and they're terribly helpful.

When I'm doing research, if I go on a trip, I'd work as many days as the libraries are open. When I'm home, I work five days a week, starting at eight in the morning until I can't stand it anymore. I make myself sit there for three hours, no matter what, even if nothing is coming into my head or nothing is happening. I'll go longer if it's coming out and if it's all working. With the research you can keep going all day—I can—just getting it in there and getting it organized and mulling it over.

There are difficult moments where you think you're never going to get a handle on it. You end up with a bulging computer with all these little disparate items of information. Some of them you got four years ago and you can't figure out where in the world they fit. They look like they belong to a different jigsaw puzzle, and [as if] you shouldn't be bothering with them at all. Until you get a handle on it, it can be very difficult. I always write a first draft that has everything in it, and it reads about as interesting as a laundry list—"first he did this, and then he did this." I just have a chronological laundry list of everything that happened to him and that he did on a given day. Only after dealing with that, and wrestling with that by just getting it down on the page, which is a chore, do murky shapes begin to appear. Then you just go with those, and you test them and make sure that they work before you finally decide to use them. It's really feeling in the dark for a while, and it can be discouraging. But I always knew he was there somewhere for me, and so I wasn't going to let him go.

James Thomas Flexner

On June 2, 1996, historian and author James Thomas Flexner appeared on the program to discuss Maverick's Progress: An Autobiography, *published by Fordham University Press.*

I GRADUATED FROM HARVARD IN 1929. It gave me a wonderful base. You go to college, the four years, really, when you're moving from being a boy to being a man. It was a wonderful place for this to happen, because you are moderately well shut in, and, at the same time, you were in a tremendously lively community. And Harvard was very, very good because it encouraged eccentrics, and I was pretty much of an eccentric.

On the other hand, I was allowed to address the Harvard commencement, in what was really a radical speech, on what should be the subject matter of poetry in a machine age, in which I argued that you couldn't really write a poem about daffodils these days. I was a little extreme about this. But not only did they let me deliver it at the commencement, but they printed it up and sent it out, as a college [news] release, all over the country. Started my being a maverick and spoiling me.

Some of the more eccentric things I have done in my life are, well, for one thing, I've written books on every kind of subject. Usually, say if you were a good boy, you'd take a subject and you stick to it. And I have written on many subjects—always on my own. I never allowed anyone to see a manuscript of mine until it was finished. I never discussed it with anybody.

My first publisher was Viking Press. I stayed with Viking through three books, and then they played dirty on me. I can say that now because it was an altogether different firm then. I started doing a book for them, *The History of American Painting.* They told me that—this was all people who are now dead and gone, so I'm not talking about anybody alive—and they told me that they had showed it to a distinguished critic, and he told them my reputation would be ruined if it was published. And I happened to know him, so I asked him. And he said, "I've tried to get them to publish it, and they just wanted to get rid of it." But, at the same time, I was not heartbroken, because Houghton Mifflin's editor in chief was mourning that Viking had it. So as soon as I got this letter, I called him on the phone and I said, "You know, I think I can get this away from Viking." And they [Houghton Mifflin] published it.

I did five or six books with Houghton Mifflin. Then there was a sort of a chop suey of publishers. I had books published by one publisher, and then they didn't like the next one. Of course, one of the things I did that was very unsuitable was I didn't continue writing on the same subject in the same way. So, as soon as the publisher was sitting down and thinking, "Ah, we've got something nice here," I'd give him something else, and then I'd have to find a new publisher, who would sit down and say, "Aha!" But I didn't want to do the same thing over again. I tried to finish off with what I was doing and then find something else.

I tried to write a biography on John Adams, but I didn't get on with him. I never got on with him. I found it was of interest to write about people whom you didn't particularly like, because it widened what you could understand, if you come to understand them. But John Adams, I just couldn't get on with. He kept all kinds of theoretically revealing diaries, and then I discovered, as I was going through these and I was starting to write, that the really important thing that was happening in there was that he was getting interested in the woman he married.

So I was writing various books [set] in the period of Washington's lifetime. He kept appearing as a secondary character in these various things I was writing. And he never seemed to fit the Washington that I had learned out of legend. I gradually built up the idea that I ought to try to really do something new about him altogether. I wanted to get back to the original material and pay no attention to anything that was published after his death, except, of course, if it dealt with his earlier times. But there were thousands of biographies of Washington.

My own book on George Washington was published by Little, Brown. I had signed the contract with them for one volume, and I very quickly realized that I couldn't possibly do it in one volume. And there was some difficulty on that. But finally, they decided to let me publish a volume on Washington's early career before the Revolution, and that was a great success. So . . . then we signed a contract for three [volumes], and that grew to four. And then I decided, after all this, that I *could* do it in one volume, by using those four books as a sort of a base. Then I had great fun with it because I didn't have to do any research; I knew that [all] I had to [do was] cut it down to one-fifth. And one happy summer, I sat in the garage in the country and did nothing but write. I didn't have to do any research at all.

I started out by doing a lot of research in books, in what was printed in manuscripts, and one thing or another, because I thought that I would better understand [George Washington]. Then I went to Mount Vernon, and they could not have been more helpful. I wasn't allowed to sleep in the mansion house, but I was allowed to have the cabin right next door. And if during the night I wanted to go out and see what the moon looked like as Washington had seen it, I would call up and get them to get the guard dogs in, and I was allowed to wander around. It was tremendously informing.

I think I spent about—I forget—something like six or eight years, but that produced the big four-volume and the one volume. They sold very well. The four volumes won a special Pulitzer Prize which has only been given about ten times in the history of the Pulitzer Prize. The [books] didn't make me a vast fortune, but on the other hand they supported me quite nicely.

THE STORY BEHIND THIS TITLE, *Maverick's Progress,* is very interesting. In the good old days when the cattle out in the West were all put out together, the various cattle were branded . . . by the owners. A man by the name of Maverick, who was politically powerful, had it arranged that if there was no brand, it [would become] his brand. So not only did that get him his own cows, but all the cows that escaped from being branded by others. And so "Maverick" meant someone who ran with the herd that was not carrying anybody's brand.

I write with a typewriter. I learned the hunt-and-peck method. I've never learned the touch system. As a newspaperman, anyone who tried to use the touch system on the good old typewriters at [the *New York*] *Herald Tribune* wouldn't get anywhere. You had to go after them with a bang. I wrote this autobiography on a very ordinary typewriter, electric, nowadays. But not on any kind of those modern machines. I don't believe in them. I think they make books much too long.

Robert K. Massie

Robert K. Massie is known for his Pulitzer Prize–winning biography Peter the Great *and his book on Imperial Russia,* Nicholas and Alexandra. *He appeared on C-SPAN's* Booknotes *on March 8, 1992, to discuss his book* Dreadnought: Britain, Germany, and the Coming of the Great War.

I WRITE LONG BOOKS. One reason I wasn't very good as a magazine journalist, a news magazine journalist, was that news magazines have space limitations. I'd be assigned to do a story or a cover story, and you'd have a couple of weeks, maybe longer. I'd get into the subject and would be absolutely fascinated, but I felt, you can't understand what this man or woman is doing unless you go back much earlier, both in the history of the subject and in the biography of the person. Finally, after doing that for a while, I realized that I belonged writing longer stories.

"Dreadnought" is the name of a ship, the first real battleship. It was an old ship name in the Royal Navy, the British Navy, which goes way, way back to the time of Queen Elizabeth I and the Spanish Armada. And in the British Navy, these names are handed down just as in our navy—names like *Wasp* and *Hornet* and *Enterprise,* that have come down since our Revolution. This ship, the *Dreadnought* in this book, was built in 1906 and was the first real super battleship: big, fast, heavily armored, lots of heavy guns. I chose it because it was the centerpiece and the symbol of the arms race between Great Britain and Germany before the first World War, which was a naval building race, both countries building battleships.

I got the idea for the book a very long time ago. When I was a boy, I was a Rhodes scholar at Oxford, and I spent two years there in the fifties. One of my courses was modern European history. One of the term papers I did was the history of the period 1897 to 1914, which is what this book is about—the diplomacy leading up to the war and the threats. I found it absolutely enthralling: the kind of Greek tragedy aspect of the coming of this war. Nobody wanted the war. Nobody seemed able to avoid it, and the personalities involved were all extraordinarily interesting to me.

Years passed. I became a journalist. I wrote some other books. Along the way, I had spent three and a half years in the U.S. Navy during the Korean

War. I was born in Lexington, Kentucky, grew up in Nashville, Tennessee, so I was a landlubber—but I loved the ocean and the sea, and I spent these years on aircraft carriers. I used to like to just go up and stand on the deck at all times of the day and night and just look at the water. Then when I moved east, I spent my summers in Maine. I started sailing, and I got a small boat, a little bit bigger, and then a little bit bigger, not very big. I loved the sea.

So there was the navy aspect, and then in the middle seventies, I was interested and worried, as all of us were, about the arms race between the U.S. and the Soviet Union. I had done two books on the Soviet Union, on Russian history rather, and I saw a lot of parallels between our ICBM [ballistic missile] race with the Soviets—both sides building and building and trying to achieve security, and in fact never, never getting absolute security, because you couldn't—with what England and Germany were doing before the First World War: building battleships, spending huge sums of money, and really levering themselves, edging themselves into war. And all of these things sort of came together. I had just finished a long book. It was a biography of Peter the Great, and I thought I'd like to do something fairly short that I could do in a few years, and I'd go back and do this pre–World War I arms race. That was ten years ago, and I've been working on this book ever since.

John Keegan

This Booknotes *interview with John Keegan on his book* A History of Warfare *was recorded on May 8, 1994 in Taunton, England. Mr. Keegan taught military history for twenty-five years at Sandhurst, a military academy which he described as "Britain's West Point." Mr. Keegan is now the defense correspondent for* The Daily Telegraph *in London and continues to write books on military history.*

I WRITE IN THE ROOM at the head of the stairs on the second floor of my house in the country, looking out over a very beautiful garden my wife's created towards the edge of the chalk plains of Salisbury Plain at an Iron Age fort, which was dug by the Celtic people of Britain in, perhaps, the century before Augustus conquered the islands in 43 A.D.

It makes a difference where I am when I write. I'm very conscious of that. In front of the house, just a few hundred yards away, runs a primitive trackway called "the hardway," on which Alfred the Great brought his army up from Somerset to fight the Danes at Edington in the ninth century. That means a great deal to me.

I write all day. From ten in the morning till seven-thirty at night, with a short break for lunch. My wife is a writer, too, so she doesn't object too much. She objects a bit. My wife has her room for writing. We have a long, long, thin house and she has a room at one end and I have a room at the other end.

Now I write increasingly by pen. I've got every sort of writing instrument known to man, from a word processor to a fountain pen and a marvelously unreliable forty-year-old portable typewriter, which I do like writing on. But increasingly, I write just with a fountain pen and ink on lined paper. I used to type on my portable. I did have an electric typewriter once, which was a monstrosity. I just get a backache now if I type for long periods, so it's easier to write with a pen.

I have written about twenty books, I suppose. The one that's done the best is titled *Face of Battle*, which I published in 1976. In a curious way, it's always called a classic—so I suppose it is a classic. It was not a difficult book to write. I knew exactly what I was going to say before I began. It just came out. It was not a difficult book to write in the way that this one was because in *A History of Warfare,* I was trying to put so much that I know into such a small space.

My books are more successful in the United States than in Britain, without any question, except, curiously, for this one. This one's been enormously successful in Britain, and it won a major literary prize. Usually, I have a great American readership. It's not the only reason I love the United States, but it's one of the reasons.

I went to America when I was very young, and I've been there many, many times in my life. I think I've got a feel for America. It's certainly a country that I am deeply devoted to and tremendously interested in. I think Americans like the practical. They like the human. And I like both of those things myself, and I try and put them into my books. I like to try and pick problems to pieces in a practical way and also pick them to pieces in a human way. I think that's perhaps—it's not a deliberate formula, but it may be a formula that appeals to American readers.

The title is *A History of Warfare.* I don't think there is *the* history. I think there can only be history and each one . . . ought to be called *a* history, because ultimately, it's a personal view.

The book's range is from the Stone Age to modern times, since *Homo sapiens* came into being. *Homo sapiens*—you and me—have been here for about 40,000 years. There have been one or two other books like this, but not many people have had a go of the whole thing. It is a bit arrogant. The reason why it's arrogant is that you're pretending inevitably that you know most of world history, which I clearly don't.

I blocked the book out over a very long period of thinking about it. I suppose I eventually wanted to write so as to try and put this extraordinary phenomenon—men killing other men and sometimes other women, too—in a book. Men killing other men really is an extraordinary phenomenon. Why does it happen? How long has it gone on? Have the motives changed? Clearly, the methods have changed, but have the motives changed? I wanted to do it before I knew I wanted to do it, but eventually, I knew I wanted to do it. That meant beginning right at the beginning.

It also meant having some means of organizing it. I think you can't do it chronologically. If you start at the beginning and go on to the end, century by century, the book would be too thick. You had to have some way of chopping it down. In the end, I hit on the idea of what was the dominant technology, really? It's not a technology book, but I thought, in the end, that that was the only way of simplifying and organizing it.

What I've always wanted to do is write the sort of book which fellow historians would have to take seriously, but which was really a book for the educated general reader who would like to be informed, to have his view of the world enlarged about a particular subject. I think this is the highest of all historical callings. I almost despise—in fact, I do despise—the direction that university history writing has taken, in which enormous effort and years of work are given to writing books that really only interest a few hundred others, that address problems which only a few dozen others were aware of as problems at all, and that increasingly use language which perhaps only other academics can understand. That seems to me to be a perversion of the historian's calling. The historian ought to be an educated person, writing for other educated people about something which they don't know about but wish to know about in a way that they can understand.

I suppose by "educated" I would mean what Jefferson meant. I have got a sort of an eighteenth-century view of what being educated is, which is having read the major works of literature, having an understanding of the broad periods of history into which the world's past is divided, perhaps speaking another language or at least being aware of other languages, and having some competence. But I don't look to find an educated person in the ranks of university graduates, necessarily. Some of the most educated people I know have never been near a university.

For years, I taught at Sandhurst, which is Britain's West Point. Sandhurst has the most wonderful library. I mean, truly, the most wonderful library. It's a library whose origins go back into the eighteenth century. It's housed in a very beautiful building. It has very liberal rules about borrowing and working and that sort of thing. It is, as far as I'm concerned, the perfect library. Most of what I know in life, I learned in the Sandhurst library.

I enjoyed writing my earlier book enormously—more than anything I've ever written. When I wrote *The Face of Battle,* I felt, for the only time in my life, I knew what [Rudyard] Kipling meant when he said that a sort of demon, a sort of spirit, descends on you and the book—your hand moves in an unconscious way. I didn't feel that for this book. It was an effort, but I still enjoyed writing it very much, indeed.

Paul Kennedy

Paul Kennedy is the J. Richardson Dilworth Professor of History at Yale University. He appeared on the program in March 1993 to discuss his book Preparing for the 21st Century.

I<small>T WAS, I GUESS, THE MIDDLE WEEKS</small> of January [1988] when [David] Broder had written his column, [and Morton] Kondracke his. They somehow got the same phrase or the same sentence: "If Alan Bloom's *Closing of the American Mind* was the sleeper best-seller of 1987, we predict that Kennedy's *Rise and Fall of the Great Powers* will be the sleeper best-seller of 1988." Now, that appeared in about three places at once, and Kondracke repeated it on some Sunday morning television show, and the next week, there was a large, full-page, front-page and then two successive pages reviewing it in *The New York Times Book Review.* I think that combination together was enough to fuel the interest.

Then the phones started ringing: Could I go on *CBS Morning Edition,* could I go on *MacNeil/Lehrer [NewsHour],* could I do this, could I do that? Then—as certain Republicans began to feel that this might be used against them, Jeane Kirkpatrick, for example, or Mr. [Caspar] Weinberger—they began to criticize the book. Of course, the more they criticized, the more delighted my editor at Random House, Jason Epstein, became. He knows that nothing sells books faster than controversy. Now I hadn't expected this, and this really knocked me off my feet. It took me some time to recover. By the middle of February 1988, my wife on a few [occasions] found me sleepwalking in the middle of the night. I've never sleepwalked in my life. She found me crawling over the furniture, muttering to myself, because the pressures were so intense.

Since then it's been very difficult to readjust. You try to normalize yourself. You find ways of protecting yourself, and I have to say that the resources which flow in from the royalties allow you to put up certain barriers around your free time—to get yourself a small cottage a little [distance] away, which doesn't have a telephone or a fax so I can't be got at; so I can do my quiet writing and grading essays, etc. But it is a transformation I had not expected, which took a lot out of me in a physical sense.

It made me much more tired. Simple things like a profound hatred of the telephone, because you could no longer have the phone ring at your breakfast time and assume it was a friend, or a colleague, or another soccer coach calling you up. It could be somebody from Dutch television; it could be a Japanese newspaper; it could be a crank; it could be somebody who disliked what he heard about you because you had said America was in relative decline.

Your mail explodes to the factor of ten, twenty, thirty. I could no longer use the secretarial facilities of the History Department at Yale. It's difficult to go many places without people stopping you and getting in a conversation with you—sometimes nice, sometimes less nice. You become a public figure in the way that most academics don't, and we're not trained to become public figures. It made me immeasurably richer, because the sales were just far beyond expectations, and they continue to pour in from all of the foreign editions. I think there are 223 different foreign translations.

Right in the middle of the controversy and debates over *Rise and Fall*, I was asked to talk to a large meeting of chiefly economists at the Brookings Institution in Washington. One economist got up—a brave man; I don't know who he was—but he got up and he said, "I don't understand why such a fuss is being made of this book; it's actually very traditional. It's about great powers, it's about diplomacy. Why didn't Professor Kennedy use his energies to look at things which are much more important for broad, long-term world history [such as] transnational forces for change, like shifts in the demographic balances, the environmental damage we are doing to our planet?" That person was then turned on by his fellow academics who wanted to debate *Rise and Fall* and tried to push his point to one side.

But for some reason his remark had lodged itself in the back of my brain, and months later when things began to die down a bit, I was starting to notice some of the topics he had referred to. I began collecting data on that and getting intrigued enough that I went back to Jason Epstein and said, "Look, I know I'm a historian, but I've got these bees going around in my bonnet now. I want to write this out."

I don't know how other authors do it, but I find I'm reading into this topic; I'm beginning to get the ideas; and they're beginning to tumble around in my head like clothes in a tumbler dryer. Now, I don't want to go on reading, and reading, and reading until I get it perfectly. At a certain stage, I want to get some of the ideas out of the tumbler dryer and get them on paper. Very early on in this process of drafting, I'm very happy to start showing people my work. There are some authors who are very, very private and hardly anybody will see it before they send it off to an editor to comment on. I much prefer to have it circulated—the drafts all come back, sometimes with detailed comments—just to make sure I'm not getting things too terribly wrong. So I get the feedback, and then I would be getting more information, and amending, and altering. This is a long process—you're snipping, and chipping, and turning it around.

I was rather amazed, when I was sending my editor drafts of the chapters of that book, that he would haul me into Manhattan and take me through for hours and hours in a line-by-line editing, saying, "What do you mean by that? Who is he? This is repetitive!" I used to roll away as if I had been in a prolonged Oxford tutorial where your tutor had torn you to pieces. So I think I was prepared for it a second time around—and, boy, he did it a second time around! But he also did something I think few editors do. It was Jason who said, "Look, you've got to not only rewrite this in terms of syntax and improving the style, but you have to make much more of the interconnectedness of all these chapters." And so, he would push me back to the drawing board, to think it through and to redraft.

You don't finish [a project like this] even when you've sent off a completed, revised manuscript—and this was the third version of the manuscript. Even when that went off in May 1992 to my formidable editor, it goes through a process of copyediting by a very skilled copy editor who will be double-checking the smallest detail. Do you have a capital *H* for history on page 29, but a small *h* for history on page 200? Then there are a lot of queries which come back. In the meantime, there's a new article that has come out on this or that pertinent subject. When the page proofs come, that is absolutely the last time you can make amendments. So at that final stage, you just might be able to insert something. Anything that happens after that—no good. You're deep frozen in what you've said by then.

Francis Fukuyama

On February 9, 1992, Francis Fukuyama, former deputy director of policy planning at the State Department and author of the book The End of History and the Last Man, *appeared on the program.*

THE BOOK THAT I'VE WRITTEN grew out of an article that I published in a small magazine called *National Interest* two years ago, just prior to the fall of the Berlin Wall when all of these great events were happening in the Soviet bloc. What I was referring to was, really, the growth of a kind of universal consensus on the justness or the rightness of the principles of liberal democracy.

But I'm afraid that what happened was a lot of people simply saw the title, and they said, "Well, what's this? It's absurd, you know. History's not going to end. We still have wars and poverty and a lot of struggle in the Third World and things of that sort, so, prima facie, it's an absurd thing." There was a lot of controversy simply over the misinterpretation, I think.

Underneath that, there really is a more serious question. It used to be that there were many alternative forms of government . . . and for many years we thought communism was our major rival and alternative type of civilization. One by one, in this century, every one of those has collapsed. And [even] now, not every country is a liberal democracy; there are many dictatorships to the right and the left remaining.

It's an imposing title. The book is about the question of whether there exists such a thing as what I would call "History," with a capital *H*. We usually associate history with just the routine flow of events—the war in the Persian Gulf, the fall of the Berlin Wall. But my book tries to ask a larger question: whether there is such a thing as a history of human society, taking into account the experiences of all peoples and virtually all times. And whether there's a kind of coherent evolution in the nature of those societies as they progress from very primitive, agricultural, tribal societies up through various monarchies and aristocracies, up to the kind of liberal democracy and technologically driven capitalism that we have today.

THE FRENCH REVOLUTION, for [German philosopher Georg Friedrich] Hegel really represented the coming of the end of history, so to speak. Now, by the French Revolution, we don't mean just the limited historical event; what we mean is the emergence of what we understand as modern liberal democracy. The French Revolution, ultimately, was about a revolution in favor of the principles of liberty and equality. Now, you could substitute the American Revolution for that because, I think, in that kind of ideological sense, those two revolutions were equivalent. They were both revolutions to create a liberal democracy as a political system based on popular sovereignty with guarantees of individual rights.

For Hegel, the coming of the French Revolution was the event that heralded the end of history because it meant that the principles of liberty and equality on which modern liberal democracy is based had finally been discovered and had been implemented—only in a small corner of Europe—but back in the late eighteenth century at least the principle was established. I think the modern Hegelians would argue that what's happened in the two hundred years since the French Revolution is simply the implementation of those principles around the world. In other words, we haven't progressed in any fundamental sense since the French Revolution.

Besides Hegel, I think the other towering figure that is really by far the most important was the German philosopher Friedrich Nietzsche. It's from him that the part of the title *The Last Man* comes, because he, in a certain sense, was the philosopher that argued that, "Well, yes, there's been historical progress, perhaps, but it's led not to greater human happiness but to a total disaster." In a way, the book is about a dialogue between these two philosophers as to how we ought to evaluate goodness: how satisfactory is our society at the end of history?

I wanted to address the very difficult philosophical issues: the question of whether there's a universal history; whether history has a directionality; whether we can say that there's such a thing as the end of history. But on the other hand, I had wanted to make the book accessible to a general reader who was educated, broadly speaking, but not a specialist in either philosophy or political science, or any of the topics that I cover. So, in a way, I had a rather schizophrenic sense of my audience: that on the one hand it was this general audience, but on the other hand I knew that there'd be a whole battery of specialists—specialists in Hegel, and specialists in development theory, and economists and sociologists that would also be there with a microscope analyzing the different parts of the book that dealt with those [specialties] as well. It was a very challenging thing to do.

I think one of the ways that I tried to deal with it is simply by putting the stuff for the specialists in the footnotes so that a general reader doesn't have to be bothered with references and complicated counterarguments and that sort of thing.

I'm going to be talking about this book in this country, and then it's being published in about fourteen foreign countries at the same time. That's one of the interesting things about this particular idea—it stirred a comparable degree of debate and controversy in a lot of places outside the United States as well, and I think that's going to preoccupy me.

Robert Leckie

On September 3, 1995, our Booknotes *guest was the historian and author Robert Leckie. He joined us to discuss his fortieth book,* Okinawa: The Last Battle of World War II.

I CAME FROM A CULTIVATED FAMILY. My father was an advertising and sales-promotion manager for Joseph Dixon Crucible Company, and he named all those famous pencils—Ticonderoga and so on. He was very proud that every year the Associated Press would put out a story saying it [the pencil] was something they haven't ruined yet, and that Ticonderoga No. 2 was always number one.

He's dead, of course. But he was a very cultivated man. He had a big library, and there were dictionaries and encyclopedias all over the house. It was an intellectual atmosphere. You got a head start. There was a blackboard in the kitchen [for vocabulary words] and things like that. I never wanted to be a writer until I realized that books were not the works of nature or of God but of men and women, and then I was writing poetry since I was twelve or thirteen.

In the service, I was in the marines, in the First Marine Division. I went into the service on Pearl Harbor Day. But the doctor said to me—now, you may want to edit this out, I don't know, but I'll say it—he said, "I'm going to accept you because you're a fine physical specimen, except for one thing." I said, "What's that?" He said, "You'll have to get circumcised first." I said, "Circumcised? What do you think I'm going to do to the enemy?" So he said, "You know something?" He said, "I know you're going to come back."

My typewriter was in the *George F. Elliot,* an African slaver, if it was anything else. They wouldn't even let us paint the thing because if we chipped the sides, they were afraid the plates would fall off. We were all ashore when a Zero [a Japanese plane] crashed amidship. I don't know whether he was the first *kamikaze* or not. But anyway, my typewriter was aboard and it sank. I came home and the girl next door—I saw her, I fell in love with her, I married her, and I'll tell you why. She had a Royal typewriter just the same as mine.

ONE THING STANDS on the shoulders of another. So I do research on the Colonial Wars, and then I do research on the Revolutionary War and then the 1812 and Mexico and the Indians and so on. It keeps building, and you keep the notes, and you buy the books. I buy everything I can because then I have all the sources at my hands. So I have about 4,000 or 5,000 books, almost all on military history, also on theology and religion because that was my first interest.

There are no notes in the back or a bibliography. That's what my editor wanted. All the other books are footnoted. Most of the other books, in the beginning, were footnoted and with a bibliography and everything, as you're supposed to do, but this has no bibliography. He didn't want one. And it's selling better. Maybe that's telling me something. I would imagine that the ordinary reader is more satisfied with a smaller book and thinks that the footnotes and the bibliography are pedantic and boring.

I write, preferably, staring at a blank wall. That's not the best scenery for a writer—better for an artist, but not for a writer. I have a lovely study, but once you're into it, it doesn't make any difference. But the difficulty is cranking up the machine, getting it started. You can sit there for hours, actually. When you're at an impasse, you have to go back to it. Every morning or afternoon, whenever you write, you have to go up and shoot that old bear under your desk between the eyes. That's right. You have to have enormous discipline, especially if you like your drink. I know so many good writers who went down the drain. If you like to drink, you can't do it. It's a reward. It should never be a crutch.

My wife would get up earlier [than me] and feed the children, put them off to school, and I would exercise, play handball, and so on in the morning, as I said, to exercise, with an *e,* to stay in shape, and to exorcise, with an *o,* the devil booze. But I would always start writing about one until five or six [o'clock]. Now I only write from about one until three.

I have four typewriters now, but they don't make Royals anymore. I tried to get the so-called word processor. Now, when I write, I put my hands on the keyboard to think. Well, what the hell—that sends the cursor thing crazy, and if you have a power outage—say you've got three months in that thing—pow! The text is gone. I'm serious. So I decided, no, that's not for me.

I'm doing a series of novels for Tora, a branch of St. Martin's Press: *Americans at War.* It will take the fighting Flynn family through all the wars. I began this book more than fifteen years ago for New American Library, but then somebody who was a higher-up in New American Library gave an unknown, unpublished author an advance—listen to this—of $850,000. The exodus from NAL, as it was called, was enormous. And I just quit. I mean, I had four editors on one book. It was terrible. [NAL is] now owned by Viking and it's quite different, but I'm doing these for a different outfit and it's a good change of pace.

I love to write. But you cannot turn a phrase very well in fiction, but, in fact, in history, you can. Somebody like Churchill—a woman came up to him, and he was a master of repartee—and she said, "Winston, you're drunk." And he said, "Bessie, you're ugly. But tomorrow, I shall be sober." You can do that in dialogue, maybe, but you can't do that in fiction because the editor will write in the margin, "purple prose."

Stephen Carter

Stephen Carter, Yale University law professor and former clerk to Supreme Court Justice Thurgood Marshall, appeared on Booknotes *on September 29, 1991. Professor Carter joined us to discuss his book* Reflections of an Affirmative Action Baby.

I HAVE LOVED WRITING ever since I was a child. When I was a little kid, I used to write short stories. Literally, when I was in fifth and sixth grade, I was writing short stories, usually for my own amusement or for the amusement of friends. Indeed, I think if you asked me when I was in junior high school what did I want to do with my life, I would have said, "I want to be a writer." Writing is my passion—one of my great passions. One of the things I love about academic life is that I get to write, and I do a lot of writing. I'm talking here about writing in scholarly and professional journals, and I think there are few law professors in the country who do as much writing as I do because I just love it so. It's so much fun. It's one of the reasons I enjoy the job that I have.

Actually, I now put the words into a word processor. I like to have an idea and then to sit there and begin to type or, occasionally, begin to make notes, and have it slowly flow out onto the paper, and then begin to fiddle with it and fiddle with it, and sometimes get mad and throw it away and start over again. Eventually something emerges that makes sense, that I hope is creative or thoughtful and sometimes is even a little fluent. I think that one who writes as much as I do sometimes runs a risk that things will not be as well polished as they might be. But I always have another idea. There's always something else I want to write about. There are students who work for me as researchers who get very frustrated because I might tell someone that I'm doing this great project about law and religion. The students will say, "It's very exciting." They'll be working and working on it, and suddenly I'll say, "We're putting it aside. I've got this great idea about copyright law. I'm writing this now. You've got to go do this research." They get very frustrated because they have to move from project to project, but that's the way my mind works. I'm quite intellectually peripatetic. I write mostly in my office, although more and more I've taken to writing at home since I got a home computer. I do some writing at night at home, but I've got two kids. When I'm home, I find I'd much rather play and tumble around with them than sit at my word processor.

I HAD AN EXPERIENCE WITH HARVARD that was, at the time, something of considerable bitterness to me, although in retrospect I've seen that it shouldn't have been. When I was a senior at Stanford, full of my arrogance, full of my love of standardized tests, I naturally assumed—don't even think about affirmative action—I naturally assumed that I would get into law school everywhere that I applied. That was just the kind of assumption I've always made through life. Well, it didn't quite turn out that way. I got into law school everywhere I applied except Harvard. I got a letter of rejection from Harvard, and then I got these telephone calls from a couple of school officials and also from a professor. What they said has always been to me quite telling: they said that a letter of rejection had been sent out, but that it was an error. And they said that they had uncovered additional information. They said somewhat coyly that it should have been accounted in my favor. Then subsequently they said that the information was that I was black. I said something like—this part actually isn't in the book—I said something like, "Why didn't you know I was black? After all, there was a comment in there that I was a member of a black pre-law society," because that was on my application. They said, "Well, we assumed from your record that you were white." Those words have always burned in my mind. There were a kind of stunning reminder of what was expected of me. What they were saying by saying, "We assumed from your record that you were white," was that in their view, my record was too good to have been compiled by a black undergraduate. To have that record I must have been white, but not quite good enough for a white Harvard law student. I went off to Yale in part because of that episode.

IT'S ACTUALLY A KIND of interesting story—how this became a book—at least interesting to me. I became interested in the subject in 1989. At about that time, I got interested in some other events that led me to write an op-ed piece in *The Wall Street Journal* that described exactly the story about my admission to Harvard and Yale. A few days later I got a phone call from an editor at a major publishing house in New York, who said, "That was a very interesting op-ed piece. Do you want to write a book about it?" I said,

"That's a kind of interesting idea." So we talked about it a little bit, and we corresponded a little bit over the next few weeks.

Then my father said, "Stephen, you are not going to sell a book without an agent." So I said, "Okay." My father loves me, and he wants the best for me. I think his view was that when you sell a book, you negotiate a deal, and that I couldn't do it myself and someone—an agent or at least a lawyer—should be doing that for me. He kept reminding me, "A man who is a lawyer in his own case has a fool for a client." Through a series of connections, I ended up with an agent who found the book interesting, and that was how it ended up going on the market. It did not end up with the publishing house that first expressed interest in it. The publishing industry is not an industry where one worries about those things, I realize, but I've always felt loyalty and things like that were very important, so I did feel a little bad about that.

The title I always had. The title was always in the back of my mind and it has never changed. There was a lot of talk with the publisher about the shape [the book itself] would take. Indeed, when I talked to the various publishers, that was one of my big concerns—in what direction they thought the book should go. I should explain that although the title may suggest the book is just about affirmative action, most of the book is not. Most of the book is on other topics, and in some ways it's the other topics that I am as passionate about, if not more passionate about.

There have been a lot of reviews. So far, I'm relieved to say, they've been more favorable than unfavorable, but there have been some unfavorable reviews as well. Whether it's sparking dialogue, I think, remains to be seen. I will confess that I've been a little bit uneasy about how a lot of black people will react to the book and [I'm uneasy] about how a lot of white people will react to it in two different ways. But you can't worry too much about that because if you write, your writing is out there. People will do with it what they want to do. I'm simply trying to raise some questions about some aspects of affirmative action and to prod us all toward dialogue.

Daniel Boorstin

Pulitzer Prize–winning historian Daniel Boorstin was appointed Librarian of Congress by President Gerald R. Ford and served in that position for twelve years. Mr. Boorstin, with the assistance of his wife of over fifty years, Ruth Frankel Boorstin, has been working on a history series. The first volume published in 1987 was called The Discoverers. *On December 6, 1992, Mr. Boorstin appeared on* Booknotes *to talk about the second volume,* The Creators: A History of Heroes of the Imagination.

I HAD THE IDEA FOR THIS SERIES about twenty years ago. My wife, Ruth, and I were on a vacation in the Bavarian Alps, and we went to the top of Zugspitze, and there we found ourselves overnight because the train left without us, and we had only each other and our thoughts. We had just completed the third volume of *The Americans: The Democratic Experience,* and we had to decide what to do next. My wife's been my closest editor and my inspiration, of course. We thought about it and came up with the idea that it was about time that I should de-provincialize myself, that I should grow up, reach out, and try to write about the world. So out of that came a notion of doing a kind of world history, which would not be about wars and empires and politics, but be about human fulfillment. How does mankind fulfill itself? This was a rather large assignment.

Out of that grew the first volume, which was *The Discoverers,* a history of man's search to know the world and himself. That was only the first part, because the search to know is only part of man's quest for fulfillment. The second part, which has just been published, is *The Creators: A History of Heroes of the Imagination,* and that is about the search to make the new. That also took about nine years, and it's been a great delight.

I consider my vocation being a writer partly because I can't explain why I want to do it. As long as I can remember I wanted to be a writer, but I didn't start out by studying how to be a writer. My father was a lawyer in Tulsa, Oklahoma, and he loved the law and played a role, as you can do in a small city, sort of like that of a parish priest. He advised people on their problems. He never got rich, but he loved the community. He was a booster for Tulsa. He wanted me to be a lawyer. He would have been happy if I'd come back to Tulsa and join him in Boorstin & Boorstin law firm. I didn't do that.

I became interested in words, I suppose, mainly in high school, because in those days people had what they called oratorical contests. You memorized the great American speeches of the past like Patrick Henry's plea or Zola's plea for Dreyfus. Back then, you had a feeling for the spoken word and the nuance of the word. Then I went away to college—I went to Harvard—and I spent much of my time there studying English history and literature. But in my junior year my grandfather died, and that was a shock to me because I loved him. He'd lived with us. I thought maybe one should try the sciences. Could you prevent death somehow by finding a cure for diseases? So, for about half of my time at Harvard as an undergraduate, I studied biochemistry. I finally graduated in English history and literature, and I wrote my honors thesis on Edward Gibbon, which was a great good fortune for me because he became my idol and my model of what a great historian should be.

I then went to Oxford as a Rhodes scholar and still had thoughts of being a lawyer, so I studied law. I did two degrees in law, the B.A. in jurisprudence and the bachelor of civil law. At Oxford, the law program is very much historical and philosophical. In fact, almost half of the program, when I took it, was in Roman law; and I had a chance to use my Latin, which I enjoyed, and to learn about Roman history, which I especially enjoyed. Then at the same time, I did what was very unusual for an American. I became a barrister-at-law [an English attorney-at-law] so I could wear a wig. Now, unfortunately, I need one, but I didn't so much then.

The great thing about Oxford was the time when you were not at Oxford. There was a six-week Christmas vacation, a six-week Easter vacation, and I spent all those times traveling and much of it living in Florence, a place which I came to love; and some of that affection is reflected in *The Creators,* where I describe the great works of the Italian painters.

I HAVE MY OWN WAY of taking notes on five-by-eight-inch pads oriented toward the book that I've been reading, so that then I have a very complete system of files for the outline. You see, the most important thing in making a big book like this is the outline, seeing where you're going. I spent, I would say, almost as much time on the outline and revising it—I have a whole file cabinet full of outlines—as I spent on the actual reading and writing, for a number of reasons. In the first place, a nonfiction book, especially if it's on a complicated subject, must have a dramatic structure. If you're writing a novel, the author has the advantage over the reader because the reader doesn't know whether this figure's going to be a hero or a villain, so you can do what you want with him. But if you're writing a nonfiction work about famous and important people and about the major events in history, people know how it turned out. They know that Michelangelo was a great painter and that Picasso was going to be one of the most famous painters in the world and so on. So the writer has to create what I would call a willing suspension of knowledge and make a drama of the facts of the past.

I think one of the weaknesses of modern historical writing is that too much of it is a by-product of the growth of the profession; that is, that historians tend to write for other historians. I want to write for the human race. That's what I try to do.

THE BOOK IS DEDICATED TO MY WIFE, RUTH. That is one of the conspicuous understatements in the book. All my major books are dedicated to Ruth because she was not only dedicated to the books, but we had a wonderful, companionable life together exploring these subjects. She's never been my research assistant or . . . typed or done any secretarial work for it, but her editorial advice has been incomparable. Among other mottoes, she has the motto, "If in doubt, cut it out," and that has helped make the books, I think, a little more readable than they otherwise might have been. But that companionship has been very important and her encouragement, her willingness to go with me—these are long projects, you know; *The Americans* took thirty years, and *The Discoverers* and *The Creators* took nine years each. Ruth has not only been patient but she's enjoyed it with me, and that's been a wonderful thing.

Stanley Weintraub

Booknotes guest Stanley Weintraub, author of Disraeli: A Biography, *appeared on February 6, 1994. Mr. Weintraub teaches biographical writing at Pennsylvania State University.*

WHAT I REMEMBER MOST about my father was that he was a tremendous reader although he had very little education. I think he didn't have formal education beyond the fourth grade. But when he died in his sleep, he was found [to have been] reading Shakespeare's *Othello*.

I WROTE A BIOGRAPHY OF QUEEN VICTORIA, published in 1987, and was fascinated by the character of [British prime minister Benjamin] Disraeli as he came across in the biography of Victoria. At that point I decided I wanted to write about Disraeli. Very often what happens is that a subject of a book comes out of the index to the last book—because you get fascinated by somebody in the book, and you want to go on and write more.

Disraeli was a novelist; Disraeli was twice prime minister, the first time in 1868. He was probably one of the major figures of the nineteenth century in England. What has happened is a lot of politicians have adopted Disraeli the same way, in America, that they've adopted Harry Truman. In other words, they've adopted somebody who is a feisty, fighting character who came out of nowhere, who came out of rather low beginnings, not an aristocrat by any means, and who fought his way up. So you find Republicans having adopted Truman over here, and you find people of both parties adopted Disraeli because they like the fighter. They like the fact that he had the audacity to do what he did.

[Disraeli's] first novel was written when he was twenty or twenty-one. It was a great success until people discovered who wrote it. It was published anonymously, and people thought some great writer must have written it and published it anonymously. They praised it, bought copies, and then they discovered that this young kid had written it, and they were embarrassed—and it hurt the future novels of his for a while.

Vivian Grey was his first novel, and he wrote a number of others after that that also dealt with his own background, but in between he tried to write one that would sell a lot of copies, in other words, a sort of romantic dream fiction. He called it *The Young Duke.* His father scoffed at this saying, "What does Ben know of dukes?" He didn't know anything about dukes, but by the end of his life Queen Victoria was ready to make him a duke. He got as far as being an earl. He became earl of Beaconsfield when he was prime minister. So he went from obscure Jewish boy ineligible for office to [, at] the end of his life, earl of Beaconsfield, and he could have had a dukedom if he wanted it.

What is very striking about his novels is that [they] made some of the other novelists of the time very jealous. Some of them were successful. They were all very greatly talked about, and finally at the end of his life, when he was about to publish his last completed novel, *Endymion,* he received the highest sum for signing the contract that any novelist had ever received in England. It made people like Anthony Trollope and some of the other novelists who were popular at the time very jealous. They couldn't imagine why somebody like Disraeli would be getting that kind of money. But he was a public figure; people would read what he had to say because it was Disraeli even it didn't turn out to be an exciting novel.

There are possibly a dozen biographies [of Disraeli]. There were biographies written of Disraeli before he became famous, before he became prime minister. And they were often very negative, very derogatory, very anti-Semitic, because he never lost the tag of being a Jew all his life. How could he? He was converted at twelve, but he remained Benjamin Disraeli. And if your name [was] Benjamin Disraeli, you're going to be identified with the background from which [you] came.

The toughest thing about writing this book was not to get diverted into writing too much about all of those other interesting people who turned up in Disraeli's life. Perhaps I shouldn't have even been diverted by his two illegitimate children [for] half a chapter because one doesn't want a book to get too long. You want to be able to lift it up in your lap, and hold it, and be able to read it. So there [is] a practical limit as to how long a book should be. The first official biography, and the only official biography, of Disraeli was six volumes, and I don't think it went into nearly as much detail about what he was really like as this one does.

You learn how to write by writing. I guess that's the only way one can do it. I'm teaching a course in biographical writing, but I don't think that's how you learn how to write. I think you learn to write by writing and writing and writing. I want to be read. I don't want to be read only by scholars who number maybe 30 to 300, and that's it. If I'm going to work very hard to try to reveal what somebody was really like and I think the person was a fascinating individual, I want to communicate that. I think Disraeli was just compellingly fascinating as a human being and as an achiever, and so I'd like people to know about that.

Robert D. Richardson, Jr.

Robert D. Richardson, Jr., a retired professor of literature at Wesleyan University in Middletown, Connecticut, appeared on the program on August 13, 1995, to discuss his biography of philosopher Ralph Waldo Emerson, Emerson: The Mind on Fire.

I STARTED THE BOOK with the moment when the young Emerson, who is a minister, is walking out to Roxbury [Massachusetts] to visit the grave of his wife, and he opens the coffin of his wife, who has now been dead a year and two months. He says in his journal that he walked out and opened the coffin. Not the tomb—he opened the actual coffin. And the reason for it has been speculated on a great deal. For some biographers and some readers, it seems so macabre an act that they've thought that perhaps he imagined it or hallucinated it, but it's right there in the journal. I think the reason—one has to guess and one has to say that it's a guess, but I think it was because he couldn't really believe she was dead. He was writing in his journal to her as though she were alive.

EMERSON IS TAUGHT NOW in somewhere between twenty and thirty percent of American literature courses. One of the reasons I wrote the book was that he seemed to me to be losing his place in American literature. I didn't write this book as a political act, but because I have found Emerson personally inspiring. Emerson and [Henry David] Thoreau are the people that I read when I'm feeling bad. I come away from reading them feeling better about myself, and the world, and my friends, and the country. This ability of Emerson to reach the individual, to reach me alone, not as part of a party or a group or anything else, but just the individual, I think is something he still has. I find that when one puts this in front of young people, they respond, and they take it up.

You do a book like this because you want to get it straight. There are lots of biographies of Emerson and there are many terrific ones, in fact, from earlier, but I never found one that got it right for me. And it began to matter to me that Emerson was so condescended to and so dismissed as a kind of minor figure to Henry Thoreau, who was the great hero of the moment. It took me a long time to work up the nerve to think of writing a biography of Emerson because, as I say, there are so many, and so many good ones, but I finally thought maybe I could do it as a study of his reading and as a kind of an inside narrative—to try and work it from the reading and the journals and get as close as I could to doing an "inside" book.

I WROTE THIS BOOK WITH A PEN, by hand, on yellow sheets of paper mostly in Middletown, Connecticut, and Cape Cod. I never went to Concord [Massachusetts] to write, but I would go to Concord to read, to walk around, just to feel the place, to look at the house again, to look at pictures, to talk to friends up there. There are a lot of experts on various aspects of Emerson; Emerson's life and family were up there, a lot of wonderful friends [were] there.

One of the interesting things is that Concord doesn't look all that different from the Concord of the nineteenth century. I mean, if you go hunting for [Edgar Allan] Poe's house in Baltimore or in New York, or [Walt] Whitman's place in Brooklyn, you just can't find anything that reminds you of these times. But Concord is still full of slow-moving rivers, and marshes and fields. And so the physical surroundings of Concord, the natural world, the nature that meant so much to Emerson is still very much there in Concord. You can take long, long walks through the woods in Concord still to this day.

Henry David Thoreau was just fifteen years younger than Emerson. He died in 1862, just as the Civil War was under way. He died young, and Emerson lived on, but they were both in Concord at the same time. They were very close friends. They were both people with a lot of intellectual horsepower, and they didn't always get along perfectly. There were some spats and some fallings-out, but Emerson, even when his memory was gone as a very old man, remembered Thoreau was his best friend. And without Emerson, I don't think there would have been a Thoreau.

IT TOOK EIGHT YEARS for me to write this book. I'd been working on some of the material before that, and I'd worked for about nine years on the Thoreau biography before that with a lot of the same material. I've been reading this material for the last thirty years.

I called it *The Mind on Fire* because the picture that I used to have of Emerson was of a kind of cold, plaster saint, his bust was up in schoolrooms everywhere. I think a lot of other people sort of picked up the notion that Emerson was this kind of cool, distant saint. One day, I was in his house in Concord, looking on the walls, and there was a picture of a volcano in eruption right where you come in the front door, and it's very striking—because it's not a very good painting, but it's very vivid and very colorful. I kept wondering and wondering and wondering about this painting. Finally, I began to notice that the image of fire and volcanoes, and the notion that humanity is all connected the way volcanoes are all connected by a fire under the earth, was his leading idea. He came to think that just as each volcano was an outlet for the fire under the earth, so each person is an outlet for the humanity that unites us all. This notion of fire, and the volcano, and the power of passion is all there, and it became the way to start the book.

I spent many years reading Emerson's reading because both this book and my previous one on Henry Thoreau really were conceived as intellectual biographies, meaning studies of what they read. Then you'd look at their writings and interpret their writings and their lives in this way. That is what is novel about this biography, if you like, that I really did try to read Emerson's major reading and then see how it relates to the rest of his life and work.

Instead of writing in the margins, Emerson would write in his notebooks, so you would have the notebook alongside and you'd have the book and you could look at the very page and the very book that he'd been reading. You sometimes got this little uneasy sense that you were really walking in his footsteps and tracing some of these books through. And sometimes you could look at a big, long book and tell that he really hadn't gotten much out of it, and you could look at his [library] checkout record and notice that he'd checked out the same book over and over and over again and never made a note on it. I think he took a lot of those books home the way I do sometimes, intending to read it and never getting around to it.

I read and researched most comfortably, probably, at home with a big pile of library books, or deep in Widener Library or the University of Denver library. Widener is the big library at Harvard. Or perhaps at the Boston Athenaeum, which has many of the books that Emerson himself looked at. That was a wonderful place to go and work.

Basically, Emerson wrote by hand. The typewriter hadn't come in yet, and he started out writing with pens that were quills made of feathers, and in the middle of his career, he switched over to the steel pen, and you can see it. You can see the ink splattered all over from these horrible, scratchy, early steel pens that were just beginning to be made. That's in his journal, it's in his letters.

The letters of all his family have been saved. The Emersons saved everything. There's a mountain of material on Emerson. His own notebooks and journals run to over 250 volumes, each one with 300 or 400 pages, and indexes to each one of these; and his correspondence now runs to nine published volumes; and nobody's even begun to collect the correspondence to him, but there's a lot of material.

WALT WHITMAN WAS AN UNKNOWN YOUNG POET and newspaperman in New York who published a little volume of his own poems at his own expense and had the very good sense to send a copy—free—to Emerson, and Emerson liked it very much and sent Whitman a wonderful letter, saying, "This is the greatest piece of wit and wisdom America has yet contributed. I greet you at the beginning of a great career." It's the most wonderful letter Whitman had ever gotten and the most famous letter in American literary history. It was Emerson's announcement to Whitman that he had made it, and Whitman was so pleased that he went out and put out a second edition and stamped Emerson's words right in gold on the binding of the second edition.

Neil Baldwin

Neil Baldwin appeared on Booknotes *on March 19, 1995, to discuss his biography of Thomas Alva Edison,* Edison: Inventing the Century. *Mr. Baldwin also is head of the National Book Foundation.*

ONE OF THE FIRST THINGS I did before starting this book was I read every single word that had ever been written about Thomas Edison. And it went in phases. There was a big burst of stuff right about the time that he reached middle age and he was becoming famous, and there was another burst in the 1920s when he was becoming revered as a deity, almost, in American culture. But in the last thirty-five years, which is what I was sort of focusing on, there had only been two biographies that are of any note, which I talk about as having some strengths and some weaknesses. But I think mine is the most balanced and the one that deals the most with him as a human being, as a person as well as a myth.

Thomas Edison lived from 1847 to 1931, so that's eighty-four years. And that's why the subtitle, *Inventing the Century,* was a concept that I thought very carefully about. I feel Edison represents the era and is a representation of the era at the same time. He exemplifies the century, the waning of one era and the beginning of another, as well as being a major prototype of the time. He defines the time and the times define him—both.

I WRITE IN MY STUDY on the third floor of my house, in a little room under the eaves there, with a computer. I mean, it's not very romanticized, but it's on the third floor so the rest of the family activities take place on the first and second floors, and I can be somewhat—I have to be somewhat isolated to do the work. But the fieldwork and the collection of the data is the social part that I also enjoy.

I am proud of the fact that I went to every single place that Edison lived in this country, that is to say: Milan, Ohio; Port Huron, Michigan; Boston; New York; Newark; Menlo Park; West Orange. And then I went to Florida, where he had his major winter estate, which is in Fort Myers on the

Caloosahatchee River in Florida. He has a beautiful home there which, of course, he designed himself and landscaped himself. I also went to England [and] did research at the Institution for Electrical Engineers over there. They have a whole archive from the time when Thomas Edison electrified a ten-square-block section of the City of London.

I've been very concerned in all my biographies about [being in touch] directly with the family of the subject. So I had worked my way in [to meet a son of Thomas Edison, Theodore Edison]. I had met the nephews and some of the cousins, and ingratiated myself. Finally, I was given permission to enter the inner sanctum and go up to his home in West Orange. He lived in Llewellyn Park, which is a very exclusive suburb of West Orange, New Jersey.

The nurse let me into this very old house—very, very secluded, way off the beaten track. Theodore Edison was lying in a hospital bed. The shades were drawn; it was very dark. The nurse introduced me to him, Mr. Edison. He had very bad arthritis. His hands were sort of clenched on his chest, and he could hardly speak. He was in the last stages of Parkinson's disease.

But he knew who I was, he knew why I was there—and he had read my book on [the poet and physician] William Carlos Williams, which really astonished me, that he actually knew of that book. I started chatting with him. I asked him about the celebration of the Fourth of July, which was a big holiday in the Edison family, and how Thomas Edison used to make his own fireworks and have the kids run barefoot on the lawn. He would throw firecrackers at their feet, and they would jump up and down. Then they would eat watermelon and have a grand old time. Theodore was able to conjure up this image of a bygone American time as if it were yesterday, even though he was laboring very, very deeply with the problems of Parkinson's disease.

The impression was of a person with an ember of thought in his mind, even though his body was very, very infirm. I felt this was a person with life in his brain but dying out slowly. Three or four months later he died, but I call him the last Edison because none of Thomas Edison's male children had offspring. So, in fact, Theodore was the last person with the surname Edison, and now he's gone.

I studied his [Thomas Edison's] notebooks very carefully because I think they are the true chronology of his career. He left over 3,000 laboratory notebooks behind. They are housed in the Edison historic site in West Orange, New Jersey. That's where the major Edison archive is located.

I read the actual notebooks, and I also studied them on microfilm or microfiche. I wanted to read them in both ways, actually. I have a background in studying manuscripts as a way to build my biographies. I decided to approach these notebooks almost as a freestanding literary genre in and of themselves, because Edison says in one of the first notebooks, "I am going to make a full record of my career," knowing the importance of them from a documentation point of view, knowing that if you're going to create a patent, you have to keep a record of the time, the place, the date of the invention. You have to keep a record of who was working on it with you. You have to have a witness for the invention. You have to have the most assiduous documentation when you're trying to create a patent for the consumer industry.

So on that level, the notebooks are important because they are Edison's chronology of his work. But they also contain ideas and half-formed thoughts and sketches and perceptions for other works and other creations that he had thought of that did not become fully realized in the marketplace. That's where you get the vision of Thomas Edison's imagination. That's where you get the vision of him as an introspective, creative person. He writes down all the names of all the books he's reading. He writes down the names of people that he meets who give him ideas. He writes down chemicals that he wants to purchase, tools that he wants to purchase. You get some sense of what direction he's going in his research.

These are really the chronicle of his entire life. I think that it's significant that he kept writing in these notebooks long after he was able to visit the lab. When he was a sick man, when he was in bed, when he couldn't lift his head off the pillow, he's still writing in the notebooks because it's the process that's important to him, not just the manifestation, not just the thing, but the process of how you get through an idea, how you track your thoughts and how you monitor your thoughts.

I'VE BEEN THINKING A LOT about the relationship of the subjects for my biographies and my job, and I think the point is that the American story is a very big story and a very varied story. Since my first roots are in literature, I feel deeply committed to bringing great, quality writing to a larger audience and making it the province of more people, even though the publishing industry is fundamentally an East Coast phenomenon and the corporate structures are in the East Coast. But the public is very wide and very broadly based, and I think we have a responsibility to them.

As a matter of fact, of the three subjects I've written about [Thomas Edison, the photographer and painter Man Ray, and William Carlos Williams], I think that Edison would have been the one that I personally could have connected with the best, I think because of his many, many times stated appreciation of the combination of imaginative thinking and hard work.

Someone asked me the other day, "Where does genius reside? Does it reside in the imagination or does it reside in the hard work?" And I said I think it's a synthesis of both, that it's not a "eureka!" kind of thing. It's not a flash. It's the understanding that the tributaries of hard work feed into and out of the creative mind, and you cannot just expect to have ideas spring fully formed out of your mind from beginning to end. They require a consciously directed effort. I believe there would have been an intuitive understanding of that dynamic in a human being. I think that I could have communicated with Edison on that level.

I think I am a student of the human condition. I've always been interested in others' words. I think my interest in biography is built upon my interest in people in general and in understanding what motivates people, people that I've known throughout my whole life. I think biography—the craft of biography—is a sleuthing job that requires you to act like a detective. You have to build and collect all the evidence. I always like to get all my research together in one place before I start writing. I like to have my entire case, as it were, laid out for me from beginning to end before I start to actually work on the book.

Robert Remini

Robert Remini appeared on Booknotes *on April 5, 1992, to talk about a new biography he had written,* Henry Clay: Statesman for the Union. *Previously, Professor Remini wrote a three-volume biography of President Andrew Jackson. He is a professor emeritus of history at the University of Illinois at Chicago.*

I STARTED THIS BOOK seven or eight years ago. I had completed my Andrew Jackson biography, and in doing Jackson of course I came upon Henry Clay. I found him funny, fascinating, and a man, I thought, that really needed and deserved a modern, full-scale biography. He was Abraham Lincoln's ideal of a statesman, I think. Most of the ideas that Lincoln had early on about economics, about slavery, come right out of Henry Clay. Lincoln is like Henry Clay to a very large extent, I found. Lincoln quotes Henry Clay in the Lincoln-Douglas debates a total of thirty-seven or thirty-eight times. Clay told whimsical stories the way Abraham Lincoln did. [In the late 1850s,] I think Lincoln moved far beyond Clay and is a greater statesman, as such, but this man [Clay] is the man who provided many of the ideas and programs by which the nation was held together when it seemed to be breaking apart.

Henry Clay really believed that the slaves had to be freed and they all had to be sent back to Africa; that the two races could not live together. He feared what would be the consequence, in part politically—he thought the blacks would assume political power and would do to the whites what the whites had done to them—and socially and economically. He thought there would be conflict and that it was something that could not be bridged. The only solution, he felt, was a gradual emancipation in which, as [slaves] are emancipated, they are returned to Africa. These are thoughts, I believe, that Abraham Lincoln had, until the end of the decade of the fifties, then I think he is radicalized and his views do change.

[Clay] freed some slaves in his will. His plan was that—it sort of reminds me of the problem between Israel today and its Arab neighbors. How long can the killing go on? It's got to be resolved. But who has the solution, in which justice and fairness will be done on both sides? With Henry Clay, he knew that slavery couldn't last. I think these are men of the Enlightenment who did believe that all men are created equal. In principle. Henry Clay said that several times. In actual practice, no two people were equal.

COMING FROM NEW YORK—when I went to graduate school, I was really interested in urban politics in New York, and I did my master's essay [at Columbia University] on John Mitchell, who was a reform mayor of New York. But my mentor at that time, who was Richard Hofstadter, suggested doing a book on Martin Van Buren, who was in politics and a New Yorker. It wasn't the twentieth century and it wasn't exactly urban, but I thought it might be interesting, that he was a president who really needed to be done. I thought he would do for my doctoral dissertation, just his early political career. But I no sooner got deeply into Van Buren's life when the great figure that loomed up before me was Andrew Jackson. My attention was refocused, so to speak, temporarily, and I did a book on his election, always intending to go back and finish the Van Buren. Finally, when I decided that nothing would satisfy him [Hofstadter] or me, except a full-scale scholarly work, I did the three volumes on Jackson.

In the meantime, several other people produced fine biographies of Martin Van Buren, and I decided then to try somebody else. And Clay really fascinated. He's a funny man, and Andrew Jackson didn't have that element of humor as this man did. Many of his speeches still have, I think, an emotional wallop that few others have, and of course the fact that a man of Lincoln's stature would regard him as his ideal of a statesman fascinated me even more.

I would love to have a conversation with Andrew Jackson—and I would also love to have a conversation with Henry Clay, which would be of a different kind. The people who knew Henry Clay thought that his natural talents and intellectual ability far exceeded [those] of Jefferson and Madison. . . . In the sources [of the period], I found that some would say, "That's ridiculous, he couldn't write as well as Jefferson. He didn't have the ideas of Madison," but other sources, who insisted on his [Clay's] superiority, would say, "Their great achievements were the result, not only of their talent, but of the education that allowed them to do so much." Think of what Henry Clay might have achieved had he had the education that those two did. His education, he himself admitted, was rather meager.

.   .   .

THE ROCKEFELLER FOUNDATION provided a month's residence at its study and conference center in Palagio, Italy. You apply to them, you tell them what you're going to do, and they decide whether they think it's a good idea. They don't have any research facilities there, but they provide that kind of atmosphere, the collegiality of scholars in many other fields, in which you can do whatever work it is that you say you want to do. So you have to bring with you your materials.

What I told them was, I had written twelve chapters of the Henry Clay, and I wanted to get away and study it carefully to be sure that it wasn't prejudiced by my deep feelings for Andrew Jackson. I still regard myself as a great friend and advocate of Jackson and his ideas. Henry Clay was his enemy. He called him a Judas. When he was dying, supposedly somebody said to him, "General, have you left anything undone?" And he said, "Yes, I didn't shoot Henry Clay, and I didn't hang John C. Calhoun."

My mother-in-law used to say, "How many books can you write on Andrew Jackson?" And I said, "Well, until I get it right." There must be about ten or so. I began just attempting small phases of his life, his election and the bank war, for example. Then I realized I had to do a really big book, and the big book grew into three volumes. When I was in Nashville once, a woman asked me—after I had finished the Jackson—what was I going to do next. I said, "Henry Clay." She was aghast. She said, "General Jackson isn't going to like this. He may shoot you."

I DEDICATED THIS BOOK to the memory of my brothers, Vincent J. and William Remini. My second brother lived in Louisville, Kentucky, and he worked for Brown Foreman [distributors]. Every time I came down to do research, I would stay with him. He was retired by that time because he had a heart condition, and he would go to the library and help me locate the documents. He knew a great deal about Henry Clay because he was in Kentucky. He knew people who were descendants. They knew a great deal about him and his home. My brother was very anxious to assist in research for this book. Unfortunately, he died before it was published, and so I decided to dedicate it to him and to my younger brother too, who was killed tragically in an automobile accident five years ago.

THIS WAS A BOOK that almost wrote itself, for some reason. I really did find it in some ways easier. Perhaps it was easier for this reason: I did not have to traipse all over the world looking for documentation, as I had to do with Andrew Jackson. With Henry Clay, the papers had not only been gathered at the University of Kentucky, they had already been published. I believe it was, at that time, eight or nine volumes. It was so much easier for me to sit in my own study and read—not manuscripts, which, in their handwriting, can be so dreadful it is almost impossible to decipher them— but to read printed text and to have the footnotes, which help to explain what's happening and who they're referring to, and not have to do that kind of research myself.

These books are not easy, but I was obsessed. I would get up at four o'clock in the morning. Suddenly I had an idea I had to develop. My poor wife didn't know what was happening. She thought I was ill.

James Billington

On September 13, 1992, our guest was Librarian of Congress James Billington. Dr. Billington, appointed to his position in 1987, oversees 25 million books and a staff of 5,000 employees. Dr. Billington, who has traveled to the former Soviet Union nearly thirty times, joined us for a conversation on his book Russia Transformed: Breakthrough to Hope.

WE HAD A LOT OF BOOKS IN THE HOUSE [when I was] growing up. And the interesting thing is they were all used books, partly because we couldn't afford any other kind. My father was a book collector. He collected used books from Leary's, and that was a wonderful introduction to scholarship. We had maybe 2,000 or 3,000 books.

My father was an insurance broker. But he really was a teacher of people. He went into the insurance business and never got to complete his education, but he did complete his education, as he said in later years—when they asked him for his biography, he always said—he went to Leary's University, because it was this used bookstore. I guess that's why I'm Librarian of Congress, because my father kept bringing back used books from Leary's Bookstore in Philadelphia.

It was very interesting reading these used books growing up because they had underlining in them. They were worn. And so, very early, my curiosity was stimulated as to, you know, why did they underline this passage and not that one. What kind of a person is this, that read the book? Not simply, who wrote this book and what were they trying to say, but who's read this book and what were they trying to say about it? This is a bad thing for a librarian to say. You're not supposed to mark up books in libraries but in bookstores you can. It was a kind of an education far better even than the very good education I later got at Princeton and Oxford.

I first got interested in Russia—I was sort of interested in the world—when I was a young kid in Philadelphia in the public schools of Philadelphia. It was during the war [World War II]. I was young, in junior high school, and I kept asking my teachers, "Well, how come the Russians are able to hold out against Hitler? Everybody else caved in." Nobody could give me a good answer. Finally I went to an old Russian lady who worked in the drugstore up the street, and everybody used to make fun of [her] because she had such a foreign accent, and I said, "How can you explain— you came from Russia, didn't you?" She said yes. "Why are the Russians able to hold out?" She looked at me very sternly like that old woman on the barricades—that's where you get your wisdom in Russia, from the old ladies. They don't say much, but when they speak, they have something to say. . . . "Young man," she said, "You go read *War and Peace.*" So I did. I felt, you know, it's not very often that young people are told what to do by an older person who commands authority, and this woman did.

So I went and read it. And it was, of course, the great story, the great novel of Tolstoy, that tells of the resistance to Napoleon, which was being eerily reenacted by the resistance to Hitler—I mean gloriously reenacted, to be sure. But as I read that story and saw the sort of strength of family that Tolstoy depicts so much, this strength—the sense of defending their land, a link between the land and the people, and this strange sort of religious quest of these people. All of that was very fascinating to me, and it helped explain what was going on in the world and, at the same time, it intro- duced me to a people—I'm not at all of any Slavic background or origin— that were very different. So that became my great passion.

But it was also a wonderful bit of advice, "Go read *War and Peace,*" because it taught me early in life that if you want to really learn about something, it's better to read yesterday's novel than today's newspaper. That's where you get some wisdom, some perspective on things. Also, it made all books seem short after reading *War and Peace.* It's 1,200 pages.

THE LIBRARY OF CONGRESS has about 25 million books, but we have about 100 million objects, because the Library of Congress isn't just books. It's the world's largest movie collection. It's the world's largest map collection. And as far as books go, we're not only the world's largest collection of English language books but also Spanish language and Portuguese language books. And we tend to be the largest collection of books outside the countries of ori- gin—we have a very large Russian collection, for instance. But it's also prints and photographs, music—it's the world's largest music library. So it's a uni- versal library, and we're just about to reach our 100 millionth item in the Library of Congress, so that's the dimensions of it, all on about 575 miles of shelving. Almost all of it's in Washington, D.C., which is another rarity for large libraries, in that almost all of it is in one place and accessible.

We have this wonderful library system and so forth, but we're not using what we have as dramatically and as effectively as we could. One of the great things about a universal library is that it can help overcome the narrowness of so much of academic scholarship. I think people are busy taking things apart without putting them together in academia. The Library of Congress, because we have all languages, all formats, and a lot of people—wise people—to draw on, it's the perfect place to put things together rather than take them apart; to make some synthetic leaps, to see some new connections between different formats, different cultures, and so forth. It's a wonderful place for creating the links, the bridges, and the unities of the human adventure, which we're going to have to do on this planet if we're going to get along and if we're going to have Switzerlands, rather than Yugoslavias, in the future.

William H. Chafe

William H. Chafe, who appeared on the program on January 30, 1994, is a professor of twentieth-century social and political history at Duke University. He is the author of Never Stop Running: Allard Lowenstein and the Struggle to Save American Liberalism, *about Rep. Allard Lowenstein (D-NY), who was assassinated in his New York office in March 1980, at the age of fifty-one.*

ALLARD LOWENSTEIN is a figure who helped to shape a great deal of our history in the years since World War II, and yet he's someone who, because he was assassinated thirteen years ago, has in some ways dropped from our public attention and awareness. Yet, if we think about some of the pivotal moments of American society and political life, the whole issue of the civil rights movement, the whole anti–Vietnam War movement, the "Dump Johnson" movement—none of these things really can be understood or even comprehended without paying attention to Allard Lowenstein.

One of the things that Al Lowenstein was really gifted at doing was bringing people together from very different places, politically. He was such a magnetic figure himself. Intellectually, he was very, very powerful. Bill Buckley, I think, had a repartee with Al Lowenstein that they both enjoyed because they were sparring partners in politics. Ted Kennedy viewed him as—what he said in his eulogy—as a brother, as a member of the family. What Al had, I think, was the ability—through his own personal magnetism and charisma—to bring people together, to have dialogue with them that was really quite remarkable, and which made it possible for this extraordinary event to take place, with Buckley and Kennedy both giving the most moving eulogies. Buckley, in particular, gave a eulogy which, whenever I read it, I almost start to cry because it's so powerful.

I was very active in Democratic politics as a graduate student. I was involved in the West Side reform movement and in anti–Vietnam War politics. Al's first race for Congress was on the West Side of Manhattan in 1966. I knew him, not well, but I knew him during that campaign a little bit. So I knew what a charismatic figure he was, because I'd seen him operate in person. He was always late, an hour or two hours late, but we'd come into a room and he would be very effective at being able to turn around an audience and make them his followers, give them a real sense of being part of a crusade.

I had found that I really loved writing about individual human beings. I had done a long biographical essay on Eleanor Roosevelt on the occasion of the celebration of her one hundredth birthday. And I loved writing about individuals. I'd written these books about social movements, but I really wanted to write about a human being—an individual human being. What I decided to do was . . . a biography that would provide a window from a personal point of view on the whole question of whether, in fact, one can achieve social change by operating through liberal political activism.

I started the book in 1986 and I completed it in December of 1992. The reason it took a while to write was that Al Lowenstein was someone who always was known for being disorganized, chaotic. Every picture you have of him is with newspapers stuffed under his arm, with a suitcase, duffel bag open—with stuff, clothes, piling out. And his convertibles—he always drove convertibles—were stacked with [copies of The] New York Times. He was someone who you couldn't believe ever was organized. Yet he saved every piece of paper he ever wrote on or received from the time he was eight years old—all of his elementary school papers, school plays he wrote, scraps of paper he wrote notes on during political conventions. He had an extraordinary collection of papers, which just provide a written archive remarkable in its complexity, in its detail. Of course, he was someone who knew thousands of people. He had an address book with 5,000 names in it, and he at least communicated by postcard with most of those people every year. That's how he created his network. It was, therefore, very important to talk to a great many of those people. I interviewed about 150 of the people that were part of Lowenstein's life. Because of the archival work in the library and all those interviews I did with many of the people [who] are now still very well-known political figures, it took a long time to write the book.

I wrote this book on the coast of Maine, near Bath. It is a place where one part of my family actually comes from. My relatives go back [to] and were born on that island in the mid-eighteenth century—back to 1732 is as far as we traced it.

I wrote it over a period of three summers. I did it looking over a harbor, from a study in an old house which is over a hundred years old. I just looked out and was inspired by the material I was reading and using, and the interviews I'd done, and the remarkable amount of dramatic and powerful and passionate stories of this man's life that I had. This is a book that I care deeply about. He is someone I think I came to understand very well. I found it very moving and illuminating for myself and, I hope, for others to be able to write about his life, which is not just his life: it is also the life of a generation. It's a life of a group of people who lived through a very dynamic and critical part of this century, whose history needs to be understood and recorded. When someone like this man has such an impact on that history, it's important to understand.

BASIC BOOKS HAS BEEN a wonderful press to deal with. They're part of HarperCollins, but the reason I was at Basic Books was because of my editor there, who was an historian and executive vice president there. His name is Steve Frasier—a terrific person, great historian, wonderful critic, very engaged human being who actually wasn't sure that he liked Al Lowenstein, and wasn't sure he wanted to do a book about Al Lowenstein. But he did sign the book up because he thought I was a good historian, etc., and then read it and said, "I'm convinced." He said, "You have made me a believer."

I suppose if the book sold 15,000 or 20,000 copies, it would make Basic Books very happy. I would be happy with that. I decided a long time ago that because I care so much about the book, that the most important thing was that I feel good about the book. Obviously, you care deeply, as you know, about what reviewers say. You care deeply whether you get to appear on a show like this. You care about what the critics have to say. And for the most part the critics have been wonderful. But what I also discovered, in sort of preparing for this period of time and thinking about this period, was that the most important thing was that I feel good about the book. And when this book went off to press, I felt as though it was as much what I really wanted to say, in the way I wanted to say it, as anything I had ever written. So I felt good about it, I guess, in the end. I take solace in that.

I ACTUALLY WENT THROUGH a very interesting series of reactions as I did the research for the book and as I wrote the book. I think initially I liked Lowenstein very much, then I became much more critical because he was very manipulative, and could—and frequently did—use people, and sometimes in a not very helpful and good way. In the end, I came to feel very strongly empathetic toward him and to feel much more a part of him, which is not to say that I feel as though I end up praising him, but I think I do end up being fair to him. I try to understand why he was the kind of person he was and how difficult it must have been for him to deal with some of the issues he dealt with.

David Remnick

Booknotes guest David Remnick appeared on the program on July 25, 1993. Mr. Remnick, a staff writer for The New Yorker *and former Moscow correspondent for* The Washington Post, *discussed his book* Lenin's Tomb: The Last Days of the Soviet Empire.

I FIRST GOT INTERESTED IN WRITING very early on in junior high school and in high school where nobody had an interest in making a school newspaper. I was doing basically the whole thing at my bridge table at home, staying up until two o'clock in the morning.

My parents are readers. My father is a very serious reader, my mother to some extent. It's like anything in life. If you're lucky enough to hook into a friend and find something to share, it's very exciting. It doesn't seem like homework. I went to a pretty good high school, but they didn't assign books in any serious way, unfortunately. But I had a friend, and we would go to used book sales and trade books. Things Russian I was really always interested in, but not Russian politics. When I was growing up, Russian politics were a bore. It was a kind of stolid, ideological, off-there-ness that I wanted nothing to do with. I was interested because Chekhov was so interesting, and Dostoevsky and Tolstoy. It sounds pretentious to say, but there it is.

I went to Princeton because I got in. At Princeton I was a disastrous Russian student. I had had some Russian in high school. I had insisted on advancing a little bit and that was a fatal mistake, so my Russian was no good when I left Princeton. But afterwards, especially when I found out I'd be going to Moscow, I really intensified Russian language study. I studied with a woman here in Washington, [D.C.] but the real breakthrough was at Middlebury College in Vermont, which has a remarkable language program. My wife, who started from nothing, and I, who started from just slightly more, after a while were getting pretty good. Certainly in Moscow we got a lot better.

The first quarter of the book is about the opening up of history. Many people feel that [Mikhail] Gorbachev's primary project in the beginning, in the mid-eighties, was to improve the economy. That's true enough, but he was a dismal failure at it, as we see to this day. What I think was the key moment was when he got up in November of 1987, the anniversary of the revolution, and all the assembled communists were there [in Moscow], even from other countries, and they were very nervous about what he was going to say about the history of the revolution. Because, after all, the legitimacy of their regimes depended on the stability of the Soviet regime—Castro is an example, [as is] all of Eastern Europe. He got up and he gave what we now see as a very mild speech, an outdated speech, but for the time extremely important. He said, "Comrades, of course things are going splendidly. Of course the revolution is glorious and we should never spit on it. But there were moments in our history that were awful." He used the word "criminal" to describe the regime of Stalin. This was an incredible breakthrough.

I had read a lot of the journalists' books about Russia before I left and am an admirer of many of them. But some of them seem to have a certain quality of John Gunther–type books. In other words, they were the books on everything about Russian society—education, the economy, sports, medicine—and I didn't want to repeat that performance. I wanted to tell more of a narrative story. The revolution certainly provided a hell of a narrative, and my job was to find some shape to it.

PREVIOUS PAGE: Neil Sheehan, author of *A Bright Shining Lie: John Paul Vann and America in Vietnam,* in front of the Library of Congress. All of Mr. Sheehan's letters and research on the Vietnam War and those of John Paul Vann are housed in this building. (Photo: *Brian Lamb*) ABOVE: Truman biographer David McCullough in front of the vice president's office at the U.S. Senate. Mr. McCullough retraced Harry Truman's steps when, as vice president, he was alerted that FDR had died and ran from a meeting on the House side of the Capitol to this office. That night Truman was sworn in as the 33rd President of the United States. (Photo: *Brian Lamb*)

David Halberstam at Eli Zabar's coffee shop on Madison Avenue in Manhattan. The author said on *Booknotes* that he likes to have "a very lazy cappuccino" before he starts his writing for the day. (Photo: *Brian Lamb*)

Colin Powell on the *Booknotes* set.
During the program, he described
how he signed 60,001 copies of
My American Journey on his
book tour. (Photo: *Susan Kennedy*)
INSET: General Powell used a
Sharpie pen, "principally because
it gives you a nice bold signature
and it's round and soft with no
edges, so it didn't give me any
calluses." (Photo: *Brian Lamb*)

George Will at work on his laptop in his Georgetown office. Mr. Will finally started using a computer to write his books and columns instead of his favorite Pelikan pen after he fell on the ice and broke his arm in February 1995. (Photo: *Brian Lamb*)

ABOVE: Shelby Foote's writing table. Mr. Foote wrote 1.5 million words on the Civil War with this dip pen. He described on C-SPAN how he has trouble today finding steel-tip replacements for the pen and often has to bargain with the few stationery stores that still sell them. (Photo: *Brian Lamb*)

OPPOSITE: Eighty-year-old Shelby Foote at work in his Memphis home. In the upper right corner is a portrait of Marcel Proust. While I was taking this photo, Mr. Foote told me he has read all of Proust's works nine times. (Photo: *Brian Lamb*)

BACK PAGE: The author is reviewing one of the many handwritten bound manuscripts for his three-volume series on the Civil War. Mr. Foote started working on the trilogy in 1954 and continued to research and write the volumes for the next twenty years. He has now returned to writing novels. (Photo: *Brian Lamb*)

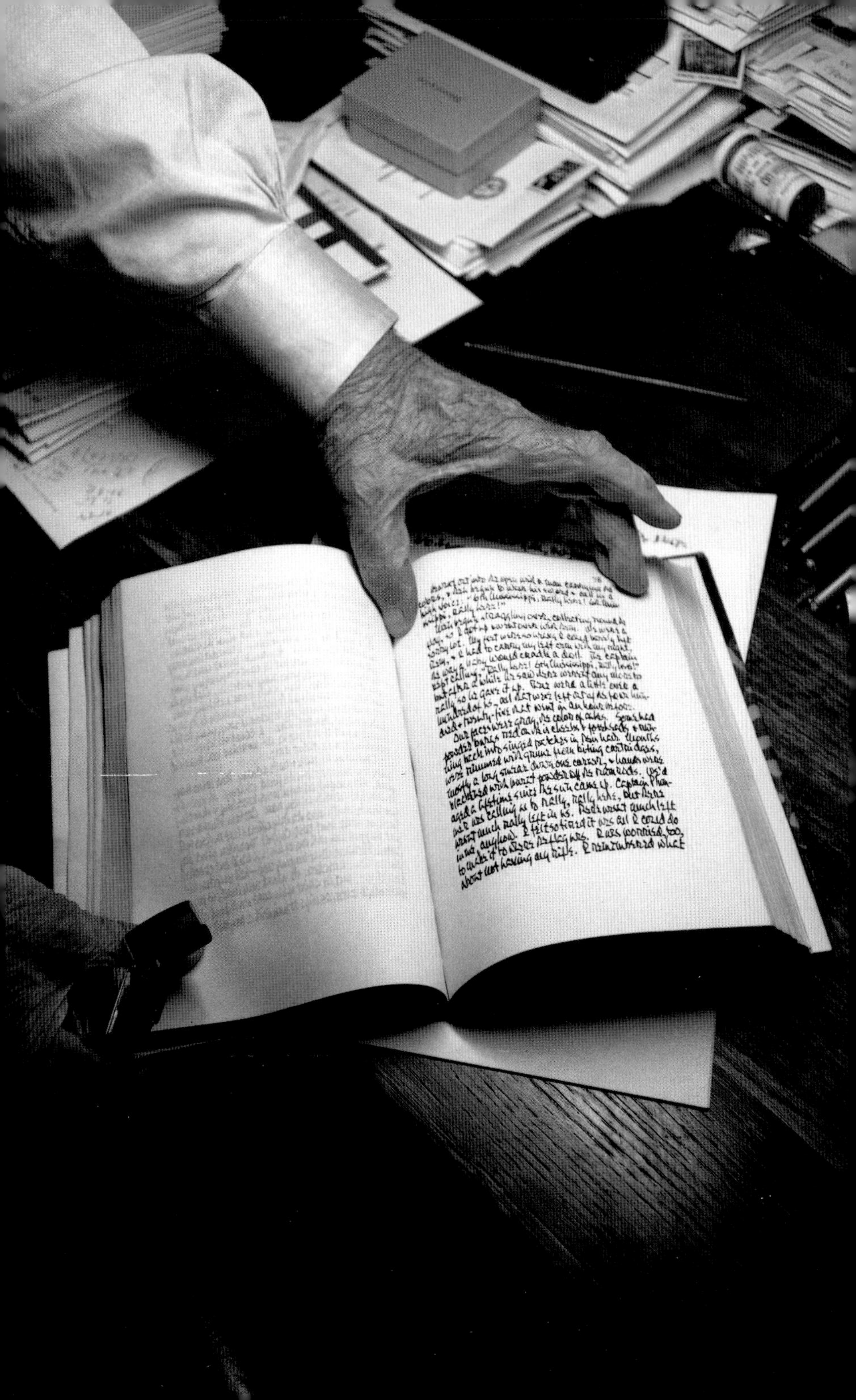

ABOVE: William Chafe wrote his biography of the late congressman Al Lowenstein, D-NY, overlooking Harmon's Harbor in Georgetown, Maine. (Photo: *Gary Bonaccorso*)

RIGHT: Broadcast journalist John Hockenberry writes in his loft on 23rd Street in Manhattan. (Photo: *Brian Lamb*)

PREVIOUS PAGE: Albert Murray in his Harlem apartment with his yellow legal pads and the music cassettes he listens to as he writes. It is here that Mr. Murray has written nine books since 1962. (Photo: *Brian Lamb*)

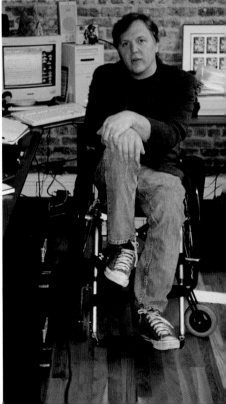

Speechwriter and author Peggy Noonan is pointing at a mass card that once belonged to playwright Tennessee Williams. For inspiration, she keeps it taped to the side of her computer in her brownstone on the Upper East Side of Manhattan. (Photo: *Brian Lamb*)

ABOVE: Stanley Crouch writes in his apartment on West 11th Street in Greenwich Village. An avid jazz lover, Mr. Crouch surrounds himself when he works with the music and photos of Duke Ellington, Ella Fitzgerald, and Louis Armstrong. (Photo: *Brian Lamb*)

OPPOSITE TOP: Writer Christopher Hitchens working in his preferred location at the Timberlakes bar near Dupont Circle in Washington, D.C. When the jukebox is playing, Mr. Hitchens says his concentration improves. (Photo: *Brian Lamb*)

OPPOSITE BOTTOM: Author and former school principal Madeline Cartwright takes a break from her computer to play with her grandson Jared, aged seven, and a family friend, Destini, aged eighteen months. On the program, Ms. Cartwright described how she wrote her book on this bed in her home in Philadelphia. (Photo: *Brian Lamb*)

ABOVE: Journalist Johanna Neuman with her cat, Smokey, in her lap, working out of her Bethesda, Maryland home. Her husband, Ron Nessen, who was the press secretary to former President Gerald Ford, is in the photograph behind her. (Photo: *Brian Lamb*)

OPPOSITE: Lynn Sherr, ABC *20/20* correspondent and Susan B. Anthony biographer, in New York City, reviewing microfilm of the Anthony papers that she purchased for her book research. (Photo: *Brian Lamb*)

BACK PAGE: Former CBS reporter Charles Kuralt in his writing office located on West 57th Street in New York. Mr. Kuralt said he wanted to re-create "the feel of a seedy, failing, small gentlemen's club." (Photo: *Brian Lamb*)

Nell Irvin Painter

On December 8, 1996, historian Nell Irvin Painter came to Booknotes *to discuss her fourth book,* Sojourner Truth: A Life, A Symbol. *Ms. Painter is the Edwards Professor of American History at Princeton University.*

SOJOURNER TRUTH WAS an itinerant preacher. "Sojourner Truth" means itinerant preacher. She was a woman who had been born Isabella. She was born a slave. Her original name was simply Isabella because if you were born enslaved, all you had was one name. She was not born a slave in the South, as many people assume. She was born a slave in Ulster County, New York, along the Hudson River, in about 1797. She died in Battle Creek, Michigan, which was kind of the Berkeley of its day, in 1883. She spent the first part of her life in freedom in the late 1820s until 1843, working as a household worker. That's how she supported herself. But she also belonged to a group of enthusiastic religious folk. Then, in 1843, the Holy Spirit told her to change her name. She became Sojourner Truth and she started wandering off to Brooklyn and then to Long Island and then up the Connecticut River Valley, and stopped in Northampton. Over a period of time she became a feminist and an abolitionist. And we know her as a feminist abolitionist.

She's often confused with Harriet Tubman. The difference is that Sojourner Truth was born in the North and made her vocation [that] of speaking aloud, as one of her biographers, Erlene Stetson, says, and Harriet Tubman was born in Maryland and escaped from slavery, and then went back [into slave territory] several times during the 1850s to bring out others, perhaps as many as 200. So Sojourner Truth [was] speaking aloud and Harriet Tubman was a "train" [for] the Underground Railroad.

I've been interested in her [Sojourner Truth] since I was a kid growing up in California. We didn't have any black or Negro history in school. But my parents made sure that I learned something. So I knew the names of Harriet Beecher Stowe, Harriet Tubman, and Sojourner Truth from as long as I can remember. And when I started becoming a historian, I was interested. The idea of doing a book on Sojourner Truth, though, didn't come until the mid-80s.

Harriet Beecher Stowe was Tom Clancy back then. Harriet Beecher Stowe was Stephen King. Harriet Beecher Stowe's brother was the most famous preacher in the land at the time. She wrote the best-selling novel of the nineteenth century, *Uncle Tom's Cabin.* It first came out in serial in 1851 and then as a book in 1852. It was a runaway best-seller. And she wrote one other antislavery book, called *Dred[: A Tale of the Dismal Swamp],* in 1856. By 1863, she had stopped writing antislavery stuff and was talking about her travels. She had become a VIP; she went to Rome for the winter and so forth; she built this big ugly house in Hartford, [Connecticut] which was expensive. So she was writing to the market. In 1863, we have black men going into the Union army, we have the Emancipation Proclamation, and the reading public in the North is saying, "Tell us about the Negro. Tell us about the Negro." So people were telling us about the Negro, and she was, too.

They had actually met ten years earlier. Sojourner Truth had gone to Harriet Beecher Stowe for a blurb [about her book] and gotten one. So when Stowe wrote about Sojourner, I suppose she was writing from memory. Her version of Sojourner Truth doesn't ring true to me. She makes her into a kind of a quaint figure of fun. And when I first read *Sojourner Truth, the Libyan Sibyl* [by Harriet Beecher Stowe], I even winced myself. But it was extremely, extremely influential.

WHEN I FIRST STARTED ON THIS in about 1989, I thought if I were sitting here and Sojourner Truth came and sat down, we could have a comfortable conversation. And it would just be hunky-dory and we'd get along just fine. And as I learned more and more and more about her, and more and more and more about the antebellum North, which was a crazy, crazy time and place—there were all sorts of people. You know, if you went out in Westchester County [New York], for instance, in the 1830s or '40s, you'd probably encounter about six or eight people telling you, "Come to Jesus. I have the Word." People were always hearing the Holy Spirit telling them to go preach their word. And there were lots and lots of itinerant preachers.

At any rate, as I learned more about Sojourner Truth herself, more about Isabella, more about the period, her closeness to me receded and she became less and less and less familiar. And so now I think if she were sitting here, I would just have to listen.

To research this book, I went to the American Antiquarian Society, which was extremely valuable for me. It is in Worcester, Massachusetts. And it's a great collection of printed matter from the United States, from

Colonial period down to about 1876. So I could read the newspaper accounts of what was going on while she was doing various things.

So I did historian's work, but I also did two or maybe three different kinds of work. I learned how to "read" the photographs. That was something new to me, and I thought it was important for this particular project. I also worked on psychology, and that's where I began to really focus on what it must have been like to live in a family where your parents were lamenting the loss of their children. That's where I began to understand the psychological weight of having been enslaved, of having been beaten, of having been fondled by your master.

In many of these photographs, Sojourner Truth is holding knitting and I wondered if she had been holding that to convey a sort of motherliness or womanliness or gentility or hominess. And at one point in the American Antiquarian Society, I was reading the papers of the Northampton Association and I found in the ledger book where Sojourner Truth, there called Mrs. Sojourner, had purchased yarn. So I squealed. That was really lovely for me to find.

In college, I studied anthropology. I was in that generation that was tested, tested, tested, tested, tested, and it was very clear that I was smart. It was clear, according to the tests, that I not only loved history but I was very gifted in history, and I thought, "Well, that just proves the tests don't make any sense at all because I hate history." What I hated was the history I'd learned in high school, which was cold war history, and I was fully aware of what was going on around us in the South. I knew about segregation. I knew about lynching. I knew about white supremacy. None of that was in my schoolbooks. So I thought, "Well, I don't want to have to do it."

Then I went to France, and I got interested in French history. I lived on one side of Bordeaux, and then I would go around the cathedral and then get to the university. And I found myself wondering about the history of the cathedral, so I ended up studying French medieval history, and I was good at it. It was one of my four fields for my general Ph.D. exams. And then when I was in West Africa later on, in Ghana, I started a master's degree in African studies, but I finished it in African history at UCLA. And so, doing other people's history, I discovered that, yes, I did love history.

I don't feel that I am all black people. I feel like I'm myself. And I come from a particular family and a particular place. Sojourner Truth came from a particular family and a particular place. She grew up in rural upstate New York; I grew up in urban Oakland, California. And I and my family are not particularly Pentecostal. She was Pentecostal after she became free. So in that sense, we were very different. She never learned to read and write, and she learned by hearing reading, which is, of course, how people did it from time immemorial. And I was an inveterate reader from the time I came out of my mother's womb.

So, in that sense, I don't feel connected. But I do know that for the rest of our country and perhaps for the rest of the world, Sojourner Truth and I are grouped together as black women. And I don't mind that. So in that sense, I am connected to her, just as I am connected to all other black women in this country and over time. But we do have extremely different experiences. And one of the things I was trying to do here was to humanize Sojourner Truth, to show her as an individual, with her own life and her own experiences, in addition to this symbolic black woman.

I DID MOST OF MY WRITING for this book in Stoneham, Maine. It's quiet. I don't get interrupted. It's comfortable. It's on a mountain lake, a little house in the woods. I write looking out over the water. It certainly does work for me.

At the height of writing this book, in the summer of 1995, I think I probably wrote from 5 A.M. until 11 P.M. I just about knocked myself out. It was too much. You need to take a vacation, but I wanted to finish that book.

In the old days, when I used to write on a typewriter, I would start my drafts on that yellow paper. I just opened my mind and just kept going. I would never know exactly what I was going to say until my fingers were on the keyboard and I'd just type. And a lot of it would be junk, so I'd retype it, and then I'd put in more, and it would get better. These were called "zero minus drafts," and they were on the yellow paper. And then I would cut them up, and cut and paste, and I'd have these cut-and-paste yellow pie sheets. Then finally it would begin to look like it should, and then I'd start typing on white paper, and then I'd have white paper with yellow parts on it. By the time it got to all white paper, that was the first draft. Now I write on a computer, but I just do endless drafts. This book is longer than I wanted it to be, actually. I wanted it to get into people's hands, and everybody told me that readers like shorter books.

I knew that I wanted this book to be accessible to general readers, so I was not writing to my historian peers. In fact, I published a separate article in a learned journal for my historian peers. So this one, I tried not to have any jargon in it. I wrote it for you. I wrote it for my cousin Charlie. I wrote it for my parents and their friends. I wrote it for all the black women who were interested in Sojourner Truth.

David Herbert Donald

Booknotes guest David Herbert Donald is a professor emeritus at Harvard. He joined us on December 24, 1995, to discuss Lincoln, *his best-selling biography of the sixteenth president of the United States.*

I FIRST GOT INTRODUCED to Abraham Lincoln when I came up from Mississippi, my home state, to the University of Illinois to write a history of Mississippi, and I fell under the spell of the great professor at the University of Illinois, James G. Randall, who was working on his Lincoln biography, ultimately published as *Lincoln: The President in Four Volumes.* I was captivated by him. I became his research assistant, worked with him closely, and became an apprentice, which is the best way for a historian to be trained, I think.

This was, oh, goodness, this is about 1942 through '48—along in there, so it was a long time ago. And [after I] got immersed in it, he suggested, "Well, why don't you go ahead and do a Lincoln subject for your dissertation?" I had already done something [on Lincoln], and so I said, "Well, what shall we do?" He said, "Lincoln's law partner, [William Henry] Herndon, has never been properly studied. His papers have just become available. Why don't you try?" So I did. And my first book was called *Lincoln's Herndon,* a biography of Lincoln's law partner, published in 1948 and, I'm still pleased to say, recently reissued in paperback after all these years. So I have been in this field for a long time.

I hope that any reasonable, intelligent, and literate American interested in the past of this country could and would read [this book]. It was written for them, particularly, and written in a special way. My way of writing might be worth about two sentences. Anyway, I sit at my computer and write, and then when I have a couple of sentences, I read them over aloud to see how they sound—not what they look like, but how they sound. Could a reader get the meaning of this? Could he follow the words and the sound of it? Sometimes it leads to rather amusing results. I had a couple of carpenters working around my house while I was doing this, and they were hammering away. And once I took a break, found them out under the

·

trees—they didn't know I was there—they were [talking] to each other. "Do you think he's all right?" said one of them. "Well, I don't know," said the other. "He sits there talking to himself all day." Well, I talk to myself as I write in the hope of getting something of the spoken language into the written page because I think that's the way people read; how you reach people with language they can both hear and see at the same time. And that's what I was trying to do.

I started the book saying that I was not going to write a commentary on previous biographies. I did not wish to explain why so-and-so was wrong, and somebody else should have known this, and so on. I was going to try to write a book as though no life of Lincoln had ever been written before.

Second, I wanted it to be a narrative—a straightforward narrative of what Lincoln did, felt, saw, and concluded; not a general history of the Civil War. I've tried that in some other books, but this is a story of how he developed, how he thought. His mental processes are my real subject here.

Third, unlike most biographies, this is not a biography that attempts moralizing contemporary judgments. I feel that biography is an art, like a novel, and they grew up together. In the nineteenth century they were very similar. [In] nineteenth-century novels, you'd have a character and he would appear, and then your novelist interjects and says, "But what a stupid thing it is to do this," or "How unwise it was. He should have done this, that, and the other." And biographies tended to do the same thing. Novels, of course, have progressed beyond that. If you tried to write a novel like that today you'd never get it published. Biographies, by and large, continue in that mode. I thought it important to get the author, me, out of it, to let the story tell itself and have it as ambiguous, as ambivalent as a modern novel, so that you could read it and draw one conclusion; I could read it, draw another; somebody else could read it and draw another, just as a modern novel should be.

[LINCOLN'S PAPERS] WERE INHERITED by Robert Todd Lincoln, Lincoln's surviving son, who was very sensitive about the family reputation and about his father's reputation. He didn't want people sort of mucking around in the family history, and he didn't like any kind of stories that reflected at all on his father. So he let nobody but [John G.] Nicolay [Lincoln's personal secretary] and [John] Hay use those papers. He ultimately presented them to the Library of Congress, where they were sealed until 1947. Nobody could get at them, even to index them. They were just there. We all knew they were there, but we didn't know what was in them. This means that [authors of] the great biographies—Carl Sandburg, Albert Beveridge, James G. Randall—they didn't have access to Lincoln's papers. They couldn't see what came upon his desk as president. Now we can. We've got all those papers. We've got ninety-seven reels of microfilm—1,500 pages per reel, something like that. You can sit at Lincoln's side and see what did he know about the Sumter crisis? Or about his reelection campaign in 1864? As the papers come upon his desk, how does he know, when did he know, from whom did he know, how did he make his decisions? This is the sort of thing that previous biographers have not been able to do.

The Lincoln legal papers have been under way in Springfield [Illinois] now for about seven years, something like that. They've collected papers on every case in which Abraham Lincoln was ever involved. They searched the county courthouses all over Illinois, Indiana, Missouri, other places as well. They've collected not merely what Lincoln had to say, but what his opposing lawyers had to say, what the judges' rulings were, what the jury decisions were, what the fees [were]. We can, for the first time, see the whole pattern of the cases and his career.

The amount of work that Lincoln went through is just almost unbelievable. After all, there were no secretaries, there were no copying machines, there were no fax machines—everything was done by hand. One memorable document runs to fifty-three handwritten pages that Lincoln himself laboriously writes out by hand. He worked very, very hard, not merely at the papers but at the research behind those papers. So the image that some people have of Lincoln as sort of a good country lawyer who shambles into the courtroom, cracks a few jokes, wins over the jury, gets his case won—this isn't the case. He was a very hardworking, well-prepared lawyer.

I worked on this book seven years, full time. Now, fortunately, I had a backlog of materials from earlier studies of Herndon, of Samuel P. Chase, of Charles Sumner, things that could be sort of assimilated into this larger picture here, but full-time work on this book was for a little more than seven years.

The original cover for the book was very different from this. We had a younger Lincoln looking rather ideal. And abstractly, I think, in the distance behind him was the unfinished dome of the Capitol and so on. We liked it. It was quite colorful. The sales representatives at Simon & Schuster said, "It won't do because people will look at it and say, 'That's a book for young adults. That's not a grown-up book.' " So back to the drawing board, and we tried several, and this came out and I'm very pleased with it.

It seems to be a distinguished jacket. Especially since I can't draw or anything like that, I can only report how I feel about it.

I worked on the audiotape for the book in the sense that I reviewed the script. This obviously had to be an abridgment of this very long text to get it under six hours. So a lot had to be left out. I reviewed it in the hopes of getting it as complete as one can in six hours and to see that not too much was left out. I had nothing to do with the recording of it, except from time to time I was called to ask about pronunciations. "How do you pronounce this," they said, "Is it Chick-a-ha-manee? Chick-a-homey? How do you pronounce it?" I'd say, grandly, "Chickahominy River," that kind of thing. So in that sense, I had a little to do with it, but not much.

I LIVE ON LINCOLN ROAD in Lincoln, Massachusetts, I'll have you know. But, alas, they're named after another Lincoln, though vaguely related way back. Some people have asked how this happened to me—and people always believe in long-range plans as conspiracies. "No doubt," they said, "when you moved to Massachusetts twenty-three years ago, you had all this in mind, so you moved to Lincoln Road in Lincoln, Massachusetts, so you could capitalize on it." It isn't true; it's near the good schools that my son went to.

If one thought how ridiculous it would be to make some kind of a comparison with my early books, I would say they would be my *As You Like It* books. They are sort of young and vigorous books of a very green young man. Then in the middle, like Shakespeare, there are my histories. Then comes my tragedy of the two-volume life of Charles Sumner, who had a tragic life, I think. And then at the end, there comes maybe a period of tranquility and reflection. This book is my *Tempest*. This is my last reflective book.

Henry Louis Gates, Jr.

Henry Louis Gates, Jr., has been chairman of the Afro-American Studies Department at Harvard since 1990. Mr. Gates came to Booknotes *on October 9, 1994, to talk about his book* Colored People: A Memoir.

MY BOOK IS A MEMOIR as opposed to an autobiography. An autobiography is something that attempts to explain how John Smith became John Smith. A memoir is more of an attempt to record an era, the sepia-toned era of the 1950s for *Colored People.*

This is a book about black vernacular culture. This is a book about what black people thought and felt when no white people were around. I tried to imagine myself as a video camera on the sofa of our living room circa 1955, 1960, 1965, and finally 1970, and we use the word "nigger" all the time. Sometimes it's used very lovingly, sometimes it's used in a mean-spirited way, but it's a natural part of our culture, of our language.

In 1957, Nat King Cole became the first black person to have his own TV program and it was wonderful. I remember we—not only all the members of our family gathered around the TV to watch it, but neighbors came to watch it. It was a real test for the race. I mean, would we be able to pull this off? It was a major breakthrough. He would have white guests, and he was just the straight host. Of course, he would sing at the beginning, in the middle, and at the end of each of his programs. Whenever there was a "bro"—a black person—on TV, we rooted for him like you'd root for your home team. We wanted the brothers to make it; we wanted the sisters to make it.

My father's family had been Episcopalians for 100 years. My great-grandmother Maude Fortune founded the colored Episcopal church in Cumberland, Maryland. This was part of my tradition, but when my father married my mother and moved to our village, he just stopped going to church because the white Episcopal church was very upper class, was not integrated. And when he had tried to go there, they told him he would have to sit in the back of the church, at the last pew, because each family had its own pew. And he just said, "Thank you very much, but I'll pass on God."

Then when I was fourteen, I had broken my hip playing football, which was misdiagnosed by this racist doctor. I ended up in the hospital for a long recuperation—about six weeks. And the local Episcopal priest, Father Smith, who was from New England, starting driving sixty or so miles out to the University Medical Center in Morgantown, West Virginia, to see me, and he would talk to me about ideas and religion, and he said, "I understand you're very religious." He was white. And he started giving me books like *Are You Running with Me, Jesus?* by Malcolm Boyd, and he gave me the works of James Baldwin and lots of books that named me as a person of color and named me as an adolescent who wanted to be religious but who also wanted to be rational. I wanted to believe in reason. I wanted to be an intellectual. And I didn't want the two to be mutually exclusive. I found that I could do that through the Episcopal church. So when I was fifteen, my mother and I converted to the Episcopal church.

That summer was the summer of transformation in my life. It was the summer of the Watts riots. On the day that we saw the headline that Negroes were rioting in this place called Watts—I didn't know where Watts was. Well, Watts might as well have been on Mars as far as Piedmont, West Virginia, was concerned. That day, Father Smith gave me a copy of James Baldwin's *Notes of a Native Son*. I looked down and saw this face. It was Jimmy Baldwin staring at me. I couldn't believe it. Here's a black man—I mean, visibly black—who had written this marvelous book.

I used to keep a commonplace book where I would write down great quotes—quotes that named an emotion or an idea that I wanted to remember or often that I had vaguely felt but couldn't articulate. And basically, I just rewrote James Baldwin's chapters. I fell in love with James Baldwin's use of language. I fell in love with the idea of being a writer though I had been primed to be a doctor, just like my brother—and because all smart little black kids were going to become doctors, right? Then all of a sudden there was this possibility of being a writer which was opened up for me through James Baldwin's example, and it was an exhilarating experience. Between retaining a belief in God as an intellectual—as a budding intellectual—and learning how to name aspects of what we might call my racial self, you know, my black racialized self to an American racist society, it was a summer like one experiences once in a lifetime.

I have two daughters, Maggie and Liza, ages fourteen and twelve, going on forty. They have both read the book [*Colored People*]. And they've attended two readings that I've given of the book—of parts of the book. I always read the preface when they're in the room because it's in the form of a letter written to them. The whole book, in its first draft, was written in the form of letters to Maggie and Liza.

I wanted my daughters' generation of black people to know about an era that will never come back again for good and for ill. To be able to encounter, at least through one memoir and, no doubt, others are being written and some recently published, what that world was like for them. That world is as strange to them [Maggie and Liza] as Tibet—they have no more idea. As I say in the preface, one day we were riding along on Route 2, which connects Cambridge with Lexington, Massachusetts, and it was 1991, it was on Martin Luther King's birthday, and they were hearing for the ten thousandth time "I have a dream" on the radio. Maggie said, "You know, Daddy, what was the civil rights movement all about?" And I said, "Well, you see that motel?" And she said, "Yeah." And I said, "I couldn't have stayed in that motel thirty years ago." I said, "Your mama could have stayed at that motel, but your mama couldn't have stayed at that motel with me." And I looked in the rearview mirror, and she was nudging Liza like, "God, you know, here's another lie."

I mean, they couldn't believe that this could be true. So the idea of separate water fountains; the idea that you would have dogs sicced on you if you were trying to integrate Lexington High School; maybe, at one point, the idea that any of the ridiculously pernicious forms of racism that were visited upon persons of African descent in this country could actually have been visited upon us is alien to them, thank God, because we've made so much progress in certain ways.

On the other hand, I want that memory to be part of their historical consciousness. I want them to know how far we've come. I don't want them to take their "freedom," as we would have put it in 1965, for granted. It's important that we remember even the painful details of our past, but that we do it not through grandiose, abstract statements like "Racism was a terrible thing," but [that we] particularize it. What it was like not to be able to sit down at the cut-rate drugstore with your white friends after a basketball game which the black players had won, a game in which the black players had played pivotal roles, and then be forced to stand at a counter and drink your vanilla rickey out of a paper cup and not be able to drink it out of a glass, sitting down with your white friends?

It sounds like such a petty thing, but it was of enormous importance. It was the kind of thing that seizes your imagination. You become determined that one day you'll sit down in that restaurant, being able to date who you wanted, to dance with whom you wanted, being able to encounter yourself in the American history textbooks just like all your white friends encountered themselves.

[WHEN I WROTE THE BOOK,] I was in Italy at the Rockefeller Foundation Conference Center at Bellagio, which is on Lake Como near Milan. I woke up the first day there and it reminded me so much of Piedmont. It's on this beautiful lake; Piedmont's on the banks of the mighty Potomac. Bellagio has the pre-Alps coming down to the left, hitting the lake; and we had the mighty Allegheny Mountains.

And so by extension, I re-imagined myself at home, and it was wonderful. And the girls were back in Boston, and so I wrote them a letter every day. So each chapter was called a date—the first was July 10th, the second was July 11th—and I wrote them twenty to thirty pages a day for two weeks. I lost ten pounds doing it. I went down to Milan and came back, and then I finished the first draft of the book over the next four weeks. It was quite exciting for me.

IN RETROSPECT, I think I wrote the book because I was grieving for my mother. My mother and I were very close. I come from a very close family, but my mother and I were particularly close. She died in 1987 and contrary to what people say, the grief didn't go away. It became muted, it assumed other forms, but it didn't go away. I really missed my mother. And the older my daughters got, the more I missed my mother, the more I understood, as a parent, what she and my father had done—things which had made me angry or which had hurt my feelings, which had confused me. And I always wished that she was still around so I could call her and say, "Hey, Mama, you know, I remember—now I understand why you did this. Now I understand why you did that."

So I wanted to write the book as a tribute to my mother and father, a portrait of my mother, but in my father's voice. My father is a brilliant storyteller. My father puts Redd Foxx and Bill Cosby to shame. If my father had been trained, I mean, he would have been a great actor. And we were raised hearing these stories every night. He would come home from work in the afternoon from his day job at three-thirty, and we'd get off from school at three-thirty. Then we'd all eat dinner at about four o'clock, and then at four-thirty he would go to his second job as a janitor at the phone company. He'd get back about seven-thirty or eight o'clock.

Then we would gather around the television, just like you imagined— if you were growing up in Piedmont, you imagined that New England families [gathered] around the fireplace in the wintertime—and you would watch television till nine-thirty or ten, whenever our bedtime was.

My dad would do a running commentary on whatever we saw on television. He would read; he'd do crossword puzzles. He subscribed to Alfred Hitchcock's magazine. He loved detective stories, which is why I love them, too.

In between reading and looking at the TV, and [doing] our homework, he would comment on everything and say, "This reminds me of," "Once upon a time," you know, "One day when we were at Camp Lee, Virginia, during World War II, such and such happened." So these became our canonical stories, and many of the stories in *Colored People* are my father's stories.

So I was imitating that voice. I was hearing my father's voice. I think the most satisfying response that I got to the book . . . was [from] my brother, who is a very distinguished oral surgeon here in New York. My brother called me after he read it in galleys and said, "You got Daddy's voice." That's what I was striving to do.

THE TRADITION OF LITERATURE in the English language is sublime. There's no question about that. I would never want to get rid of Shakespeare or Milton or Virginia Woolf or any of these people. But I want to make room for other great writers—writers like Wole Soyinka or Derek Walcott or Toni Morrison or [Gabriel García] Márquez or—you know, the list could go on and on and on. That's been a very important battle—and it's a battle, quite frankly, that I think we've now won because most major schools of education now accept the principles and premises of a multicultural literary or a multicultural historical curriculum.

What we're trying to do at Harvard is to create, well, quite frankly, what I hope will be the greatest center of intellection concerning persons of African descent in the Old World and the New World. There are many great centers—Yale and Stanford, and the University of Chicago has great scholars; Wisconsin and Michigan, and at Princeton. Lord knows Princeton has a wonderful assemblage of scholars who do African-American studies, and we want one at Harvard.

Over the last three years, I have been able to make several major appointments. Evelyn Brooks Higginbotham and the federal judge Leon Higginbotham and, most recently, Cornel West from Princeton and Anthony Appiah, the great African philosopher who was at Cambridge with Soyinka at the same time I was. We've been able to bring all these people to Harvard, and we expect to make at least four or five more distinguished appointments so that we can eventually have a graduate program, what I hope will be a Ph.D. program in African-American studies.

See, my generation of African-American scholars takes African-American studies for granted. We have always been in the presence of African-American studies at historically white institutions. Cornel West went to Harvard, I believe, in 1970. I went to Yale in '69. Afro-American studies was there. There was a math department, there was a physics department, there was the history department, and there was Afro-Am. So it's not out of place in the academe of our generation. Curiously enough, many of us who have Ph.D.'s, many of us who have chosen to be academics have chosen to be scholars of African or African-American studies, almost as if it's satisfying a vague political commitment—and I think because Afro-Am was under siege when we were undergraduates, that left a certain sort of imprint in our minds.

So some of us liken our task, our privilege, our obligation to that of a Talmudic scholar in the Jewish tradition: that you preserve the text, you resurrect the text, you interpret the text, you live with the text, and you take a stand for your community.

Peggy Noonan

Peggy Noonan, a speechwriter for Presidents Reagan and Bush, and the author of What I Saw at the Revolution: A Political Life in the Reagan Era, *appeared on* Booknotes *on February 18, 1990.*

CONSERVATIVES HAVE, by and large, tended to be a little rough on the book. Ronald Reagan was a really terrific political leader. But I had some ambivalent feelings towards him, and I let them out, and sometimes I'm a little rough on him. So that's one thing that's bothered them. Another thing that has bothered them is I have written as a speechwriter about writing speeches for Ronald Reagan, and there are some people who feel that as a speechwriter you should never be out there and say that you wrote anything, or ever write about the writing of it, that you should pretend that the president didn't have speechwriters, that that is our job. I think that's silly. I think once that was legitimate and now it's just untenable. So the book didn't do any halo-polishing, or if it does, it's not quite enough.

I tried to write a serious book, and I wanted it to be a book that taught people things. I wanted it to have weight. I wanted it to be dense. In a way I think you have no right to be boring. A book is a form of aggression; you're aggressing and saying, "Hey, look at me, I can tell you something, I really have things I want to tell you, and it might be worthwhile listening," and if somebody says it was worthwhile listening, you feel, "That's wonderful! I just spent the last three years the right way." So, it's a delight.

In the morning, when I was working on speeches for [George] Bush, I was always going over notes of things Reagan had told me. And I was always trying very much to listen, to re-summon in my head the sound of his voice or the way he was using words when he told me something that I wrote down. So the morning was sort of trying to re-summon him, and keep him in my head. Then I'd go have lunch with my son, and in the afternoon I'd sort of try to shake it out, and remember what it is that I think, and how it is that I express myself. I've spent all of my professional life writing for other people. And they have mostly been men—[Dan] Rather, Reagan, and Bush. There was a part of me that was a little bit afraid when I first decided to do the book, and signed the contract to do it, and got a deadline for it. There was a part of me that was afraid that I didn't really have my own sound anymore because I had so subsumed, in a way, my own sound in order to hear others. Maybe this is a smaller point, but maybe not. I was just really afraid I couldn't get my voice back—I couldn't get *me* back.

When the manuscript was done, I sent it to a few close friends, and they all told me, "You know, we were afraid this might sound like Reagan, but it sounds like you." I said, "Oh, does it really?" And they said, "Yes, it sounds like you at dinner," which is precisely the quality I wanted it to have—a conversation, as if you were talking to someone you respect at a dinner table.

I WROTE THE BOOK IN TWO PLACES. At a word processor at my home out in Virginia, in a very quasi-rural Virginia, out there by the Potomac. Then, when I moved from there, I wrote the book in a big leaky Victorian town house in Georgetown. A marvelous old place, full of books, that was owned by an elderly lady who was a liberal Democrat, and who had worked—apparently, from what I could see of her books—for Johnson in the sixties. I would open up her books at night when I was done writing about Reagan. I'd just pick at random a book and I'd go through it and out would flutter little leaflets in which the woman who owned the house had clearly written this essay answering Lyndon Johnson's conservative critics. And there was something so funny about that, you know, that I was in . . . not just another writer's house—but a woman who was somewhat clearly obsessed with a time and a person.

When I had finished one of the final drafts—I think not quite the final draft, but one of the final drafts of the manuscript, Random House and my agent sent the entire manuscript off to a number of magazines, so that the magazines could buy an excerpt. This is standard operating procedure. And you hope that a magazine will buy for almost any price; you're not even that interested in money at this point, you're interested in exposure. You hope that a magazine will buy a chapter, say, of the manuscript. We were very lucky. We were hoping *The New York Times* would take a chapter. Every few months, the *Times Magazine* does take a chapter of a book—they took Thomas Friedman's *From Beirut to Jerusalem*—and so they bought a chapter from us, and we thought, "Well, terrific, that is just wonderful, that is the best thing that could possibly happen for the book." Then, within a few weeks they told us, "Guess what, we want it to be on the cover [of the *Times Magazine*]," and that was really stupendous. And we were surprised and delighted.

I hope I'm not talking out of school to say this; I don't think I am. We had somewhat of a disagreement about the cover. The editor of the magazine, a very talented man named Jimmy Greenfield, had decided, having read this chapter, that he wanted to use the [life-size cardboard] cutouts of President Reagan that you see on the streets of Washington. You still see Reagan ones, now you see Bush ones, you see Jesse Jackson, they were all over, but we remember when they were new. He wanted me to pose on the street between a Reagan and a Bush cutout. I thought, "Oh gee, that doesn't sound good. I don't think so." So we sort of tussled around a little bit. We kind of thought we weren't going to be on the cover anymore after we said we didn't like that. But they came back with another idea having to do with a teleprompter and words and such coming out of the presidents' mouth[s]. That still didn't feel right.

Ultimately they said, "Well, what about a picture of you at a type-writer—did you ever write at a typewriter?" I said, "Sure, when I got to the White House I did." They said, "Good, with a picture, a sort of campaign picture of Reagan in the background." I said, "Gee, that's really wonderful," so they put us back on the cover. It did get a lot of attention when the magazine came out. So my editor, Peter Osnos, said, "Terrific, wonderful picture. That's the cover of the book."

I HAD TWO GREAT NERVOUS MOMENTS on this book tour. One was before I did the *Today* show. I had never done live national TV. And I was so nervous, a producer had to walk through the halls with me at 30 Rock [Rockefeller Plaza] and take me around from office to office, just parading me around so I could burn off the nervousness—because, you know, you have horrible fantasies. It's one thing to write for people who go across the nation on live TV, but it's quite another thing to be your own self, un-scripted and afraid, perhaps, that your tongue will get caught in your throat and you'll go, *Aggghhh,* like that, on national TV, and frighten your friends. So that was the most frightening moment, the *Today* show, and the second most frightening was going on with "Bombastic Bushkin," John McLaughlin, yesterday up in New Jersey, with his audience. He has a cable show [*McLaughlin* on CNBC], and he has an audience full of people, and a little panel of reporters questioning me, and I thought, "Oh, I'm not up to this, I'm new at this game." So I was really nervous about it. But it went OK. I was a little dull, but it was OK.

WHEN [EDITORS] WOULD CALL and say, "We need a photo of you for the review," I'd say yes, feeling it was definitely a good review. Because I'm not Gore Vidal, and I'm not worth denouncing at length. And if you're going to denounce me, why have a photo of the hapless person you're being tough on? So, this is a small clue to future authors: if they want to take your picture [for the book review], say yes. It's good news.

Charles Kuralt

On December 31, 1995, veteran CBS News *reporter Charles Kuralt joined us to discuss* Charles Kuralt's America.

I DON'T KNOW IF I KNOW HOW to write. I think writing is derivative. I think it comes from reading. I was what they call a voracious reader when I was a little boy. I read every book in the house, and luckily they were adventurous books, many of them would appeal to a child—[Rudyard] Kipling and Richard Halliburton—all those sets of books that were fashionable back in the thirties. I read my way right through them and never did stop enjoying sitting down with a good book.

I can hear the rhythms of writers I admire when I sit down to write. Sometimes I could even tell you which writer's rhythms I'm hearing, whether it's Red Smith today, or John Steinbeck, or Eric Sevareid, [or] some other writer whose work I have admired. I do not mean to . . . put myself in that kind of company as a writer, but I do think that that's how young writers learn: . . . from growing very enthusiastic about something they're reading.

I write most anywhere. I'm a slow thinker and a slow writer. I wrote this book on kitchen tables and beside the fire in rented houses or under an inadequate lightbulb in a motel room someplace. Writing the notes amounted to writing the book. Since leaving CBS, I knew that I didn't want to hang around the house all day, so I have rented a writing room on top of a building [on] Fifty-seventh Street in New York and fixed it up to look— I think, rather successfully—like a seedy, failing, small gentlemen's club. There are lots of mahogany cabinets and shelves and an old eighteenth-century desk with a leather top on it. It is just the sort of room I've always imagined would be a wonderful place in which to work, and it's turned out that way. Somehow or another, it makes me feel like a writer, and I guess that's half the battle.

I HAD ALWAYS HAD THIS NOTION that it would be great to take off and spend a year in America—a perfect year, choosing twelve favorite places and going there at just the right time of year to be there, and, moreover, not going there to work, not going with a purpose or with a camera crew or with any promise of reward; just to have a long one-year vacation, a perfect year in America. And it worked out that way. It was a dream for me, and it was the best year I ever spent in this country.

I had been to these places before. They were all familiar to me. This will sound like bragging, but the truth is there's no place in America I haven't been. Thanks to Mother CBS and all those years of wandering for the *On the Road* program, my camera crew and I went to every corner of every state over and over again. These twelve locations are the ones I thought might be most fun to revisit.

I went utterly alone with no plan, no company, just a notebook in my hip pocket. And at the end of the day, I would sit down and see what was in the notebook. I have a lifelong habit of making notes, so I did that. I had great fun summing up the day on my little laptop computer after the sun had gone down and I had time to maybe sit by a fire somewhere and think. When it came time to write the book, almost all I had to do was go back and look at those nightly notes in which I'd also ask myself questions, things I should have learned that day—if I had been a real reporter—and didn't bother to.

I don't remember ever getting lonely. This country is so full of interesting characters, and they're so different, one from another. Vermonters are not a bit like Louisianans, it seems to me. I remember hearing from one fellow, "Oh, my gosh, you mustn't leave town without meeting this totem pole carver who works out here on the edge of town. He's a real craftsman and an interesting fellow to talk to." I think that's what kept me going without being lonely. I had the company of a totem pole carver all the next day.

Since everybody else in television news is covering politicians, I've always made it a point of honor not to cover them and not to talk about politics with folks. I must say, of the 150 or so people I write about in the book, I don't think I know the politics of any of them. We just didn't talk about that subject. They may have strong political opinions, but I was talking [to each person about his or her experience] as a saddlemaker or a chef or an orchestra conductor.

On this trip, I didn't [read much]. I was so drunk with the joy of going out and talking to people, and spending time with them, and remembering things that had happened in these places before that I didn't have a chance to read. But I always took a few books that I'd meant to read. There's an obscure story by Anthony Trollope in paperback that I found in my suitcase just the day before yesterday. I started out with that a year ago, and I don't think I ever opened it.

I suppose I was lucky. I think I had the best job imaginable in journalism. For twenty or twenty-five years, *CBS News* didn't even know where I was. They would let me just wander at will and occasionally send in stories, all of which I found myself. I never had an assignment. And that became a purpose. I still have—somewhere at home—several big cardboard boxes full of story ideas from the seventies and eighties that I never got around to doing. I guess just showing up, spending a day or two with somebody interesting, became a purpose in itself.

When I was in high school, I went into the school library and somehow picked up a book of radio plays. Some of our younger viewers will not know what I'm talking about when I say radio plays, but there used to be marvelous drama on the radio. And the best of it was written by Norman Corwin, who is still with us, still teaching at the University of Southern California, and, I'm happy to say, has become a friend of mine. I read those plays, the language, and it just sent an electric chill down my spine. I thought, "Oh, if ever I could write like that, then I would be happy in life." Well, I never did learn to write like that, but I think all writing comes initially from an enthusiasm about writing.

I write on a computer now. I was a little late coming to the word processor. I have an old typewriter. It must weigh fifty pounds. It's a Swedish job called a Facet, and the clatter and clack of that machine used to confirm for me that I really was getting some work done. I needed the noise. But then I was persuaded by someone that rewriting and revising is much easier on a word processor, and so I went out and bought a used Toshiba laptop, the kind you had to plug in. After I learned to use it, and learned the mysterious commands that were needed back then, it did change my view of how one should really proceed.

My editor might say I only write under dire deadline threats. I find it hard to actually get going without a figurative guillotine hanging over my head. Toward the end of finishing this book, which was many weeks late, I wrote from dawn until midnight just because I had to. I find that having to finish really helps.

I DEDICATE THE BOOK to Catherine. Catherine is a little bit of a mystery. Some friends, thinking that she must be a secret lover . . . have sidled up to me and asked me that question, "Hey, who's Catherine?" Catherine is my well-loved sister, who, with her family, lives on Bainbridge Island out in Washington. And she and I became very close during this year because we, along with my brother Wallace, were mainly responsible for taking care of our dying father. Something about a brother and a sister who have lived, as people do these days, far apart from one another for many years, coming together again at a moment like that endeared her to me all over again. I knew that when the time came to dedicate the book, it was to my angelic—and I say the word without the slightest bit of irony—my angelic and beautiful sister whom I wanted to dedicate the book.

Most people say they enjoy my [books]. They say nobody else is writing stories like this. And I suppose that's more or less true because most people are writing about important things, and these subjects are determinedly and intentionally about unimportant things. Things you wouldn't expect to find on page one of the newspaper. I think people maybe get a sense of reading about their neighbors because there's nobody in the book that they might not know. Certainly no one is inaccessible to a traveler through America.

I guess this book is about number six. I was signing books at a bookshop in Virginia and a man came up with a book called *To the Top of the World.* It was a record of a polar expedition, an attempt to reach the North Pole by a bunch of madmen from Minnesota back in 1967. That was my first book. I didn't think a copy of it existed. I have only one copy and his was in a good deal better shape than mine, but I was glad to sign that book. And I told him he had a rare volume there because I don't think that book ever sold more than 6,000 or 7,000 copies.

As I look over this book now, I see that it's not quite finished yet. I left out a lot of things. I just forgot some stuff that I meant to put in there, and I wish I had a chance to rewrite it. Maybe that's the way all authors feel.

I went to Montana when the book was finished but before it had been published, thinking that after this yearlong vacation, I owed myself a vacation. I went to Montana to go fly-fishing for trout. And the high altitude there always gets me for a day or two, but this time I couldn't get over it. I was short of breath, and found it irritating, and knew something was wrong. When I got home I had some chest pains that didn't feel right. So I went in for the usual examinations, and they found that I had one coronary artery that was pretty well blocked, and my doctor, who happens to be a cardiologist, recommended a bypass. I think while they've got your heart stopped and your breastbone cut in half and all of these violent things they've done to your chest, they figure, "Well, here's some other arteries that could use a little help, too." It turned out to be a quadruple bypass. My friends and acquaintances who have had the same operation assured me that it was like being hit by a truck, but they also assured me that within a few weeks I'd begin to feel better than I'd felt in years, and that part of the prediction is just now beginning to come true, I'm happy to say. The hit-by-a-truck part lasted quite a while.

The biggest surprise of the operation was waking up and finding out that I was still alive, because I had made the mistake—the typical reporter's mistake—of reading in detail what was about to happen, and it just didn't seem logical to me that one could live through that. But, of course, nearly everybody lives through it and goes on to a more comfortable life.

I met a fellow in Key West, which is undoubtedly our most laid-back American community. [His name was] Clyde Hensley. Clyde says human beings were not made to labor from dawn until dusk. Human beings were just made to hang out. And I learned a good deal about how one really should live while I was in Key West, and much of it was from Clyde. Human beings were just intended to be on this earth to enjoy themselves a bit. It's a philosophy you don't hear much in this intense, work-oriented society of ours. But to the extent that one can survive without working from dawn to dusk, I've about decided Clyde is right.

Norman Mailer

Norman Mailer, the author of more than twenty-five books, appeared on Booknotes *on June 25, 1995, to discuss his first nonfiction work in over a decade,* Oswald's Tale: An American Mystery. *When he appeared on the program, Mr. Mailer had just celebrated his seventy-second birthday.*

I WRITE IN MY STUDIO. I've got a little studio in Brooklyn a couple blocks from my house—no telephone, nothing there. When I go there, the only thing I ever do there is work, so it's wonderful. I'm like a dog with a conditioned reflex. There is no television, no telephone, nothing. My wife wants me to get a portable telephone. I refuse. I don't want to be tempted. There's an old Jewish belief that you build a fence around an impulse. That's not good enough, you build a fence around the fence, so no telephone.

I write longhand with a pencil, and I've got a marvelous assistant named Judith McNally, and she will type it up the next day, and then I go over it. Since at my age you begin to forget things very easily, it's marvelous because I hardly remember what I wrote the day before. Now it's typed as if someone else wrote it. I'll go through it, and I'll say, "Who is the idiot who wrote that stupid sentence?" And I'll fix it up, and I'll edit it, and as I edit it I give it back to her, and she sends it back each day. I don't work with a word processor, but I do have the benefits of one.

Generally, I'll start writing late in the morning. If we're not going out that evening, I won't finish till nine o'clock at night, so it plays hell with our social life.

I DON'T USUALLY HAVE writer's block, but I think I may have had a certain sense of how to avoid it. I'm keeping my fingers crossed. It's a foolish author who'll brag they never had writer's block. When I was younger I had years when I used to wonder whether I'd ever write another book, and I wouldn't write for six months at a time, but since I wasn't [trying to work] on anything, I didn't see it as writer's block. Or I had a couple books I started and didn't know how to go on with and I dropped, but I never called it writer's block because it didn't feel that way. I think what happens is there's something deep in the unconscious that says to you, "You can go ahead with this. This book can be written." There's certain books you can't write. If you're writing about terribly charged, emotional material and you're not ready to live with [it], I think you're not writing anymore. You're engaged in a transaction with yourself that probably is analogous to a patient with a psychoanalyst, where psychoanalysts are always talking about how they can't get patients to deliver certain sorts of obvious material because they won't face it.

So I think a writer's block probably is related to that, but all writers have certain strengths and weaknesses. I think one of my strengths has been that I've been able to avoid writer's block; it isn't a preoccupation of mine. What I'm concerned with is, how good is it going to be?

I like to give a lot of value for the dollar, so the readers are going to get a good bit [in *Oswald's Tale*]. First of all, they're going to get an informal biography of Lee Harvey Oswald, which starts in the middle. The first half is about him at the age of nineteen, going into Russia and leaving Russia at the age of twenty-two. That's the first half of the book. It's got a lot of new material about Oswald in Russia, living in Minsk, getting married, having children there, trying to get along in the Soviet system, becoming disillusioned. A lot of detail on how he got out of the Soviet Union. People always think that it was very mysterious that he got out and came back, but in fact it wasn't. He just wore out two bureaucracies.

Then he came back to the United States, and the second half of the book is all about Oswald in America, starting with him as a child and carrying him through to the day of the assassination. What the book became as I wrote it was a portrait of the cold war as seen by somebody who's living at the bottom in both countries.

I started this book because of Lawrence Schiller. Larry had worked in the Soviet Union off and on from about 1983 because he was directing the movie *Peter the Great* that was put on television, in a miniseries with Maximilian Schell, a couple years later. So he had contacts in the Soviet Union, and he had learned how to work with the bureaucracy there. At a given moment, the Soviet Union started to fall apart and everything began to open up, and it looked like some of the KGB files were going to indeed open up. He called me one day and said, "Listen, would you be interested in doing a book about Oswald in Russia because I think I'm going to have access to the Oswald file?" It came at a perfect time for me. I had finished [writing] *Harlot's Ghost* [the 1990 novel] about which some people may remember that at the end of page 1,300, I had written, "To be continued."

So the second half of *Harlot's Ghost* had to do with the narrator being in Russia. I was wondering, how am I going to deal with the KGB? I don't know enough about the KGB; I've got to learn more. This Oswald project was the perfect opportunity.

Also I'd been obsessed with Oswald for more than thirty years—had he done it? hadn't he done it? was he part of a conspiracy?—so I said yes without any great palaver back and forth, and in September of 1992, I moved over to Minsk.

Larry and I worked together with a young lady, a translator named Ludmila, whom he in the period of time [we all worked together] married and divorced. He had known her for years, but he married her while we were still in Russia, in Minsk, Byelorussia. Then they got divorced later. The point is not that they got married and divorced but that the three of us were there all the time, working in Minsk, where there's nothing to do except eat an indifferent meal in an unhappy restaurant every night—because Minsk will never be famous for its cuisine, or at least not in the next decade or two. We worked. We worked constantly. We interviewed people. We had the great good fortune that the KGB had shut down all talk about Oswald after the assassination because they were horrified by it; they got paranoid. They felt that the United States had a master plan to start a war with them and that Oswald was the point of this war, and so in Minsk they immediately went around to everyone who had known Oswald and said, "Don't say a word about him," and nobody did. So for thirty years no one had talked about Oswald. You can imagine what a time capsule we entered when we started interviewing people who had known him and were his friends.

In Minsk, I lived in an apartment house that was like every other apartment house in Minsk. There's no differentiation as such. In other words, you can be a worker, you can be a doctor, you can be a professor, you can be a manicurist—everyone lives at the same level, which is a fairly low level. I had a small three-room apartment, which was pretty good, in a dreary quarter, which was like all the other dreary quarters in Minsk. The difference is that in Minsk if you were an intellectual or if you were a doctor or scientist you lived no better—unless you were very, very high [in rank]— than a worker. In fact, you may have even earned less money a month. But what you did have is . . . your superiority, which is [to say] you had your essential class superiority—which is, you were cultured and they were not.

The problem in researching the book was we'd be interviewing a Russian, so we needed one hour for the English, one hour for the Russian, and one hour for arguing with our translator because she had a very definite idea of how you spoke. I learned a lot about Soviet society, which was just ending at that point, by her attitudes. For instance, we might ask a question on the order of, "What year was it that your father was in the Gulag?" since this had come up earlier in the conversation in a roundabout way. She said, "I will not ask that question. It will wreck the interview. You will insult them by such a question. They will not be able to go on." So we said, "Ask the question the way you want to ask it." So she'd ask the question; she'd get an answer. Then we'd turn to her and say, "What did you ask them?" She'd say, "I said to them, 'Was there a year that was worse for your family than other years?' " Through that, you began to get a sense of how roundabout everything was in the old Soviet Union, that people became—not evasive, but they phrased questions in such a way that there were no sharp edges. There was no handle to the conversation, so that [it] could not be repeated definitively afterward in such a way as to incriminate you. It opened a great deal because you had that contrast between the essential brusque approach of Russians. I don't know the finesse in Russia—there's a great deal of it, apparently—but immediately, in the little bit you can learn, there's a great deal of brusque approach. There are no definite articles; there are no indefinite articles.

Altogether in Moscow and Minsk, I think we must have interviewed fifty or sixty people, but [the interviews] were in depth. It was different than my earlier books. During [the writing of] *The Executioner's Song* [the 1978 book about Gary Gilmore, a convicted murderer who asked to be executed and was given the death penalty], we must have interviewed 300 people, but here, first of all, the number of people was limited. Not everyone had known Oswald well enough to bear an interview. It took so long. You really had to work very slowly and carefully. But we interviewed in depth. There were certain people we saw ten times, and conducted ten interviews.

I had all the information about Russia that I needed, 95 percent of it. When I came home I started writing [about] Oswald in Minsk, but by the time I finished that, as I say, I thought I was going to add a hundred pages about Oswald in America. That hundred pages became 400 or 500 pages because I began doing new research. I'd stop writing for long periods and do the new research, and so the second half of the book took as long as the first half, easily. Then you finish it, and then you go over it, and then you start to shape it more and more and more. Once you know what you have, you shape it more. So the writing of this book, I'd say, was easier than the writing of other books I've done. On the other hand, I got more out of it. I'm fond of the book because I had this extraordinary experience of living in Minsk. I just felt, well, hell, I'm in my late sixties—I had my seventieth birthday in Moscow a couple years ago—and I just felt, I'm not dead yet. This is not so bad. I can live in a strange place and get a lot out of it, and I'm working hard. All that was fun.

Reporters

ভেত্

*One of the great advantages of being a freelancer is that you
exist outside the rules that grown-ups make.*

—Michael Kelly

David Halberstam

David Halberstam started his career as a writer in 1955 as editor of The Harvard Crimson *at Harvard University. His first newspaper assignment was as a reporter at* The Tennessean *in Nashville and he later won a Pulitzer Prize for his reporting on Vietnam. Now the author of numerous best-sellers, Mr. Halberstam appeared on* Booknotes *to discuss* The Fifties *in July of 1993.*

I WRITE AT HOME. In addition to our regular apartment, we have a very small apartment in the back. My wife wanted to get me out of the main house, where I work, because she thought the steam and angst that came out of my ears and nose during the day while I was working there significantly detracted from her calm and her control of space. So we got this back apartment, which is really quite nice. I get up in the morning when I'm writing, if I write in the morning. I get up, and I have a very lazy cappuccino—I love the cappuccino—and a very light breakfast.

Then about nine-thirty or so, I go up to what I call the cage, which is where I write. I've got a nice little CD player. Sometimes I play the blues, or sometimes it's Mr. Vivaldi or Mr. Mozart. Then I work for about five hours. There's some exercise machines there and whatever and some books, and it's a nice place, but when [my work is] done, I want to get out of there. Jean, my wife, says, "Come on. If you're going to read, why don't you read in the office?" I said, "It's a cage when I'm there. I'm exhausted. I'm writing. Everything I think about in that office is writing. The moment my writing for the day is done, I want to get out. I want to be here. I want to be with you." The pressure of writing and being in that room is so great that when it's over, I don't want to be in the room. I can't relax almost until I'm out of the room.

In New York there's a wonderful library that I love going to called the New York Society Library. It's a small private library [on] Seventy-ninth [Street] between Park and Madison. It's wonderful. It's not very expensive. While I do go to the New York Public Library, there's something about the New York Society Library that I really love.

A friend of mine named Eli Zabar runs a wonderful little food shop, the most expensive food shop in America—probably a roast beef sandwich is about $200 these days—over there [between] Eightieth and Eighty-first [Streets] on Madison, so if I work until about two-thirty, I often go and have a light lunch, and I can get cappuccino there, and then Eli will come over and talk with me. I check in with a friend, I have this great cappuccino and a light lunch—maybe a salad—and I've had five hours in the library. Five hours in the library is just wonderful. It's always an adventure. It's like eating salted peanuts. You never know what you're going to get next.

I USED TO BE an old-fashioned typewriter, hunt-and-peck. I never went to an electric typewriter. Then about ten years ago, friends convinced me to try word processors, and it has liberated me and probably doubled my productivity. It's a great instrument with which to rewrite, to clean up. In the old days, you made one typo and you had to retype the whole page because of a typo. I make a lot of typos. I'm a fast hunt-and-peck man. Now it's like playing Pac-Man cleaning up the typos, so it's really made my life a lot easier. It's really damn near doubled my productivity.

I envisioned the book six years ago. Another reason I wanted to do it was that the last long book I'd done was *The Reckoning,* which was a story of the American economy coming under pressure, becoming vulnerable from the challenge of the Japanese, so I wanted to look at America when it was rich in a world that was poor, when everything seemed to work. These were the dual things, and I had a vision of the book about six or seven years ago before I started out. The vision was that there would be sections on television, sections on the affluence, sections on the McCarthy period, and, if possible, near the end of the book they would begin to twine together. As one person said, they would braid, so that you would have television and then you would have civil rights, and then late in the book television would be covering civil rights. That's what I had. I wanted to show the impact, among other things, of television on the society, so that you get the speeding up. I had that in my vision, that these different parts would begin to braid together.

During those six years, I also did a small sports book, *The Summer of '49,* which was great fun, and which, by the way, informed this book because this is a book on the coming of television to society and *The Summer of '49* is on the last radio era in baseball—before big money, before television—when you hear a game on the radio and you form a mythic vision of a [Joe] DiMaggio or a [Ted] Williams. They live larger because you create the myth for them in the fantasy of your mind. I did that book in the middle of this one.

. . .

I THINK MOST INTERVIEWS should be done in person. I think it's great fun. I think you interview better when you see someone. As you show up, you get a higher validation. You've made the effort to come to their house, you see people. It's more fun. The real fun is in doing the interviews.

When people talk about America in the fifties and they talk about it as an innocent time, they think of those early shows—*Leave It to Beaver*, *Father Knows Best, Ozzie and Harriet*—and they were the all-American family. Yet the fifties were not that innocent. Even in this all-American family, no one knows what Ozzie does, but he's a good, easy, relaxed guy. In real life, Ozzie was a workaholic, quite authoritarian—really dictatorial—wrote, directed, and produced all these shows, used his own children in the shows, and really in some ways, you could argue, took away part of their childhood. Particularly with [his son] Rick, he took away the one thing that mattered, his music, and put it into the show. Ricky, I think, was always unhappy with that. You could make the argument that in the end the Nelsons were something of a dysfunctional family even though they were the ideal to all those other American families back in the fifties.

I MUST TELL YOU that my friend David [McCullough] is an appallingly good speaker. He came to Nantucket last year and spoke at the Athenaeum there, and every seat was taken, and it was as [if] Harry Truman had walked into the room. And three weeks later, I was supposed to give a comparable speech as part of the same series, and I thought, "No, I'm not going to compete with this on my home territory." So we worked out a format where a friend would just interview me, and we'd just do a dialogue, not unlike this, because I was not going to compete with McCullough.

The next morning, I saw David walking down the street, and I drove by very slowly, rolled down the window, and said, "Get off this island, McCullough. It isn't big enough for the two of us."

It's a wonderful privileged life, you know, being a book writer. I'm about to be sixty on my next birthday, and I go out and I write books. I live a good life, and I can have both my private life and my professional life in a way that an anchorman on television or a superstar television reporter can't. There's a wonderful level of privacy and a wonderful level of engagement in the society. I have the best of both worlds.

George Will

Columnist George Will appeared on Booknotes *on October 18, 1992, to discuss his book* Restoration: Congress, Term Limits, and the Recovery of Deliberative Democracy. *Besides being a writer, Mr. Will is a panelist for ABC's Sunday public affairs program* This Week with Sam and Cokie.

I WRITE ALL THE TIME. It's a metabolic necessity for me. A lot of writers, I don't know what you found—but I think that a lot of writers hate to write. They like the research, they like thinking about it, they like the end product, the book or the column or something with their name on it, but the putting words down, they hate. I love it. To me, it's more fun than anything. It's a tactile, physical pleasure. And I'm not one of those who despairs about the printed word. I think book sales are strong and robust. I believe that the book still is the primary carrier of ideas. I write books when I get impatient waiting for someone to write them for me.

I write about 125 columns a year for *Newsweek* and the newspapers—and if I don't write twelve to fifteen a year on books, I'm not doing my job right, because books are news, big news.

I write with a fountain pen, a big, huge Montblanc pen. I write everything with a fountain pen including my books. I write on yellow tablets in my office in Georgetown, on airplanes, everywhere. I have an itch to write. I would explode if I couldn't write.

It's hard to be alone [while writing]. One does want to be alone a lot, so I find I compensate by staying home a lot, and not socializing very much in Washington. But that's not giving up very much. The best thing about celebrity is it gets your books read, because people say, "I'm interested in him; I know something about how his mind works—and what [does] he think about this?" So to the extent that it serves to get people to open the books and read the columns, then it's wonderful.

WHEN I USE THE WORD "RESTORATION" as the title of the book, it was precisely to say I want to restore Congress by term limits, by the end of careerism, by bringing in a more deliberative kind of legislator. I want to restore Congress to its rightful place as the first branch of government. Conservatives used to believe in this profoundly.

This book came out of a kind of an epiphany I experienced. I know all the arguments against term limits, because I used to make them. I was opposed to term limits for a long time for lots of reasons: you don't change the Constitution lightly; you do not limit choice lightly; you have to have a good reason. Then one day I found myself making the usual talk, and I said, "I'm against term limits because if we didn't have the seasoned professionals we have in Washington today, we wouldn't have the good government we've got today." And I said to myself, "You can't say that with a straight face." And I also used to say, "We can't have amateurs in Washington." Then it dawned on me that the word "amateur" comes from the French word meaning "to love." It's somebody who does something for the love of it, not a bad motive even in a federal city.

Another one of the little epiphanies I had on the road to conversion on the subject of term limits occurred when I got up in Denver one morning. I read a headline in the *Rocky Mountain News* that said that Congresswoman [Pat] Schroeder [D-CO] had got one of her committees to vote an appropriation to make a federal project out of the midnight basketball program. Now, midnight basketball, I think, started somewhere around Washington and suburban Maryland but basically became a conspicuous and well-publicized phenomenon in Chicago where basketball leagues play in the middle of the night. It takes at-risk young men, basically inner-city black men, seventeen to twenty-two or twenty-three, and gives them something to do after midnight when they might otherwise be in trouble. It's funded by the private sector with some help from the city government of Chicago for uniforms, referees, award banquets, league standings, the whole thing.

I wrote a column about it. This was a big mistake, because then it came to the attention of the people in Washington whose premise is that any good idea should be a federal program. It just goes without saying. So Mrs. Schroeder got a bill through, and it suddenly dawned on me that this epitomized the complete absence of any sense of what is and is not a proper federal responsibility, but, more than that, [I noticed] what a strange mentality [this] was—that a congresswoman who's been here, by now I guess she's been here twenty years, should not think there's any question, any problem with the federal government making midnight basketball in Chicago a federal program.

Now, all these came together for me in this epiphany because, at the time, I was reading a biography of Henry Clay, and I was just at the spot where Clay arrives in Washington in about 1806. He's jarred into town from Tennessee: he's come over corduroy roads, and up the rivers on the steamboats and barges, and it was hell getting here. And he gets to town— and Congress is arguing with President Jefferson over whether or not to pass a national roads bill, and Jefferson said, "All right, I'll sign this, but I'm warning you it doesn't say anything in the Constitution that Congress shall build roads, and if you're not careful, in 150 years you're going to be subsidizing basketball in Denver." Jefferson didn't say quite that, but that was the import of what he said.

My parents were sort of academic liberals. They voted in the thirties for Norman Thomas several times, I think, a Socialist candidate. [Like] most academics . . . and certainly [most academics] in Illinois, they were supporters of Gov. [Adlai] Stevenson against Eisenhower, but they followed, I won't say their son, but they followed the trend of the country a little bit to the right since then.

Nixon was not a strong president. There was a huge outpouring of important legislation under Richard Nixon, but that was just because he wasn't interested. He was going to save the world, and go to China, and negotiate with the Russians. He actually said once that the country pretty much runs itself.

In '64, I voted for [Barry] Goldwater. I voted for him by absentee ballot from Illinois while I was at Princeton for three years—'64 through '67— getting a Ph.D. in political philosophy. Then I taught for a year at Michigan State [University]. They offered me a job, and I was glad to go back to the Big Ten, back to the Midwest.

Then I got a very attractive offer and went to the University of Toronto, where I was when, one day out of the blue, I got a call from the office of Gordon Allott, of whom I had never heard. By then he was the senior senator from Colorado. They said that Dirksen had died, and they were shifting the Republican leadership around, and Gordon Allott became, I guess, the number-three-ranking position of the policy committee. He had some more staff slots to fill, and he wanted a Republican academic to do some writing. Well, Republican academics were pretty thin on the ground in those days, and through sheer luck, someone at the University of Denver who'd known me at Princeton told him I was in Toronto, and the phone rang. So he said, "Come to Washington." I never looked back.

Working on the Hill was great. Three years was probably long enough, but it's a crash course on American politics, a great immersion and a wonderful institution. I loved Congress then; love it now. It's one of the reasons I wrote the book. I got to admire a great many of the people, a great sense that there's a lot of talent there, a lot of public spiritedness, a lot of intelligence; a lot of the opposite of that, also. After that I started writing a column instantly.

I had written a couple of things both as an academic and while on the Senate staff for *National Review,* and I called Bill Buckley and said, "I think you need a Washington editor," and essentially he said, "OK, do it." That's the way Bill often ran *National Review.* He'd spot people, you know; most great editors are that way. They trust their instincts.

Also, in my third year and final year on the Senate staff, I had attended a conference on one of those politics-and-the-media things at Kenyon College, and it was attended by Meg Greenfield. At that time, she was the deputy editor of the editorial page of *The Washington Post,* and she liked some of the stuff [I'd written and] what I said. She asked, "What are you going to do?" and I said, "I'm going to leave at the end of the year and start writing for *National Review.*" She said, "Well, submit some stuff to us." So I did, right then in 1973. At that time, *The Washington Post* was just starting its in-house syndicate, principally to syndicate David Broder to a wider audience, and I think they figured it's just as easy to do it for two as for one, so I went along as ballast. They said, "Do you want to start a syndicated column?" and I did, I guess, in January of '74. That's how it started. I'd love to say it was a heroic, uphill struggle, but it was effortless. I kept saying, "Make me a columnist," and they kept saying, "All right," and off I went.

I LOVED THE BOOK *Friday Night Lights* [by H. G. Bissinger]. If someone said, "What book from the last five years do you wish you'd written?"— that's the one. Here's a guy from Philadelphia, I don't know the fellow. He went down to Odessa, Texas; hung out with the Permian Panthers [the football team at Permian High School] named after the Permian Basin, the great oil basin down there, and watched the culture of high school football in this windswept part of Texas. And it's a stirring, heartbreaking, wonderful book. You look at that, and you say, "Where'd he get the idea?" Suddenly the whole vista looks different.

By the way, among the things that are getting better in America are bookstores. There's a chain—I don't mind giving them a big plug—called Borders, and I now go into cities, and if I'm going to have some time, I look up where there is a Borders. You go there, you find people who love books, and you find all this serendipity happening. People go into bookstores, and it's the great bastion of impulse buying, and they go in, they may not know they ever wanted to read a very fat book about the Brooklyn Bridge, for example, but they say, "Oh, what's there to know about building a bridge?" And that's how these books take on a wonderful life of their own that will outlive all of us. No civilization had anything like what we have now.

I WAS IN THIRTIETH STREET STATION in Philadelphia, just the other day, and I went into a bookstore they have there. And they had fiction, and science fiction, and all the usual stuff, and they had a philosophy section. And in the philosophy section is quite an eclectic collection—a biography of Sartre and some Aquinas and there was Ortega y Gasset's *Revolt of the Masses*. Now what a wonderful thing a book does. This Spaniard sat down and wrote that book eons ago and somehow, in Thirtieth Street Station in the 1990s, there's that book sitting there—that's as close to immortality as I think you can get.

James "Scotty" Reston

James "Scotty" Reston wrote Deadline: A Memoir *about his years as Washington bureau chief, columnist, and executive editor of* The New York Times. *Mr. Reston retired in 1988, after spending fifty years at the* Times. *He appeared on* Booknotes *on December 8, 1991.*

I WENT TO WORK for *The New York Times* on the first day that the war broke out in 1939. I'd been working at the AP in London since 1937, before Munich. I'd tried to get a job on the *Times* for two and a half years, and I couldn't make it. But when Hitler went to war, they had to have somebody in a hurry, and I happened to be around. That's how I got on.

At *The New York Times,* I was in the scoop-artist business for a long time, including during the critical period right at the end of the war when we were trying—with the Soviet Union and the British and the French and the Chinese—to work out a basis for the postwar world; that is to say, a charter for the United Nations. It was a great period for the scoop artist because all relations at the end of the war were new, all kinds of new political procedures and relationships, so you could go around and pick up news all over this town. It was great fun. But I suppose I liked doing a column more than anything.

I made a deal with *The New York Times* that if they would allow me to hire a young man or a woman just out of college, with or without any newspaper training, I would settle [for] that instead of a secretary. My theory . . . was that there is a great danger in my business that you'll get out of date. There is also a great danger of writing [something] and not having somebody read it before you publish it—to say to you, "Reston, that is a stupid column," or, "You are repeating in the fifth paragraph what you had in the second," which is an old failing of mine.

Tom Wicker [another longtime columnist at *The New York Times*] was ahead of us in using computers. I said to him one day, "Do you like this thing?" He said, "Well, I do in a way, but the damn thing is programmed for clichés." I said, "What do you mean?" He said, "Well, that cursor there blinks at me all the time and says, 'Come on, Wicker. Get going, Wicker.'

The first thing that comes into my mind is the cliché." But I have found it a wonderful instrument. I wish I had had it when I was on the daily beat.

I think it is the reporter's job in Washington, really, to be the watchman on the walls and apply a critical eye to whatever party and whatever president is in power. It is very dangerous to get close to people in power in the White House for the very simple reason that they are faced with such agonizing problems that, if you have any human sympathy for them, it's really quite impossible not to sympathize—and therefore [you will not] be objective. Our job is to be fair. I use these big words like "objective," but fairness and fair criticism [are] what is required.

In this town, people fail when they begin to think they are what they merely represent; when secretaries of state think they are the State Department, when presidents think, as Lyndon Johnson said, "I will not be the first president to lose a war." He's thinking about himself. I've always thought that the role of wives is terribly important. I've tried to write a chapter about the role of wives in this book. But I believe there should be a constitutional amendment under which the wives of presidents and members of the cabinet are obliged to say, at least once a month, to their husbands, "I love you, but I think you're a stupid numbskull. Why are you doing that?" Now, if Mrs. Nixon had said that to Richard Nixon at the time of Watergate, it might have saved his presidency. And if Lady Bird [Johnson] had said it to Lyndon during the Vietnam War, it might have been different. But that's merely a silly fantasy of mine.

I'm not really happy with [the title] *Deadline*. There's a paradox in it, I think. "Deadline" is a pessimistic word. . . . And "deadline" suggests the end of things, even the end of life. Actually, it is an optimistic book.

[This book is] a story of a love affair, and of a wonderful family life, and of a wonderful journalistic life in what is, I think, without any doubt the greatest era of journalism in the history of the republic. The story I see that is so interesting is to have lived to be an old man and to have lived in the political world of the last fifty years, which was really a revolution in the history of our country. It was a marvelous experience.

Stanley Crouch

Stanley Crouch, a columnist for the New York Daily News, appeared on the program on May 12, 1996, to discuss The All-American Skin Game, or the Decoy of Race: The Long and the Short of It, 1990–1994, *a book nominated for the 1995 National Book Critics Circle Award.*

MY DAD WAS A BAD GUY. He was a criminal. I don't know if he is now. I haven't seen him in thirty years. But he wasn't a good guy. He was involved in car theft, and drugs, and various things like that. My mother, though, was a domestic worker, and she was a real all-American aristocrat. If you were to meet me and my mother in a store in 1960 when I was fourteen, going on fifteen in December, you'd never know who she was. She had this way that she carried herself and the way she spoke that was really something. She was special. She was also very big on reading and studying. When I was young, if I would be staying up late—and listening to records, or reading books, or something—[and] my brother and sister would complain about it, she'd say, "You know, he's the artistic type. Don't bother him. You know, they're different from other people."

I write a column every Sunday for the New York *Daily News.* It gets me right to the sidewalk. I like that. See, I don't mind writing—as any writer likes to—to the intellectual elite, if you will, of the United States, whomsoever they might happen to be. But there's something great when you're in a cab and the cabdriver says, "Don't you write for the *Daily News?*" Or, the Puerto Rican messenger kids, age seventeen or eighteen, saying, "Are you Stanley Crouch? I read your articles. Very interesting articles." Then you get on the subway, and a guy's getting off duty, and he drives the train, and he says, "Oh, you're Stanley Crouch." He says, "I'm glad you're X-Y-Z." Of course, you also meet people who say "Oh, you jerk. You blah, blah, blah." But I just like that. I like the interplay with the public.

. . .

FOR ME, ALBERT MURRAY AND RALPH ELLISON are the twin towers, as I say in the introduction of the book, of a certain kind of intellectual and cultural clarity, authority, real inventiveness, and a very broad sense of American meaning that's not sandbagged by racial divisions. I'm a person who has always had trouble, even when I was trying, to embrace black nationalism. It meant that I had to let go [of] too many things that I liked, you know, like James Joyce, and [Herman] Melville, or John Wayne, or fantasies I had about being at Kitty Hawk the day that the Wright Brothers went up, because I used to read books about guys like that.

Then, when black nationalism came along in the late sixties, and I started going toward that, I realized I would have had to give all of that up and just focus on one thing, along with a certain kind of fantasy about Africa. While I was battling with that, I came in contact with Albert Murray through [an author] friend of mine named Larry Neal, who was also trying to get out of that and go [in] another direction. I was very attracted to what Murray was like. That was around 1970, so I've known him for twenty-five years, and I've learned something important from him every year.

I thought James Baldwin was a guy who had an incredible gift, but I think veered off course after the black-nationalist nut wing began to influence the civil rights movement and eventually devour it. I think that he used that incredible gift to start ranting in very irrational ways about the United States, and I think it affected his novels. He wrote progressively worse novels. I think the last book, *The Evidence of Things Unseen,* was a truly terrible book.

Ellison died a couple of years ago. You know, he was from Oklahoma, and he grew up listening to the bands. He used to talk about seeing Lester Young walking down the street in Oklahoma City with a white sweater and a silver tenor saxophone. He wrote *Invisible Man,* which is considered one of the great American novels of the second half of the century. He wrote many essays that are extraordinary; [they] have been recently collected.

I dedicate a whole group of essays in the book to "Ralphus" [Ralph Ellison] because I used to call him on the phone and call him Ralphus. You know, there's an old slave name, Rastus. He used to pick up the phone, he'd say "Hello." And I'd say, "Is this Ralphus?" And he'd say, "Oh, Stanley." And we would go on, and we'd talk. He was a great man. A very big man. He saw the interconnectedness of American life. He recognized that all white Americans are part Negro; all Americans—all black Americans, so-called, are part white—not necessarily genetically, but that our culture, what makes us American, is something that has influenced all of us, wherever we are from in the United States. We are all, essentially, variations on a certain set of propositions that make us American.

I'M PREPARING ANOTHER BOOK OF ESSAYS right now that will either be called *Possession Over Judgment Day*, *Blue Light*, or *Bittersweet*. Those are the three titles I thought of in the cab on the way over here.

Evan Thomas

Evan Thomas is an assistant managing editor for Newsweek *magazine. He came on the program on December 17, 1995, to discuss* The Very Best Men—Four Who Dared: The Early Years of the CIA. *The book is a study of Frank Wisner, Richard Bissell, Tracy Barnes, and Desmond FitzGerald, who ran the agency's clandestine service in the 1950s and early 1960s.*

To WRITE A BOOK, I take a leave from *Newsweek* to write. I've always taken a three-month leave for a book, and I've done this three times now. I just write as fast as I can for three months to get a manuscript down, to get a basic, rough—and I do mean rough—draft. Then I spend a lot of time and odd hours reworking it—early in the morning, sometimes late at night, sometimes at lunch—whenever I can get a spare hour.

I GOT THE IDEA FOR THE BOOK from writing *The Wise Men*, which was a book that came out about ten years ago about the old foreign policy establishment. Two of the wise men were Chip Bohlen and George Kennan. They were senior foreign policymakers after the war, and one of their social friends was Frank Wisner. Frank Wisner killed himself in 1965. I thought, "Boy, there's got to be a story in there. The man who started the CIA's clandestine service, who started the department of dirty tricks, as reporters later called it, shot himself." And I thought, "Why? What happened?" I started pulling on that string, and it led me to these four characters. What I wanted to do was bring stick figures to life. It's really a social history as much as anything else. The goal is to make you understand that all the spooky stuff the CIA was doing had a human dimension, and the human dimension was this insular, clubby group that lived in Georgetown, that went to places like Groton, that had a certain mind-set, a certain ethic. I try to explain that and to understand that.

Mrs. [Katharine] Graham, who runs *The Washington Post*, still has dinner parties in Georgetown where she has policymakers and they eat good food . . . in a kind of a glamorous setting, and everybody's vaguely self-satisfied. They're fun to go to, but they're a vestige of something that was once a very powerful institution. You cannot understand the CIA, in fact, you can't understand the government of the United States, at least the foreign policy part of it, unless you understand what Georgetown was like in the late forties and early fifties: They were all friends, they all knew each other, they had gone to school together, they had been in the same clubs together, they were godfathers to each other's children, they drank together at the Sunday night supper. They were a world unto themselves, and they made policy.

Joe Alsop [the columnist] was the center of the universe. His dinner parties were the most important dining table in Georgetown and, hence, Washington, and hence the world. That was Joe Alsop's in the 1950s. Jack Kennedy, when he was president, would come for dinner there and hold forth, and it was a kind of forum. Alsop was a brilliant, loyal, belligerent, slightly sad homosexual who was an imperious figure. "Well," he would say to Kennedy, "now why aren't we doing enough about the communists?" And Kennedy, sitting at his table, would try to answer him in quite specific detail. In those days, public officials trusted journalists, and they would, over dinner, reveal state secrets, trusting those journalists not to print them. There were different rules in the 1950s.

To research the book, I interviewed sixty-six former and current CIA agents. Actually, "agents" is a misnomer. Case officers and officials. An agent is somebody that the CIA hires to do their spying, usually a foreign national. These are all case officers or officials. The interesting thing about it was how free they were in talking to me. You would think the CIA would be clammed up, that they're keeping secrets. But the cold war is over. A lot of these men are older and facing their maker and thought, "Well, now's the time to tell my story."

Their personalities tended to be larger than life—and lively. They are such a distinctive contrast, to me, with bureaucrats I see today in my day job, working for *Newsweek,* who tend to be pretty cautious, by and large. This group was not cautious. They were very bold, and they were bold in their actions as CIA officials in the 1950s. By the time I got to them, they were pretty bold in talking to me. I think only five of them refused to talk at all. There's only one unattributed quote in the entire book. Everything else is on the record.

I spent about four days interviewing Richard Bissell [one of the four former senior CIA officials]. He could talk all day long even though he was, then, eighty years old. He drank a lot. We would sit there drinking wine and by the end of the day, I'd be looped, and he seemed completely sober and always lucid.

I SIGNED A SECRECY AGREEMENT [with the CIA]. It was a complicated process. I was afraid that if I signed an all-purpose secrecy agreement for clarity, [it] would allow [CIA officials] to censor my book. I refused to do that. I hired a lawyer, Sven Holmes, who is now a federal judge in Oklahoma, who had been the chief counsel of the Senate Intelligence Committee. He represented me for over two years in long negotiations. We worked out a deal that worked this way. I wrote an entire book without any access at all. I submitted that book [to the CIA]. I did it based on my interviews. I wrote a book based largely on sources that already exist and my interviews with old spooks. I submitted that manuscript, and I said, "You tell me what bothers you in this manuscript. What are you going to want to take out? What don't you like?" They [CIA officials] gave me a list of about fifty items, and then we went through each one, and I found basically public sourcing, or I convinced the CIA that these items were in no way a harm to the national security in all but, I think, about two cases.

Once we had settled that, we put that manuscript aside, and they made an agreement not to touch it, to ask for no further changes, but just to accept what I had written. Then I was allowed in [to read the CIA's classified documents]. I read the [CIA's secret] histories. I took notes. I submitted my notes to them. They looked at that and they decided what, from my notes, they were going to let me print. They let me have just about everything. The thing that they're still sensitive about are some code names, for reasons I'm not entirely clear about. They're sensitive about code names, the identities of agents; they don't like to print them for obvious reasons. If I had read the record of them bribing a foreign official, they weren't about to allow me to print that. But generally, they [the CIA officials] were pretty open. They allowed me to use specific details about covert operations all the way back. They withheld virtually nothing.

The CIA has a whole history staff, and they write secret histories that nobody can read because they're classified. It's kind of like librarians who love books so much they don't want anybody to read them. But I was allowed to read these histories, which are interesting, but it's important to note they are incomplete. They don't promise to be complete records. They're also turgid: they're written by intelligence officers, not professional historians. [But] they are very interesting windows into the way the CIA viewed itself at the time. And I took them as that—and I found some interesting tidbits. No shocking revelations. All the big secrets are out. Only in this country would we really know all the big secrets of our intelligence service. In fact, we probably know more about the CIA than we do about the history of the Department of Agriculture or the Department of Housing and Urban Development.

I'M TORN ABOUT THESE MEN. I admire the courage of these men. I admire their idealism, their sense of grandeur, which you don't find in Washington today. You don't find the same, "Boy, we're going to try to save the world here. We're going to be confident in our world leadership." You don't see that. What I don't miss are the mistakes, obviously. These guys made a lot of mistakes. The Bay of Pigs was a fantastic blunder. It was profoundly humiliating to the president of the United States—and dangerous. One reason why we had a Cuban missile crisis is because the CIA spent so much time trying to kill Castro that Castro said to the Russians, "Sure, I'll take your missiles. The CIA's trying to kill me." I don't think those missiles would have been based in Cuba but for the CIA's nutty plots to try to kill Castro. So there was a real downside, to put it mildly, to what they did. They suffered from the ancient Greek disease of hubris, a kind of overweening arrogance. They were good and idealistic men who went too far. They were too brave, too confident.

Anna Quindlen

Anna Quindlen, a former columnist for The New York Times, *discussed her book* Thinking Out Loud: On the Personal, the Political, the Public and the Private, *on* Booknotes *in May 1993. Ms. Quindlen is now a novelist.*

Y OU KNOW, I FEEL SORT OF FUNNY about pulling together collections of my columns because I think, "You already did this." You know, when I was publishing my novel *Object Lessons,* I felt that [it] was a brand-new thing and I'm sort of entitled. But readers tell me over and over again that they like it [*Thinking Out Loud*], first of all, because they've clipped these things out and saved them, and they turn this horrible orange color and start to fall apart after a couple of months or so. And second of all, because putting them together with like-minded columns gives them a way of looking at the issue[s] that they didn't quite have before.

I'VE GOT TO TELL YOU, I was never so blindsided in my life as when I filed my first column, and after I had filed it, the copy editor called me and said, "Well, what's your headline?" I said, "Wait a minute. I don't write headlines. Editors write headlines." But once I got used to it, I got to really like it.

To get to be a columnist for *The New York Times,* I certainly think it's helpful if you have a good deal of reporting experience and a career in the newspaper business. But Mr. [William] Safire proves that that's not necessary because before he came to us, he worked for Richard Nixon. I think the most important thing a columnist really needs is a clear voice, an identifiable way of speaking to the readers and looking at the world, and a real ability—not necessarily to take lemons and make lemonade, but sometimes to take a little bit of string from here and a little bit of string from there and to weave them all together into whole cloth. It's quite a different skill than being a really good reporter or a really good writer because of the self-starting aspect of it. I mean, no one calls you on a Monday morning and says, "For Wednesday, do a column about this. And for Sunday, do a column about that." It all has to come from whatever motivates you.

Pete Hamill

Pete Hamill began his journalism career at the New York Post *as a nightside reporter in 1960. He went on to become a columnist and, later, editor in chief of the* New York Daily News. *Mr. Hamill, the author of seven novels, appeared on* Booknotes *to talk about his book* A Drinking Life: A Memoir *on May 29, 1994.*

A NUMBER OF MY FRIENDS were either getting in trouble or dying. I had gone to two or three funerals of friends who had died from, not necessarily straight alcoholism, but from the consequences of it. I had friends—really close friends—who were in awful trouble. They kept asking me at some of these [funerals], "How did you do this?" They knew I had stopped drinking twenty years ago and that I had been a really good drinker. I found it was not easy to give an easy answer. If I could have given a three-minute answer and said, "Here is the magic key," I'd have done it. But I found myself sitting down and writing a book about it.

I think the one thing you find out when you stop drinking is just how much time you have. You have time to read. You have time to listen to music—not just [to] have music as background on a jukebox in a bar, but to listen to it. In my case, I found time to write. I wrote one book before I stopped drinking; I've written ten since then. So I found an enormous amount of time.

One of the ways that drinking is bad for a writer—it's bad for a carpenter, too—but it's bad for a writer because it erases your most important quality, your memory. We're the rememberers of the tribe. That's what the tribe hires us for. They say, "You remember. I'm too busy." Later on in life, as drinking began to take over in my thirties, I couldn't write very well about a lot of what happened then without doing research—without having to research my own life.

The first twenty to twenty-five years of my life I remembered very clearly. I used some mechanical devices to trigger memory. For example, I got the *Billboard* lists of hit songs, and I made cassettes of some of those songs. I would play them in the car when I was driving somewhere alone—

a popular song in particular is a great trigger for memory because of its repetition. When a song is a hit, it plays over and over again, and it weaves its way into your life, and [hearing it again helps] you remember everything of that period. A lot of it I remembered myself, and then . . . where I had problems with detail I would call my sister Kathleen, to whom this book is dedicated. She is the only one in the family of seven kids who didn't drink, so she was the one whose memory was the most reliable.

I THINK AN AUTOBIOGRAPHY really should be done when you're seventy-five, when you get as close to the way the story ends as possible. A memoir is a fragment, and in this particular case, it's a fragment geared to a theme. I don't know how the story is going to turn out. I could be hit by the D train tonight, or live another twenty-five years, so who knows?

Elsa Walsh

Elsa Walsh, a reporter who has worked for The Washington Post *and* The New Yorker *magazine, came to* Booknotes *in September 1995 to discuss her experiences writing the book* Divided Lives: The Public and Private Struggles of Three Accomplished Women.

I WRITE ABOUT THREE WOMEN in my book, all of whom are very accomplished. The first is a woman named Meredith Vieira, who is a television correspondent. Her story is the story of a woman who was offered the very top job in her field, [as a correspondent for] *60 Minutes,* just as she gave birth to her very first baby, a child that she had desperately wanted to have but put off having because she wanted to build her career. Her story is one of a career woman who was really struggling to be the very best at her job but at the same time really wanted to be a very good mother. And the conflict was sort of never-ending for her. She eventually left *60 Minutes,* and [my book tells] the story of her trying to sort out how to be both a good mom and a good journalist.

The next woman is a woman named Rachael Worby, classical music conductor, very talented, who performed all over the world, met a man in her early forties that happened to be the governor of West Virginia, fell in love, married him. And her story is really the story of a woman who is searching for an identity within a marriage, one that a lot of women, I think, can relate to.

The third story is about a woman named Alison Estabrook, who is a breast surgeon, who really had to fight a kind of classic old boys' network to become the chief of breast surgery at Columbia [Presbyterian] in New York City, one of the biggest hospitals in the country and one of the best.

I wrote this book because I thought that women weren't telling the truth about their lives, that they were presenting—particularly, prominent women were presenting—a very idealized version of what it was like to be a woman in the '80s and the '90s. That was a picture that didn't at all reflect what I heard other women talking about, my friends talking about, and women I'd interviewed as a journalist. I knew it was a lot tougher out there than the little blips in the road that you heard about when women talked in public . . . presentations.

I interviewed dozens of women around the country. Initially, I thought I was going to cover the whole spectrum of women's lives: demographic, geographic, age, socioeconomic. What I quickly discovered was, in fact, that that wasn't going to work. That [concept involved] too many women, and to travel deep, you couldn't travel broad. So I quickly narrowed it to about a dozen women—and then, after about a year, narrowed [it] to seven, then five, and at the very end, my last draft, narrowed it down to three women, primarily because they were women who were really committed to telling the truth. They were very honest, but also [made good subjects] because they would let me use their real names, and the other women really didn't want their names to be used. I recognized at the end of my book that one of the real powers of it was its honesty, and that I couldn't write a book with a couple of names being used and then a couple of names not being used because that would undermine the whole message.

Writing a book is much harder than I anticipated. It's something that you really have to be committed to doing. But it was also fun. It gave me a good life during the period I took off. I was a reporter at *The Washington Post*. I'm still there, and I'm on leave. It gave me an opportunity to realize that, in fact, you could have both a work life and a day life, which I didn't really have at *The Washington Post*.

My husband [Bob Woodward] has had a remarkable influence on my writing style. I mean, he would probably say, "Oh, you know, not as much as you think." But, in fact, what Bob has really taught me as a journalist and as a thinker is that people tend not to tell the truth initially, when you first interview them. It's not because they're always purposely not telling you the truth, but oftentimes they don't really know what the truth is. I learned that you do need to go back and back and back and back, and peel back those layers. What was really interesting to me in the process of doing this book—I interviewed the women very intensely for two years, but really covered them over about a three-and-a-half-year period—was that oftentimes, things that they didn't even know they believed . . . came to the surface.

When I was out on my book tour I did an interview with a woman at a local NPR [National Public Radio] station who said, you know, "I picked up this book. What am I going to learn from this book? I make $22,000 a year. I'm a single mom." Her child has cerebral palsy. And she said, "I saw myself on every page." The internal conflicts that women feel are the same, whether you're making half a million dollars a year or you're making

$20,000 a year. There are a lot of women like Meredith who feel that they really want to be at home taking care of that baby, but they [also] feel they've got to do their job.

Nora Ephron, who's a writer, wrote me a letter a couple of weeks ago and said, "You know, I think your book is a real Rorschach test for people." I found myself, which I'm sure a lot of other women will, filtering my own life and my own reactions through these women's stories. I think there's a lot of comfort that women get in discovering that, in fact, women who they think so-called "have it all" don't really have it all at all.

I HOPE I AM GOING TO WRITE another book. I've got a couple of different ideas, but I think that one of the problems that you have sometimes after you write a book is you live so much in your own head, and you live so much in your own room, that you do need to get back out as, "I'm a journalist. I'm not a novelist." You do need to get back out and see what people are talking about, what they're thinking, and what's interesting. Because what's interesting to you after you've lived in your own head for several years could be pretty boring to other people.

Neil Sheehan

In September 1988, Neil Sheehan agreed to do C-SPAN's first extended author interview. He spent two and a half hours discussing his book A Bright Shining Lie: John Paul Vann and America in Vietnam. *Viewer response to this interview prompted the launch of our* Booknotes *series.*

THERE WERE A NUMBER OF REASONS for writing *A Bright Shining Lie.* First of all, as a reporter, I never could escape from Vietnam. It was my first assignment in 1962 as a wire service reporter. I spent two years there, then went back to New York, got a job with *The New York Times* and was sent back to Vietnam for a third year, came to Washington in '66 to cover the Pentagon and all the antiwar protests, etc. Then one day I found myself at Arlington [National] Cemetery at the funeral of a friend, John [Paul] Vann, and realized that I wanted to leave something behind other than another magazine article or another newspaper story. And I felt that through him, I could write a book that would really tell a story of the war.

At the time of John Vann's funeral in 1972, I was a reporter for *The New York Times.* I had, the year before, obtained the Pentagon Papers for the *Times,* and the intervening year had been one of turmoil. I was just about to settle back into work as a daily reporter, when I went to this funeral of a man who'd been my friend—because I had gotten to know John, I thought, quite well. As a young reporter in that first year, I'd gone to Vietnam [where we met], and I'd seen him since then. I had not thought he would die in Vietnam. None of us did. He took so many risks that after a while his friends began to think that the odds, as he said, did not apply to him. One day I picked up the paper and there was the news that he was dead.

It took me fifteen years to write the book, and then it spent another year going to press. I was as impetuous as Robert McNamara in thinking, at the beginning, that I could do this work in three to four years—that is, write a biography of John Vann and a history of the war, which is what the book is. It's the two combined. It tells the story of the war through the man, and tells the story of the man through the war.

But it turned out to be a vastly greater task than I had imagined. I also had some setbacks; I had an auto accident in '74 that took a year out of my life. And I had to lecture to earn a living and that sort of thing. But, basically, most of those fifteen years went into that book.

The title of the book, *A Bright Shining Lie,* originated from a remark by John Vann. When he came back here in July of 1963, he said to a U.S. Army historian, "We, too, were, to all the visitors who came out there, among one of the bright, shining lies." So I used that because he had said it and also because, to me, it reflected the ironies—the many, many ironies of the war and the many, many illusions of the war. To me it was a very apt title because the war—our war, our venture in Vietnam—was fueled by many, many illusions. The title is meant to reflect those ironies. It is not a simple title, in other words.

John Paul Vann was the closest we came in Vietnam to an American Lawrence of Arabia. He was an extraordinary character—at least to me he was an extraordinary figure. I met him when I first went there in 1962 as a young reporter on my first assignment for United Press International. He was a lieutenant colonel in the army, and he was the senior adviser to the South Vietnamese infantry division in charge of the northern Mekong Delta. And he left the army after that first year under controversial circumstances. He got into an argument with a commanding general as to whether we were losing the war or winning it. Vann said we were losing, and the commanding general said we were winning. Vann left the army.

Then he went back as a pacification adviser, a civilian, for AID [Agency for International Development] in '65. He finally rose to be the first civilian to command troops in wartime as a general—in a general officer's position. He was killed in June of '72 after the better part of ten years there. I went to his funeral at Arlington because he was a friend. When I walked into the chapel, it was like going to a very strange class reunion. I got there only about ten minutes before it started, and the chapel was already full. This man had pulled—had drawn together—everyone, or almost everyone, who was of significance in that war.

Here was William Westmoreland, who was the chief pallbearer of this former renegade lieutenant colonel who had retired from the army in 1963. Daniel Ellsberg was over on the other side sitting next to the family. Edward Kennedy came in a few minutes before the service began. And I thought of the one Kennedy who had started us into Vietnam, John. And the second one, Bobby, who'd been murdered during the presidential campaign of '68, which was after he turned against the war. And then Edward, who had known John Vann.

I guess my favorite part of the book would be the funeral itself, maybe one reason being that it was the easiest to write. I wrote it back in 1976 and didn't ever change it substantially. I had an enormous struggle to come up with a structure that worked for the rest of the book, that is, to meld biography of this man and the history of the war. My favorite sections within the book, then, vary. The chapter on his childhood and youth is, to me, a favorite section.

I HAD SPENT MY CAREER involved with Vietnam, not because I was obsessed with the war, but because I couldn't get away from the war. As I said, I was sent [home] from Vietnam in '66 to be the Pentagon correspondent in the Washington bureau of the *Times*. Then they sent me to the White House in 1968 for the last six months of [President] Johnson's administration, when Johnson was driven from office by the war. Then came the Pentagon Papers in 1971. I could never get away from this war. It had dominated my newspaper career.

There's a considerable misimpression about the role of the press in Vietnam all along and particularly in this early period. The reporters who went to Vietnam early on, like myself, were not antiwar dissenters. We were very much in favor of American intervention in Vietnam. We had the same set of illusions everyone else did. We felt our duty was to report the truth, so that the president [and the rest of the leadership] would know what was happening in Vietnam . . . and win the war. The advisers in the field, like John Vann, told us, "Look, this isn't working. The policy isn't working. We're losing. And here's why." And we were writing these stories, and they were being denounced.

If you watched . . . *The CBS Evening News,* Walter Cronkite sounds like a Pentagon spokesman in 1965 and 1966. I hope I'm not making Mr. Cronkite angry by saying this. But he's essentially repeating—in an enthusiastic way—what he's being told. It is only after 1968, after Tet '68—the Communist Tet offensive of '68, which disillusioned the general public— that you find an antiwar bias coming into the news media in general. You find figures like Cronkite really questioning the war. That [skepticism] was crushed again by Agnew and Nixon in '69 and '70 with their attacks on the press. You don't find it really asserting itself again until '72, when the country begins to absolutely get fed up with the whole thing—and there's another crisis in Vietnam.

.   .   .

I DID 385 INTERVIEWS FOR THE BOOK. Almost 400. I think I acquired about 670 [audio]tape cassettes. The tapes were extraordinary. They helped me to gather detail and, if you will, to retain detail. The tape recorder is a wonderful memory device. It can be a trap for you if you depend on it, but I didn't depend on it. I used my notes, primarily. But it was a wonderful memory device.

The experience of doing the research deepened my conviction that much of the history of this war had never been written down; that it existed only in the minds of people, in their memories and perhaps, in some cases, in notes and diaries they'd kept, or letters. But in most cases it hadn't been written down. One of my tasks was to capture the history of the war before it disappeared, as people's memories faded, as they moved on. I thought a reporter was uniquely qualified to do that.

I interviewed at such length because it was absolutely necessary. If you look at the [official] documents of Vietnam, you find that [it is unlike] World War II, in [terms of] the thinking of the people at the top. [The documents] tell you what they thought, but they don't tell you the realities of what was happening on the ground—because in Vietnam the people at the top didn't know what was happening on the ground. So I interviewed as extensively as I did for that reason. It was very fruitful. A lot of people were terribly good to me.

I've kept the audiotapes, and they will eventually go to the Library of Congress. Some of them will have to be sealed because there are some private [classified] things there, but they'll all go to the Library of Congress.

I WROTE THIS BOOK for the general reader because I wanted to try to write a book that would help my countrymen in general come to grips with this war. This book is deliberately written with what I hope is a powerful narrative, a driving narrative, that retains suspense and narrative force. I felt that that was the way a reporter ought to write a book. That is the kind of training a journalist gets. I was influenced in my writing very much by Truman Capote's book *In Cold Blood.* He made me realize that you could write a book about real events. That a book could have the narrative drive of a novel and yet could be about real events, which are often much more interesting than those that appear in a novel. Certainly it's true, I think, in the case of Vietnam.

Now it's much more difficult to write that way and to retain truth, and to retain subtlety, and to retain all of the complexity that you want. I was writing a biography of a very complicated character and a history of a very long war. But it's written deliberately with what I hope is narrative drive because I wanted people to read this book. I did not want to write a scholarly book. It would have been easier to do it in scholarly form, with footnotes, etc. There are no footnotes in the book. There are source notes at the back because I wanted to give full documentation for what I had written. But I deliberately kept it to source notes at the back because I did not want anything to get in the reader's way. It made it much more difficult to write. But I hope it was worth it.

Peter Arnett

Peter Arnett, author of Live from the Battlefield: From Vietnam to Baghdad, 35 Years in the World's War Zones, *appeared on* Booknotes *on February 20, 1994. Mr. Arnett, based in Washington, D.C., is a CNN international correspondent. From 1962 to 1975, he reported on the Vietnam War for the Associated Press.*

*W*E WERE SORT OF A JOURNALISTIC cabal thirty years ago. I had the good fortune, early in my career, to encounter those three gentlemen, David Halberstam, Neil Sheehan, and Malcolm Browne. I was a young reporter, enthusiastic, headstrong, poorly trained because Commonwealth journalism was not particularly strong on adequate analysis, on having a very deep factual base for your stories. Australian journalism, in particular in Sydney, it was hit and run to some degree—headline-happy newspapers. In Saigon in 1962, where I was assigned by the Associated Press, Malcolm Browne was my bureau chief. Neil Sheehan and David Halberstam also covered Vietnam in those days. From them I learned of the principles of American journalism—freedom of expression, the need to delve into stories, to question decisions made by government, to present the obverse side of the story. And the intellectual courage of all three men, in addition to their physical courage, impressed me and made an imprint on me that has lasted to this day.

From the time I arrived in Saigon, in the early sixties, to the time that I left—when everyone else left—in the middle of 1975, I made it a point to be in the war theater and out of Saigon 75 to 80 percent of the time. I had the good fortune to be part of the Associated Press bureau in Saigon. We had, at the height of the war, twenty members of that bureau—ten reporters, ten photographers. The duty fell on others to go to the "Five O'Clock Follies" military briefings, to interview General Westmoreland and others, to cover the activities of politicians. I was there early. I had won the right to go and cover the big actions. I felt it was a privilege, really, to be out of Saigon and in the field with the troops. It was a responsibility that I wanted to bear, and I also realized, as the war became more controversial, that my reporting had to be accurate, right on the button, or my career would be destroyed if I was ever wrong, if my assessments were inaccurate.

There was an outspoken American adviser, a colonel called John Paul Vann, who was so angry at the ineptitude of the Vietnamese soldiers he was advising that he talked freely to the press. He talked to Sheehan. He talked to Halberstam. He talked to Browne, and he talked to me. We quoted him at length, and—in writing of this debacle in Vietnam—the story made headlines. It was a quiet weekend in early January of 1963, not much other news. Suddenly there were headlines and the name of John Paul Vann was propelled into the spotlight. There was great concern in Washington about what was going on. We had thrown the spotlight on the war in a negative way, and from then on in, the questions came even more loudly phrased and more vehemently phrased, about whether or not we should be in Vietnam and, if we're there, what the nature of our commitment would be.

John Paul Vann is a man who, for me and for other reporters, was a beacon of realism in Vietnam. John Paul Vann, after the battle at Ap Bac, left the U.S. military service, for various reasons that Sheehan details in his book, but mainly because he was a critic of Vietnam policy. He did return as a civilian adviser and lived in various provinces, and was an acute observer of what was going on. But John Paul Vann, by 1965, had learned his lesson about going public to the media. But he wanted the truth, as he saw it, to come out. So he used reporters such as myself. He leaked information. The leak is a standard ruse in Washington to put out information into the mainstream. John Paul Vann would meet with me. I would ask him questions, and I could always believe he would give me candid assessments of what was going on. Were the South Vietnamese really effective? What was the level of corruption? Should American troops be fighting? In fact, when American troops were committed, what were they doing? What about tactics? What about strategy? And I would look him up several times each year, as the war got bigger and bigger, and more violent and bloody, and more controversial. He was a beacon of realism for me.

When he finally died in 1972, shot down in a helicopter outside Con Tho, by then he had become nationally well known because he basically had become the last hawk left in Vietnam—the last American hawk. In the end he did believe that maybe the war could be won. When he was shot down, I thought I'd lost a friend and a great news source. It was with genuine sorrow that I learned of his death. I'd flown with him a couple of weeks earlier. And I wrote an obituary with Horst Faas, our photographer, about John Paul Vann, and it was probably one of the more emotional stories from Vietnam that I wrote.

In the case of [Daniel] Ellsberg, I would bump into him occasionally in Vietnam. I would learn from these people, but he and John Paul Vann were simply two of the many sources that we used in Vietnam. And as I point out throughout the book, not only in Vietnam but elsewhere my main sources of information were my own two eyes, and my ability to get to where the action was and to make assessments of the nature of the war and its direction from my own experience and observations.

AFTER ALL THESE YEARS of reporting, I decided to do a book because I had an offer from Simon & Schuster that I could not turn down. In addition, there were more questions raised by my [Persian] Gulf [War] coverage than at any time since the Vietnam War, and I felt I had enough under my belt in 1991 to write my life story, in a sense, as a cautionary tale to young correspondents who want to become war correspondents, pointing out the dangers; but also, in a sense, [as] an explanation of why people like me and many others—and you can go to Ernie Pyle [American journalist Ernie Pyle (1900–1945)] or go right back into the earlier years of the United States when reporters were out covering conflicts, or to the young reporters of today, such as Christiane Amanpour [CNN international correspondent]—why we do this sort of thing, and why we're out there covering wars, getting the information back, even though it's dangerous and, in my case, often controversial.

When I started writing this book, I wasn't quite sure where it would go. I started writing about my beginnings, and it was exciting to talk about my early newspaper jobs. It was when I got to the Vietnam section, though, that I felt that the meatiest part of my life began to emerge. The Vietnam War was the defining experience of my life. I spent basically thirteen years there, from '62 to '75. And even though the Gulf coverage was controversial, the real questions that remain in American society and within American journalism and government today revolve around the Vietnam War, the nature of that commitment and the coverage of that conflict. So I had good reason to write in depth about the war. This was encouraged by my editor, Alice Mayhew, at Simon & Schuster in New York. She said, "Write as much as you can about the Vietnam War. People need to know more about what went on. And try to define, in your eyes, what really happened there."

I had never written a book before in my whole life, and I began by writing about the Gulf War. And I wrote seventy or eighty pages, and I sent them to New York. My editor said, "Ah, you know, this is no good. Try again. Start with your youth." And I thought, "Well, I won't start at my youth. I'll start with my forefathers." The family legend went back to the sealers and whalers, the progenitor of the family who arrived in a whaling ship in Riverton [New Zealand] in 1834, came ashore with a group of settlers, and married a local Polynesian woman, and they built the family line 150 years ago.

When I started writing that section, I felt I had found a voice. I started to learn who I was, just this kid from New Zealand who wasn't quite sure where his destiny would take him but knew that he had to go somewhere, that he felt very confined by the little community he was brought up in. Fortunately I was a prolific letter writer when I was a kid. My mother kept everything I ever wrote her, and years ago I'd got all that mail back—so a lot of what I was able to describe in my early years came from my own letters to her a long time ago. I've kept every clipping I ever wrote, and I've kept carbons of every story I ever did in Vietnam. So every quote you see in that book has been published before, and every incident I can verify from my own notes and my own stories.

It was a long and painful experience, digging out all that color and information and anecdote, but [with] each section I finished, I had a degree of satisfaction. I thought, "Well, hey, it's down on record." All the stories I've told in bars, all the stories over dinner, all the times that Halberstam, Browne, and Sheehan and I and Faas have got together and told stories to each other—most of them are there. All the publishable ones are there. And it was a great delight to slowly go through my life.

I will put it this way: I wouldn't have been surprised at any point that death would have taken me—not surprised at all. At the end of my Vietnam experience, I suppose I was surprised that I had not been injured, that I hadn't even sprained an ankle in the war. But anyone who gets close to combat has to know that a bullet will have his name on it, or a piece of metal will have his name on it—and so it should not come as any surprise to those who do the kind of things I do.

I know that the public has mixed feelings about the media today, and questions our mission and our motive, but I think in the field that I specialize in, foreign correspondence, you've got really dedicated people. You've always had them, and they're still there now. And I think they're largely unsung—and I think most of them would prefer it that way—but I am really proud of what they do. And I hope this book, when they read it, they'll grin and say, "Hey, that's what we're doing right now."

William Prochnau

William Prochnau, a former national affairs reporter for The Washington Post, *appeared on* Booknotes *on January 14, 1996, to talk about his book* Once Upon a Distant War. *During his interview, Mr. Prochnau discussed four noted Vietnam correspondents, all previous* Booknotes *guests: Peter Arnett, David Halberstam, Malcolm Browne, and Neil Sheehan.*

THE BOOK WAS an eleven-year project. People have asked me, "When did you come up with the idea of this book?" And I respond, "About five years after I began." It was a real wrestle. The book started out as a totally different idea. I had gone to the Westmoreland-CBS libel trial to cover that as a book, as a flashback to the media and their battles with the military, and vice versa, in Vietnam. But that just sort of fell apart on me. So then it was a question of, actually, many years of trying to wrestle this thing into place and going from what originally had been a book with the working title *The Last Battle* to a book about what is essentially the first battle.

I was always intrigued by these half-dozen or so young war correspondents in their twenties who caused such an uproar in the very early stages of Vietnam, in '61, '62, '63. It was always going to be a couple of chapters in the book, and one day I just said, "Hey, this is your book." So I made two start-overs. At one point, I threw away 70,000 words and started writing again.

This book is set in the Kennedy years, the very first years. It's the early part of Saigon and Vietnam that I think most of us have either forgotten or never really knew because people weren't paying that much attention then. It's before the combat troops went in. It's the time of the advisers. In the book, I take you back to a Saigon that's still French, in a way. It was a fascinating and romantic place. I mean, it's hard to think of any war as being romantic, but these young reporters were. Kennedy at first had decided to run a secret war over there. We were violating the Geneva Convention by adding these advisers supposedly secretly.

Reporters would have none of that. But they also got no cooperation from the government. So they would get their tips on battles and that sort

202 / William Prochnau

of thing in little Saigon bistros along this romantic boulevard, Rue Catinat, which later became known as Tu Do Street. And they would, literally, catch a cab—go out and hail a little French Renault—and take the cab to war, which might be ten miles out of town. Peter Arnett came in about six months later and revolutionized the whole thing. He bought a white Karmann-Ghia and he would watch the helicopters take off and chase them to war. It was that different from the war that we came to know via Hollywood and via our experience.

I went to Vietnam for *The Seattle Times* in 1965. I was still the Washington bureau chief of *The Seattle Times* at that time. *The Washington Post* had an extraordinary reporter over there at that time, Ward Just, and he was their first real full-time correspondent there. The *Post* was still growing. It wasn't the paper that it is now, and they had very few foreign correspondents. Actually, they played a small role in the time period that I write about.

PETER ARNETT WAS THIS BRASH young New Zealander from the bottom of the world, who had no place to go but up. He came into Vietnam, turning his head at the swish of every Asian silk he heard and charging into battle and into combat the way few of the others did and became, of course, probably the preeminent correspondent in Vietnam. But at the time this book covers, he was pretty much still the rawest. He was the rookie among rookies.

In Vietnam, he was twenty-seven, which was actually older than, say, Neil Sheehan. But he had been beating around, almost as an adventurer in Southeast Asia. He had been in Bangkok, and he'd been in Laos. All of these places were very romantic places, at that time, of opium smuggling and intrigues and little mini-revolutions. And he had covered all those and then finally caught on with the AP [Associated Press] and came into Saigon in '62.

David Halberstam I describe as a brilliant brat. He worked for *The New York Times.* The *Times,* at that point, was clearly the dominant and most prestigious newspaper in the world. And television was not what it is today. Television came in occasionally with stringers and part-time correspondents, and you'd see a little blip here and a little blip there about Vietnam, but Halberstam represented the most powerful media institution of all. He was twenty-eight years old. He was a man of great passions, great angers. He felt the government was deluding itself as much as deluding the American people. It drove him to fits. At one point, in one very famous episode, he slammed his fist down on a table in a little cafe in Saigon and said that the commanding general, the American General Harkins, Paul Harkins, should be court-martialed and shot. Everybody in the room turned around and looked at this twenty-eight-year-old making this kind of announcement. He was clearly the driving force.

Malcolm Browne is the wonderful eccentric of the book. He's the guy who, to this day, wears red socks. In Korea as a soldier, when he was serving in the army, he found a couple of cases of red socks on sale at the PX, and he bought them all, and he wore them until he wore those out—and by that time, it had become a habit with him. He wore red socks beneath his combat boots. He wore red socks beneath his tuxedo when he went to accept the Pulitzer [in 1964] for the writing he did in this year.

I think Malcolm was the only one that was thirty in Vietnam. All the rest were in their twenties. And he was thirty exactly. However, he had had very little experience in the media. He had been a chemist and made a couple of very interesting inventions as a chemist. He had invented a rubberized blintz that wouldn't crack when it was frozen. Unfortunately, in one of his experiments, he blew up his laboratory when he was working for a chemical company in New York, and I think that helped propel him into this profession that made him famous.

Neil Sheehan was twenty-five years old. A sometimes brooding, sometimes absolutely wildly humorous and wonderful Irishman who had worked exactly two weeks for UPI [United Press International] in Tokyo before the Saigon correspondent for this second-rate, second-best news agency quit. When the Saigon chief quit, they rustled around in Tokyo to see who could speak French. He spoke French. And suddenly, after two week's experience, he was the Saigon bureau chief for UPI. It was thirty years before he really rid himself of Vietnam after that.

I spent I would say probably twenty to thirty hours taping interviews with Neil, and then a lot of little spot phone calls and checking this and checking that. I did a long profile on Neil for *The Washington Post Magazine* at the time his book *A Bright Shining Lie* came out. The title of the piece was "The Last Prisoner of Vietnam." He pretty much liked the article, I think, but he didn't like the title much. I bumped into Neil a few weeks ago in New York, and he looked at me and smiled and winked and said, "Aha! Here comes the real last prisoner of Vietnam." Because eight years later, I had finally finished my book about the subject.

I surely was a prisoner. I'm not so sure it was of Vietnam. I was a prisoner of the book. You know, you become a bit of a recluse; you pull off. You can't get rid of it even when you do something else. I don't think it was an obsession in a normal sense. It was trying to pull this thing together properly. I am a bit of a perfectionist, and I wanted this to be something. I couldn't grasp it for a long time. My wife says—I think she has the best line. Some people asked if it was an obsession or what caused it. And she said, "Oh, that. Bill was *Apollo 13*. He got out there as far as he could go, everything blew up on him, and then it was just a question of getting back alive." And I did. Like *Apollo 13*, I got back with a few interesting scientific bits and with a hell of a good story, I think. And that's really the obligation of a writer, to bring back a good story.

Malcolm Browne

Veteran war correspondent Malcolm Browne, author of Muddy Boots and
Red Socks: A Reporter's Life, *appeared on* Booknotes *on September 26,
1993. Mr. Browne is now senior science writer for* The New York Times.

W̲ʜᴀᴛ ʟᴇᴅ ᴍᴇ ᴛᴏ ᴡʀɪᴛᴇ this book now, I suppose, is the feeling that
I'm probably nearing the end of my journalistic career and possibly my
life; and while I still remember so much of the contemporary history that
I was privileged to watch, I thought it would be nice to leave some of it
behind. It might be useful to my grandchildren, if no one else. I'm coun-
seling them to take up careers in burglary because I'm not sure that journalism has a future, but in case it does, why, this book is something to
think about.

I̲ ʟɪᴠᴇ ɪɴ Mᴀɴʜᴀᴛᴛᴀɴ in the shadow of the Empire State Building. I was
born and raised in New York City. I think I'd be quite happy to move away
from the city at this point if the opportunity were to present itself, but I
work for *The New York Times,* which is a fond and loving family for me,
and have done so since 1967.

I'm technically called a "senior writer." I have been covering science for
the last decade, but I have interpreted this to mean that, since science covers just about every aspect of human activity from crime to wars and so
forth, I can sort of do what I please—within the limits imposed by my very
indulgent editors, of course. So I went to the Gulf War. I expect probably
to be in Yugoslavia at least for a while because I lived there for four years. I
have [been] very, very lucky. My life is terrific; it affords the greatest possible variety of experience. That, after all, is why I became a journalist.

I was born in Greenwich Village, which used to be sort of the bohemian
and artistic quarter of Manhattan. In later years it's become a rather dangerous area in some respects. Because my mother was a Quaker, I went to a
Quaker school, from kindergarten all the way through twelfth grade, called
Friends Seminary. For me it was wonderful. It happened that that school

had marvelous teachers, and the only objection I had was that they got me so interested in everything that it took me a while to settle down on a career. Then I went to Swarthmore College, also a Quaker school, in Pennsylvania, where I studied chiefly chemistry. After college, I worked as a laboratory chemist for about four years. This was in New York City for a consulting firm. Clients would come to us. I remember that a French chewing-gum company came to us in 1954, I think it was, when [Jacobo] Arbenz [Guzmán], the president of Guatemala, was overthrown in a coup that had been engineered by the CIA. Many Americans didn't realize at the time, I think, that Guatemala was the world's principal source of high-quality chicle, which is one of the ingredients in chewing gum. So part of my job was to devise substitutes for chicle for this French chewing-gum manufacturer and that sort of thing. It was not very high-level science, I must say. When the time came for me to abandon it, I left with no serious regrets.

I was then drafted to go to Korea. The army actually taught me two trades. It first taught me how to drive tanks, both Russian and American, and sent me to Korea. In Korea, shortly after I arrived there, the army, for reasons best known to itself, decided that I would probably do less damage writing for *Pacific Stars and Stripes* and military newspapers than I would driving a tank, and so I was taught the rudiments of journalism . . . by a little army organization that I worked for. I was there for two years, the minimum for a draftee. That was the normal tour of duty for draftees.

After getting out of the army, I worked first for a small newspaper about a hundred miles north of New York City, with a very enlightened view. I conned them into sending me to Cuba just after the revolution. I spent some time in Cuba, where I had a marvelous time getting my feet wet as a correspondent and filing, incidentally, for what had then become UPI. United Press had merged with International News Service to become UPI. I was among the correspondents who were there during the final days [of the revolution in Cuba that ended January 1, 1959]. Soon after that I was hired by the Associated Press, the archrival, sent to Baltimore for about eight or nine months, and then miraculously got the very job that I wanted, bureau chief in Saigon.

I won the Pulitzer Prize but the Pulitzer committee doesn't ever say specifically what for. . . . I think basically it was for coverage of the political events and war as they unfolded in 1963. It was a tempestuous year. Dave Halberstam was my cowinner. We were both awarded the prize for the same reasons. The same year I took photographs of a monk [who immolated himself in the streets of Saigon]. [One of them] was submitted for a Pulitzer in the photo department. The Pulitzer that year, however, was awarded for the famous *Dallas Morning Herald* photograph of Jack Ruby shooting Lee Harvey Oswald. But, at any rate, this series of pictures sort of made me famous overnight because they were simply so horrible—and it happened that I was the only one present to photograph it.

This event revolved around the Buddhist monks who had been conducting antigovernment demonstrations for about a month and a half prior to this incident. They were demanding certain changes in what they regarded as kind of a pro-Catholic bias on the part of the government, which made it difficult for Buddhists to hold high-ranking jobs and all that sort of thing. [These antigovernment demonstrations by the Buddhist monks] were essentially political protests rather than religious ones. They conducted these street demonstrations virtually every day, and I think most of the resident correspondents in Saigon got thoroughly sick of having to get up at five-thirty or six o'clock every morning and march around with the monks when nothing much was happening, but the monks had threatened some time in advance that, unless they got their way in some of these political matters, they would commit some protest suicides, either by disembowelment or burning. I think after a while my brother correspondents simply couldn't take them seriously because nothing ever happened, but as a wire-service man I couldn't afford to take that chance, so I just kept covering them day after day.

On this particular occasion I was the only one there. There was a procession of about 200 or 300 monks, all of them on foot excepting for those at the head who were riding in an old gray Austin. There was a driver in that car, two younger monks, and this old monk named Thich Quang Duc, all of them in orange saffron robes, chanting. [They] marched as far as one of the street corners in Saigon, the corner of Phan Dinh Phung, and all at once the whole group stopped and formed a circle. Thich Quang Duc and his two acolytes got out of the car, walked to the center of this intersection, put down a little cushion. Thich Quang Duc seated himself in the lotus position on this. The two young monks then got out a jerry can of gasoline from the car and poured it all over him, and he lighted a match and set himself afire, and the rest of us watched in horror. I think it was one of the worst things I've ever seen. I've seen a lot of death. Thich Quang Duc, I think, took about eight or ten minutes to die. It was not a rapid death. His face was clearly in agony. The whole region was just pervaded by the smell of burning flesh by the time he finally collapsed and fell over. I was able to, I guess, continue watching just by refusing to perceive what I was seeing and concentrating on the details of making sure that the exposure of my film was correct, that the camera was working properly, and so forth. That's one of the things you do, I think all journalists do, when . . . confronted with something really ghastly. They can sort of defend themselves by working and trying to not be conscious of the thing that they're recording. It was published all over the world. Many morning newspapers in the United States refused to publish it on the grounds that it was just too awful a picture, *The New York Times* among them, by the way. The *Times* did not publish it.

Some interesting surveys were done. I think the Columbia School of Journalism [did] one, [sounding] out newspapers as to whether they had run this photograph or not and why, whichever way they answered, and I think it was sort of interesting. I think possibly today the *Times* would run it, but I do know that it made an impact on the White House. Ambassador Henry Cabot Lodge told me later that while he was being briefed by President Kennedy to take up his new assignment in Saigon, he had noticed this photograph on Kennedy's desk—and that Kennedy had commented that this is really bad, that we were going to have to do something about that regime.

I have to say one thing about my own feelings about the Vietnam War. We who were covering it, I think, never really experienced the kind of polarization that was going on in the American mainland during that period. Americans [on the home front] seem to have been divided up between hawks and doves at that time, and the tone of argument became increasingly strident, while [we who were] in Vietnam saw things quite differently. There was nothing black and white. It was shades of gray. For example, the communists were charging that the American forces were committing atrocities nearly every day, whereas the so-called hawks were charging that the atrocities were all on the other [Communist] side. [But all of us who were there knew.] I knew. I saw plenty of atrocities on both sides. There were no nice guys in Vietnam. It was not a nice-guy war. So to say that I was on one side or another would have been unrealistic, and yet I must say I felt friendlier toward the likes of Martin Luther King and Senators [Ernest] Gruening [D-AK] and [Wayne] Morse [D-OR] [the only two members of the U.S. Senate to oppose the Gulf of Tonkin Resolution] simply because I think that they were better plugged in to the reality of the situation.

Parts of this book were very hard to write because there are things in there that I've never really told anyone. It's like going to a father-confessor or to a psychoanalyst, I suppose. I had never written before on my feelings about leaving Vietnam. After the fall of Saigon, I hadn't written about Vietnam at all. This is the first time I've girded my loins to do it.

Morley Safer

On Sunday, May 6, 1990, 60 Minutes *correspondent Morley Safer appeared on* Booknotes *to talk about* Flashbacks *on Returning to Vietnam. Mr. Safer opened CBS News' Saigon bureau in 1965, serving two tours in Vietnam.*

*I*N VIETNAM, THERE WAS NO FRONT. What front there was, reporters and soldiers had equal access to. I think they [the military establishment] were naïve and expected that we were going to be a kind of cheerleading squad. Well, journalism had changed. Warfare had changed. In the lifetime of the people fighting and reporting on it, this was probably the only war that Americans were engaged in that did not have a clear-cut purpose—if not a strategic purpose, at least have some kind of moral base to it. Whatever moral base that the administration tried to apply to that was so transparent—it was transparently propaganda: "Protecting democracy in Vietnam." That was hardly a moral base for sending half a million men.

I was in my early thirties, which was, relatively speaking, older than a lot of the guys. I think we all felt that we had a great story in our teeth, and we were going with that great story. At the time, at least I can speak for myself, I had no sense of what would happen after Vietnam. I never wanted to be anything more than I was, which was a foreign correspondent. It was a childhood dream come true.

I like to think that those guys who were pretty good reporters in Vietnam, would have been pretty good reporters in covering anything else. No question that it was the central fact of journalism for—really, for ten years, or at least eight of those ten years of the big war, from '65 to '75. I really can't speak for anybody but myself. There's no question that the reporting that I did in Vietnam affected the perception of my bosses at CBS because it was one of those stories where you were on the air every night, sometimes seven days a week. You were covering the most dramatic kind of human tragedy.

War is—and some people get annoyed when I say this—it's about the easiest kind of story to cover, really and truly, because it happens *for* you, generally speaking. I'm talking about the dramatic stuff, the bang-bang stuff, the stuff they want at CBS and NBC and ABC and the AP and every-where else. The dramatic stuff is easy. It happens for you. All you have to do is keep your head down, in one sense, and up in the other—at least up enough to be able to report the story.

And we all got praised. Some of us accepted the praise, and some of us feel that no one came away clean from Vietnam—no one. As every reporter on every story, we exploited the story. And in this case, the story was hun-dreds and hundreds of thousands of deaths. I think we did a good job. I think I did an honest job. But there is a shadow of something over it.

We all want to revisit scenes of lost innocence, or our youth. But in Viet-nam, I think there's so much poignancy involved in so many people's lives about that place. While I was curious—the left-hand side of my brain said, "Aren't you curious?" And the right side said, "I don't care how damn curi-ous you are, it's going to be traumatic for you." So I wanted to go and I didn't want to go [when the Sunday evening news program *60 Minutes* asked Mr. Safer to revisit Vietnam for a segment that aired in March of 1989]. But [the *60 Minutes* producers] made the decision for me. There was no way I was going to say, "No, I—you know—can't stand the trauma. I can't stand the thought of doing it." So I went. And I advise anyone who has even had the mildest case of post-Vietnam blues to go. It's an exhilarat-ing thing to do.

I HONESTLY CAN'T THINK of anything else I'd rather do, week in, year in, year out [than *60 Minutes*]. My reporter's blood still gets up—not as often as it did before, but still enough to make me want to do it. It pays very well. It's a very popular broadcast, which is good. It's popular without speaking down, which is good. I mean, what more does a reporter want?

Writing this book, however, was a bit of a diversion for me. To realize there is another life out there that's very, very satisfying, as writing this book was. And I'd like to do it again, perhaps in a year or two.

Robert Timberg

On August 27, 1995, Robert Timberg, deputy Washington bureau chief for the Baltimore Sun, *came to the program to discuss his book about five Vietnam War figures* The Nightingale's Song.

My BOOK, *The Nightingale's Song,* is a tale of five men—five larger-than-life men: Oliver North, John Poindexter, and [Robert] "Bud" McFarlane, the three men who were caught in the Iran-Contra scandal; Sen. John McCain [R-AZ], who was a prisoner of war for five and a half years in North Vietnam; and James Webb, perhaps one of the marines' most honored heroes of the Vietnam War, a critically acclaimed novelist and later secretary of the navy. This is their story, but what it also allowed me to do was to explore a fault line that I think first appeared within a generation—a generational divide, if you will, a fault line that first appeared during the Vietnam era in the 1960s, and which I believe continues to haunt the nation three decades later. Essentially this fault line is between those who fought the war in Vietnam—and I'm talking about liberals, conservatives, and everyone in between—and those who used money, wit, and connections to avoid serving in that war.

This is the key: all five men are graduates of the U.S. Naval Academy at Annapolis, as I am; all were touched in varying ways by the Vietnam War and its aftermath; and all became well known during the Reagan years. I also, like Oliver North, like James Webb, and like Bud McFarlane, served as a marine officer in Vietnam.

Interestingly, though, when this so-called Watergate of the 1980s broke—the Iran-Contra scandal—I was the White House correspondent for the *Baltimore Sun.* And suddenly, in this strange juxtaposition of circumstances, there were three men—Oliver North, Bud McFarlane, and John Poindexter—at the heart of this scandal, and there I was, as the White House correspondent, with a very similar background. And it was this background, I think, that made me feel I needed to go off and try [to] answer the question of: how the heck did this happen? After a year of covering Iran-Contra, that's what I did.

Everybody spent a lot of time with me. McFarlane, Webb, and John McCain spent a lot of time right from the beginning. John Poindexter wouldn't agree to speak to me until something like three and a half years into it—and Oliver North, probably [didn't participate until I was] four years into my research. At that point, though, he had written two books of his own, and his story was very well known. At the same time, because I didn't think I would get a chance to speak to Poindexter or North, I did a lot of research around them. And so when I got to the point when I could speak to them and explore things with them, at that point I knew a lot. I had spent a week in their hometowns. I had talked to everything that moved. I had talked to everything from Boy Scout leaders to [their] old girlfriends to family to people on the fringe. So I knew a lot when I finally had a chance to actually speak to Poindexter and North. It was very important for me to hear their voices and for their voices to be in the book; particularly Admiral Poindexter, who was perhaps the least known or, least known with any sort of depth and perspective. That was really important to me, and it would have been a major loss if Admiral Poindexter hadn't taken time to talk to me.

But at no place in this book do you hear my story. I'm a reporter. I'm a journalist. And it now looks like I'm an author. But this isn't my story. My story is of interest to close friends and family, and a few have heard it. But this is the story [of these five men] and it's a better story.

Even the people who were in the rear echelons in Vietnam saw something approaching combat. I mean, no place was safe. We were always out [in the fields], but we weren't always, on a daily basis, under fire. I was wounded over there. I came home and I had a few bad years, and I then said it's time for me to go on with my life. And I did. I mean, I put Vietnam very much off to the side. I think in a way, I feel particularly close to Senator McCain, who said, "Whatever happened, it's over. And whatever I'm going to be—good, bad, whatever—whatever destiny has in store for me, I'm going to make it happen, Vietnam or no Vietnam." And I essentially moved on from there.

I BECAME A JOURNALIST almost by throwing a dart. There comes a time sometimes when you just have to do something, and it doesn't much matter what it is. And I was at a stage in my life where I just needed to do something. I decided I was going to go to journalism school, and I went and got a master's in journalism at Stanford. And I became a reporter. And I went from there. I found out I was good at it. But I had no reason to really think that at the time. All I knew was I had to do something.

If I had done this book in 1973, '74, '75, it would be junk. I needed to get away from this. I needed to get it way, way out of my life, and go on and do what I needed to do. And I never, frankly, had a compelling need to write this book until twenty years later—when suddenly things happened, and I could provide [the] journalistic distance [needed so that] I could do something that I thought was worthy and not just a complaint.

People have said to me, "This must have been really hard for you, to go through this again, to go back through all of this." And the fact of the matter is, it was hard but it wasn't hard for that reason. It was hard because it was a hard book to research and write. And whatever frustration or anger that I felt, it was the anger and frustration of a journalist, because sometimes I thought this story wasn't coming together. It was just journalistic craziness, if you will.

I worked on it for seven years. I had a one-year leave of absence that lasted five and a half years. I figured I'd be finished in two years. It wound up taking me seven. And so for five and a half years, I was doing nothing but this book, and then for a year and a half I was doing a full-time job and this book.

A lot of what I wrote is new. I probably did 400 interviews for this book, beyond the reading of the documents. This book is not a recycling of old clips. This is original research. And I was glad to give the time because the story demanded it and, you know, good reporters follow the story to the end.

Back when I started the book, I was working in [the basement of] . . . my house in Bethesda, Maryland, a place that no one dare venture anymore because there are files everywhere. I began to think of myself as the troll of Bethesda. I'd just get up in the morning, go down to the basement. If I had to do interviews, I did that, but my life was pretty much it.

Initially I had an advance from my publisher, Simon & Schuster, and that was going to be terrific if it took me, as was my original plan, a year where I would just do my research and then I would try [to] write the book at night. Well, it became clear fairly quickly that that wasn't going to happen. So then I applied for and received a fellowship called a Woodrow Wilson fellowship at the Woodrow Wilson International Center for Scholars here in Washington [D.C.]. [Originally,] that was going to be for ten months—and then it was extended to twenty-two months, and that helped. The [fellowship] included a stipend. If you're ever going to write a book, the Woodrow Wilson center in Washington is the place to do it, because you have an enormous support structure, everything from notepads to research assistants to Xeroxing, and they ask virtually nothing in return, other than that you do something of value.

The thing that was hardest for me [was that] when I started this, I said, "This book's going to start at Annapolis, and I'm going to look at the early years of these men . . . [using] flashbacks." Well, as I started my research, I realized just how powerful their early years had been, and for [each of the] five men I wrote a chapter about his childhood, a chapter about the pre-Annapolis years. And they were some of the most colorful chapters in the book, and they were among my favorites.

NEIL SHEEHAN IS A GREAT REPORTER and I'm a good reporter. And sometimes when you get something that makes you say, "God, this is a good story"—there's just nothing that stops you until somebody shoots you or you finish. Vietnam is—actually, Ben Wattenberg quoted it to me, but I think it may have been Daniel Yankelovich, the pollster, who used the term. He said, "Vietnam is an undigested lump." For those of us who went, we've never quite come to grips with what we found [out about ourselves] when we got home. Now, that doesn't mean that we were immobilized by it, that our lives couldn't go on.

This book is a book about survivors. This is about people who said, "OK. That happened and there are a lot of parts about it I don't like, but I'm not going to join the unemployment lines. I'm not going to, say, turn against the war and say I shouldn't have gone." These people—McCain, Poindexter, North, Webb, McFarlane—they somehow put whatever anger, frustration, hostility that they felt aside and went on with their lives. And they have been very successful lives—until Iran-Contra popped, and it became evident that McFarlane, North, and Poindexter, at least, had failed finally to put this aside—[or] as far aside as perhaps they should have. Essentially, it came out of the wings and blindsided them. That's my sense.

David Maraniss

David Maraniss, a national reporter for The Washington Post, *won a Pulitzer Prize in 1993 for his coverage of Bill Clinton's 1992 presidential campaign. He came to* Booknotes *on May 7, 1995, to talk about his biography of President Clinton,* First in His Class.

To try to find out about what Bill Clinton's early childhood was like, I moved to Hope, Arkansas, where he was born, and spent a few weeks there interviewing dozens of people who knew the family. I talked to a lot of his aunts and got a lot of the letters of that era and tried to re-create what it was like in that small town in the South during the late 1940s and the early 1950s. Then I moved up to Hot Springs, where his stepfather was from, and stayed in the same hotel that Al Capone used to hang out in, in the Arlington Hotel up there, and tried to talk to as many women of [Clinton's] mother's generation, many of whom also dealt with the same problems that she did in terms of being treated as equals with men and being abused by their husbands. So I spent a lot of time trying to re-create that generation.

I would like to know how much violence and alcoholism President Clinton saw as he was growing up. I think he saw a lot. That's why I said I would have liked to have been there during that era. That's not to say that every day in that household was a terror or that it was terrifying. I know, from re-creating Bill Clinton's life through his letters and conversations with some of his friends, that it did not dominate the exterior of his life. His friends didn't even know that his stepfather was an alcoholic or abusing his mother, but I think that there were many occasions when it got pretty nasty inside that house. And I think that's what drove him in a lot of ways.

I first interviewed Bill Clinton in December of 1991. I interviewed him six times in long interviews during the campaign. I wrote a number of longer stories about Bill Clinton and his life and career. The day I started writing a book, I contacted his press people, who all knew me, and said, "I'm doing a biography." From that day until the day the book was published, I tried to get interviews with him, and he denied all of my requests.

I'm not always satisfied with the [reasons I was given] for being turned down. I think that, largely, the reason . . . was that Bill Clinton is a person much more comfortable with the present and the future than with his own past. I was told, actually by Hillary [Rodham Clinton], his wife, that their lawyers recommended against him talking to me. I could only surmise that one of those reasons was monetary, that they thought it might affect their own future memoirs.

The reason why I decided to write a book about a sitting president is that I thought it was a great story. That was really the underlying motivation—that whatever anyone thinks of Bill Clinton's presidency or his ideology, that his life is a great American story. And it's a narrative that I thought revealed a lot about ambition, the clash between ambition and idealism, coming out of nowhere, that part of America, dealing with a troubled family, rising out of Arkansas from the point where he shook John Kennedy's hand in 1963, to actually living in the White House himself. I mean, that's just a great story. The other thing that intrigued me was that I am of his generation. I'm three years younger than Bill Clinton, but I thought I saw him and Hillary as a means of writing a book about the postwar baby boom generation, using them as the main characters.

The hardest thing was to decide in my own mind what I felt about this guy. I'd go back and forth violently because there were chapters in his life where I liked him and chapters where I didn't. So I would beat myself up, saying, make up your mind; you've got to decide. Then I realized that he is a dual person and that I had it right.

Lou Cannon

In 1991, Booknotes spent two hours with the author Lou Cannon, the first on May 12 and the second on May 19, to discuss President Reagan: The Role of a Lifetime. *Mr. Cannon is a reporter for* The Washington Post *based in California.*

THIS IS THE THIRD BOOK I've written about Ronald Reagan. I always said I was going to keep writing about Reagan till I got it right. I don't know whether I did, but I tried.

The first book on Reagan was written in '68. I guess it was published in '69. It was called *Ronnie and Jesse: A Political Odyssey.* It was about Reagan and Jesse Unruh, this larger-than-life character, unfortunately now dead. Jesse "Big Daddy" Unruh was the most powerful Democrat in California.

The second book I wrote about Reagan was when I was working for *The Washington Post* and that was right after he became president. It was published in 1982. It was called *Reagan,* a title that a friend of mine in the White House said, "Good. It's so simple, even he'll remember it." There was no subtitle either.

This book is the last one. I have been working on it since the day after he left the presidency. I was one of the small cadre of correspondents who flew out with him to California—[I] got off the plane, and spent the next two years on the book. Actually, I had been doing interviews on this book going back into the eighties. Different groups of people, for instance, would leave the White House at the end of the first term. I tried to interview them then because I knew that after four or five years, they would remember things differently. So I had done a lot of the interviewing before, but I actually wrote it over a two-year period. I started writing in June of '89, and I guess I finished November of last year [1990].

I've been interested in journalism all my life. When I was a kid, I remember we played football games on the farm. I must have been all of seven or eight, and I'd go and I'd write a story of the game. I've always wanted to be a reporter. I don't know why. I was editor of my high school paper. I started out as a sportswriter. I used to write sports for the local paper in Reno, Nevada, when I was still in high school.

I was actually drafted during the Korean War. I went into the army. I never got to Korea, although I volunteered for it, but probably very fortunately for me I didn't get there. Then when I got out of the army, I sort of bummed around. I drove a truck for a while. I did different things. I worked in a political campaign, but I really had this view that I ought to be a reporter and that I ought to write books. I've always wanted to do that, and I went into some little paper in Northern California. They gave me a story test. Remember there used to be those things? The facts were in scrambled order. I was able to put them into good order, and since I didn't have much experience, they could hire me very cheaply. That was always a great premium at newspapers in those days, and so I got the job.

I went to work for the *San Jose Mercury-News* after working for two or three other papers in the early 1960s. I stayed there, really, until I came to Washington in 1969. I came back to Washington for what was then Ridder Publications. They merged several years later with the Knight newspaper organization. Knight-Ridder is now one of the largest newspaper chains in the United States.

I think that one of the duties of a biographer is to examine the contemporaneous record. Part of that record is in the books, the so-called kiss-and-tell books. I like Ken Adelman, who wrote a very good book about [the Reagan] administration. I like his phrase of "kick and tell" even better. There are also books by David Stockman and by Don Regan. What you see, running through these kiss-and-tell books, is sort of a disenchantment with Reagan, I think partly because the people involved never really felt that he took to them. Somebody asked me just the other day, did I like Reagan? I said, "Yes, I liked him well enough." This person knows Reagan very well and said, "I don't dislike him, but to like somebody, he has to be a person who extends to you some kind of friendship." Reagan didn't do that. He was the friend of the American people. He had a bond with the people. But up close, if you formed an attachment to Reagan, it was often one way. That was harder for some of these personalities.

It's often said that they wrote all these books just because there's so much money, that they got such huge sums. I'm sure that has something to do with it in the case of some of the books, but I don't think that that's the real story. I think the real story is that they didn't feel the kind of loyalty that you often see. People like Lyndon Johnson, Richard Nixon, Jimmy Carter produced a kind of a personal loyalty, personal attachment of people that, with some conspicuous exceptions, didn't last in the Reagan case.

There's no last word on a president. Even the presidents who are most written about—Abraham Lincoln, Franklin Roosevelt—a new book will come out almost every year. So, if anybody is so full of self-delusion that they think that they're going to do the last word on any subject, they should do something other than be a biographer or historian. That doesn't bother me or even really interest me.

I'm sure that fifty years from now there's going to be a whole different look at Reagan and everybody else, but I hope that this book, because it has the living recollections of people when they were close to this process, will be of help to those historians who are writing long after I am dead, let alone these people who are far older than me who worked for Ronald Reagan.

RONALD REAGAN CALLED ME after my mother died. My mother had been sick a long time before she died. When he called me, I thought, as you do, that I had been prepared for her death, and like most of us, I wasn't. I said that to him. I thanked him for calling me and I said, "I thought I was prepared for this." He said, "You're never prepared for the death of your mother." Now, Ronald Reagan's mother is the most important person to him. He's influenced by his mother. But I thought that was such a wise, comforting thing to say. He may have called me because somebody told him to call me and his opening words may have been a script, but he didn't know what I was going to say. That wasn't from a script. That was from his heart, and it was also wise. But that's not part of an interview. That's kind of a personal thing.

I guess the favorite moment that I ever had in an interview was also personal, but it was personal about him. I had never heard this story. It was an interview for this book. We were talking about his father, and Ronald Reagan, like a lot of us, romanticizes his boyhood. It's ideal. Everything was wonderful. But he was talking about the alcoholism, his dad's drinking. By this time Reagan was a young man working as a sports announcer in Des Moines [Iowa], I think, and his father apparently had been drinking kind of heavily. His mother had visited him regularly. Reagan wrote him a letter. This is what Reagan told me. He wrote his father a letter and said that he wanted him to stop drinking because he, Ronald Reagan, had this problem, too. Reagan said this was a lie. By the way, in all the time that I knew Reagan, he had this marvelous ability to tell something that is factually not true and make himself believe it's the truth, but this was the only time that I had personal experience where Ronald Reagan said, "Yes, I told a lie."

I put this in a footnote: My father was named Jack, as was Reagan's father; he was an Irish American, as was Reagan's father. I think, since I pay a lot of attention to the influence that this had on Reagan, it seemed to me that a biographer owes it to his readers to say, "Hey, maybe I'm interested in this because I had a similar circumstance." Actually, I've always thought it gave me some empathy to Reagan, and maybe it did. It's sort of a truth-in-advertising label. I think that people should know where their biographers or where their reporters are coming from.

Stanley Karnow

Journalist Stanley Karnow began his professional career as a correspondent for Time *magazine in 1950. On May 28, 1989, he appeared on* Booknotes *to talk about the book* In Our Image: America's Empire in the Philippines. *During the program, Mr. Karnow also discussed his 1983 book,* Vietnam: A History.

I CONSIDER MYSELF to be a journalist rather than a writer—if there's perhaps a conflict in those terms. But I've really spent all my life, professional and nonprofessional, in the field of journalism. The difference between being a journalist and a writer is, well, let's put it this way: journalists are writers, but not all writers are journalists. I use the distinction because the word "journalism" contains the French word *jour,* which means day, and there is a temporal quality to journalism as opposed to literature or poetry. You really are under pressure as a journalist. That same pressure exists, I discovered, if you're working for a wire service or you're working for a daily newspaper or you're working for a weekly magazine or a monthly magazine or even if you're writing books. Books take a long time, but still you have a deadline. You want to accomplish it; you want to finish it within a time framework. I'm not saying that poets don't try to finish their poems with a certain deadline.

The other aspect of journalism is that it is nonfiction. It may be vivid, it may read like fiction, and I try in my histories or current affairs books to make it vivid and to bring the journalist's instruments and tools to it— depicting things as if they are actually happening under my very eyes, even though they may have happened a hundred years ago. This requires a lot of research. I go back and read old newspapers, or, if I can, interview people who have recollections. I try to get that kinetic, live quality into it because I believe that history is made by people. It is not made by cosmic forces. It's not ordained or preordained. I want to tell it in terms of people.

I started out as a sportswriter in high school. I was the sports editor of the paper. I don't pay much attention to sports anymore, but that was a glamorous thing to do when you were a high school kid. You went to all the football games, and the cheerleaders got to know you, and it was a nice avocation [for] a high school student. Later in college as an editor of the paper, I mostly concentrated on editorials but I also liked to write light feature stuff. In those days my inspiration was *The New Yorker* magazine, which was funny and lively. I think it's gotten a bit ponderous in recent years. So I got launched, if you want, or I launched myself in that and, like everybody getting out of college, went out to look for a job and had a very odd way of finding a professional job. I went over to Paris after I graduated from college. I went over there for the summer, liked it, was intrigued and captivated by it, and stayed on. Fortunately, in those days we had the GI Bill. I had been in the army during the Second World War so I had something like three or four years of GI Bill coming to me. Those were the days when the dollar was strong and, believe it or not, you could actually live in Paris on a hundred dollars a month. Today, it barely pays for lunch. So I kind of hung out.

I enrolled in school in order to get my GI Bill, did go to classes, did get the required diplomas and so forth, which are really valueless in a way, but by some chance I got hired by *Time* magazine, first as a spear carrier and a general factotum. I spoke French by this stage and eventually became a correspondent for *Time,* and that was the beginning of my professional career back in 1950.

The idea of the television series on the Vietnam book was proposed to me by Lawrence K. Grossman, who was then the president of [the] Public Broadcasting [System], in a rather nice setting. We were lying on the beach in Nantucket, the summer of 1977, I think it was. And he said, "What about doing a television series on Vietnam?" I had spent a lot of time in Vietnam, longer than I like to recall, in fact.

I started going to Vietnam in the fifties, so I was there from the fifties— and then for the television series and the book I went back in the early 1980s, so I clocked about twenty-five years [going] in and out of Vietnam. At any rate, Grossman proposed the television series. I thought it was a very good idea, and I thought it was very farsighted of him at that particular time. This was two years after the fall of Saigon to the communists. The American public was thoroughly uninterested in the subject, and it took us seven years to do it. By the time [the series] did come out, I think attitudes had changed. I like to think that maybe [the series] contributed . . . to changing the attitudes, but by that time the Vietnam [Veterans] Memorial was going up in Washington [D.C.]. Veterans were getting a new look. So, we were part of this whole new interest in the Vietnam story, which of course has proliferated and expanded since then. At the very beginning, when the idea of doing a television series attracted me, I also began to think that I wanted to do a book that went with it as a companion. I actually did the book [on Vietnam] with the television series. It wasn't as if I wrote the book and then the series was derived from the book. I [would] do my interviews or do my writing for the series, then [go] back and work on the book for a while. The research of one helped the other. So I was doing them in tandem, which was quite a load to carry.

I felt that a television series based on my earlier book, *Vietnam: A History,* could do a lot of things in telling a story. You can't really dramatize certain events in words in the same way you could do it on the screen. The old Chinese adage about a picture being worth a thousand words is modest. I think a good picture might be worth a whole chapter in a book, and certain very dramatic events are just almost impossible to capture in words. But television has its limitations. It's very hard in an ongoing documentary to analyze things. Television requires images and visuals; it requires photographs or film. For example, if you were trying to deal with a diplomatic negotiation, what have you got on television? What have you got to deal with? Usually, you can't get into the room to listen to people bargaining, so you either have the opening shot that the negotiators allow the television cameras to do or you get pictures of people getting in and out of cars. None of that's very satisfactory. There's a limited attention span, I think, on the part of the viewer, for an analysis of what's going on inside that room, but you can do that in a book.

The Vietnam book was published in late '83. It's still on the shelves. It's being used in schools along with the television series. I must say that I get a great sense of satisfaction and gratification when some high school student or college student calls me up and in effect asks me to do his term paper for him. My wife hands me the phone. She says, "Here's another call from Iowa State," or the University of Florida, and there's some college sophomore there who's taking a course on Vietnam and wants to ask me some questions. If [they] were a little more enterprising, they could probably find the answers in the book. But maybe they just want to talk on the phone, bounce some ideas, and that's very good. I get a lot of satisfaction out of that.

I get a lot of letters from veterans, from Vietnamese refugees or immigrants now living in this country, so you get some sense that you've put something into the world that's still there, that wasn't one of those quickie sensations that came and went. So I find that gives me some sense of achievement. I find the same thing if I go out lecturing, which I do as often as I can, at universities. What is interesting about Vietnam is that you have a whole generation of Americans who lived through it, either veterans of the war, GIs—or "grunts" as we called them. You have the Americans of that generation who lived at home, either students who were protesting against the war, people who were supporting it, and then you have a whole generation of Americans who weren't even born when we got involved. There's an intense interest in Vietnam in the universities and even in the high schools, so that all contributes to this continuing interest in the subject. I do feel that it does give me some role to play in dealing with the subject.

IN ORDER TO SURVIVE WRITING A BOOK, you want to get a handsome advance, if you can, although it's not a way to make money. Working on these things, you could be a teller in a bank and probably make more money than you make writing, even though a lot of people think I became a multimillionaire because the Vietnam book sold remarkably well. I was doing other things on the side. I was doing some other writing and editing, and I'd saved some money, and I was getting paid in a modest way by the television project as well, so while I wasn't getting rich, it was all right. It was comfortable. I don't work for money. I like to earn money. Dr. Johnson once said, "Nobody but a blockhead writes except for money," but there are other satisfactions, I think, in writing. If you looked at the average [for] writers across the country, you'd probably find that the mean income is something like $6,000 a year. So while you read about these glitzy contracts, of people getting multimillion-dollar advances, you also have to bear in mind that there are a lot of writers who are struggling.

Every step of the way, I feel some sense of satisfaction in writing a book. First, you organize. You plan what you're going to do, and you know perfectly well as you start it, when you've got a grasp of the subject—this is before you've even done the research—you have a kind of road map of where you want to go. That's very important. You may not follow that outline. I think it's very important to do a good job of outlining what you want to do, even if you throw it away. Usually, you don't follow it exactly. When I was a young reporter in Paris, I interviewed the great abstract painter Georges Braque, who said to me, "If I knew what was going to come out on the canvas, I wouldn't bother to paint it, because things develop as you go along." So that first sense of satisfaction is getting an idea of where you're going. Then you start researching, and researching is a little bit like panning for gold. You can just lie by that stream looking for those nuggets to come along, and every once in a while something does come along, and that gives you a great sense of satisfaction.

Interviewing people is fun in many ways, especially if you have time to do it, and you can let it spread out a bit, and you can help the person you're interviewing get over that initial nervousness, especially if you're doing it jointly on camera. Many of the interviews I did in the book were being done [simultaneously] on camera, or sometimes I would do a pre-interview to determine what I was going to ask them when we taped them on camera. That takes time. Then you begin to hear those things, not that you're trying to direct the person to say something, but maybe you're getting something original from this person or some new anecdote that hasn't been told before. Then you plunge into archives and start digging out all kinds of things, and there again you're down there with your helmet light on in that coal mine chipping away or that gold mine looking for material. Then you get it all and—pardon me if I mix my metaphor—you're a bit like a sculptor with this enormous piece of granite, and then you've got to chip away at that granite in order to mold that sculpture. It is a very hard process.

I don't know any writer who thinks that writing is fun. It's hard work, and the way I do it is just as if I'm doing any other job. I get up in the morning and I have breakfast and read the newspapers and shave and shower and get dressed. But [then] I go down in my cellar, where I have my study, and work. I try to get to my machine by eight or nine o'clock in the morning. Sometimes I'll run out of steam in the afternoon, but sometimes I'll go until midnight. But you have to treat it as a job; you have to be disciplined. You don't sit around waiting for inspiration. If you do, you're never going to get anything done because it's much more fun taking the dog out for a walk along the canal than sitting down there and writing. But the thing that keeps you going, I think, is that you have these peaks in which you really do begin to feel that you're getting the story told and this chapter looks pretty good. Very often it looks good, and you put it aside; you look at it two weeks later and it looks terrible. So you go back and work on it again. Or maybe your editor doesn't like it very much, or only partly likes it.

So what I'm trying to say is that there are troughs when you're not feeling like working. The best thing to do in those moments is just to get up and take a walk. When you get the whole thing finished, there is that great sense of satisfaction of having completed it and kept it within some sort of reasonable bounds. I write books for the public. I'm not an academic, and I don't want to throw twenty-four volumes at people. I assure you that I had enough material to do a twenty-four-volume account of this story, but I wanted to keep it within, obviously, reasonable bounds. Then you wait, and you're in limbo until the reviews start coming out. With this book, *In Our Image,* I must say that I've been extremely fortunate. I've had much better reviews than I would have dreamed of having. *The New York Times, The Washington Post,* the *Boston Globe* have all been very kind.

Then again, because you put in so much time, you cock your ear for the ring of the cash register to see whether the book is going to be a good seller or best-seller. I think that in my own mind I'm much more interested in the longevity of the book, what the publishers call the shelf life of the book, than I am in the immediate impact. I'm not going to dissimulate and say I don't like to sell books—I think every writer does—but I really hope that the book is around for a long time.

Richard Ben Cramer

On July 26, 1992, journalist and author Richard Ben Cramer came to Booknotes *to discuss* What It Takes: The Way to the White House, *personal portraits of the 1988 presidential candidates.*

*T*HIS BOOK IS 1,047 PAGES at last count. The size of the book wasn't really a problem [with the publisher] once you've got them involved with the idea. It was my idea from the first to try to write a real human story about these guys [the 1988 presidential candidates] and to try to let people connect with them in a visceral way so that they felt with them and exulted with them, and felt their tragedy and their triumphs. So by the time I started feeding the manuscript into the publisher, everybody was on board and they really weren't too worried about the length.

The hard part was in the beginning, trying to sell a book like this. As I'm sure your viewers know, most books are signed up and contracted for before they are written. And in this case, I had to go to a publisher, Random House, and tell them, "Well, look, I don't have chapter 1 yet and I don't have an outline for you. I can't tell you who the characters will be yet. I can't tell you what the story will be, but you just give me all this money and I'll see you in four or five years. Don't worry, it'll be great." So once you sell a book [in this way], after that, convincing them about the length is just a walk in the park.

There were months at a time when I thought it might finish me and that it would not emerge as a book, that it would never finish itself and come to any roundness or fullness as a story. But I never had the temptation to stop trying because it was driving me. I didn't have to. It wasn't something that I had to force myself to do at all.

While working on the book, I had every stress-related illness that can be listed in a medical textbook. Along the way, I thought I had a heart attack, liver cancer, and phlebitis. My back was so bad at one time that I had to work lying down. I actually had a little "space pen." It's a by-product of the NASA years, and it writes upside down. This brilliant man developed a pen that would write in weightless, zero gravity, so that's what I used. I was lying there on my back with a paper over my head. I had to do this for a couple of weeks on and off.

I did tape some of the interviews that I conducted for the book. After the book was published, we [my wife and I] actually had a very happy ceremonial pitching-out of all of the things we had lived with—boxes and boxes of newspapers, 300 or 400 notebooks, and hundreds of audiotapes. We tossed them out. Got them out. You can have no idea how necessary, psychically, it was to rid the house of the book. It had come to dinner six years ago and it had never left.

David Hackworth

An early Booknotes *guest, retired army colonel David Hackworth appeared on May 7, 1989, to discuss* About Face: The Odyssey of an American Warrior, *written with Julie Sherman. He is now a military writer for* Newsweek *magazine.*

I HAD A LOT OF PEOPLE come to me during my eighteen years of rumination when I thought about writing this book. A lot of potential coauthors came to me to write it with me or for me, and I waited for the right one. And Julie Sherman came along, and after looking at her work and talking to her I concluded that what I really needed was a woman's feel, a woman's touch. War is about men and men take life, but the horrible end result about war is it takes the life of young men, in the main. It's the sons and the husbands of women. Women give life. And I felt that if we could discuss war and discuss it with that man's passion from my own experience but with a sensitivity and the depth and feeling of a woman, we could tell the complete story.

During the eighteen years since I left the army, I seriously considered writing this book probably a half-dozen times. But I wanted also to ensure that I had my head together. I wanted the message that I was going to give to be clear and objective, and without bitterness and vindictiveness and the need to even the score.

In 1971, I said to the nation that Vietnam was a bad war. I said it from my heart, from the experiences of almost six years in Vietnam. I said that it was a bad war. We were losing it. We were bleeding unnecessarily. There was just simply no way we were going to win it, and we should get out now. What I didn't realize was that when you sound off against a big institution like the U.S. Army and say they are all wrong—I didn't realize what happened to whistle-blowers. I got thumped about the head and shoulders in a very severe way. That created the bitterness that caused me to leave America, leave my roots, and go to Australia and be angry for a long time.

But no one listened. No general came down and said, "Gee, how did you guys do this? How did these untrained troopers win battles like this time and time again?" Because we didn't want to learn. The government, the army specifically, has no real deep reflection. They just don't look at the past to learn from it or to grow from it. This frustration built up and caused me to sound off.

As a little kid, when I was fifteen, I was in Italy and General Eisenhower, who is a five-star general, stopped in front of me, and probably because I was just a little fifteen-year-old kid, he said, "Well, how do you like it here?" So I said, "Oh, just fine, General." And he said, "How's the chow?" You know, the normal thing that a general is going to ask a little boy. And I said, "Oh, it's terrible. We eat Spam every day." Then he went down the line and asked, "Why do these guys eat Spam every day?" It went from the lieutenant general to the major general down to the little major, and the reply came bubbling up, "Oh, the depot from the war is filled with Spam. We've got to get rid of it." So Ike said, "Stop it! Give these guys fresh food."

From that point forward, as long as I was a soldier, I sounded off. If I saw something wrong I told them. When I look back I realize that when I sounded off in '71, I tried it through the system. I told everybody in the army that would listen to me. When I realized that wasn't going to happen, I went to the people via the media and told them the truth of what was happening in Vietnam.

I entered the army when I was fifteen. You could do that if you lied. And I had been in the merchant marines for a year before, so I had merchant papers from my experience in the Pacific. I used those documents to get me in the army. I was an orphan, so the army became a home for me. It became my family. It was something I loved very much. I was very protective towards this institution. I always loved my soldiers because I was a soldier and I wanted to keep them alive. I believed in winning battles and fighting wars. I was a warrior but not at the expense of my men. I think it was also that great love for my soldiers that made me stand up and shout, "Stop the madness."

On the battlefield, you're frightened all the time. You live with it. The beauty of being a leader, of being a squad leader, a platoon sergeant, a company commander, and so on, was that you were busy. You were looking after your troops—shepherding your herd, so to speak. You were calling in artillery fire, bringing in air, maneuvering your unit, talking on the radio, and you simply didn't have time to be as concerned as that warrior is who's just waiting behind a wall for someone to say, "Let's get up and go." So that's the real problem. Another problem is the brighter you are, the more imagination you have and the more things your brain can conjure up that can happen to you. So if you're not too clever, you might make it through the night without a lot of stress. I think that one of the things from Vietnam with this Vietnam stress syndrome is that those kids endured something that the American soldier in the history of our country, from 1776 forward, didn't experience in battle. In Vietnam, it was that minute-to-minute experience of walking through a field laced with booby traps that were carefully camouflaged. You know 50 percent of all casualties in Vietnam came from mines and booby traps. You were lucky to survive for the 365 days our infantry fought in Vietnam—that would sear your mind. And I think that that is one of the causes of disturbances among the men that fought in Vietnam.

THE BOOK TOOK FIVE YEARS. Five long years. What Julie and I first did was work out a game plan. We decided to tape every experience that I had, and before the taping—audiotaping—we took all of the documents, the notebooks, the papers, the things I had saved throughout my twenty-five-year military experience, and we compartmentalized them into eighteen chapters that we envisioned. Maybe it was a notebook, a little small book I'd carried in Korea, which had only six or seven lines in it, or a letter from a friend, or a letter that I had sent home that was saved by my brother or my sister-in-law or someone. Once we'd organized those eighteen boxes of information, we went through them and recorded those experiences. That became a transcript of about fifty-seven tapes' worth. Julie went through that and set out what the story was. Then she would write a chapter and give me the chapter. I would rewrite the chapter—while she was doing [chapter] 2, I would be doing [chapter] 1. From that, names would fall out. We only started with about three or four names, and we ended up with almost 400 people who contributed to the book, which made the book alive—in that we were drawing on the experiences, on the memories, of a lot of other warriors. By the end of the book, it was like I was driving this truck and there were 300-odd guys in the back of the truck whose voices we could use. It added to the wealth and the knowledge that's contained in the book. And to the accuracy, too, because your memory is a funny thing. On the battlefield, you can only see over the sights of your rifle, so you don't see the big picture. We wanted to tell the big picture as best we could.

So then these chapters would go back and forth, and we'd integrate the input from the letters from the people that we were tracking down, and we'd crank their stuff into it. Then the thing would be rewritten and rewritten and rewritten. Some chapters were written twenty times. So that put a big strain on Julie and me. Julie's a screenwriter, not a book writer, and there's a thing in her trade called "abandon." You just get so much information—and in my case, I was so passionate about the subject because I felt the book would cause people to learn, the book would cause people not to make those horrible mistakes again. So I wanted to get in every little detail. For example, one chapter called "The Wolfhounds" deals with

Korea of 1950 and '51 and early '52. When it was completely done and locked in concrete, I then got some information from the National Archives that really lent a lot of information to that particular chapter. I went to Julie and I said, "Look, golly, this is great stuff, we need to put it in." But she felt we had reached a point of abandonment on that chapter. So we had that kind of friction. A give-and-take friction to get the book together and to get it done correctly. That's why it took five years, which is a lot of your life.

We wrote it in Australia. This was supported by three or four visits to the United States by Julie, [who] went and interviewed the people that we had tracked down in their hometowns. So she traveled all over America, recording people's comments, and collecting data, and so on. We made it a full-time job. We decided it was such an important message: that war has changed so significantly from the time that my ancestors came to America in 1622 and landed in Jamestown. They were firing old musket weapons at the Indians, and the Indians were firing bows and arrows back at them. But by the time I was to leave the military, we had [such] awesome weapons in our inventory that one alone could bring about the destruction of humankind. I felt that we had to bring out the point through our story that war is no longer, probably, the means to resolve conflict. We have got to find a new way to do it. That's kind of one of the bottom lines of the book.

We spent most of our own money on the book; we sure did. The advance was small because Simon & Schuster didn't know us from Adam. We had never written a book before of any significance and so the advance was really small. Julie dipped into her savings, and luckily I was retired army so I had my little magic blue [veteran's pension] check coming in every month. That's what kept us going.

The introduction was written by Ward Just. Ward Just is a writer. He wrote for *Newsweek* and *The Washington Post*. He's now a novelist, and a very good one. Ward Just had a profound influence on my life. It started in June of 1966, during the battle of Duc Tho. Ward was with one of my platoons—a reconnaissance platoon—[whose men] found themselves in a very tough firefight deep into enemy positions. They were surrounded and had a great number of casualties. Ward was wounded in this action. That night, we couldn't get to this sieged unit with infantry to reinforce them. We were working toward that end, and the unit had eight seriously wounded men. The medic that was on the ground reckoned they wouldn't make it until first light when we could get them out with choppers. So we got an all-volunteer air force chopper crew that flew over the battlefield and took a lot of fire but winched them out. While I thought that this reporter would come out too—he refused. He gave up his seat so a fellow who was, in his judgment, more severely wounded could get out. He stayed on the ground, stayed surrounded, when he had had a free ticket out, which was so untypical [of] reporters in Vietnam. He won me for life. He joined the brotherhood. He joined the brotherhood of infantryman. When the fight was over, I went to the hospital and I awarded him the Combat Infantry Badge. I took him a rifle that we had captured in the fight—a Chinese rifle—and he became my friend for life.

Coincidentally, after that assignment, I was assigned to the Pentagon, right here in this city, as was Ward. He became *The Washington Post* military correspondent. So we dealt with each other a lot, and I learned from him. He wrote his very brilliant book *To What End,* and he asked me to review the manuscript. I realized then that the war wasn't only a war of tactics and strategy, but a war of winning the people to the side of the government in South Vietnam. There were so many other political implications other than the wham-bam of the battlefield. So Ward became my teacher and caused me to kind of wake up. I knew that he had the sensitivity to write an introduction that would really tell what our book was all about.

I CAME HOME MAINLY to promote the book. But I think I discovered an important part of this which I didn't understand. Last May, my son graduated from [the University of California at Berkeley] and I came to his graduation. At the same time, I brought the manuscript back—the final manuscript—to Simon & Schuster. Then I went out to Montana to spend a few days with my best friend. And I suddenly realized that I wanted to come home. The book had had such a cathartic effect on me, such a healing effect, such a purging effect, that it had taken all of the bitterness out. It had taken all of the need to strike out and get revenge for what happened. And I realized that I wanted to return home and return to my roots.

I think when I return to the States, I will live in Montana or Colorado. Someplace up high where I can be out in the country. I like the wilderness, and I'm not into the big cities. I've just been in New York for three or four days, and I couldn't sleep from all the noise. In Australia, I live on top of a little hill all by myself—and when I hear a car coming down the road, I know they're coming to see me. And I don't hear that many cars coming down the road. So to suddenly be thrust into New York City, where they're collecting the garbage at midnight and there's crash, bang, boom—it was like living on a battlefield. So I'll live probably up in the hills where my family came from. I really have this passion to return to my roots.

Johanna Neuman

Johanna Neuman, the foreign editor at USA Today, *joined us on March 10, 1996, to discuss her book* Lights, Camera, War: Is Media Technology Driving International Politics?

IN SEPTEMBER OF 1993, I was blessed with a fellowship at Columbia University to study the issue of whether media technology was driving diplomacy, whether those pictures of starving babies in Somalia had forced President Bush to intervene, and whether the picture of that body of an American soldier dragged through the streets of Mogadishu had forced President Clinton to withdraw. And I came to it convinced that there had been a revolution, that satellite television had changed the way nations interact and the way diplomats do their job.

I had traipsed around the globe with then Secretary of State James Baker, and I had watched him use CNN. Once we were in an air force hangar in Taiff, Saudi Arabia, a couple of days before the Persian Gulf War began, and he made a very impassioned speech about the brink of war and how if Iraq doesn't withdraw from Kuwait, there will be hell to pay. He told me later that he was making this appeal not to the audience, not to these airmen and airwomen in that hangar, and not to the journalists who were traveling around with him, but to one guy in his bunker in Baghdad, Saddam Hussein. It was the fastest way to convey that information.

I thought then—and many people did later, at the time of the Somalia incidents—that there had been a revolution, that CNN was running things, that diplomacy had ceded something to satellite television. When I got to Columbia University, they gave me the run of the library, and I started reading history. I found instead that we, in the satellite television generation, were just going through a familiar pattern that all new media inventions go through, that whenever a new invention of media technology comes along—whether it's the telegraph, or film, or photography, any of them—they all evoke the same pattern, and we're going through it now with satellite TV.

The Butler Library [at Columbia University] is a very special place for me, and it was just very exciting to read, for instance, about the telegraph and see some of the same kind of hysteria from the diplomatic community about how it was cutting their time for deliberation and how this new medium was just robbing them of time for thought and of their rightful role at the helm of diplomacy. I spent a year at Columbia gathering research. I had two able research assistants, and I did a lot of reading. I probably did more reading in that year then I had in some years before that. Then I took some months off back in Washington [D.C.] and just wrote with my cat, Smokey, in my lap [by a window] looking out into the trees.

As I wrote this book, I wished that I had become a historian instead of a journalist. I love delving into the history and finding these little nuggets. And it put into context that which we think is unique for us. There's always a precedent. At one point, I almost called the book *Echoes,* because to me there were so many echoes in it of our own times, and that it was just a great comfort to know that all of these things had precedent.

The "inverted pyramid" is how journalists write in most newspapers and newscasts that you see. The inverted pyramid is where you tell the most important thing first, and then you tell the rest of the story in descending order of importance. Newspaper stories used to be written in the narrative style as if they were telling you a story. In the beginning this happened, then this happened—it was sort of a chronological approach to news. Then the telegraph arrives, and what happens is that because it can cut off in transmission, reporters start packing in the most important stuff at the beginning of their cables in case they should get cut off in mid-sentence.

For journalists and military people, speed of information is a great asset most of the time. For the journalist, you just want to get your information. You want to beat the competition, you want to get information to the public as quickly as you can, and likewise for military. If you have advance word on what enemy positions are, if you have a faster flow of information from your capital, it's all an asset.

For diplomats, delay is often the secret weapon. Delay, the calming of tempers, of fever, of emotion, is often something that diplomats use quite well. And so, for them, these are harder intrusions to absorb.

I WROTE THIS BOOK without a book contract. I decided to just go write the book and then see if I could sell it. When you write a book without a book contract, you have to have a great deal of confidence in the topic and also a great deal of support at home. Whenever my spirits flagged, my husband [Ron Nessen] would come by and assure me that someday I would be on *Booknotes.*

I married Ron Nessen in 1988. He's the former press secretary to Gerald Ford. He was a wonderful source of support. He was a wonderful intellectual colleague. I could bounce things off of him and debate things [with him]. We are not always of the same mind, so we tend to have a lively debate in the house anyway, but he was more than that. He was a great emotional support.

Nathan McCall

Nathan McCall came to the program on March 6, 1994, while a reporter for The Washington Post, *to discuss his book* Makes Me Wanna Holler: A Young Black Man in America.

*T*HE BOOK STEMS FROM A PERSPECTIVE that I wrote for *The Washington Post.* I had moved here from Atlanta, and as soon as I moved here I realized—I mean, I could feel it—there was a difference in the intensity in the crime, in the violence, [from that] in Atlanta. After I moved here, I was able to go home [to Portsmouth, Virginia] much more frequently and visit my parents and hear about all that was going on with some of the guys I grew up with on the streets. Some of them were being killed, some of them were going to jail—some of the same things I was hearing about here in Washington. And it struck me that the difference was when I read about these stories here in Washington, they were stories about faceless people.

I decided to write about the feelings of going home and hearing about all these tragedies, and how it compared to being here and reading about the tragedies, and just my ambivalence about it all. I wrote this piece, and it appeared in the "Outlook" section of *The Washington Post,* and I was scared to death. I had never written about my life. As a journalist, I could always write about other people. When I wrote about my life, the response was overwhelming. I got a lot of letters, I got a lot of phone calls, and I got some phone calls from book agents as well. They said, "I think you've got a book here." So I settled upon an agent and things started happening, and we got a book contract. That's how it happened.

I got the title of the book from an old Marvin Gaye album, *What's Going On.* The album came out in 1971 and it is a classic. There was a song on the album, called "Inner City Blues," that I really could identify with. They had a line in there that said, "Makes me want to holler and throw up my hands." I used that line in a piece I wrote for *The Washington Post,* and so it sort of caught on. The line was talking about, well, the song itself was talking about the times, the social strife, and some of the same issues we're dealing with today: crime, depression, and the struggle of black people.

When I sat down to write this book, I said I wanted to be brutally honest. I wanted to be honest about myself, about my life, talk about the pain I felt in life, the pain that I think a lot of black men feel. I wanted to write about things that a lot of black men don't publicly discuss. I decided I wasn't going to pull any punches anywhere. So, I write about what I did outside the mainstream—the white mainstream, I called it. I also write about what it was like for me crossing over into the mainstream, and how this world that was controlled by white people looked at me and how it felt to me. In the chapter that was about the *Post,* I talked about the racism. The competition I felt at the *Post* was really, really intense, and it made me tense and it made me uncomfortable. So I wrote about it.

Shortly after we got the book contract, we got a movie deal. I learned a lot about just how closely entwined the book industry and the movie industry are. As soon as we had the bidding war for the book, we began getting calls from Hollywood. We got a good offer from Columbia Pictures, and we were eventually able to do a contract. And they bought the rights to the book, to the story. The director will be John Singleton, who was the director of the movie *Boyz N the Hood.* He's about to start on another movie project, and they have said that this will be his next project. We're having discussions now about what—if any—role I will play in the making of the movie.

I don't think you can go through this experience and not change in some way. Especially when you write this kind of book. When you write a book about your life, it forces you to sit down and think about your life in a way that, perhaps, you've never thought about it before. I had to put my life together in a story in a way that would make sense to a reader and in a way that it would help readers understand the journey that I've taken—from the streets to the mainstream—and why I took that journey.

Lewis Lapham

Lewis Lapham, longtime editor in chief of Harper's Magazine, *joined us on August 15, 1993, for a conversation on his book* The Wish for Kings: Democracy at Bay.

IN THE NEW YORK LITERARY WORLD, the conversation is much more apt to be about the author's standing in the market [than about the book]. Everybody has read the reviews, and everybody knows whether the book is up or down, or in or out. And everybody has something to say about it in a couple of sentences. Also I find that—at least within the court world of the New York literary scene—relatively few people have had the time to read all the way through the book. But I find that when I travel across the country—that if I'm in California or I'm in Ohio or Texas—and I run across somebody who has read the book, they're apt to have read the whole thing and are prepared to really talk about it. Whereas in New York, I get the current opinion.

The chapter called "Versailles on the Potomac" is about the splendor of Washington that has been the magnificence of its marble, of its pretensions, of its bureaucratic vastness, so that it has become like a palace at Versailles. It is a court society, a world unto itself, sometimes called "inside the Beltway." It's grown and multiplied since the end of the Second World War so that the expanse of government, the number of functionaries, of people who serve government in its many facets—I think there's something like 100,000 lawyers and lobbyists who work on various degrees of regulation. The staff of the Congress has multiplied to 35,000. It's this sense of a vast Versailles-like court, the Hall of Mirrors, in which the various servants of government flatter one another or blame one another, strike poses, issue bills, make announcements, stage pageants of one kind or another—that's the view of it in that chapter.

I first came to Washington in the late 1950s, during the Eisenhower administration. I'd come from university, and I was trying to decide what kind of career to follow. I approached the CIA, I approached *The Washington Post*, and I also approached the White House and I was sent to talk to

Mr. [Robert] Gray. Gray eventually became an enormously successful lobbyist and trafficker in influence and patronage. He had his own lobbying firm for many years and is now with Hill & Knowlton. But then he was a young man and was an aide to Eisenhower. I can remember being interviewed by him. He had very little time; he was hard pressed, and the interview took place in the basement of the White House, in the barbershop. There was a barber chair down there those days, and the only other place for me to sit was on the toilet. I sat on the toilet and Gray sat in the barber chair, so I was at the level of his shoes, which I remember as being very beautiful shoes.

I started to talk about democratic theory. I was very young, very idealistic and Gray waved all that off and sort of said, "Please don't waste anybody's time." He said, "The whole thing about government, about Washington, or about power is simply to acquire the right sort of friends and make connections and do what you're told until the great day comes when you can tell others what to do. Carry whatever water must be carried." And so on. It was a very realistic assessment and a very clear statement of the principle, which I never forgot. He made it very articulately.

What happened to me? I went into the newspaper business. I became a newspaper reporter first for the *San Francisco Examiner* and then for the *New York Herald Tribune.* Then I became a magazine writer in most of the sixties for *The Saturday Evening Post* and for *Life* magazine. After that, I became a writer for *Harper's* in about 1970. In 1971, I became, by default, a managing editor. There was one of those office-politics things that happens in New York offices fairly frequently. The then editor resigned; so did some of the other editors. I didn't agree with their unhappiness, so I stayed. And on a Monday I was a writer and on a Tuesday I became a managing editor. I was the managing editor for four years, and then I became the editor in 1976.

I was the editor from 1976 to 1981. Then I was fired and spent two years in exile and [was] rehired in 1983. The glorious return. I was recalled as the editor of the magazine. So I've been the editor twice—once, 1976 to '81 and again from 1983 until now.

I HAVE A STORY IN THE BOOK about Robert Mosbacher, the former secretary of commerce. Mosbacher was appointed by Bush, and he came from Houston, and he thought that a man of his stature and magnificence should have had more notice by the media, more time on television, more space in *The Washington Post,* and so on. He was constantly seeking means of his own self-aggrandizement. He hit upon having a private entrance made for himself at the Department of Commerce on the other side of the building from the entrance in which the mere populace was to come and go. He had the entrance built at great expense, with a long awning, sort of like a canopy in front of a nightclub or a restaurant. I think he wanted to have it red because [then Secretary of State] Jim Baker's canopy at the State Department was blue, or he wanted it blue because Jim Baker's canopy was red—I can't remember which way it went. But there were only six people allowed to use that entrance. There was Mosbacher himself, his wife, his secretary, his deputy, his lawyer—for all I know, his valet. Then after he had gotten that all together, it still wasn't quite grand enough. He practiced walking in and out of that entrance for a number of weeks. And then he decided that, once he got inside the building, there was [quite] a distance to go [until] his own private elevator. But between the entrance and the elevator there were offices, sort of cubicles in which the "poor" people worked, wearing shirtsleeves—I mean, it was an unseemly display of manual labor. So he had the entire inside of the Department of Commerce—that part of it, anyway—reconstructed. The offices were moved so that there was a properly open grand space between the entrance and the elevator. I believe there was a table put there with simply a decoration of flowers. But it's that kind of attitude that too often captures people, not only, of course, in Washington, but elsewhere, within any organization large enough to sustain its own theory of reality.

Kissinger was a man who knew how to play the court world extremely well. He was discovered by Nelson Rockefeller. He'd been an academician at Harvard, a history professor, I believe, and then somehow he managed to get to Nelson Rockefeller. Nelson Rockefeller was then governor of New York and had presidential ambitions, and [Kissinger] provided him with theories of the cold war, theories of nuclear disarmament, theories of nuclear exchange. I forget in what succession they came, but Kissinger, again, was a man always willing to arrange the world to fit the desire of his patron, whether it was Rockefeller or Nixon or, sometimes, important senior columnists in the media. He understood that the world was a world of poses, of the right word at the right time. Whether the theory was actually true of not, whether it had any relation to the facts or not, was less important than the way it advanced or failed to advance Kissinger's career.

I've been told and I think it's true that Kay Graham of *The Washington Post,* shortly after Nixon [resigned]—I mean, the same month—sent him a nice note and said, "Don't worry. When it's all over, we'll have dinner." The relation is always to power. If you're out of power nobody can remember your name, and if you're in power everybody's your best friend. Nixon's career is a brilliant demonstration of that—a man who was considered a used-car salesman, nearly impeached. Twenty years ago his name was synonymous with scoundrel and crook, and now his name is synonymous with statesman and philosopher.

Jack Kent Cook is the owner of the Washington Redskins, and one of the most valued places at court in Washington is in Jack Kent Cook's box at RFK Stadium. It's a large box. I believe there are fifty or sixty places in it. Of course, during the long period of a Republican administration, the box was filled with important Republicans. Shortly after the election of Clinton—I believe within two days—suddenly it turned out Cook discovered all of his Democratic friends. Their seats were changed, and with a new administration the court brings in new courtiers—and Cook was very quick to see that. It's the constant game in Washington of who's in and who's out. I mean, who will come, who will go, who will get to write the senator's speeches or carry the general's shirt or sit in Jack Kent Cook's box or have a parking space at National Airport? These are questions of vast weight.

We, as Americans, like to pride ourselves as individualists constantly, and one of the images of ourselves that we like the best is that of the Clint Eastwood figure, the man against the system, the cowboy facing west in the rain. But we, in fact, are people that are very much dependent upon our institutional identities and identifications. I am "of" this bank; I am "of" that paper; I am "of" the studio or whatever. This, of course, is one of the premises or theses of the book: which is the courtier spirit, which is the accommodating spirit? The democratic spirit is the one that simply speaks out and says whatever is in its mind, and candor is one of the great democratic political virtues. We're democrats to the extent that we try to tell each other what we know, what we've seen, what we feel. We're courtiers to the extent that we tell each other what each of us wants to hear.

I wanted to write the book because I was trying to describe what I saw. I was trying to report accurately the circumstance of what I kept encountering. Again, it's not only about government; it's about universities, it's about corporations, about the media, and I don't exempt myself from the conditions that I describe.

Nan Robertson

Our guest on the March 29, 1992, Booknotes was the Pulitzer Prize–winning journalist Nan Robertson, author of The Girls in the Balcony: Women, Men, and The New York Times. *Ms. Robertson was a reporter for* The New York Times *for over three decades.*

THE "BALCONY" IS—or was—the balcony of the National Press Club, an all-male institution until just twenty years ago. And when in 1955 the men decided that they would let women in to cover—to report on—events taking place there, they put us in a very narrow, extremely uncomfortable balcony at the far end of the ballroom. We stood there while some of the most important men in the world spoke. It was hard to hear them; we were crushed together; we couldn't even do our job right.

I wrote [this book] because the story had never been told before, because every major book ever written about *The New York Times* almost ignores the women who contributed to it—such books as Meyer Berger's *Authorized History of The New York Times,* in 1951; Gay Talese's compulsively readable *The Kingdom and the Power,* which came out in '69; Harrison Salisbury's *Without Fear or Favor;* and David Halberstam's *The Powers That Be.* Women were invisible, and we've added a great deal to this newspaper. I thought I would like to tell their story.

I wanted to tell how a group of very brave women pushed the *Times* into the twentieth century, made it live up to its own ideas and public image of being a humane, liberal progressive, lecturing newspaper—lecturing the nation in its editorials about how white males would have to give up power. How, of course, they felt uncomfortable with the minorities and the women pushing for equal rights and equal pay. And at the same time, this great institution, which I loved, was fighting the women's [law] suit tooth-and-nail, and historically has not been welcoming to women, until very recently.

It's a great story. It's full of heroines, not many heroes. There are very few villains, however. I think it has a lot to do with ignorance, insensitivity, and the fact that nobody who has power and is part of the status quo will move or voluntarily give away any of that power without being pushed.

I knew that they [the *Times*] would have to review it, and the *Times* is big enough to review it. I thought that the person who reviewed it—whether male or female—might think that if they wrote a favorable review about a shadowed series of episodes in the *Times's* history, that they might never be able to write for the *Times* again. Many outsiders think of the *Times* as a monolith instead of a newspaper with thousands of diverse personalities in it. There are a thousand people on the news staff. There are 6,000 employees altogether. And we do not think and act as one.

I think I'm seeing [a reaction to this book] already. Women who have read this book are saying, "This is my story." And they are already identifying with the story and sharing the fact that this has happened everywhere. They want to get some sort of hope from all that has happened to women in the working world.

Howell Raines

Howell Raines covered Ronald Reagan's first successful presidential campaign in 1980 for The New York Times *and then served as White House correspondent for the* Times *for the first eighteen months of President Reagan's first term. In January of 1992, Mr. Raines became editorial page editor of* The New York Times. *On May 1, 1994, Mr. Raines talked about his memoir* Fly Fishing Through the Midlife Crisis.

SEVERAL PRESIDENTS have been fly fishermen. Hoover was the devoted fly fisherman and Cal Coolidge fished with a fly rod but with worms most of the time, and that irritated Hoover and he used to tease his fellow Republican about that. President Eisenhower liked to fly-fish. President Bush is an ardent fisherman but a novice—a self-described novice, as he says in my book, at fly-fishing.

President Carter was the best fly fisherman ever to occupy the White House, according to my research. I haven't fished with them all but I think people in fly-fishing generally believe that President Carter has the highest level of expertise. He's very knowledgeable. He took up fly-fishing as a diversion fairly late in life, as people often tend to do, and became passionate about it. In fact, if he had spent a little less time at fly-fishing and at the fly-tying bench while he was in the White House, perhaps he might have been there a bit longer. But he's a good fly fisherman.

I started fooling with the idea of this book when a friend of mine asked me to do a piece for his [new] magazine . . . called *Southpoint,* which was an original magazine in the South—my home area. So I told him I wanted to write a piece about the Rapidan River in Virginia, since it was a magazine about things in the South. Rapidan is in the Shenandoah National Park, in the Blue Ridge Mountains of Virginia, about two hours west of Washington.

And the story about the Rapidan—it turned out to be less about the Rapidan than about the experiences my sons and I, and a man named Dick Blalock, who's my fly-fishing guru and really the hero of this book, had on the Rapidan. That article was so much fun to write that I decided to see if I could do a book.

I wrote this sentence down, "It's a good day to die," and put it by my telephone in my office. I mention this in the book because I thought, if you're going to write a personal book you have an obligation to the reader to be candid about all of your emotions, including the ones that are not particularly pleasant, in this case fear. "It is a good day to die" was the battle cry of the "dog soldiers" of the Cheyenne tribe of Plains Indians.

The dog soldiers were the most feared fighters on the Plains. And their power came from their embracing death as central to combat. "It is a good day to die" is not about fatalism; it's about a celebration of life and doing what one is put in the world to do. In the dog soldiers' case, that was to make war. So the joyfulness of that, the affirmation of it, made them both powerful and admired.

I was divorced in 1990. It happened when I was in the course of writing the book. I didn't anticipate that at the time, but I was writing an autobiographical book, and I felt that I couldn't fairly leave out that kind of major event, particularly if you're writing about the midlife passage, because divorce is a part of that experience for many people. It turned out to be for me. Some of the critics have faulted me for not telling more of the details of that. And I'm willing to take that criticism. I'm pleased with the way I handled it in the book because I wanted to try to sketch some things in life without necessarily drawing them in stark crayon, and I hope I succeeded in doing that.

The greatest influence, probably, on my writing in my mature years is Yeats, the poetry of Yeats. I'm not a poet, but you can learn from the study of Yeats's poetry, if you're interested. The language is very powerful. I keep the collected Yeats poems on the table in my office, and I try to read one a day—or, by now, reread. But the magic of that language is very powerful, and so that's been a great influence on me.

I wanted to write a book that was very personal, and that was about me, and in which I did not edit out the parts of my opinions that I had rigorously kept out of my work as a journalist. One of the things that I think we in journalism have not done a good job of educating our consumers about—and it's our fault, not theirs—is that what we do is an intellectual discipline. And we do have opinions, but part of the professional craft of journalism is separating opinion from non-opinion journalism. I do opinion journalism now. I don't simply exercise my personal opinion. Institutionally, my job is to form opinion that speaks for *The New York Times*. But I felt free in this book to explore my own political opinions. And I think part of every personality is how you come to form your politics.

· · ·

WHEN I WAS YOUNGER, when I wrote my first two books, I did [so] by getting up at five A.M. and even some more atrocious hours, and working three hours before I went to the newspaper. But as I've gotten older I find that hard to do, so I work on weekends a lot. But the morning hours are my hours of preparation. As a general rule, when writers are in full production, they have about four hours of good composition time a day. And it's just a matter of when your unconscious mind is pushing stuff forward, as to when you work. Some people work late at night, some in the afternoon, some in the morning. For me, over the years I've sort of trained myself— that [the morning is] when I can access the creative imagination, and that's very important for a writer to learn, when his or her unconscious is going to offer up whatever's in there.

Writing the book was an important lesson for me, and it was connected with a larger point. It was during the time when I was working out the whole business about death and mortality. And I don't take this as a general universal law, any more than I think every midlife crisis has to encompass divorce. I don't say that every midlife crisis is about mortality. I know mine was. And I think that's a common experience, and I would say to anyone who's going through this period of their lives, particularly men, that you need to look at that issue very carefully because a lot of people have had the kinds of experiences that I have.

Andrew Ferguson

On November 3, 1996, Andrew Ferguson, senior editor of The Weekly Standard, *appeared on* Booknotes *to talk about* Fools' Names, Fools' Faces.

I SHOULD PREFACE THIS by saying I hate to hear writers complain about how hard it is to write, because anybody who can make a living at it is so lucky. I don't care how good they are, but anybody who can actually make a decent living at writing has no right to complain. That said, I hate to write. I mean, I would rather go to the dentist sometimes than write a piece. But there are a lot of people who really enjoy writing and who find it liberating and expressive. George Will once said that he wakes up every morning and says, "Do I have to write a column today?" And if he does, it's going to be a good day. To me, it's the exact opposite. If I wake up and I've got a deadline looming, it's just awful.

To get through it, you just make coffee. You make a lot of coffee, and you sit down in front of the [computer] screen and you just type out a word. Then you go and talk on the telephone. You go get some more coffee, you come back, and you make yourself type out [a] sentence. Then, if you're at home, you rearrange your ties or you clean off your dresser. Then you go back and do it again. You make another phone call. And pretty soon your editor's on the phone saying, "Where is my copy? I need your column." So then you sit down, and you just do it. It's very unpleasant.

I try and do it as early as possible in the day, mainly because I postpone things. It takes a lot of time to get all those cups of coffee and talk on the phone. So if I don't start early in the day, I won't actually get to writing till about six o'clock at night. But also I'm much fresher in the morning. My mind is much livelier.

When I was at the *Washingtonian,* I wrote at home all the time, almost all the time. I was also a big smoker in those days, and you couldn't smoke in the *Washingtonian* offices, so I smoked at home and wrote at home. "I write where I smoke" would have been my motto in those days. Now I work at the office, usually, unless it's a really big piece that's going to require a lot of concentrated effort.

HUMOR DOES PLAY A ROLE in my writing. I hate to be too somber when I write about something. I guess that's just my disposition, but it's also a way of keeping people reading. It's also an effective way of arguing people out of a position. If you just kind of poke fun at a position or a person, you can bring them around to your way of thinking without too much boring argumentation and logic and things like that. So I use it as a way of avoiding argument, I guess.

When I was a kid, I was always drawn to writing by people who were funny: Mark Twain, of course, and Robert Benchley, and some of the other great humorists. But I would hate to be called a humorist. It sets the bar too high. I don't write because I want to make people laugh; I write because I want to say something, and I hope that people enjoy it as they go along.

I always liked writing when I was kid. I like it less and less as I get older, but now it's too late; I can't do anything else. I can't. When I was young, I just loved using words and writing about my feelings about this great diarist or that great writer. But now that I have to do it to put food on the table, it's not nearly as much fun. I never really wanted to do it seriously, as a way of making a living, until after I was out of college. I had a number of failed attempts at other endeavors, except I didn't fail up, I kept failing down.

[THE TITLE] COMES FROM a quote from that famous author Anonymous. If you look in Bartlett's, that's where you'll find it. It's an old saying from the earlier days of America. I think it goes, "Fools' names, like fools' faces, are often seen in public places," which means the public square draws people who tend to make clowns out of themselves.

It's a book of essays, all of which have been published over the years. I think the earliest one goes back to 1986, but most of them are [of] much more recent vintage. And they look at various prominent people like [Louis] Farrakhan and Barbra Streisand, who are on the cover; a lot about Washington and Washington politics; and then about some of the larger trends over the last few years. It's sort of a book of cultural criticism, which sounds slightly pompous, but it's about large trends in the culture over the last ten years.

I use [Robert] McNamara as sort of an example of that fact that in Washington, people fail up. He's a guy who's gone from failure to failure to failure. He first came to public prominence as the head of Ford Motor Company. The great innovation of the Ford Motor Company when he was president was the Edsel. He did so well that President Kennedy made him secretary of defense where he was one of the architects of Vietnam, which is sort of the Edsel of American foreign policy.

After messing up our foreign policy, he went on to the World Bank where he presided over one of the great calamities of foreign aid, which was this free flow of money to what are called "kleptocracies," these terrible dictatorships that just swallowed up money. And McNamara just kept the spigot open.

But, astonishingly, he really had not paid a price until his book came out, which was the occasion for my piece. He wrote a memoir that I thought was just shameless in which he sort of semi-apologized—but didn't really—for Vietnam. He finally got the criticism that I think he deserved, but not in Washington. In Washington, he was still the toast of the town. When the book came out, the Vietnam veterans were suing him. He was getting lambasted. And here in Washington, Kay Graham threw him a book party—and everybody who's anybody in Washington was there.

I'm not sure why this happens. It's partly that Washington is such an inbred culture—I'm talking about official Washington, federal Washington. Once you reach a certain level, people tend to protect each other. Kay Graham is a great friend of Bob McNamara's going back to the fifties, I think. She is the doyenne of Washington society and the president of *The Washington Post* publishing company. Now she's sort of emeritus, but she's one of the most prominent people in town.

John Podhoretz's [contributing editor of *The Weekly Standard*] mother, Midge Decter, a great figure in her own right, a superb writer, once said to me, "Sooner or later, you have to join the side you're on." For a long time, even given my affiliations with various conservative magazines, I always hemmed and hawed when someone asked me, "So you're a right-winger, huh? You're a conservative." I thought it was an easy label to dismiss somebody, especially in a culture where so many of the institutions are taken over by people on the left. So I resisted it. I thought it was bad, for professional reasons and others. That's a very long way of saying, "Yes, I think I am a man of the right."

In an amazingly short amount of time, *The Weekly Standard* has become a must-read in Washington among political and journalistic types. It's a funny thing, when you write, you're never quite sure who the audience is. And when you're in Washington, which has this incredible concentration of journalists, you measure your feedback by what other journalists tell you about what you've written. It's very incestuous, but it's one of the few gauges you have of how a piece is going over.

No matter how much journalists beat their breasts and talk about how cynical and skeptical they are, there isn't enough debunking going on. It's part of the job of a journalist—and there's not enough of it. This is true particularly within the culture of journalism itself because it is so monochromatic. It's filled with people who think alike and talk alike and see the same movies and read the same books and go to the same parties. The culture is so incestuous that there are some targets that are simply left untouched.

Christopher Hitchens

Christopher Hitchens, a contributing editor to Vanity Fair, *is a British native who's now based in Washington, D.C. He came to the program on October 17, 1993, to discuss his book* For the Sake of Argument.

I DON'T REALLY KNOW if I enjoy writing or not. I'd hate not writing, I know that. I sort of do it because I feel I have to. Sometimes it's a real pleasure doing it. Usually the pleasure comes, though, when you see it in print—not until then, and usually not until some time after.

I sometimes write in bars in the afternoons. I go out and find a corner of a bar. If the noise isn't directed at me—in other words, there's not a phone ringing or a baby crying or something—I quite like it if the jukebox is on and people are shouting the odds about a sports game. I just hunch over a bottle in the corner. I write in longhand anyway, so I can do it anywhere—sometimes in airport terminals. Then when I've got enough [written] down, I start to type it out, editing it as I go. I don't use any of the new technology stuff.

I wrote this book as a reply. The pieces are very various. They're a salad, but they have a common theme, which is a reply to all those who say that since the 1989 revolution there's really no need for the left critique of society or politics anymore, that we've moved beyond all that, that society is just basically a liberal, problem-solving matter and no more, though the conservatives, I notice, are still allowed to have their say. Implicitly, everything in there is about the origins of the 1989 revolution in Eastern Europe, which I covered in some part, and its consequences. I define it as a real emancipating revolution that I'd long hoped for and worked for and supported, but one that by no means makes politics any more one-dimensional. I think, actually, it restores the left as a very necessary part of the political argument, so even when I'm writing about something else, I'm always trying to bear that in mind.

Some of the articles come from *The Nation*. *The Nation* is America's oldest political weekly magazine, founded in 1865, towards the end of the Civil War, by a group of abolitionists, and it's basically upheld the liberal left end of the rope ever since. It still proudly comes out every week, and every other week it features, and has for the last ten years, a column by me called "Minority Report," which is sometimes about politics, sometimes about a new book, sometimes about a personality, but is, again, an attempt to mount a left critique of society and politics.

It can be hard. George Orwell used to say, "I won't have lunch with X or Y because I'm going to write about him soon, and I'm sure I'm going to find he's really quite nice, and, therefore, I don't want the corrupting effect of an acquaintanceship or friendship. I'd rather keep clean and keep pure." I. F. Stone in Washington used to do the same thing. He wouldn't go to briefings and little soirées because he wanted to be able to say what he thought about people. I'm not that fortunate; I'm impulsively social.

THE [LONDON] *Times Literary Supplement*, THE *TLS,* AS IT'S CALLED, sells independently as a weekly—and, actually, half its subscribers are in the United States. I used to be its American columnist. In there I've written about more general subjects, like the work of Graham Greene or P. G. Wodehouse, who is perhaps my favorite author, and a couple of other more literary pieces. But, again, I try when I'm writing about literature not to leave the political dimension out. When I'm writing about politics I try and recall that politics isn't all there is to life, and try and import what you might call cultural or literary or aesthetic points to it. This must make me sound insufferable, but that's my ambition, anyway.

George Will also writes about P. G. Wodehouse all the time. You get into terrifically bad company some of the time if you're a fan of Wodehouse. That's true of also being a fan of Kipling or Orwell or many other people. P. G. Wodehouse is the author of the most imperishable double act in fictional history, Bertie Wooster and his manservant Jeeves. Of course, a joke is never a joke if it has to be explained, so [to] those who haven't discovered and immersed themselves in this, I can only say they should start today. It sounds a bit cultish, but those who have already done it will already know what I'm talking about.

P. G. Wodehouse died at the age of about ninety-three in the mid-seventies. He was an English comic writer who got driven out of England, partly by poverty, and moved to America, which he adored, and stayed for the last fifty or so years of his life on Long Island. He was always writing about the mythical golden past of the English country house and of the English gentleman of leisure and man-about-town Bertie Wooster, who's a complete chinless idiot and can't get himself out of any scrape without the

254 / Christopher Hitchens

help of his amazingly impassive, brilliant, classically educated—as he's called in the stories—"personal gentleman's gentleman," the butler Jeeves, who's always rescuing him. It's not unlike *The Importance of Being Earnest.* These are guys who would be nowhere without their servants and are always getting involved in ridiculous love affairs that have to be explained to them and [that] they have to be hauled out of and stood up on their feet.

I think George Will's stuff is very affected and overwritten. It's full of, I think, rather bogus shows of learning and classical tags and things of this kind. I have a weakness, sometimes, for quotations of that sort myself, so I think I recognize the disease in others. It's in a very advanced stage in his case. I think he's a courtier. I think especially during the Reagan era, he basically was making a living as a professional flatterer of the Ron and Nancy court. I don't think journalists should do that. I think it's even more important not to do it when your friends are in power. I think it'll congest your style very badly. You'll be full of things you can't really say, things that are half-confidences that have been given to you by people in power. Your stuff will start to puff up. Your paragraphs will start to get rotund with all the things you could say if you really wanted, but you can only hint. That's bad. It's bad intellectually, and I think it's bad morally. It means that your contract is no longer with your readers.

WHAT I TRY AND DO, and the reason I write in longhand and write in isolation, is to say the only person I have a deal with is the person who might read this, and I'll give them my best. I don't care what the editor thinks, the advertising department thinks, friends and colleagues think. You try and live as if none of those people counted. What's the best account I can give the customers of this? Most of Washington punditry is nothing of the kind. It's private letters, written to other pundits, appearing in public space.

Mark Twain said if you give a man a reputation as an early riser, he can sleep until noon. Kissinger has, somewhere or another along the line, picked up a reputation as a statesman and peacemaker and negotiator and sort of miraculous dealmaker and bridge builder. I invite people in this piece to consider any instance in which he's left a country or a cause or a problem better off than when he found it, and I also point to what I consider to be a record of crime in his past. He's been complicit in the commissioning of assassinations and in the covering up of mass murder, and I think there are some signs in his memoirs and his behavior that he enjoys it, that he's a very dangerous person, a war criminal. I give the list of instances where I believe that to be true, and I'll give them here and now if you like.

P. J. O'ROURKE IS A GUY who gets away, in my opinion, with murder. He's another ex-leftist, sixties radical dropout, who wrote very funnily about what it was like being permanently stoned and bummed out and paranoid in the sixties. Then he saw the light, put on a collar and tie and became a young Republican and has been cashing in this chip ever since— and has a terrific following as a humorist for his books of essays. The first one is quite funny. It's called *Republican Party Reptile,* and the next one is called *Holidays in Hell,* and the more recent one is called *Give War a Chance.* These sell terribly well among the young, much better than any of my books ever have, and it gets me down; so this is my revenge upon him.

My favorite conservative writer in the United States is William Safire. I'm a very great admirer of his. I think he's a wonderful writer. I think he's a very humorous writer. He's quite a brave writer, too. He tries to remember even when his own team is in power that that doesn't mean you're obliged to stop criticizing.

I don't think liberals make very good writers. I think liberals are always trying to have it both ways. They want to share in the idea that capitalism is basically the best humanity can do, but they want to be able to be compassionate about it. I think that leads to a lot of sickly writing. I find it very hard to read, and I think it is harder to read than it is to write.

I WAS BORN IN PORTSMOUTH, Hampshire, England. I'm a navy brat in other words. My dad was a lifetime naval officer in the service of the king and, indeed, of the empire. Until I was about twelve, I wanted to do the same. My father and mother are no longer alive, alas. It's just me and my brother. My brother's a very conservative journalist who writes for a conservative tabloid in England called *The Daily Express.* He's just become its Washington correspondent, having been in Moscow for a long time. He's a very brilliant guy, very thoughtful, a very good writer, with political views the opposite of mine. He's just arrived in Washington this week, so I'm looking forward to it. I'm going to have to give a party or something and say, "Here's the Hitchens family secret. Now you know everything."

I was the first member of my family to go to a university, or certainly to go to Oxford. We had, as a family, sort of worked out the steps. If you want to be upwardly mobile in Britain, that's the key thing, so that step one is you have to go to a private school, basically, if you're starting from where we were. My parents made a big sacrifice to send me to a private school in Cambridge, actually a Methodist public school, a pretty good school.

There I decided that I knew exactly what I wanted to do. I wanted to become a writer.

I came to the United States in 1980. I'd been coming ever since I left university. I came here on a scholarship in 1970. It was a traveling scholarship. You got to travel all around the U.S., and I decided then and there that I'd rather live in America. I thought it was great. I nearly didn't go back when the scholarship ran out, but I sort of had to because I was out of dough. Actually, there was a woman in the case and I had to go back to England. I didn't come back again for about another five or six years, but then I started coming more and more often, and then *The Nation* offered me a job. I took about ten seconds to decide, yes, I'm coming for good.

MY FAVORITE RADICAL JOURNALIST in history, I suppose, is George Orwell. I know it's a cliché, because everyone now pretends to admire him, but there was a long time when he wasn't well known and certainly not well liked. I think it shows in his prose, and it's those bits of his prose that I admire. He didn't go to university at all; nor did my living favorite, Gore Vidal, go to college, either. I've always thought that's a good counsel for people who think that credentials are everything. You don't have to do any of that. Orwell went to a privileged public school, but because it was in his family, he went off to be a colonial policeman in Burma.

George Orwell would follow logic and honesty to their full conclusion. He would not be deflected by the fact that this might offend someone he knew or some cause with which he was associated or, more important, wouldn't even discompose himself. In other words, he thought, "Okay, if I don't like this conclusion, I'm still sticking with it if it's been arrived at honorably." It sounds like an easy thing to do or to say, but it's actually very hard to live by, and I think he really did live by it. And then I think he was a very witty and brilliant stylist. His writings on other authors, like Dickens, for example, his reflections on eternal subjects like capital punishment or family life, ordinary things, arguments that never go away, are always worth rereading.

MOST OF MY BOOKS DON'T MAKE BACK the small sum of money that I'm paid to write them. I don't know why. I don't have any knack there at all. There are very, very few publishers these days who will take a risk on a book that won't make money, and I'm probably exhausting the patience of Verso Publishing. That's the publishing arm of New Left Books. It's a very fine publishing firm. It's published some wonderful books, but it has to take permanent risks on opposition writing and unknown writers. They probably would never let me down, but increasingly the mainstream publishing industry wants an assurance up front that everything's commercial and that you've got a tie-in of some sort, a serialization or maybe a movie deal. I'm no good at that. I wish I was.

FOR A LOT OF PEOPLE, their first love is what they'll always remember. For me it's always been the first hate. I think that hatred, though it provides often rather junky energy, is a terrific way of getting you out of bed in the morning and keeping you going. If you don't let it get out of hand, it can be canalized into writing. In this country where people love to be nonjudgmental when they can be, which translates on the whole into being lenient, there are an awful lot of bubble reputations floating around that one wouldn't be doing one's job if one didn't itch to prick.

Robin Wright

An early guest on Booknotes *was Robin Wright, author of the book* In the Name of God: The Khomeini Decade. *A former national security reporter for the* Los Angeles Times, *she appeared on the program on November 19, 1989.*

IN BEIRUT, I LOST an apartment from a car bomb and a hotel room from artillery fire. In every war there's been something. The side of my rib cage is crushed. You pick up these little war injuries, even being a correspondent. I don't get tired of this because the opportunity to witness history is just so amazing. For a little girl from Ann Arbor, Michigan, to be able to have traveled with the pope and to have interviewed [Mu'ammar al] Gadhafi and to have seen some of the great turning points in modern history—I mean, what an opportunity.

I wrote the book because of my own experience in the Middle East. I lived in Beirut for years as a correspondent for *The Sunday Times* of London, and during that period I witnessed the marine bombing in 1983, when 241 American military personnel were killed, the two embassy bombings. Two of my very best friends are [former] hostages, including Terry Anderson, who had the office next door. It was my own sense of rage and misunderstanding of the situation. I wanted to find out why this was happening to the United States, why there was this tremendous antagonism between two countries that had been such good friends, and so I kept going back to Iran. I'd first been there during the shah's era in 1973, and I kept going back, and back, and back; and finally I came to grips with why it was happening, what it meant, and answered some of my own questions. I don't have any sympathy for the revolution, but I certainly understand now.

I wrote a long chronology of the revolution, trying to group events—military, political, whatever—together so that those of us who have seen only those limited pictures on television or read little bits from correspondents who got in during the windows of opportunity, could fill in the gaps, could see what happened, could fit together the pieces. The goal of the book was to give an overview of the ten years. I didn't want to have to deal with every specific event, so I chose to put that in a chronology.

The last date in this book that I was able to write about was [the Ayatollah] Khomeini's death. He died the weekend I was writing the last chapter. I may be the only American grateful to Khomeini for anything, because it was going to be subtitled *The Khomeini Era*. And so I got in the complete time of his rule in Iran.

MY FATHER ALWAYS TAUGHT ME, as a child, that when there was some major issue, that one had to distance oneself from it, to try to stand on top of the world without having the subjective values that can impede or limit judgment. He was always interested in foreign policy. We traveled a lot as children, and he would try to explain other cultures to us. So I guess what I tried to do with Iran was to go there, to stand on top of the world and look down at Iran—not just as an American with my own bitterness, but as someone objective, trying to see what the revolution set out to accomplish. And the book actually begins from something called "the roof of Teheran," which is the top of a mountain reached by antiquated cable car, and looking down at this extraordinary capital, and looking at life a decade after the revolution and what it's like.

I guess a journalist always has this divided feeling. I'm in my 40s now and I want to do serious things, but yet you don't want to give up the opportunity to get out there and see what's going on in the world. You can't give it up completely. So when I wrote the first book, I taught at Duke University and did a Poynter fellowship at Yale to give myself some of the media credentials, but . . . there's something addictive about journalism.

Colman McCarthy

From 1978 to 1997, Colman McCarthy wrote a twice-weekly column for The Washington Post *that was syndicated in newspapers across the country. He joined us in July 1994 to talk about his book* All of One Peace, *a compilation of columns he had written over the course of his career.*

I DECIDED AFTER I LEFT [the Trappist order], I would not eat any meat or any animal products. I don't wear any animal products. I don't patronize circuses, aquariums, zoos. I don't go to horse races. I'm very much opposed to how we treat animals. These shoes are not leather. I think it is wrong to eat animals. They have the same kind of life force that you and I do, and we have no right to inflict any suffering on another sentient being. I do it for health reasons and ethical reasons. We slaughter for food about 12 million animals a day in this country. I've been to slaughterhouses, and once you see that you never would do it again. It's abstract for most people. . . . It's also healthy [not to eat meat]. I've been working on you for a number of years, Brian. You're a Lamb, you know. You especially should not be eating meat. But to bring you along a little bit, I've brought something along from the farm. I want to give you this [*holding up a squash*]. This is from my garden, right here. This is a squash for you, Brian. There's your dinner right there. You can take that. I hope you'll accept that. This also is from our garden [*holding up another squash*]. These are the first ones that I've grown this summer. Now, I want everybody out in the country to know that we here inside the Beltway can grow things.

I was such a hedonist in college, always on the golf course and never really studied very much and kind of frittered it all away. I was coming home from Alabama to New York where we lived, and I stopped off at a religious order, a Trappist monastic order in Georgia. I went to stay for a week and I ended up there for five years, living with the Trappists. It's a Catholic order. I've written about that, I think, in the book a little bit. I was never a monk; I was a laborer. We did all the heavy lifting. I shoveled cow manure for four years, and some of my critics on the right say I'm still shoveling cow manure. So it's worked out fine. But it was a lovely five years. I came out before taking any kind of vows. The reason I did it is because I wanted to read and I wanted to get away from the world for a little while.

But [while at the monastery], I also read about 300 books a year and wrote a lot and kept a journal. I wrote, I guess, about 10,000 words, at least, a week in my journal. I studied English and really did what I probably should have done earlier, but I was doing it on my own now. I read the books I wanted and really studied writing then, and really, I guess, put my heart into it.

I left monastic life after five years, in 1966. Then I started to freelance write around the country, and I wrote for some of the small magazines. One of my readers then was Sargent Shriver, who saw an article I wrote about him, a little bit criticizing him. I didn't have a nickel. I was out in Kansas City, and he tracked me down somehow and found me, and said, "I read this piece and thought this was somebody who thinks he knows everything," and he was kind of joking like that. He said he was looking for someone to help him with some of the writing of his articles and speeches, and so he hired me, and that's how I came to Washington in 1966. In fact, I dedicated my book to Sargent and Eunice Shriver, and also to my mother-in-law. I've been very close to Sarge Shriver all these years. I think he's one of the great, great political servants.

[THE BOOK] IS A COLLECTION of essays I've written for the past twenty-five years, mostly with the theme of nonviolence and pacifism. I've been writing those all this time, and that's how I make my living. I picked the columns for the book. Rutgers University Press said, "Pick out the ones you really feel passionately about and arrange them in order," and so there are about seven or eight chapters, where I arranged everything from my teaching in school to the nonviolence of bicycling. I commute to work every day by bicycle, which is a lovely experience, and I've been bicycling to work since the early 1970s. I've been urging you to bicycle to work also, Brian. Stephen Breyer from the Supreme Court, I think he bicycles to work, so I'll be eagerly watching to see if he keeps that up.

I asked Ben Hogan, "What's the most crucial shot in golf?" and he said, "The one you're about to hit." And your column, the next one you're writing, is the one you really put your heart into. I do about four or five drafts of every column. It's always 800 words. I guess I've developed an 800-word mind over the years. I go over them with great diligence and take out the clichés, the slogans and the hackneyed phrases, and put all I have into it.

I've been doing that since 1978 when I joined the Post Syndicate, and I joined in 1968 *The [Washington] Post* itself.

University presses make their hardbacks kind of high priced because they sell those to libraries. They make a lot of . . . sales to libraries. Paperback is a lot cheaper. I think it's almost a third or half the price. The paperback of my book costs, I think, about $15. It's out in bookstores this month. The university presses get to a lot of books that the big houses wouldn't go near. This probably wouldn't be a big house book, but that's okay.

If you read the history books, how they teach the kids, it's almost war-centered, and so you don't hear much of the pacifists. It's a one-sided schooling which we give our kids, and that's why I teach that there is another side to this question of how do you solve conflict. If you don't know how to solve them, if you haven't studied the history and the methods of nonviolent conflict resolution, you're not going to know about it, and so as a result we graduate kids who are peace illiterates. I'm trying to do a little bit about that.

William F. Buckley, Jr.

William F. Buckley, Jr., founder and editor at large of The National Review, *came to* Booknotes *on October 24, 1993, to talk about his book* Happy Days Were Here Again: Reflections of a Libertarian Journalist.

WILLIAM SHAWN BECAME THE EDITOR of *The New Yorker* in 1953, right after Mr. [Harold] Ross died. He was its editor for about thirty-five years, up until three or four years ago. He was a man of spectacular talent and of very idiosyncratic personal manners. He was terrifyingly shy and a very reclusive man, enormously well organized. When I sent a manuscript of a book in which I simply recounted what I had done during a week of that year, and he accepted it for publication, I couldn't believe it—because I'm a conservative and *The New Yorker* was pretty liberal.

This was in 1970. Then I sent him a second book and he accepted it, and then a third book and he accepted it, and then a fourth book, and then a fifth book, so that I had this extraordinary hospitality by this extraordinary man. Now, about once a year he assigned himself the job of editing, line by line, a book that had been accepted by *The New Yorker.* And it fell to me to fall under his personal direction for the first of these books, which meant having a lunch with him.

Having a lunch with William Shawn was—well, the next thing to a defloration. You felt that you were getting in the way of his privacy. He was very formal and very genial, always, "Mr. Buckley"—I mean, he wouldn't think of calling me by my first name. But it was an enormous experience because of the care and love that he devoted to every single sentence. He once said to me, "Mr. Buckley, I really don't think that you know the proper use of a comma." Enormously amused me, and it's true that I take sort of liberties in the use of the comma, intending certain effects, which every now and then dismayed him. But he would never publish anything except after your approval of exactly the way it appeared. He was very fastidious on that point.

Richard Rhodes

Richard Rhodes, author of the Pulitzer Prize–winning book The Making of the Atomic Bomb, *appeared on* Booknotes *on December 24, 1989, to discuss* Farm: A Year in the Life of an American Farmer. *The book is Mr. Rhodes's fourth work of nonfiction. He has also written four novels.*

I WENT TO YALE, and then I worked at *Newsweek* a little bit, and then I went off to teach college for a while. It took a long time for me to start writing. I think that writing is something that people find hard to start, primarily because they are afraid—afraid they don't have the right to speak, afraid no one should care about what they have to say. I certainly went through that. I think I was thirty-two before I really wrote something that was worth putting my name on.

WRITING THIS BOOK gave me the chance to look into something that had been puzzling me for ten years—which was what happened to the family farm and what happened about those bad times in the early eighties—so I wanted to go out and live it for a while.

I was on a farm for six years as a teenager. It was a boys' home. My brother and I had been in an abusive situation with a stepmother, and the court removed us to this absolutely wonderful private institution outside of Independence, Missouri, which is no longer, but was then a 360-acre working farm. We raised all of our own food except for white bread, which we saw perhaps once a month. I had a lot of good farming experience. It was very different from what farming is today.

I tried the title *Family Farm.* In fact, my first idea was *The Last Family Farm,* but Tom Bauer, the farmer who is in the book, and a very straightforward man, said, "Well, you know, Dick, that's not true." So, then I thought, well, *Farm.* We have Tracy Kidder's *House* and a lot of other one-name books. *Farm* made sense.

I sat in New York with my editor trying to think what sort of family would be the right family for this book. We decided that it should be a family that survived the bad times . . . a family that had children, maybe sons, who were thinking about whether they should go into farming. Then I went back to Missouri and tried to think how on earth I would ever identify such a family. I imagined myself going from door to door for a year. But I called a friend, who [later] illustrated the book, and told him my problem. He said, "Well, I have a cousin down the road named Sally Bauer, let's go see them." We went to the Bauers and had supper and started talking. After a month of sort of a tentative arrangement, we agreed that we would go ahead with this book.

I bought myself a seed cap, and put on some jeans and boots, and went out and started farming. The first day that I was there, Tom was working on a hog that had a prolapsed rectum—this hog had been kind of mixed up in hog manure—and he said, "Grab that leg, Dick, and let's get this animal fixed up." And I swallowed hard and grabbed that brown hog leg, and we got busy.

I don't see any difference, from a technical point of view, between writing fiction and writing nonfiction. The only difference is that with nonfiction, every fact in the book must refer to a document or a source outside of the book. But technically speaking, as a piece of work, the two have very similar requirements. When I wrote *The Making of the Atomic Bomb,* I tried to arrange the story so that it was dramatic and interesting, which it is inherently. There are some things in the book that a novelist might invent. I did not invent it, but I positioned it.

I think that nonfiction and fiction are very similar tasks for the writer. Here I had this story of a family living day by day on a farm, doing what they had to do to get their crops planted and maintained and harvested, the kids going to school. In other words, a family and its life. Again, I had to figure out what shape it should be in the book. I started with the harvest because I thought that most of us would like to know what the results in farming are before we put any seeds in the ground. I left some things out because they were repetitious. He fed the hogs every morning of the year. In the book he feeds them once, and that is as much as we need to know about that.

I like writing very much. I often ask my writing friends if they like to write, and they always say that they don't. They love the research, perhaps the fun after a book is published, but not the task of writing itself. I think that it is the glory of the work. You have assembled all of this information. You have thought about it. You have dreamed about it. You're ready. You are bursting with all of this and then you have this meticulous, but somehow not entirely rational, process of organizing it so that you communicate it transparently to other human beings. That is great fun.

Interestingly, I think that the most often asked question has been, "Why this book, after *The Making of the Atomic Bomb?*" which I find a curious question. I am a writer. I am not a physicist. I am not a scientist. I am not a nuclear weapons expert. I have published novels about everything from the Donner Party in 1845, to an astronaut after he gets back to earth and what will he do then, and articles about everything under the sun. Truly, I made my living writing for magazines for twenty years. So, the notion of changing radically from nuclear physics to farming did not seem unusual to me at all. In fact, it was a delightful change. I am interested in technology. I am interested in the intersection between human beings and technology and how it threatens us all and perhaps will save us all too. I think that we forget that farming is a technology, a very old technology.

What I like to talk about with this book most is how different farming and farming people are from what I think are the stereotypes that most of us have who live in the city. Farmers are, in fact—especially these days, after all of the winnowing that has gone on in the last decade—very talented, entrepreneurial, technically skilled people. So much so that I felt sometimes as bewildered trying to keep track of everything that Tom Bauer did in the course of an ordinary day . . . as I sometimes felt trying to keep track of nuclear physics. And I say that very honestly and candidly. I kept a spiral notebook stuck in my back pocket while I followed this man around through his days, and I could not write down fast enough all of the different things that he did from hour to hour. He fixed machines. He worried about the genetics of the animals. He dealt with the types of soil that he had and what nutrients they needed. He was remarkably competent at everything that he did and he kept it all in his head. When I said, "Tom, you ought to get a computer to keep track of all of this stuff," he just kind of smiled.

Michael Kelly

Journalist and author Michael Kelly came to Booknotes *on March 28, 1993, to talk about* Martyrs' Day, *a book about his experiences as a freelance journalist in the Middle East during the Persian Gulf War.*

THE TITLE, *Martyrs' Day,* [REFERS TO] A DAY every year in which the Iraqis honor their war dead—which is a fairly large population in Iraq, since they've been engaged in one war or another ever since the Baath Party took office. On that day, by decree of the state, there is a ceremony held in Iraq at the Martyrs' Monument. I went to it on the Martyrs' Day after the end of the Gulf War and attended the ceremony as a reporter. It struck me at the time as a wonderfully emblematic moment about the Iraqi society, about the wretchedness that Iraq was.

I had a minder with me, a gentleman from the [Iraqi] Ministry of Information and Culture who was assigned to watch over me. At one point, he was whispering in my ear what each deputation was. You know, "This is the Iraqi Students Association; this is the Iraqi Doctors Association"—all of which are party organizations. At another point, he saw a deputation come up, and he got excited. He said, "What! They have no banner! Perhaps this is just ordinary citizens!" Then the wind shifted, and it blew over a banner, and he said, "Oh no. It's just the Ministry of Interior, after all." I thought, this is a moment. I wrote the first chapter of the book about that—a small chapter just to set the tone. And I took the title from that.

I didn't know at the beginning [of this project] that I had any mission. I'm not a very organized person, and I started it out almost by accident. I wanted to go to Baghdad and see the beginning of the war and write something about it. I had no larger thought in mind. But once I started it, I got more and more impressed by the remarkable things that happen in a war. The things that happen to people and the astonishing displays of emotion—cowardice, and bravery, and terror—that you see all around you all the time. I thought a writer might be able to put some of this down on paper.

I take an awful lot of notes. I suppose I filled forty or fifty notebooks during the actual war. I write every night—or I try to write every night—in a hotel room. Longer things, reflections, and so on.

I spent no time with any of the official structure at all. I did spend some time talking to American soldiers and officers, but at a very low level—people that I found on the battlefield in Kuwait City and places like that and just talked to. But I didn't have any real contact with officialdom.

I travel very heavy, which was a problem. I never know how to underpack. My last trip, when I went to Kurdistan, one of the reasons it was so difficult getting out of Kurdish Iraq was that somehow I had gotten to the point where I was carrying three large pieces of luggage. As somebody who doesn't have a car, it's a sort of insanity. I never throw anything away. I pack everything; I save local newspapers wherever I go, and I get heavier and heavier.

I had to pay for everything myself and get reimbursed and I was maxing out credit cards and rolling the debt along and beseeching the editors for reimbursements to keep going.

My mother and a few other people in my family were annoyed at me for not mentioning more at the time how sick I'd been in Kurdistan and [instead] finding out about it in the book. A few people have seen things in [the book] that I didn't see when I wrote it. I think it is, to some degree, a book [in which people see] what they want to see.

I SUPPOSE THAT I THINK a lot about the ability you have in writing a book—something of that length, and something without the conventions of journalism to bind it—to tell a story in detail and to use the accrual of detail to paint pictures. I think if I miss anything in writing [a book], it's that. It's difficult to do that in newspaper writing because of the limitations of time and space and because of the conventions of newspaper writing.

I would be happy if [people] said the writing was good. I wanted to write something that was not a journalistic account as much as it was a piece of writing. I wanted to write something that would use writing to look at the way war affects what happens in times of war—not the Gulf War, but war in general—and the way people are and the way they behave.

Garry Wills

Garry Wills, a professor at Northwestern University, an author, and a Time *magazine writer, visited* Booknotes *on December 30, 1990, to discuss* Under God: Religion and American Politics.

I STARTED WRITING BOOKS when I was in graduate school, which was in the 1950s. My first book was *Chesterton,* and I wrote that in a summer when I was over in England between my first and second year of graduate school. I wrote [my first newspaper column] in 1972. I had been approached by three different syndicates. Most people don't realize this, that it's very easy for a syndicate to say to somebody, "Write some columns," because they don't lose anything. They put you in their portfolio, and if nobody buys you they haven't lost anything. You've just lost your time writing the columns. I had heard that, so I said no. I was teaching, and I didn't have much time. But then Kent State occurred. [On May 4, 1970, four students were killed at Kent State University in Ohio when Ohio National Guardsmen opened fire during an antiwar protest.] I was writing then mainly for *New York* magazine and *Esquire,* and they both have long lead times—a month to six months between when you actually write something and it appears. I was so frustrated that I couldn't say something right away about what was going on in the country—I thought the country was really being torn apart by the Vietnam War and other things—that I said yes, I would do it just to get an immediate audience, no matter how. Fifty papers bought it, so I stuck with it.

DURING THE 1988 CONVENTIONS I was following the candidates around, and doing a series of cover stories for *Time* magazine, and a program on national public television on the campaign. And I noticed that although religion was a very big part of the campaign, it was not adverted to in anything like the proportion that I thought it should be. You had two ministers running, Pat Robertson and Jesse Jackson. You had a vice president of the United States [Dan Quayle] who had cultivated very intensively the evangelical right wing. Bush was down [south] before Jim Bakker's scandalous fall. He was down there courting him. And Gary Hart had a very strong religious upbringing and theological training at Yale Divinity School. All of this made the importance of religion to the campaign obvious to me, and yet so little of it came out.

To take one example: Jesse Jackson surprised a lot of people by the acceptance he got in some states where there is a very small black population, because people looked at him as a black candidate or a candidate of the left wing of the Democratic Party. He was not treated normally as a religious candidate, and yet he uses the Bible and religious language and religious imagery constantly. When he went to Iowa, for instance, he would go into people's homes and stay overnight and say prayers before meals, and he would speak to church groups. That was very important to his success, I believe, in Iowa; that there is a kind of natural deference and respect that is given to the clergy. So religion was playing a role there that was not being adverted to.

NOW I TEACH ONLY ONE COURSE A YEAR. I taught full time, and I found I couldn't write and do the things I wanted, and especially I found I was giving too much time to committee work. If you're a tenured member of the faculty, as I was, it's a matter of duty, it seems to me, to be a citizen of that community and to partake of its activities. So I resigned my tenure because I didn't feel that I could keep it in conscience without performing all those duties, and I was getting too old to spend all that time on that kind of work. I'd rather write.

I always say to my students, "When you talk about 'the media' a lot of people are saying *The New York Times, The Washington Post, Time, Newsweek,* or something. Go to a newsstand. Go into a big supermarket and see what people actually read." They read the *National Enquirer.* They read astrology journals. They read the most incredible range of things. There's a much bigger readership for the *Reader's Digest* than there is for *Time* magazine. Real America is something out there that's not discovered by a lot of people including some—especially Democratic—political advisers. The Lee Atwaters are very aware of what the ordinary people are reading out there. They like to pay attention to that, and to go to things like country music festivals, and to listen to country music bands on the radio. Listen to a little country music, and you'll find that God's all over the place in those songs.

Kevin Phillips

Kevin Phillips, author of The Politics of Rich and Poor: Wealth and the American Electorate in the Reagan Aftermath, *appeared on the program on June 24, 1990. Mr. Phillips is the author of numerous political books, including* The Emerging Republican Majority *written in 1967.*

MY SENSE IS THAT if you go back and you look at the history of the Republican Party—and I don't think I sufficiently appreciated this back in 1967 or '68—that it's taken power in some of the great cycles of American history. It's taken power for broad-based reasons: in 1860 with Lincoln in the Civil War; in 1896 when William McKinley fought back the William Jennings Bryan challenge; and then in 1968 when the country was, really, in some ways on the verge of disintegrating from riots in the cities, riots on the campus, a Southern sectional movement led by George Wallace. The Republican Party has played a kind of nationalizing role. It's kept things together during these particular periods. But once it's been in for ten, twelve, more years than that, it tends to get the country too close to upper-bracket economics, a kind of capitalist heyday, and it does too much for the people at the top, and it loses sight of the people at the bottom. And I think the 1980s have had a lot of that.

I have an overall view of the Heritage Foundation and the editorial page of *The Wall Street Journal,* and basically it's "they deserve each other." If there are any people who've been involved in sort of blueprinting the whole laissez-faire deregulate, cut-the-taxes, hands-off view of the American economy during the 1980s, it would be groups like the Heritage Foundation and the editorial page, which I differentiate from the rest of *The Wall Street Journal,* which is superb. But the editorial page is all these yuppies in red suspenders who miss not going to Morgan Stanley during the heyday, running around and thumping. I think that these are the people whose policies the book would be dead against. So I can't say that I'm particularly surprised that they're critical [of the book]. From their standpoint, I think they should be.

If you're going to prove the point, it doesn't do any good to simply say something. What makes sense is to go in there and lay it out and put down the numbers from a lot of different directions. There's a chart in there that shows how during the eighties, the Forbes 400 richest families roughly tripled their net worth. There are others [charts] on who made the most money in Wall Street, how much the top partners in the most prosperous law firms made.

There are lots and lots of charts. The point is that by the time you get through the charts, you've got a picture. And in this particular case, those pictures, I think, are something you can't possibly do with words. So there's a reason for them.

I GAVE UP WRITING A COLUMN because I really got sick of the column. It's called "feeding the monster." And the monster had to appear three times a week. I was willing to entertain the possibility of once a week. But three times a week was a horrible experience. You find you'll produce one out of four or five that you think is really good, and out of the other four or five, two or three will be okay, but nothing much. And there's always going to be one that's a real turkey that you whip out in thirty-six minutes when you were late for lunch. Now, there are people who are perhaps more into commentating than I am. The whole notion of going and interviewing these politicians that I regard as one notch above a melted Hershey bar, didn't appeal to me. Reporters like to do that. I basically am interested in things that don't involve actually sitting [down] and asking these guys so they tell you something you know isn't true—and you go write about it anyway.

So I wanted to get out of that, and I wanted to get to something whereby I would write [a column] only . . . twenty, thirty times a year. Then I would get to write something that was large enough to be a think piece. And I do that now. I do about twelve to fifteen a year for the *Los Angeles Times,* big ones that are like 1,200 to 1,500 words, and then usually anywhere from two or three to five or six or eight others. It works out very nicely. I haven't had a moment's twinge about not being a columnist, and when I've been asked did I want to go back into it, I've said no.

David Halevy

On March 18, 1990, former Middle Eastern correspondent for Time *magazine David Halevy came to* Booknotes *to discuss his book* Inside the PLO, *written with Neil Livingstone.*

FIRST OF ALL, I DON'T BELIEVE that the word "objectivity" exists at all. I think we all, as journalists, when we come to a story, we bring with us our background, education, nationality, religious connections—anything. Objectivity is a word that was invented by those who refuse to stand up alone. I do believe that journalism is a fighting profession. You have to fight. You fight for [a] cause, you fight against corruption, you fight against misleading information. You fight for a lot of things.

To some extent, I wrote the memo which pointed the finger, and said that behind the Palestinian massacre conducted in September of 1982 in two refugee camps in Sabra and Shatila around Beirut—that the man who orchestrated, initiated, encouraged, condoned, call it any name you want—the man behind that massacre of 730 or 750 Palestinians was Israeli Defense Minister Ariel Sharon. Sharon sued *Time. Time* won from a legal point of view, but to some extent lost in the public arena. The story is still correct. The story is still right. I have no second thoughts or misgivings. I continued to work for *Time* for another three years as a correspondent, and then I decided, and *Time* decided—we both came to the same conclusion—I mean, I was nineteen years with the company, and I wanted out. I had had enough. And they had probably had enough of me. So it was very simple.

WE GOT A CALL from a Washington-based institute, headed by Ernest Lefever, who actually called Neil [Livingstone, the coauthor] and later myself, and we went there to see him together. He asked whether we [could] put a book together about the PLO [Palestinian Liberation Organization]. He wanted really a very short . . . kind of a summary of where the PLO is today. When we starting the research, we realized that we had a huge amount of material and that we could turn it into a book. Here was information and a lesson that maybe should be learned.

We enjoy working together. I think we complement each other very much. I run around and I collect information; Neil puts it in this singing form, in this singing fashion. It's terrific to have that capability. I do believe when you operate, especially in this highly controversial area of intelligence and facts that are not clear-cut, you need to double- and triple- and quadruple-check everything you got. Four eyes, four ears, four hands make it a lot easier, and you are really walking on a bridge made of steel.

I NEVER MET YASIR ARAFAT. We deliberately decided not to conduct interviews with Mr. Arafat and his lieutenants while researching the book. The reason for that was very simple. What are you going to ask them? What are you going to get in return? Whenever you see Mr. Arafat and his lieutenants appearing on TV or giving interviews, they deny that they were responsible for terror operations. So what's the point of conducting an interview with somebody who is not ready even to say, "Hey, okay, I did those things. Maybe I'm not proud. Maybe I am proud of those things. But right now the situation has changed and we are doing something different."

I discovered in my years as a journalist that, a lot of times, when I open the intelligence archive and boxes loaded with intelligence documents—that in reality some of the journalistic reporting is better than the intelligence reporting. Journalists are intelligence officers. We work as an intelligence operation, without the huge overhead of intelligence organizations. But we collect intelligence. We present the intelligence to our readers. We are there to provide analysis to our readership, and we are responsible for that information.

I think a lot of my colleagues forget that we are really the tools. We are only a loudspeaker. We are not the issue. We are just the loudspeaker through which somebody is transmitting a message. We are not the newsmakers. We are the news carriers. If you'll remember, in ancient Greece they used to kill the messenger when he brought bad news. We bring a lot of bad news, and nobody kills us. And what does that mean, "standing up"? I stood up for a lot of things. This book does not end with a conclusion. This book does not offer you a solution to the Israeli-Palestinian/Palestinian-Israeli conflict. It does not. It's dealing with facts.

John Leo

John Leo, the author of Two Steps Ahead of the Thought Police, *appeared on* Booknotes *on August 28, 1994. His book is a collection of 114 essays. Most were originally published in* U.S. News & World Report *or syndicated by Universal Press.*

AFTER COLLEGE, I wandered into a newspaper office in Hackensack, New Jersey, right next to Teaneck, where I grew up—*The Bergen Record:* It was during the summer, and I said, "Do you have any jobs?" And they said, "Sit here." In a half an hour I was typing obits, and I guess I was hired. Nowadays you've got to stand on line for years to get jobs at the *Record,* but in those days they just took you right off the street. So I covered crime and violence and sex and trials for three years and then went elsewhere.

Later on, I edited a Catholic weekly in Davenport, Iowa, the *Catholic Messenger,* which was then the most liberal Catholic paper and the paper of record. We interviewed a lot of people and challenged a lot of received wisdom, and we had a lot of impact. After that I was hired by *Commonweal,* which was the lay Catholic weekly; in other words, it's owned by individual Catholics, not by the church itself. I was there three years, and *The New York Times* hired me. The *Times* wanted me to be religion editor and I said no, so they hired me to cover the social sciences instead. I had no background at all in the social sciences, but it was a good job. I worked there for three years.

I LIKE GRACEFUL WRITING. I like people who get to the point quickly in an 800-word column because I have to do that, too.

Anybody who writes feels that it's fun or it's fun having written or it's a joy to get certain phrases in there, but sometimes it's a grind. It's there every week whether you feel like it or not, and you feel you have to give your best, and it's not always easy. Sometimes your opinions change in the middle; that's happened to me a couple times.

One thing that you learn when you write a column is that if you're ready to be interviewed on a subject, it takes no preparation at all. You can just go right out and talk. If you're going to write and have the words frozen in print and torn out and Xeroxed, it takes a good many hours to get ready for that. Opinions, when they're framed in print, are more carefully stated and apt to have fewer mistakes and fewer outrages in them because you can see the copy, because it's compressed and goes through an editing process, whereas talk—you just go right out on the air.

I STAY MOST OF THE TIME AT MY DESK. I try to do a lot of it [my work] by phone. I travel some, probably not enough, but basically my theory is you can make the phone sing beautiful music to you if you call a lot of people, and you can do it a lot faster than you can by traveling. And I read a lot of things. I think if you're going to pontificate every week, you better read a lot of newspapers and magazines to keep up with what's going on. I try to do that.

MY ASSISTANT, BEVERLY LARSON, thought up the title of the book. I was looking for something that would reflect what I was talking about, not too brisk but a little bit jaunty, that showed that I had tried to write about serious things in a light way, and I liked it right away.

I'm talking about political correctness there in the book. A lot of the columns are about correctness, particularly on [college campuses], which I consider pretty much a disaster in America. It's organized around the principle of racial and gender equality, which I presume we're all for, but it amounts to a kind of repressive attempt to tell people what to think. Beyond that, it's organized around a radical ideology. I don't use that as a name-calling adjective; it really is radical. It goes to the root of what America's all about; it insists that there's no mainstream; it plugs into multiculturalism and insists that we're all warring tribes. In the PC [politically correct] lexicon, there is no mainstream; there is no commonality in America. It always looks for differences, and it divides us. I think when you put the division together with the repression of trying to tell people what to think and having codes that you can enforce, you have trouble.

I love to write about language. When I was at *Time* ten years ago, I started doing essays on journalese, the little clichés and weird constructions that we in the press resort to, including make-believe hyphenated terms that have no meaning at all like "blue-ribbon panel," "tree-lined streets." In the whole history of journalism, there's never been a street that hasn't been described as tree-lined. And [I wrote about] the little code words that tell us what to think about things—if a politician has his "ups and downs," they're hinting that he's manic-depressive. This is the journalese way of getting into the insults. So, anyhow, I include a lot of language essays in the book.

I try not to write on the issue of the week. First of all, I write about the culture; I rarely write about politics. My theory is, we already have 400 people in Washington [D.C.] writing about what Secretary X said to Senator Y that day, so I assume that that service is provided for Americans and for the Beltway and for the political class. I try to write about what I think is disturbing and new about the culture, whether it's political movements, or what's on TV, or how movies are being put together, or feminism, or trends that I see. I think people respond to [my writing] because they don't regularly see commentary on the culture; that's what I try to do.

Elaine Sciolino

Booknotes *guest Elaine Sciolino was chief diplomatic correspondent for* The New York Times *when she came to the program in August 1991 to talk about her book* The Outlaw State: Saddam Hussein's Quest for Power and the Gulf Crisis.

I WAS A ROVING CORRESPONDENT, based in New York, for *Newsweek*. It was very exciting, but I ran out of steam, frankly. I'd be in Grenada one week, I'd be in Beirut the next week. My editor would say, "What countries do you have visas for in the Persian Gulf?" I'd go through [them] and say, "I have one to Kuwait." He'd say, "Go to Kuwait tonight." So it was an exciting job, but it was one where I always had a suitcase packed and a thousand dollars stuffed in a book in case I had to get on a plane on a Sunday night and the banks were closed. From there, I left *Newsweek* magazine. I decided I really wanted to get into daily journalism, and I went to *The New York Times*.

[THE BOOK] HAD AN ODD GENESIS. I was actually on maternity leave with our second child when Iraq invaded Kuwait. I was called back to work for *The New York Times* on an emergency basis and was sitting at my desk and was called by John Wiley & Sons, the publishing company, where a man who I had gone to graduate school with twenty years ago was a vice president. He asked did I want to take on this project? Hubris prevailed, and I said yes. So I worked on the book from September [1990] until February [1991], and then we closed the book in April.

I will say that when war broke out, the book changed, and three chapters had to be completely rewritten because I really did not believe that there would be war. I truly believed that Saddam [Hussein], cunning man that he was, at the last minute would at least pull back some of his troops and at least stall a war. But he did not. The reason why is a question that even now I continue to deal with. I try to explain it in the book, but it will be one of the mysteries of the next decade and historians will have to deal with it.

WHEN THE TEXT OF CHAPTER 1 mysteriously disappeared from my computer hard drive, I cried. I have no idea how it disappeared. We even went to the same people who had found the secret memos of Oliver North, the same experts, and they couldn't find the chapter on the hard drive. I was quite upset for about two days. I had printed out an earlier version of chapter 1, so I knew that, if worse got to worst, I could use that as a base. But one of the technicians in our computer department [at *The New York Times*] spent hours trying to find the chapter on the little disk, which had also been degraded. There was some massive blowout so that my backup system had failed. Eventually, [the technician] found it.

I EXPLAIN IN THE BOOK [which country, Iran or Iraq, I would choose to live in]. I would choose Iran. Even though both countries are autocratic—they certainly are not democratic countries as we know them—Iran is an easier country to work in. It's easier for a foreigner to be accepted in Iran. Also there are holes in the system. Iran is much easier to break into. I could go to Iran today, and people I've known over the years would invite me over for dinner and would be seen with me in public. Iraq is very different. Iraq is as close to a totalitarian state as we have, and there's a level of fear there and a fear of the foreigner that pervades the society.

In the acknowledgments I wrote, "This book is a product of both passion and folly." The passion is that I really wanted to write about Iraq. I had felt very strongly in the mid-1980s that our policy was skewed, that the United States had shifted too much towards Iraq. I had written about this in the mid-80s at the height of the Iran-Iraq war. This book is really a logical extension of that thesis that I wrote about for *The New York Times Magazine*. So that's the passion.

The folly is that I took on this project, which was quite an ambitious project, knowing that I had to produce a book in six months at a time when I had a full-time job and two children under the age of two. Now they're two and one. But it was a bit crazy to think that I could do it all. I'm not sure I would do it again, not under these circumstances. I don't think my husband would let me because he is as responsible for this book as I am.

Hugh Pearson

Booknotes *guest and journalist Hugh Pearson appeared on August 21, 1994, to discuss his book* The Shadow of the Panther: Huey Newton and the Price of Black Power in America.

NEW YORK IS A VERY BUSY CITY. I love Manhattan, and I'm very fascinated with Manhattan. The noise really dies down anywhere from eleven P.M. to five A.M. I can go out in the day and go into practically any community and be fascinated, and then at night I can hear myself think, or read, or work at my word-processing program on my Macintosh. When I'm really going good, I might spend five or six hours working on a piece. I like to write every day. I would say, for the most part, I try to get five, six hours' worth of writing done at least five or six days a week.

THE TITLE, *The Shadow of the Panther,* originates out of my determination to find a good title to catch the attention of publishing houses when I came up with a proposal—that's one part. The other part is that the nature of what I wanted to do is like the shadow of the panther. What kind of legacy did the Black Panther Party leave America in general and black America in particular? I thought that it would be a good title to use to convey what I was trying to say about the Black Panther Party.

For the most part, you did have to be black to be a member. But a lot of people don't realize that the Black Panthers were different than black nationalists. The Black Panthers believed that the system was at fault for the problems of black people and poor people in general. They had a lot of white allies, and I think that's one of the reasons a lot of the white radical movements like the SDS [Students for a Democratic Society], the Weather Underground, the Peace and Freedom Party . . . created an alliance with the Panther Party—because the Panthers said, "We believe that it is the system that's wrong and not white people in general."

Interestingly, it wasn't until I got to Brown University, in Rhode Island, that I even came across the notion that I might be inferior because I was black, because you had the affirmative action program and a lot of whites felt that the only reason the blacks are here is because affirmative action is giving them a leg up. So I would say [about] growing up in Fort Wayne [Indiana]: there are a lot of clichés around the conservative midwestern values, the optimistic midwestern values. I think, for the most part, those clichés about their values are true. There might not be the worldliness you'll find on the East or the West Coast, but I think there is something to this notion of basic midwestern values that I grew up with. My notion is "Be straight with me and don't give me a lot of crap." I think I grew up with that notion.

I studied a variety of different things at Brown as I was trying to figure out what I wanted to do. At first I came in wanting to be a writer because I had won a major high school writing award. I was the only one in northeastern Indiana to win it, an award called the National Council of Teachers of English Achievement Award in Writing. But then I saw my first article published in a student newspaper at Brown. It didn't look like I had even written it. So that kind of turned me off journalism. The editor had edited it so heavily. It was almost like, gee, if this is what it is all about, I don't want to go into this, so I had just had the idea that this is something that I might not want to do.

From there I thought about being a lawyer, so I took some social science courses, and then eventually I found my way into premed, not so much because I loved the sciences but because I thought, looking back on my father's life and the fact that he was independent and very, very well respected, I want to do something where I can have an impact on people's lives and can be independent and make a decent living, more than a decent living—a comfortable living. So I went into premed. I guess I really started going into it hard in my junior year at Brown. Actually I took an extra year. I graduated from Brown on time, but I took an extra year between finishing Brown and going on to medical school and finished my premed and majored in biomedical ethics, which was an interdisciplinary major at Brown. But I did not get my medical degree. I spent two years in medical school and left because eventually I figured out I wasn't going to become a good doctor. I just lost an interest in the science and medicine.

At this point, I'm very much where I want to be. I've taken a lot of risks, stuck to my guns to take the risks and basically hit bottom as far as the things that a person needs to do as a struggling writer and have come back up, and I'm very much satisfied with what I've accomplished.

My dream job would be, I'd say, as an independent author who for some time, well, maybe for a few years, would be connected with a major newspaper writing commentaries. But ultimately, say when I'm fifty years old, a person who's written in fiction, nonfiction, maybe a couple of plays. Ultimately that's what I'd like to do.

Robert Kaplan

Robert Kaplan appeared on Booknotes *on April 21, 1996, to discuss his book*
The Ends of the Earth: A Journey at the Dawn of the 21st Century. *Mr.
Kaplan is a contributing editor to* The Atlantic Monthly.

THE BOOK IS ALL ABOUT TRAVELING—in the sense of John Gunther
traveling, in the sense of Herodotus or Odysseus traveling. In other words,
what I wanted to do was a sort of an old generalist's book where I would
take in travel writing, history, demographics, sociology, and blend them all
together and cover a wide swath of the Earth. Because there are so many
books out there, people don't have time to read 500 pages on West Africa,
500 pages on Asia, or 500 pages of literary travelogue and then another
public policy book. I think people yearn for the old-fashioned generalist's
Guntheresque book and that's what I was trying to do here. To do a book
that would break categories, break genres, to try to be a sort of hippie back-
packer but with the questions of a Washington policy wonk.

When I travel, I take about one change of clothes. I never bring a tie or
dress shoes. I bring Nikes, running shoes, something like that, but I always
bring a nice shirt and nice pants. If I have to go to a diplomatic reception,
I fake it, you know? I always apologize and say, "I'm traveling light," and
everybody understands.

So I take one change of clothes—two change of clothes at the most; usually a few books—that's what weighs down the backpack; a set of toiletries;
a small shortwave radio so I can listen to the BBC; a medicine kit with
malaria pills and things like that; and a manila envelope with statistics and
other sorts of information like that; and a water canteen, too.

I traveled about a year. A total of a year, but a number of these places I had
been back to several times over the past fifteen years, and I was making an
umpteenth journey for the sake of the book, so to speak. In some cases, it was
a continuous trip, in some cases, not. West Africa was a separate trip. Egypt I
had been back to about ten or fifteen times. Turkey I have been to about
thirty times, because I used to live in Greece, but I spent two months, particularly for this book, there. Iran I went through many times. But Iran, central

Asia, China, Pakistan, India were one thing; I didn't go home. Then I went home for a little bit and came back and went to Thailand, Laos, Cambodia.

To prepare for these trips I had to get visas, I had to get a lot of shots, because you couldn't get a visa without an injection. Some embassies requested cholera shots; the cholera vaccine is largely useless, but they requested a shot anyway.

I had to get maps. I would phone up people who had been there before, and say, "Who's someone I can talk to when I'm there? Where should I go? What's an interesting part of the country? What's safe?" And then I would [coordinate] my own travel arrangements, because for each part of the world, I would use a different travel agent. I found that I couldn't find anyone who could do all of this.

But more than anything, I would read. To me, reading liberates you. It separates you from other travelers. You could be among 500 tourists in a mosque in Turkey, but if you've read ten books on Turkish culture before coming into that mosque, you're occupying a different realm than the other 499 people because what you're seeing is completely different. It's infused by everything that's happened in the past in that country. How can you observe a present if you don't know everything that's happened up until that present? And you can only do that through reading.

The longest period of time I spent on one of the many buses I rode was about thirty-six or forty hours, on a bus that went from Urumqi, in western China, which is a region in the countryside where there aren't many Chinese but it's mainly Turkic Muslim people. So although you're in China, you're seeing Arabic calligraphy and Arabic script. What the bus did was to cross over that mountain range at the top right-hand corner of the picture and then go southwestward along the southern slope of the Tientsin Mountains all the way to Kashgar.

It seems short on the map but it took two days or so, and you slept on the bus in the seat, and the driver stopped about every eight hours or so in these kind of noodle stands, where you would see these guys throwing huge noodles up into the air, long noodles, about six feet long, and you'd go in the back to some very rustic restaurant. Then the toilets were always 100 yards in the back with growling dogs all around, and everyone in the bus would pour out and slurp down these noodles, and then you'd try to get some water. You would turn on a tap coming out of the ground and rusty water would trickle out. You'd fill up your canteen, and you'd have to put iodine tablets in so you wouldn't get sick from it.

Then you'd get back on the bus, and the bus was not air-conditioned, and people had all their goods on the bus. They had cooking containers.

They had burlap sacks. Everyone had taken off their shoes. And it was all very crowded. So this is how people travel. This is how people cover large distances in western China. This is a part of China where the 14 percent growth rate, the computer revolution, China joining the Pacific Rim, the new superpower of the twenty-first century doesn't exist.

I would go weeks spending maybe ten dollars a day, but other parts of the trip were enormously expensive, because to get to Iran, I had to fly in and it was hard to get a budget fare. Then, once in a while, you'd have to stay at a luxury hotel for a night or so just to clean up, take a bath, and that was a lot of money. But the most expensive part of the journeying was because I'd start off one place and fly back from someplace else. I could never buy round-trip fares. So the fact of buying one-way fares halfway back around the world kind of evened out with the weeks of ten-dollar-a-day traveling.

I interviewed Liberians, I went around its border areas, but I didn't go into Liberia. At the time I was there, it was impossible to get over the border. Also, one of the things I try to do is to avoid places that everybody knew about. Liberia everybody knew had failed. It had had a civil war. It was intensely covered. That's also why I didn't deal with Israel or Syria. I try to deal with places that are either overlooked, [or] are covered from only one layer of reality, like Egypt or Turkey or Iran, and try to get underneath. You never know what the headlines are going to be. But I try to avoid places that would constantly be in the news, or that I felt people were fed up with reading about. They knew that place was bad—"Don't tell us any more about it."

At times I would travel with a guide for a few days, and the guide was someone I found by myself. I never went to an official guide or tourist bureau. I never did that. What I would do is hang around at a university or at a youth hostel and try to find a local character or a local student who happened to speak English and was definitely not a professional tour guide. Because I wanted someone who would be discovering things just as I was discovering things; someone who wasn't quite sure what I was after, so to speak.

I LIVE IN THE WASHINGTON [D.C.] AREA, in Maryland. Usually, I sit at home and write all day when I'm not traveling or I'm not at the library. My time is spent three ways: traveling, library, writing. Occasionally, two or three times a year, I'll go to a seminar for a day or so; occasionally, two or three times a year, I'll give a speech; but mainly it's writing, traveling, library.

I'm a contributing editor at *The Atlantic Monthly* and the articles in *The Atlantic Monthly* have, for the last ten years, grown up into books. I also write for *Condé Nast Traveler* magazine, and then . . . here and there for some other publications like *The New Republic, The New York Times Sophisticated Traveler.*

I wrote an earlier book, *Balkan Ghosts,* in 1989 and 1990. I finished it in 1990. The book was rejected by fourteen publishers who said that nothing would happen in the Balkans, it was another obscure part of the world. My earlier book on Afghanistan did not do well. So they said, "This is another obscure area, nothing's going to happen." It finally came out just as the war was kicking up.

I got my interest in writing and traveling probably from my father. My father spent the Depression years as sort of a hobo and racetrack tout, traveling throughout America. He was probably at every racecourse in the lower forty-eight states during the 1930s. I grew up listening to his stories of traveling. After he stopped that, he became a truck driver for the rest of his life, but he always read a lot, and he always read about history. That's why my goal was always to come back and do a book about America, which I'm just starting now.

My father's name was Philip Kaplan, and he drove trucks for the New York *Daily News* for about thirty years. I grew up in a place called Far Rockaway, New York. That's in Queens, on the border with Long Island. It's part of New York City.

I went to college at the University of Connecticut. I got admitted because of my swimming ability. I was a competitive swimmer. But I didn't continue long with swimming. I took a few journalism courses. Then I worked for eighteen months as a reporter for the *Rutland Daily Herald* in Rutland, Vermont. I wanted to move up to a bigger paper. I couldn't get a job. Nobody would hire me. So I bought a one-way ticket to Tunisia and basically stayed overseas for about fifteen years, as a freelancer, which I still am, actually.

The book is dedicated to three diplomats and a relief worker. Dick Hoagland is a diplomat who was also the U.S. press officer in Moscow. He gave me enormous assistance in Uzbekistan for this book, and enormous assistance in Afghanistan for one of my previous books. Kiki Munshi is a diplomat who gave me enormous assistance in West Africa, and is now a U.S. diplomat in Tanzania. And Ernest Latham is someone who, probably more than any other person, inspired me to write *Balkan Ghosts,* and he's an old U.S. foreign service officer in the Balkans who's now retired. And the relief worker, Graham Miller, is an Australian who I first met during covering the Ethiopian famine in southern Sudan. We remained friends for many years, and we saw each other again in Cambodia for this book. He's a character in the book.

I didn't have a tape recorder. I used a lot of Bic pens and notebooks. It was a People's Drug notebook—what used to be People's Drugstore, now it's CVS—those kind of thick notebooks that they sell, with the spirals. I didn't use the journalist's half-notebooks because they wouldn't fit into a pocket easily. Then what I would do is, when I'd get about fifty pages of notes, I would photocopy them all and mail them back home. The reason is because the most interesting observations are often the most subtle. And the most subtle are the ones you're likely to forget the quickest. Yet you'll go through, like, ten thoughts in five minutes and you'll say, "Oh, I'm going to remember that." But a day passes, you can't remember one of them because all new thoughts come. If you lose your notebook, with this kind of writing, you're finished. You'll have to go back and do it all over again. So the thing I was always paranoid of was not losing my passport or my wallet—that's an inconvenience—but losing the notebook. . . .

I actually never lost Xeroxed notebooks when I sent them back. That never happened. They always came back. And it turned out I'd always throw them away because once I write up the manuscript, I didn't need the second copy of the Xeroxed notes anymore. Once it's in the manuscript, then you're less paranoid about your notebook. In fact, sometimes I'd get so nervous that I wouldn't leave the notebook at home after I got back if I didn't have the Xeroxed copy—because that was it. That was everything.

My wife, Maria, manages the home, manages my office and everything. I don't take her with me, not on these trips. I believe it was Kipling who said it, and then John le Carré copied Kipling as an epigram, that "He who travels fastest, travels alone." It's become a cliché by now. You can get more done when you're by yourself than when you're with someone else. You can decide at ten at night to go out and do something. You don't have to agree upon it with someone else. You can get twice as much done by yourself, I believe, than when you're traveling with someone else.

To me, fun is hard work because I love what I do. I work for a living, in the sense of what I am is what I do, and to me, the harder traveling is, the more fun it is, because you're happiest when you're getting a lot of information, when you're scribbling it down in your notebook. And when you're scribbling it down, you're working hardest, because you know you've got to come back and make sense of those notes. So one day of note-taking may mean three weeks in the study—writing, organizing it all, finding the right sentence and all of that. That's why when you come home from a month of traveling, it takes you sometimes three or four months to put it together.

I would go back to any of these places if I had the time and everything, because you never really understand places. One of the real driving forces of this book is quick study, the whole idea of somebody coming in and doing a quick study on a place. It's not *the* truth, but it's *a* truth.

Thomas Friedman

On September 10, 1989, during our first Booknotes *season, Thomas Fried-man appeared on the program to talk about his best-seller* From Beirut to Jerusalem. *In the 1980s, Mr. Friedman was* The New York Times *bureau chief in both cities.*

THE BEST PIECE OF ADVICE I got before I wrote this book was from a colleague of mine, David Ignatius, who is editor of the "Outlook" section at *The Washington Post.* He had written a novel about the Middle East [*SIRO*], a very good novel. He said, "When you're writing this book always imagine whether the reader is going to want to turn the page. Whether what you're writing, how you're writing, and the anecdotes you're telling will compel that reader to want to turn the page." That's what I tried to keep in mind. Hence the book is a really a combination of analysis of history, of autobiography, of anecdote, put into my own kind of Cuisinart. It comes out the other end in a way that I think really makes it read like a novel much more than any kind of nonfiction book.

WHY DID I WRITE IT? In the simplest sense, I just had more to say. After ten years in the Middle East, I really wanted to sit back and reflect on all that I had said—to try and sum it up, to try to see the patterns. I wanted to try to set a framework for myself to understand this period of ten years that I saw in the Middle East in hopes that that framework would serve others and help them understand the Middle East both tomorrow and yesterday.

I wrote from articles that I had published already. I used fresh interviews and notes I had taken, to a large extent. And then just whatever came out of my head that was rolling around back there in the file cabinets.

I think it depends on the writer what role the editor plays. Obviously I came at the book with a lot of writing experience. I wasn't in any way a novice. But at the same time my editor, I think, played a very important role in helping me with organization. Sometimes you don't really see the best way to organize the book as you're writing it. And it's very helpful to have someone say, "You know the second half of chapter 5 would really make a perfect first half of chapter 3, and the bottom half of chapter 3 should really be the second half of chapter 7, etc., etc." It's only an outsider that can make those recommendations for you.

WE'RE IN OUR SEVENTH PRINTING, [so there are] over 100,000 copies in print. So I'm really pleased. That's a lot of books for any hardcover book. It's certainly a best-seller. It's been number one in *The Washington Post* for two weeks of August. I never dreamed I'd sell 100,000 copies of a serious book on the Middle East.

It is a Book-of-the-Month Club selection. That's something that's negotiated ahead of time. They read the manuscript. They decide whether they think their audience, the Book-of-the-Month Club subscribers, would find this book of interest. And they give you an advance as well, against their sales.

WHAT MAKES BEIRUT such a wild and crazy and absurd place to live is not that people get killed. It's that they get killed playing tennis or they get killed taking their kids to school or they get killed playing golf. That's why I called the second chapter of my book "Would You Like to Eat Now or Wait for the Cease-fire?" which is a quote from a dinner party in Beirut and reflects the kind of absurd juxtaposition of life there, where life was always secure enough for you to go about your day but never secure enough for you to be sure that day wouldn't be your last.

R. Emmett Tyrell

R. Emmett Tyrell, who founded The American Spectator *in 1967, is the author of* The Conservative Crack-Up. *He appeared on* Booknotes *on June 7, 1992.*

I STARTED *The American Spectator* in Indiana, at Indiana University [in Bloomington] in '67 because I didn't like the looks of student radicalism. I thought student radicalism was going to destroy the universities, and it certainly did set them back. I thought it was going to be a real burden to the best of liberal values, which it was. I didn't think it was a good thing, and I think I was right. It led to a little increase in V.D. in the country, a little more mischief in the country, and that's about it.

A lot of people think [that] writers and editors were forever eggheads. Well, unfortunately, I was never an egghead. I was a swimmer on the Indiana University swimming team, which was the greatest swimming team in the world. We had three-quarters to four-fifths of all world records. I suffered a slight inferiority complex. Most of my pals were world record holders and Olympic champions, and the best I could do was to be about the fourth best in the country in my age group.

But our coach, one of the greatest coaches in the history of the sport, Doc Councilman, had the added attribute of really being an intellectual, and he is the guy who got us—a lot of us—to read seriously, to try to write, go on to graduate school and to listen to opera while we were swimming the 200-meter butterfly.

Like a lot of young people, reading books and education didn't have a lot of zest for me. But, you know, all you have to do is have a few smarts and be around people who present ideas and literature in an attractive way, an imaginative way. One of the points I try to make about the conservative crack-up is: the liberal crack-up came about because liberals had a superabundance of imagination; the conservative crack-up came about because conservatives don't tend to have much imagination. Liberals brought about their crack-up by extravagance. Conservatives brought about their crack-up through omissions. The imagination is something I try to talk about in this book. Einstein said imagination is more important than knowledge. I think there is a lot of truth to that. It's an imagination that makes a young person say, "I want to go out and read Shakespeare," or "I want to go out and do better than Shakespeare."

My parents didn't read books. They do now—my mom does. My dad's deceased. My dad worked for Pabst Brewing Company, and my mom raised three kids. Now she has the time to read books. It's amazing how many books older people—retired people—read.

The American Spectator was founded as a college magazine, and it became the national anti-radical magazine. We used these kind of fancy names [as bylines]—"the Baron Von Kannon," "R. Emmett Tyrell, Jr.," and suddenly it was 1970 and R. Emmett Tyrell was my name. Unfortunately, the name was too well known to get back to Bob Tyrell, which is what I'd been called. That's the way it goes. I was a victim of my fifteen minutes in history.

You know, *The American Spectator* is considered kind of a flashy, irreverent, joyous publication, but a surprising number of the thinkers I've admired in life have been not very flashy. I don't want to say I've been solid, sober, cheerless. But [James] Madison, that's my kind of guy. Madison never did much that was dashing, but he certainly did more solid work in his lifetime than most of my flashy friends would do in a hundred lifetimes.

Roger Gittines

Reporter Roger Gittines collaborated with the late Sen. John Tower (R-TX) on Consequences: John G. Tower—A Personal and Political Memoir. *Following Senator Tower's death in a plane crash, Mr. Gittines agreed to appear on* Booknotes *on June 30, 1991, to talk about their book.*

I SPENT NEARLY TWENTY YEARS as a Washington [D.C.] reporter, and I came to this project with lots of preconceived notions about John Tower and the material we were going to cover—and most of it turned out to be false. I was dead wrong about John Tower, and I suspect as a result of that experience that a lot of Washington reporters were also dead wrong about John Tower. John Tower, we're told, was very arrogant, a little pompous, a little stuffy. But he was a very human man. Some people misinterpreted his lack of conversational finesse as being arrogance. It was a lot of fun getting down in the trenches with him and going through almost thirty years of public life stretching all the way back to the 1950s.

We share literary agents, and John Tower had another literary collaborator at the early stages of this project. I had just finished a book and mentioned to my agent, "If you ever get another John Tower project, it's ready-made for somebody like me, having spent twenty years in Washington, so keep me in mind." No sooner had I said that than—two days later—she was on the phone saying that the ghostwriter—the collaborator—had dropped out, and would I be interested?

I probably shouldn't say this, because every Washington reporter in town will climb the wall: I've always thought that in some ways Washington reporters are ghostwriters, anyway. We spend our lives and careers covering government officials, taking down what they say. While we engage in some commentary here and there, and analysis, basically we're passing on the words of someone else. So I thought [this project] would be a natural kind of segue in my career. I've been a radio broadcaster, and a newspaper writer, and a wire-service journalist. As I gravitated toward print, [ghostwriting] was an avenue that was open, and it's one way to pay the bills. Like most journalists, I had a few novels sitting unpublished in my desk drawer, so it gave me a good option to get published and break into the commercial world of publishing. I developed an outline and submitted it to Fredi Friedman, the editor at Little, Brown, and we went from there. The first outline was rejected. I had structured it to be less on the confirmation and more on his career. But that was vetoed in favor of a book that alternates back and forth between the confirmation hearings and episodes in the senator's career. It's almost a cinema verité technique.

WRITING, AS IT HAS BEEN SAID ad nauseam, is an intense, lonely occupation. When you collaborate with someone else, it breaks the loneliness and gives you an opportunity to be exposed to the rest of the world, rather than sitting in some garret staring at your word processor. So from that standpoint, it's enjoyable. It's an unnatural act, though. Writing is a solo occupation, and when you involve another person, it becomes cumbersome. Then, when you factor in editors and agents and all the other people that come with the game, it can get pretty unwieldy.

WHEN I STARTED ON THE PROJECT in October of 1989, we were to deliver in April of 1990, which was an impossible deadline to be faced with. We pushed it off until June, but it was a real crash job. I went without a day off for all those months, worked seven days a week, often twelve, thirteen hours a day, just to do the necessary research. We all think that senators have vast archives to pull from and lots of correspondences and speeches and letters. Well, a lot of the senator's archives were down at his alma mater, Southwestern University in Texas. They had not been collated or organized in any way, so they were literally inaccessible. He never did much personal letter writing. He didn't keep a diary. His memory was spotty, as anyone's would be twenty-five or thirty years back. So I had to write in the morning, and I'd write until noon or one o'clock, and then I'd spend the rest of the day researching. I'd be on the phone interviewing former staffers, government officials, colleagues in the Senate. [Then,] I'd go out, I'd fly places and try to fill in the gaps as we tried to get this thing done. It was quite a job.

John Tower used to introduce me as "Roger Gittines, my writer." I would say, "No, Senator, you're the writer. I'm just the typist. I'll just take it down under 'Boswell.' " That's essentially what we did. We spent literally hundreds of hours in conversations, which I taped, going across all of the principal events of his career. Basically, when that was done, I sat down to, really, put a jigsaw puzzle together.

Writing is a very exhausting, very grueling process, mentally and physically, and I think nine times out of ten a collaborator, a ghostwriter, or call it what you will, probably deserves to have his or her name on the cover of the book just in recognition for all the work. But sometimes when you're dealing with these great historical figures, it's a good idea to say, "It's your book. I'm not going to appear with you on Mount Rushmore. It's not the Gettysburg Address by Abraham Lincoln with Roger Gittines."

It's a historical document, I hope, of considerable importance and so did he. That's why he worked as hard as he did on it. It gives an inside account into the political process—not just the confirmation hearings and the way they turned out, but into twenty-five, thirty years of Washington life. Readers can see through John Tower's eyes just how Washington works, just what it's like to be a START [Strategic Arms Reduction Treaty] negotiator, to be chairman of a presidential commission investigating Iran-Contra. I think you've really got a bird's-eye view on history through John Tower.

Jack Nelson

Jack Nelson, author of Terror in the Night: The Klan's Campaign Against the Jews, *was the guest on* Booknotes *on February 7, 1993. Mr. Nelson began working for the* Los Angeles Times *in 1965, and served as its Washington bureau chief for over twenty years.*

I COULD HAVE MADE MORE MONEY writing a book about Bush, about Reagan. The fact is, the editor at Simon & Schuster, Alice Mayhew, was interested in my writing a book about the presidents. My agent was interested in me writing a book about the presidents. I cover them. I didn't want to write a book about people I'm covering today. I thought I could write this book, and it wouldn't in any way interfere with what I'm doing now. I'm the Washington bureau chief of a very large newspaper. I didn't think that I could handle that, for one thing, and I never knew whether this would be a big seller or not. It may not be, and it may not make a movie. Who knows? But whether it does or not, I'll always be glad that I wrote it.

I covered this story back in the late sixties when the Ku Klux Klan decided that the blacks weren't the problem; maybe the Jews were the real problem. [The Klan] decided that because they had the idea that the Jews had the money behind the civil rights movement. They'd sent civil rights lawyers down to the South to represent demonstrators. A large percentage of the college students who came south in the sixties to demonstrate against Jim Crow laws in the South were Jewish students. So they decided that, and I covered the story. It was something that, when I looked at it—I couldn't believe what was happening, to begin with. They changed from attacking blacks to blowing up synagogues, a rabbi's house, and then one of the most unusual things happened that I'd ever seen as a reporter.

The Ku Klux Klan began to become such a problem to the white community—not the black community, but the white community—that the FBI got together with the Jewish community [, which] was very small in Mississippi at the time. This was Jackson and Meridian, Mississippi, and the community was very small but also had a lot of clout. They were people of some means. They got together with the FBI and the Meridian Police

Department, and essentially what happened was that two members of the Klan were set up in a death trap. I wrote a lot about it at the time. Some of it I couldn't tell in as much detail as I would have liked. I didn't know a lot about the Jewish community at the time I wrote my stories back in the late sixties. It was something that sort of gnawed at me, and I always wanted to go back and find out more about it; how it happened, why it happened. I worried about whether the ends justified the means here—because they did carry out this plot. It ended the Klan violence, but it was something that I always wanted to write more about.

I WAS BORN IN TALLADEGA, ALABAMA. I never knew about it, but it was a KKK stronghold. I was born there and raised in Alabama, Mississippi, and Georgia. My roots are probably more deeply planted in Biloxi, Mississippi, where my mother still lives. My sister lives there. So I'm probably more a Mississippian, I guess, than anything else.

I went to work for the *L.A. Times* in 1965. I opened up the Atlanta bureau and covered the South out of there. That's what I was doing then. For five years I covered the South—some politics but mostly civil rights. This was when civil rights was really the hottest story going, not just in the country but, [for] part of the time, in the world. I covered Martin Luther King right up through his assassination in 1968.

I didn't start going back to Mississippi to write it until about three or three and a half years ago. I'd always thought about writing this book. It's the only story I ever worked on in forty-five years—I was a teenaged reporter; seriously, right after high school I became a reporter—but it was the only story in forty-five years of reporting [for which] I saved everything. I saved all of my notebooks. I could even read the old notes. I saved a tape-recorded interview with a key detective involved in the case who gave me so many details on it. I saved all of my original documents and everything. Then about five or six years ago I began to collect more documents from the FBI under the Freedom of Information Act, always within the back of my mind that I'd go back and do this story one time. Then finally—I have a very good agent by the name of Ron Goldfarb who said, "You've got to do the book." So I finally decided to do it.

It's kind of interesting, when I went back to Meridian, Mississippi, there's a lawyer there, a good friend of mine by the name of Joe Clay Hamilton, and Joe Clay Hamilton had been a reporter on the *Atlanta Journal* back when I'd been a reporter on the *Constitution*—way back in the fifties. Joe Clay actually was a district attorney in Meridian who helped prosecute a Klansman who was caught in this death trap—an attempted bombing down there. He told me when I was there, "You know, Jack, you're timing on doing this book is perfect. If you had come in any earlier, nobody would have talked to you, and if you'd have come much later, there would have been more people dead and fuzzier memories." The fact is, of course, that some of the main players are now dead, and some do have fuzzy memories, but I got there in time enough to talk to a lot of people whose memories were very good, and most of the principals are still living.

I DON'T GUESS YOU CAN CROSS every *t* and dot every *i,* but you will have a hard time finding a book that is more heavily documented than this one— because I have [included] the daily logs that Detective [Luke] Scarbrough filled out. I went back to a secretary in the Meridian Police Department named Marie Knowles and dictated to her every day. She was a tremendous source for me for the book, too, by the way, because she was right there in the Meridian Police Department. She sat in the Meridian Police Department and listened to this ambush being played out on the police radio. She had attended all these meetings between the police and the FBI when they were plotting this thing. So Marie Knowles attended these meetings, see, and she heard them plotting. In fact, she would hear Chief [Roy] Gunn say, "When you get out there, drop him, drop him," meaning "kill him." She said that when she was listening on the radio to what was going on, she had almost a guilty feeling about being part of a murder plot; that she felt bad about it even though, as she put it, "even though they were Klan members." I had a letter she wrote to me just the other day after reading the book, and she said reliving this was very excruciating for her because she went through the same sort of fear and excitement reading it and also the same feeling of guilt. I don't know how many people had feelings of guilt about it because there are a lot of different, mixed emotions here.

Book one—I write that in the third person—that's all about what happened: the Jewish community, the background of how this tiny Jewish population in Mississippi dealt with the civil rights crisis, how they tried to walk a thin line and to fit in with the predominantly Christian and mostly fundamentalist religion there. It's about what happened when the Klan turned on the bombings and so forth, and the shoot-out at Meridian, Mississippi. That's all in the third person.

Book two is about—and I write that in the first person—how this story began to draw me in ways that I would have never expected. Detective Scarbrough, who is a principal figure in the case, told me one time, "You know, Hollywood couldn't make up this story." I think that's true, and he didn't know half of the story. But Hollywood couldn't have made it up.

I talk about then how after the shoot-out at Meridian, Mississippi, I went to Chief Roy Gunn. Now, Chief Roy Gunn was an interesting character because he was the gruff police chief of Meridian, and he was as segregationist as you get. He used to say that "the only thing we need around here to enforce the law is a bunch of nigger-knockers and burr-head sticks." That's the way he talked, and that's the way a lot of blacks were treated at that time in Meridian. Then one day Chief Gunn had sort of a religious experience in church, and he told this to a minister friend of his. He said he decided that if the law was to be enforced, and enforced fairly, that he had to do it, and he had to do it for all people. He declared war on the Klan and the Klan declared war on him. So I write a lot about that, and I write a lot about other people who had this sort of transformation.

IT WAS HARD TO COVER THE KLAN OBJECTIVELY AS A REPORTER, but not just the Klan. I think [that, when] covering civil rights, it's hard to say you're 100 percent objective, because I'd say of anything I've ever covered in forty-five years as a reporter where your emotions get involved, it has to be civil rights—because there are not many gray areas you see in some of this. It's pretty much black and white. I mean, you see justice and you know it, and you see injustice and you know it, so you become involved in the story. There's not much question about that. You want to get to the bottom of it, and you can pretty clearly see the justices and the injustices.

Terror in the Night was one of a number of titles that we discussed. I first felt we ought to have the title *Ambush: When the Klan Came for the Jews.* I tried to stick with that title for a while. I was finally convinced by Simon & Schuster editors, including Alice Mayhew, that it was a little too limited because the book is about a lot more than just the ambush. And it is.

I'LL PROBABLY DO ANOTHER one or two books, but they're tough. It takes a long time to do a book, and it's excruciating. It was Red Smith, the old *New York Times* columnist, who said that writing is easy; you just sit down and open up a vein. Writing is tough. It's real hard. It takes a lot of time and an enormous concentration. I did this book while continuing to do my job as Washington bureau chief. I wrote on weekends and early in the morning and on holidays. You'd find me writing on Thanksgiving and Christmas . . . so it was tough doing it.

PREVIOUS PAGE: Doris Kearns Goodwin was a permanent fixture on this couch while writing her Roosevelt book at her home in Concord, Massachusetts. The author is reviewing a calendar where she recorded both Franklin and Eleanor's daily activities. (Photo: *Brian Lamb*)

BELOW: Lincoln biographer David Herbert Donald, surrounded by Lincoln books, a Lincoln bust, and other materials he used in his book. When I drove to his house for the photo session, I discovered that Mr. Donald really does live on Lincoln Road in Lincoln, Massachusetts. (Photo: *Brian Lamb*)

Former president Jimmy Carter described on *Booknotes* how, when he needed a break from writing, he would head out to his woodworking shop at his home in Plains, Georgia. (Photo: *Charles W. Plant*)

ABOVE TOP AND INSET: Chief Justice William Rehnquist is the only member of the Supreme Court to appear on *Booknotes*. The interview took place in an elegant conference room inside the Supreme Court, where a portrait of former Chief Justice John Marshall hangs above the fireplace. (Photo: *C-SPAN*)

OPPOSITE TOP: One of the more unusual *Booknotes* occurred early on in the program's history, in December 1989. Clifford Stoll, who now has a program on MSNBC, surprised me by pulling out a yo-yo to illustrate a point. (Photo: *C-SPAN*)

OPPOSITE BOTTOM: Writer Colman McCarthy also brought a prop to the set. In this instance, he offered me a yellow squash freshly picked from his backyard garden. (Photo: *C-SPAN*)

Booknotes authors, clockwise from top left: First Lady Hillary Rodham Clinton, former Senate Majority Leader Robert Dole, Vice President Al Gore (a senator from Tennessee at the time), and House Speaker Newt Gingrich. (Photos: *C-SPAN*)

ABOVE TOP: Former president Richard Nixon writing in his coat and tie.
(Photo: *The Richard Nixon Library and Birthplace*)

ABOVE BOTTOM: Retired general Norman Schwarzkopf on the *Booknotes*
set visiting with (*from left*) Mem Constidine, my aunt Eileen O'Gara, and
Bobbsie Ross, all from the Northern Chicago suburbs. (Photo: *Brian Lamb*)

ABOVE: Former Soviet leader Mikhail Gorbachev explaining something to me minutes before the taping. He spoke only Russian. I did, however, have simultaneous translation coming into my earpiece. (Photo: *Tony Pronko*)

RIGHT: Professor Doug Brinkley wrote a book titled *Majic Bus: An American Odyssey.* We were so inspired by his description of his students traveling across the United States to see history firsthand that C-SPAN decided to get into the bus-tour business. In 1993 we launched the first C-SPAN bus; visits were in such high demand that we created a twin C-SPAN school bus in 1995. Our buses operate as production and presentation vehicles, visiting schools and cable communities nationwide. (Photo: *Deborah Lamb*)

ABOVE: Harold Holzer's book resulted in a C-SPAN re-creation of the seven historic Lincoln-Douglas debates. The author is in his office at the Metropolitan Museum of Art in New York, surrounded by memorabilia from the 1858 debates. (Photo: *Brian Lamb*) RIGHT: George Washington biographer Richard Norton Smith stands before the tomb of the first president at Washington's Virginia home in Mount Vernon. The author explained on the program that he has visited the grave of every former president. Intrigued by this idea, I later retraced Mr. Smith's presidential graveyard tour. (Photo: *Brian Lamb*)

Biographer Joseph Ellis surveys the marginalia of President John Adams at the Boston Public Library. He described Adams' informal notes as "in some ways, the most revealing statements of his political philosophy." (Photo: *Brian Lamb*)

ABOVE TOP: Forrest McDonald working on his secluded porch in Coker, Alabama. During the program, Mr. McDonald admitted that he usually writes in the nude on this porch.
(Photo: *Porfirio Solorzano*)

ABOVE BOTTOM: In preparation for her biography on Benedict Arnold, Clare Brandt retraced his journeys up the Hudson River and around Lake Champlain. She's pictured in a motorboat in front of West Point Military Academy.
(Photo: *Brian Lamb*)

Nell Painter, who wrote a book on Sojourner Truth, reported that Sojourner Truth spent a great deal of time knitting. Before our interview I discovered the author knitting, and I could not resist taking a picture capturing the shared hobby of the author and her subject. (Photo: *Brian Lamb*)

ABOVE: In December 1996 we took the program to the White House map room to interview President Clinton about his book, *Between Hope and History*. The president is pictured here with C-SPAN books producer Robin Scullin on the right and C-SPAN cameraman Greg Fabic in the background. Robin was the primary researcher for this book on *Booknotes*. (Photo: *Brian Lamb*)

BACK PAGE: During *Booknotes*, we began to notice many references to Alexis de Tocqueville's 1835 book *Democracy in America*. When C-SPAN decided to retrace his U.S. journey, we started our research in Tocqueville, France, at the family château, where the young French aristocrat wrote part of his book in the room pictured here. (Photo: *Brian Lamb*)

Tina Rosenberg

Tina Rosenberg, the author of Children of Cain: Violence and the Violent in Latin America, *appeared on* Booknotes *on November 10, 1991. Ms. Rosenberg was a journalist covering Latin America, spending time in El Salvador, Nicaragua, Chile, and Peru.*

THE BOOK IS ABOUT PEOPLE in Latin America who do violence. I chose the title, *Children of Cain: Violence and the Violent in Latin America,* in part because of its connotations of violence and in part because of the connotations of universality that come with a biblical title—the story of Cain and Abel; Cain, who took a rock and slew his brother. I'd always wanted some form of Cain in the title. I had played with different forms of it. It's not about children, and I think the title may somehow be misleading. The title is about Cain's spiritual children, which is [to say] people who do evil.

I wrote the book because I was living in Latin America, and in my six years there you can't get away from violence. It really does a lot to shape how society is down there, and it's something that hits almost everyone in society personally. I wanted to try and explain it. I had been reading news stories about violence in Latin America, and they normally were about the victims—about grieving widows, and children who were orphaned. Those stories, I thought, were touching, but they didn't help to explain why that violence always exists in Latin America. This book is not about the victims. It's the perpetrators. It's about people who commit evil or people who learn to live with evil and why they do it.

I loved [writing the book]. The process of working on it, of talking to people, of traveling, is a wonderful thing. You can go wherever you like, and call on anyone you want, and ask them any pending question you want. I can't think of a better job.

In Nicaragua I wrote, I walked around a lot, and tried to fix my car, which took up about a quarter of my time. You can't find parts, and this thing was held together with string and duct tape and jar lids. And I just learned about life. I talked to people. And I also fell in love with Chile. In 1987, I moved to Chile to live. Chile is a very serious country. I belonged to a salsa club in Chile, and people go to dance salsa wearing black tights and serious expressions on their faces. Salsa is Latin dance music that's usually done with bright colors and happy expressions, and in Chile it's very somber. Chile is a serious country, a country of habeas corpus and afternoon tea, where people follow the rules. I can't explain the chemical attraction I feel for Chile. I just got off the plane and felt that this was my home.

One of the overwhelming qualities of the third world is a division. There's one set of institutions, such as schools and hospitals and neighborhoods, for the rich, and one set for the rest. It's as if the two don't live in the same country. The United States looks more and more like that to me. I don't know whether it really changed while I was away or if I just see it in a different way now.

I HAD THE CHOICE OF TWO PUBLISHERS who were very interested in me. One publisher sat down with me and said, "We're going to make you a star." And the other publisher, [William] Morrow, sat down with me and said, "We're going to help you write the best book that you can write." I chose them.

This book is a book that is very intriguing to me and, I believe, is a serious book that explores why people commit violence, not just in Latin America. I feel that these people are violent not because they're Latin but because they're human, and the book has a lot of that in it. But it's not a glitzy book. It doesn't have a lot of famous people in it. I think [that if I had] gone with the other publisher and tried to write a more commercial book, it would not have been as interesting.

I AM STILL VERY FASCINATED by Latin America. I still find it a [place] where the noises are louder, and the colors are brighter, and life is more vivid and intense, and the stories are better, and all the decisions in people's daily lives are much more life or death than up here.

James B. Stewart

Former Wall Street Journal *reporter James B. Stewart was interviewed on* Booknotes *on November 24, 1991, about his book* Den of Thieves, *which covered the rise and fall of Michael Milken and other junk bond dealers in the late 1980s.*

I WAS BORN IN THE MIDWEST, in a small city right on the banks of the Mississippi River—Quincy, Illinois. Hannibal, Missouri, which was Mark Twain's home, is right across the river. There was always a big rivalry between Quincy and Hannibal. I really grew up with Mark Twain lore and Mark Twain stories and visiting the Mark Twain cave. I guess my first interest in storytelling got started with Mark Twain.

Mark Twain took the substance of the world around him and wove it into these gripping narratives. I know he's deemed as a kind of symbol of Americana. I don't know if he really thought of himself in those terms, but he was a realist and a humorist, and he took the materials of life around him and created these great stories.

I myself don't write fiction. The reason is I don't think I have that kind of imagination. I couldn't dream up, certainly, some of the bizarre events that happen in this story. I think someone like Mark Twain had a wonderful imagination, and some of his works are more fictional and imaginative than others. But I still think, at its core, he was doing much the same thing. He looked at the world around him, and that's what inspired these stories.

There was a wonderful, wonderful English teacher at Quincy High School, named Marjorie Bolt, who had a tremendous influence on me. I guess maybe everyone has had this experience—one high school teacher that just made the world come to life. She could do that. I just loved her English classes. She always said, "Read, read, read." She was constantly shoving books into our hands, and she was so enthusiastic about it. I still remember that very vividly.

After college I went to law school, and then I worked for a law firm in New York City. The big leap in my career came in 1979 when I decided to move from practicing law to writing about lawyers at a new magazine that

302 / James B. Stewart

hadn't even started called *American Lawyer*. I helped get that off the ground and stayed there for four and a half years. I wrote my first book about lawyers. It was called *The Partners*. Shortly after that, I wrote a letter to *The Wall Street Journal* because I loved their front-page stories. To me, in journalism, that's where you could be a storyteller and a reporter at the same time. I didn't know anybody there. They called me in for an interview and eventually I got hired.

When I wrote the book, I was editor of the front page at *The Wall Street Journal*. Typically, I would get into the office around eight-thirty or nine in the morning and work until about two in the afternoon. I'd try to cram a full day's work into that period of time, but then leave my wonderful staff there polishing up the rest of the day. Then I'd race home, grab a bite to eat and usually be writing by three, say, in the afternoon. Then I'd go until about nine, and then I'd have dinner. Six hours a day of intense writing is about all that I can do. I would find my stamina kind of went off the cliff at that point. That filled up my life pretty fully. I don't necessarily recommend that regimen. Sometimes I was just writing so intensely I couldn't go in to work, and I took some days off.

I've been working on this book for five years, and it was an intensely draining experience—not only because of the work schedule I described earlier, but just because of the adversarial nature of so much of the reporting. It was a very hard story to report with the array of forces lined up against me, fueled by the Milken money. I'm just thrilled to have it done. I'm just so happy that it did get out, again, looking at all of the money that was spent to stop it. Some private detective has been going around trying to find damaging things out about me. None of it has worked, and the book is out there, and I feel great about that.

Having done a story that was this engaging and consuming, my impulse is I don't want to start on anything else that wouldn't somehow be as fascinating as this. So I guess I'll sit back and watch for a while and see what comes along.

Molly Moore

Molly Moore, former senior military correspondent for The Washington Post, *appeared on* Booknotes *on July 18, 1993, to discuss her book* A Woman at War: Storming Kuwait with the U.S. Marines.

WHAT I WANT TO GIVE PEOPLE in *A Woman at War* is a view of the nitty-gritty side of the war that people didn't see on TV and they didn't see in the newspapers because, at the time, we couldn't get a lot of this out. And I also wanted to give people kind of a behind-the-scenes view of what goes on in war. I mean, no reporter that I know of has ever had the kind of access that I was lucky enough to have with this general [Lieutenant General Walt Boomer]. I mean, I was going through the course of the four-day ground war with him, living in his tent with his chief operations officer, listening to his conversations back to Riyadh with General [Norman] Schwarzkopf—just a view that I was so fortunate to see, I thought it would be a shame to lose it.

Now, "sleeping" in the general's tent is a little bit of a misnomer because, of course, you're in the middle of a war. In fact, one night as we're sitting there, we hear artillery—the Americans firing over us at the Iraqis in front of us, the Iraqis firing over us at the Americans behind us. We're sitting there, saying, "You know, God, don't let these shells fall short and land on us." All night long, General Boomer and his operations chief, Colonel Bill Steed, were working the radios. There were constant foul-ups on the battlefield. There were allied troops crossing into other allied troops' territories. So they were constantly trying to untangle these traffic jams on the battlefield so you wouldn't have . . . friendly-fire incidents.

The tent was more a shelter from these horrendous sandstorms, the cold, the rain, everything else, as opposed to a place to sleep. The most you were doing was taking off your flak jacket when you went in there. But the first night I was there, I was extraordinarily uncomfortable—because the entire time I was in Saudi Arabia, every time I went out to the field, I made a point of not letting them treat me differently because I was a reporter or because I was a woman. Their tendency was always to give you the best tent, to give you a cot when nobody else had a cot. And I always said, "No, I'll sleep where the troops sleep. I'll eat what they eat."

I had this extraordinary window on the war. The frustrating thing about it, though, and one of the main reasons that I wrote *A Woman at War,* was [that] so little of what I saw and wrote ever made it off the battlefield and got back to *The Washington Post* because the war moved so fast and the communications were so terrible. There was just problem after problem out on the battlefield [with] actually filing your stories.

I was actually more fortunate than most of the reporters. I had covered the military for five years, knew many of the commanders and the public affairs officials, and got around some of the restrictions. But during the ground war, there were many of my colleagues that just had absolutely horrendous experiences. The *USA Today* reporter, for instance, spent weeks living with his unit out in the desert, and then was writing furiously every day of the four- to five-day ground war, and thought that his copy was getting back to Dhahran; and at the end of the war, he went back to the army headquarters and they handed him his stack of stories [all of which had been intercepted] and said, "Here, you can take them back when you go."

I went in August of 1991, just a few days after the invasion of Kuwait. As people may recall, it was very difficult for reporters to get into Saudi Arabia. Even in the best of times, the Saudis don't let reporters in. Secretary of Defense Dick Cheney went on a mission to try to get these Arab countries to allow the U.S. military to put aircraft in and on their soil and ships in their ports. Much like when the president travels [with the White House press corps], [Cheney] takes the Pentagon press corps with him when he travels. And I went with him and discovered the day before I got on the plane that I had a visa to stay in Saudi Arabia thirty days, not just the four days of the Cheney trip. So I got off the plane and didn't come back to the U.S. at the end of his trip.

The ground rules then—because the war was still going on, and no one knew how quickly the war would move—were that General Schwarzkopf, of course, could read all my copy before it went out. But I had been covering the situation long enough and had been covering the military long enough [to] develop a sixth sense of what should be in the story and what should not be in the story. I mean, the American public thinks reporters are about as sleazy as politicians and used-car salesmen, [but] we did impose a lot of self-censorship on what we were doing. [One] night, he was telling me the war plan—very explicit details of the war plan for the next day. And I could not report that ahead of time. In other words, you couldn't report

. . . future operations. But that's something I knew. He didn't even really need to verbalize that.

I had a tape recorder with me and also had a notebook. I'm scribbling furiously, but much of the war, and what ended up being very beneficial for the book is [that] I had a little tape recorder with me. For example, the night that we were trapped in the mine field—it's pitch-black. You can't see to write a note anywhere. I just turned on the tape recorder, and in doing the research for the book, I just listened to hours and hours and hours of these tapes and could reconstruct entire conversations verbatim.

Now, the other thing that was extraordinarily helpful in doing the research for *A Woman at War* was that General Boomer did something that I think probably has never been done before. In every one of his war-planning meetings [which] he had every morning, he had a court stenographer [who] recorded word for word everything that was said. And after the war, I got these tapes. They were on twelve computer disks. It was just a phenomenal amount of information. And I spent weeks doing nothing but reading all of these war meetings. That helped you get inside the head of these guys, too. Some of them were very extraordinary. They were candid.

I came back from the war, and it seemed to me that the American people believe that this was a very quick and easy war. It was antiseptic. It was surgical. You saw the missiles coming through the front doors of the warehouses, hitting everything just perfectly. The war I saw was nothing like that. The ground war that I saw was chaotic. There were miscalculations. There were mistakes. There was one day where General Boomer, during the toughest day of fighting, couldn't communicate all day with one of his senior commanders because of communications problems. There were friendly-fire incidents. It's amazing there weren't even more than those we all knew about at the time—and heard about after the war.

The book is an adventure story. Even if you don't care anything about the Persian Gulf War, this is an adventure story about the human side of war and the fears, the anxieties, what's going on in the commander's head, what's going on in the journalist's head, what's going on in the minds of these young men who think they're going to die when they cross the border.

Lynn Sherr

ABC News 20/20 correspondent Lynn Sherr appeared on Booknotes *on March 5, 1995. She came to talk about her book,* Failure Is Impossible: Susan B. Anthony in Her Own Words.

I FIRST GOT INTERESTED in Susan B. Anthony when I was a reporter at the Associated Press in the late sixties, early seventies. There was this burgeoning new thing, which was then called the women's liberation front. I don't want to tell you we've mellowed, but we have mellowed. Anyway, I was a reporter sent out to cover a lot of those early meetings. As I got involved, both as a reporter and as a woman, I also was struck by the fact that this exciting new field of women's rights was to me new, different, exciting. I truly believed we had invented this. I truly believed we were the first ones to think about equal pay, to think about sex discrimination. Then I started reading a few history books, because in college, in high school, in grammar school I learned almost nothing about women's history. I suddenly discovered there were all these women that had come before, and, to my mind, the brightest star of all was Susan B. Anthony. She just got there first with everything. She said it all first. She did it at a time when it was much, much more difficult to stand up against the entrenched philosophies of society, so she became my hero, and I decided she was a great inspiration and I wanted to do something for her.

This book was either written in a year or in twenty-five years, depending on your point of view. Since, I think, I discovered her about 1970, in a way I've been collecting string for all those years. In fact, I started it a little over a year ago, and I wanted it to come out in time for her birthday. Her birthday is February 15, and 1995 is the 175th anniversary of Susan B. Anthony's birth. The goal was to try to bring her alive, particularly for the generations that don't know much about her, and to point out that she is utterly relevant to our lives today.

I STARTED OUT WITH THE PLAN of going to the several dozen libraries in this country that have the original letters, diaries, scrapbooks, and correspondence of Susan B. Anthony. I was prepared to do that; I did some of it

at the New York Public Library; I did some of it at the Bancroft Library [at
the University of California at Berkeley]. What I wound up discovering, to
my great joy, is that all the papers, or most of them, of Susan B. Anthony
and Elizabeth Cady Stanton are now on microfilm. And I wound up pur-
chasing forty-five reels of microfilm and a small microfilm reader and doing
the research at home, which was absolutely a gift. There's something called
the Stanton-Anthony Project, and through a federal grant [academic
researchers] went and got all this material together. It's a wonderful contribution to academia, and the fact that it exists on microfilm and this microfilm is now available at libraries all over the country makes it much easier
for other people to [study].

The forty-five reels of microfilm cost a little over $3,000, and I'll let you
in on a little secret. Actually, I think my alma mater is not going to be
happy about this. I thought, at first, it's a lot of money. It's quite a lot of
money. I understand that microfilm has to be expensive and it's very labor-
intensive getting all this done, and instantly, when I heard the price, I hung
up the phone and I said, "No, I can't possibly do that." Then I sat there and
I did the math, and I realized how long it was going to take me and how
much money it would cost to go to the libraries, so I thought, I'm going to
do it. Then I thought, I'm going to do it, and then when I'm all done I'm
going to donate it to my college, and I will get a tax deduction, and I will
save a little money, and I will have done a wonderful thing. Well, here's the
dirty little secret: I'll never part with this microfilm. I love having it, I love
reading it, and hang the expense, you know. It was a very worthwhile
investment.

I went to Wellesley College. So, Wellesley, I'm sorry, but I'll give you
something else. I love having this microfilm because every now and then I
just want to go through and read an old letter, and looking at somebody
else's diaries you are peering over their shoulder, reading their mail. Don't
we all love reading each other's mail? So I love doing that.

Her scrapbooks are on Library of Congress microfilm as well. The
Library of Congress has six reels of them—actually it's more than six,
maybe—Anthony scrapbooks on microfilm. They also have six reels of her
papers that they own on microfilm, so with all of this you can get a very
complete picture. But I also saw the scrapbooks in person, which is fun
because then you really get a sense of her cutting and pasting these articles.
She put all the articles about herself in there, even the bad ones. This
woman had a great sense of history.

My hope is that people will read the book and understand [that] this
woman has a lot to teach us. This woman was more than just a crazy old
spinster who ran around in bloomers campaigning for the right to vote.

ON THE BACK OF THE BOOK, I have endorsements from Leslie Stahl and Diane Sawyer and Ellen Goodman and Ellen Chesler, who wrote the biography of Margaret Sanger, a wonderful biography. You know how it works. A lot of them are my friends. The publisher sends things out, and you get what comes in. Some of them don't come in by the deadline, some do. So it's largely hit-or-miss, but people said wonderful things about the book.

What really pleases me about the blurbs, because these are women who are my friends and whom I do respect, is that all of these women called me up to say, "I learned so much from your book. I didn't know that about Susan B. Anthony." To a great extent, what I'm trying desperately to do is to reintroduce this woman to the world and make people understand. She's part of our lives and ought to be part of our lives. So I'm very proud to have those folks with those endorsements.

She was very famous and was interviewed all the time. You would have had her on this program for her books and on everything [C-SPAN does]. You would have had her time and time again because her opinion was always sought no matter what the issue was. An interview with Susan B. Anthony could make a reporter's career. That's how famous she was.

John Hockenberry

On July 30, 1995, our Booknotes *guest was John Hockenberry. As a broadcast journalist, he has worked for ABC News, National Public Radio, and the MSNBC cable network. He joined us to discuss his book* Moving Violations: A Memoir; War Zones, Wheelchairs, and Declarations of Independence.

I WENT INTO THIS PROJECT thinking that everything about me was wheelchairs and war zones. And when I was finished, I realized that no, there's a lot more to me than that.

I wrote this book as a way to, in some sense, clear out my soul and mind of a whole bunch of adventures that were building up over a period of fifteen to nineteen years, which is sort of the period that I was working on this book one way or another—of just being a journalist and being an American who went from walking around normally to rolling around in a wheelchair. And for a long time, it was something I resisted. First of all, because I'm in my thirties and you just don't associate memoirs with people in their thirties. And then I resisted it because I didn't really want to do a "John went here and John went there" wild and crazy adventure book with no other sort of intrinsic meaning than that.

I WAS IN A CAR ACCIDENT AT NINETEEN, when I was in college, and it was the kind of thing where I was a confused kid having a great time in college, studying mathematics, having really no idea what I might do with my life. I was hitchhiking, I got in a car, the car went off the road because the driver—the two women who picked us up, myself and my college roommate, had been awake driving for thirty hours as kids often do when they're driving.

I was at the University of Chicago. We were hitchhiking to Massachusetts to visit my roommate's girlfriend at Williams College. We never made it to Williams. In Pennsylvania, the driver of the car fell asleep. I woke up in the backseat and discovered that the car was out of control. We were weaving across the road in this crazy way, and I actually remember thinking, because I was in physics and math class in college, that what I was experiencing at that moment related to some of my assignments. Bodies being acted upon by forces in space. You had this tremendous feeling of gravity, this visceral sense of being plummeted and tossed about on earth. And the idea that you were alive inside this car didn't really matter. Your human personality sort of goes out the window, and you feel this feeling you get when you're in an elevator when it goes up and down, that sort of pit in your stomach. It was all over my body and mind, and we went over this guardrail and landed at the bottom of a 200-foot embankment. It was a slow grade of an embankment, but the car rolled and bounced.

At the bottom of that hill, I was in this car, and I knew I was hurt pretty badly. I was conscious the whole time, and I was scrunched up in the backseat and bleeding from my head. And I had some trouble breathing because my ribs were broken. A bunch of ribs were broken. I put my hands down, as you naturally would—you're kind of crouched in one of these American-made car backseats where they don't have much in the way of leg room. I put my hands on my knees, and nothing—it was like they were somebody else's knees. And at that moment—and I describe it in the book—that was the moment that began this other journey in this other body. I remember thinking, "OK, so something is broke in my back. So something has broke in the spinal cord. So, number one, I might not walk again"; I was sure that I wouldn't. It just seemed so, just so stark, that change. Anyway, I was in that car for a long time, and some paramedic-firefighter types came upon us—it was on Route 80 in Pennsylvania—and sawed the car into pieces to pull me out of it.

Thank God for a truck driver who was behind us, who put out this fire that was going on at the same time. The driver of the car died, so in a sense I was very, very lucky. My roommate [Rick] was okay. He wasn't hurt at all. It's a subplot in the book. Rick is [now] in Seattle. He is a kind of venture capitalist who works in that whole kind of pot of wealth associated with Microsoft Corporation. He's doing very, very well. We've been close all during the nineteen years since my accident. But unquestionably, in a kind of a mirror-image way, it both divided and brought us together. And my relationship with him is part of the book. He was very concerned for me after the accident and in a sense was afraid to address it and talk about it. We were afraid to discuss it as friends. I think a lot of relationships between men sometimes have these barriers where something immense happens and it's almost too difficult to talk about.

Time went on. We actually did sit down for the first time sixteen, seventeen years after the accident and talked—while I was writing this book—

and talked about what it had meant. It was so surprising because what I thought he thought and what he thought I thought were completely different. I remember waking up from a dream and going, "My God, I never thanked him," because essentially he saved my life. If he wasn't there, I would have burned up in that car. I was so driven to move on from that moment that I never had said, "Thanks, Rick." I was so obsessed with this idea that I'd never thanked him and that there was no acknowledgment of his role, that I was the one that was getting all the attention.

I said this to him, and I think he kind of went, "Huh?" He said, "What a silly thing." And both of us being so moved by that. We carried them in our little packet of life that we all carry around with us, these strange questions and weird presumptions about things. In a way, it was a relief to kind of move past that in the course of writing this book.

I WROTE THE BOOK IN NEW YORK CITY. I had lived in little studios and garrets in New York. I decided that when I got the contract to write the book, I really wanted a serious office that would have some space, a place where I could find quiet, a room of one's own, as Virginia Woolf wrote in her memoir. So I got this place on the Upper East Side in Manhattan that looks over the water. It actually looks away from New York City. It looks out over Long Island Sound. I would get up very early in the morning, about four-thirty in the morning, and get my coffee, and I'd be at the word processor at about five A.M. I'd stay there until about ten, and then I would hop in the shower and go off to ABC News, where I had my other job, and work there until eight, and then try to do something to get my mind off both of those things, get home about eleven P.M., go to sleep, wake up [at] four-thirty, do it again. A good day was two thousand words, a bad day was having to erase one or two hundred because you looked at it and you went, "No, it's not working." An average, I would say, was probably about eight hundred or nine hundred.

The cover photo for the book was taken at my favorite place to roll in the city of New York, which is over the Brooklyn Bridge. The two best wheelchair ramps in the city of New York are the Brooklyn and Manhattan sides of the Brooklyn Bridge; it's one of my favorite places.

In the book is the story about Martha's apartment. Martha's the one I don't want to talk too much about. It's not her real name, but suffice it to say that in a large midwestern city, I had a relationship with a very wonderful person, and it didn't work out. I had just recently moved out of what had been our apartment, and we had just broken up. Part of the reason we had broken up was that she had difficulty imagining—I think a lot of people sometimes do have difficulty imagining that they would be together forever with someone who has a disability for one reason or another. And she had been seeing this stage manager guy.

One morning, I'm on the *CBS Morning News* show, and when I got off the air I called my parents, and they were thrilled. And Martha called, and her parents called and it was, "Wow, that was great, that was really good!" So I was feeling on top of the world on that particular day. That evening I said, "You know, I'm going to just go over there, to our old apartment and just surprise her, maybe take some flowers or something." I still had the keys.

So I go over. There's nobody there, and I go into the apartment. I look around, thinking, "Oh, well, you know, she'll be home later." I go into what had been our bedroom. I fall asleep immediately on what had been our bed in what had been our bedroom in what had been our apartment. God knows what I was thinking.

When I woke up—it's four hours later—there were voices, and the stereo was on. There were two voices out in the living room. Suddenly I was terrified. Before I really even had a chance to think about what I was going to do, they started saying, "Okay, I'll get the lights," and "I'll do the stereo," "Okay, see you in a minute," "I'll brush my teeth." And I am thinking, "They're coming to bed right now, they're coming into this room." I thought for a second, "Well, couldn't I just go out and say, 'Hi, sorry I'm here. See you later.' "

Sure enough, they come into the room. I'm off the bed. I'm under the bed. I move the wheelchair, I'm huddled with all this stuff under there. Then there is like a midair collision, boom, and stuff starts falling off—shoes and socks and everything else you might imagine. They're in bed, and it's ten hours of this. I mean, ten hours under the bed and they're on top. They weren't awake for the ten hours, I assure you, but I was just like, "Oh, my God. What am I doing here?"

I found a pen and scratched a little note to her saying I was here. And it's amazing what you learn when you're underneath the bed of someone you're that close to. It's amazing what other guys will say—this guy talked a lot about *Lord of the Rings*, the J. R. Tolkien book, and Martha did a lot of, "Uh-huh, uh-huh." It just seemed like the guy was kind of a loser. But who was the loser, right? Me. I was the one under the bed.

I couldn't sleep. If I fell asleep, I would snore or something. If you're a paraplegic, you often get spastic. Your leg will, like, start twitching or something. So I was just having to lie there very, very still and monitor my legs and everything—because if I twitched. God knows what they would have thought—somebody while they were sleeping is snoring or making noises underneath the bed? So I just had to lie there completely still.

In the morning they're getting up. I had to go to the men's room very, very badly. It's not like anyone else, but it's an unmistakable feeling of extreme urgency. So I was hoping that this was going to be over soon. They're collecting their stuff. Martha reaches down to grab something, a sock or something. Her head comes down, and I'm going, "Oh, my God. Oh, my God, she might see me." Her head comes down, and then it goes up. I'm thinking, "Maybe I got away with it, but I don't know." Then her head comes down very slowly. And she looks at me—her head's upside down looking at me. I'm under there, like, "Hi."

She was great. She says, "Why don't we go into the kitchen and have some coffee." She immediately gets him out of there. They go into the kitchen and have coffee or something, and then he says good-bye. She comes into the room. I thought that she would just take out a farm implement or something, a rake or a pitchfork and just yell, "What the hell do you think you are doing?" But no, she was very nice. I gave her back the keys. "Here, keep these," I said, "I don't need them."

WHEN I FINALLY STARTED to put things down, I realized that finding the meaning in between the stories was a really interesting process. Writing the book itself was a journey. There [are] so many journeys in that book, but it was a journey to figure out, "Does it have meaning, or is it just a bunch of random chaos of a kind of crazy guy named John?" What I discovered in the end is that it does have meaning and that a lot of our struggles to make a mark or to overcome are very American stories. They relate to why each of us is a citizen of this country as opposed to any other. As I learned in my reporting assignments around the world, being an American is a very special responsibility in some ways to the broader human experience, and it's a great adventure. I was very surprised to discover that.

SOMETIMES [WRITING] WAS MY SANITY FROM TELEVISION. And some days, television was my sanity from getting through the book. In fact, doing them together was a great thing. It was very much worth it.

Public Figures

Harry Truman was a reader. He was a lifelong reader. I asked Margaret [Truman, his daughter] one day, "What would be your father's idea of heaven?" She said, "Oh, that's easy. It would be a good comfortable armchair and a good reading lamp and a stack of new history and biography that he wanted to read." He once said that all readers can't be leaders, but all leaders must be readers. . . .

—David McCullough

Jimmy Carter

Jimmy Carter, the thirty-eighth president of the United States, came to
Booknotes *in February of 1995 to talk about his book* Always a Reckoning
and Other Poems. *While* Booknotes *does not normally feature poetry books,
we thought that C-SPAN viewers would be interested in hearing about the
former president's experiences publishing this work.*

ABOUT FOUR YEARS AGO, I contacted a few publishers about a book of
poems and they said, "No. No way." They said that they didn't think they
wanted to publish a poetry book by me, and they said that my poems that
I submitted were not suitable for a book, so I backed away for a while. As a
matter of fact, I didn't exactly back away. I took a poem out of a current
issue of *The New Yorker* magazine, which to me was completely garbled. I
mean, there was no redeeming feature that I could see in this poem. It
didn't make sense. It didn't have any rhyme. It was not beautiful. The
choice of words was not notable. So I cut the poem out and sent it to the
publisher of Random House's Times Books and I told him that if *The New
Yorker* could publish a poem like that, I saw no reason why they couldn't
publish my poetry book. I didn't push it any more.

But later I felt that I got three or four poems in final form, and I began
to send my poems to different periodicals around the country, to quarter-
lies, and to the monthly magazines dedicated to poetry. Some of them were
rejected and some of them were accepted. I asked [the editors who published the poems] not to comment on the fact that I was a former president, just to put my name and not say who it was. And, increasingly, the
poems got favorable reviews from inside those places. I eventually got up
the nerve to put about forty-five poems together; and then I resubmitted
them to the publisher. They offered me a minuscule advance and decided
to take a chance on the book.

Some of the poems I would write, to a great degree, on trips in airplanes
or other places when I was away from home. But the final versions—most
of which were twenty generations away from the original version—were
usually done on my word processor in Plains, Georgia.

I have heard it said that John Quincy Adams and Abraham Lincoln wrote poems, but I have never seen any of their poems. I've asked two or three people lately who were poetry critics if they had read the poems of the two previous presidents. They said no. But that has been a story that has gone around—that Abraham Lincoln and John Quincy Adams did write poems.

I'M MUCH MORE PRODUCTIVE very early in the morning. So when I have a poem that I can't make come together, or a word I can't think of, or how to juxtapose two words that fit, my mind is much clearer, I'd say, between five o'clock and eight o'clock in the morning. I generally have breakfast with [my wife] Rosalynn and talk about things of the day when we are at home. Then I work on the word processor maybe three or four more hours that day, maybe six or seven hours during the day. I can do that much. Then my mind kind of stops working well. I have a very nice woodworking shop about twenty feet from my computer, so I go out and build a piece of furniture, or go out to my farm and walk in the woods, or do something like that.

I guess I started poems in kind of spurts. If I had a day or two at home, which is not all that often, then I would try to think of some things that I wanted to express and that I thought were interesting or that were heartfelt, and I would concentrate on those poems, about three or four poems, and revise them and put them aside. When I remembered it, I would print a copy off my computer to get a version. For about twenty of those poems, I have all the intermediary phases of it—from the original thoughts to the final version. Someday I'll put those in my presidential library so historians can see how a former president wrote poems. But then I would read them to Rosalynn, and I would share them with Miller Williams and Jim White-head, who are experts at poetry. They would give me advice on what was wrong with the poem, primarily "This line doesn't work" or "The poem has extra words in it" or "This word doesn't fit." And then I would revise the poem.

The reviews have been beautiful. The only negative comment I read in an otherwise very good overall piece—I think it was in *Newsweek*—the critic said that I shouldn't have included the poem to Rosalynn, because it was so personal and emotional that, in effect, it embarrassed him to read it. But that has turned out to be, I think, the favorite poem in the whole book. When I sign books—and I sign maybe 1,500 or 2,000 at each bookstore— a lot of the people will open the book to a certain poem and ask me to sign there instead of in the flyleaf. A surprising portion of the women want me to sign the Rosalynn poem.

I'M WRITING ANOTHER BOOK right now, and I've published two books since this one was begun. Whether I'll have another book of poetry, I don't yet know. I've got seven or eight poems now that are in the development stage, and so I've continued to write poetry. I really enjoy this. I've been amazed at how much of a self-revelation comes from a poem. I start writing a poem about things that I want to treat in a superficial way, and before I know it, I've kind of explored the inner depths of my soul, and my consciousness, and my memory—revealing things that otherwise I would never have told anyone.

Richard Nixon

Former President Richard Nixon came to Booknotes *for a special two-part program on his ninth book,* Seize the Moment: America's Challenge in a One-Superpower World. *Both parts were taped on the same day, with the seventy-nine-year-old Mr. Nixon taking a break for lunch and a nap in between. The two parts aired separately on consecutive Sunday nights in February and March of 1992.*

PEOPLE ARE AWARE OF THE FACT that I'm sort of a connoisseur of good Bordeaux. A Bordeaux should never be drunk until it's at least twenty years old. In my view, history is never worth reading until it's fifty years old. It takes fifty years before you're able to come back and evaluate a man or a period of time. So, my reading goes back to people who lived and worked fifty years ago. As far as those who work today, I'm not going to evaluate them. I won't be around fifty years from now to evaluate them.

This is the ninth book I've written and the eighth since I left the presidency. The first book I wrote was *Six Crises,* and I must say that this book, the ninth, was my ninth crisis. Writing a book is very, very hard work. I know you interview writers on your program—I've seen them on occasion—and I must say I admire authors. I'm not saying that in terms of myself, but it is a great ordeal for me. I don't write easily. I write outline after outline, then I dictate into a machine after I've done the whole thing so that it is the spoken word rather than the written word which, as you know, is very formal. And then I have good people that work with me. But when I finally get down to crafting the final product, it is a great, great burden, an ordeal, for me. Every time I finish a book, I say never again.

I received a very outraged letter from a very good supporter who loved the book. She said, "I loved the book," and she agreed with me on my attitude toward the Russians and toward the Chinese and the rest, but she's a very partisan Republican and said, "Why did you dedicate it to the Democrats?" She didn't realize that it was lower case rather than upper case. This is to the democrats of the world, and democracy, in the best sense, that is the wave of the future. In other words, government by the people rather than government from the top down, from authoritarian leaders, be they on the right or the left.

This book took, if I may say, forty-five years to write. It began when I was a freshman congressman when Jack Kennedy and I supported the Greek-Turkish aid program, which was the beginning of the Marshall Plan, the goal of which was the defeat of communism. Through the years I've traveled all over the world. I've had a chance to survey the situation, and what wisdom I learned is in this book—not only traveling in office as president and vice president, but also out of office. In addition to that, I talk to people and I listen because I find that in talking to people you can learn a lot.

In addition to [traveling], I get most of my information from reading. I read newspapers, magazines. I read everything from *The New Republic,* for example, to the *National Review*—the conservatives, the liberals, etc. I read the columns, and I read as many books as I possibly can. I don't want to indicate that I spend all of my time reading material that doesn't eventually end up in a book, but I find that only by expanding the mind, by reading and talking to people, can you then write anything that makes any sense at all.

My books will last only if the events bear out the predictions and also the recommendations that I have set forth in them. But whether they have lasting value is something I cannot judge. The jury's still out on that. What I have tried to set forth in these books that I have written are my analyses of the way things were, but also to make recommendations as to what our policy should in the future to avoid some of the disasters we have experienced in the past. I am probably wrong in many cases, but in other cases I can be right. If this book affects maybe one, two, even three potential leaders, it will be worth it.

We are not a nation of readers anymore. Unfortunately, our leaders today are so busy doing things—like members of the House and the Senate. They have to spend their time raising money, meeting potential givers to their campaigns, and so forth, attending meetings, just running around like chickens with their heads cut off. They don't have the time to sit down and read. I would recommend that they take the time. I would also urge all people who are in public life, who are trying to get into it, to spend less time in front of the tube—even if you're listening to this program—and more time reading. I would urge our congressmen, our senators, our political leaders—sure, use speechwriters, get good phrases and the rest, but you won't think the problem through unless you sit down here with a yellow pad and write it out yourself.

If I had to choose another profession, I would want to be a sportscaster. I think that would be the greatest job in the world. I like sports. I think I would do it pretty well because I like to watch how they play and see these young people, how they meet the test and so forth. I'd just love to be a sportscaster.

Al Gore

Vice President Al Gore came to C-SPAN in February of 1992, when he was still a Democratic senator from Tennessee, to talk about his book Earth in the Balance: Ecology and the Human Spirit.

ONE OF THE REASONS I wrote the book is to put in one place all the facts for anybody who is curious about why their kids are so involved in the environmental issue and what families can do to address the issue.

I wrote the book myself. Every single word of it. And people in my profession sometimes are suspect in that category. But I was a journalist for seven years before I got into politics, and I'm quite familiar with word processing and writing. Although I must say the difference between writing a daily story or daily stories and writing a book was a difference that I did not fully appreciate until I got up to my elbows in this. It is a different breed of cat.

There's a difference in the temporal reality. Stamina is one of the most important qualities you have to bring to the task. If you've got a long newspaper story, even a weekly story, and you get behind a little bit, you can pull an all-nighter and get it finished, or you can just really buckle down and set aside the four to six to eight hours and get it done. With a book, particularly one like this, that is, of course, entirely out of the question. This was a three-year effort. The first two years were focused mainly on the research and organizing the task, talking with people, getting all the ducks in a row. And then immediately after the reelection campaign of 1990, in November of 1990, after my own Senate reelection, I just cleared the decks and wrote in a very concentrated way, day and night, weekends, for a full year, after having gotten all the research lined up.

I think most people write books as if they're going to be read from front to back continuously. I'm not sure everybody reads them that way. But the arc of a book is constructed according to that assumption. A book starts in a particular place and then takes the reader through the full text and then ends in the right way. And if your experience is, as mine was, in writing thirty-word leads and relatively short newspaper stories, you have to make

324 / Al Gore

a transition to capture that sense of how long the arc of a book is. My editor was very helpful in helping me gain that understanding. I wrote it in sections, not chapters. I mention that I took a couple of years before I actually started the writing process to organize research. I pasted things up on the wall, and each area was a different part of the book. I ended up with forty-five sections and then they were aggregated into chapters and actually there was surgery from time to time to rearrange the way chapters were put together. And that again was a new experience for me.

Houghton Mifflin is a terrific publishing company. I've been so impressed with them. They're very conscious of their tradition of publishing books on the environment. They were the publishers of *Silent Spring*, by Rachel Carson, back in 1962. In fact, going farther back than that, they were the publishers of *Walden* by [Henry David] Thoreau. They just have a very strong commitment to the overarching issue, and the editor in chief, John Sterling, took a personal interest in the project. He became my editor. I worked with him, you know—the normal relationship—every single day. Since he is in New York and I'm mostly here in Washington, we really burned up the telephone lines going over every page. And I learned a lot from the editing process because the editors I've worked with in the newspaper business taught me a lot, but as we were saying earlier, a book is so different. Rearranging the flow of ideas and concepts with an eye to the arc of a whole book is something that is akin to an art. I gained a tremendous amount of respect for what good editing is all about.

If I wasn't a full-time politician, I'd be a writer. I'd be a full-time writer. I was a full-time writer for seven years, just before I got into politics. I was in it long enough to get the printer's ink in my veins a little bit, and I really do like the process of writing. I'm one of those people who finds it easier to understand something in the process of trying to communicate it and express it. Not everybody's like that, but there are a lot of us, I know that for a fact. I do like to search my own thoughts in the process of trying to communicate them to others.

James Baker

James Baker, secretary of state for President Bush, appeared on Booknotes *on December 3, 1995, to talk about* The Politics of Diplomacy: Revolution, War and Peace: 1989–1992, *which he wrote with journalist Thomas M. DeFrank.*

I WROTE THIS BOOK ON MY YEARS as secretary of state because the world has changed. The world, as I had known it throughout my adult life, changed completely in those three and a half years. It was a book I knew I could write. I knew I could find the materials necessary to write it in some detail and to write it with great accuracy. If I had tried to write a book about the five [presidential] campaigns [I worked on], or the Reagan White House, the Bush White House, or the treasury job, I never could have brought it all together. It would have been a very superficial book.

I had a collaborator, a very good one, Tom DeFrank, who is the White House correspondent for *Newsweek* magazine and someone I have known since my first experience in national politics, way back in 1976. I also had quite a few fine research assistants whose names you will find in the acknowledgment section of the book. But I wrote the book largely from memorandums of my conversations with various world leaders with whom I dealt. Many of those meetings were one on one, but we each had a note-taker. The memorandums of those conversations are on file over at the State Department. They remain classified. And of course, in order to have access to them, I agreed that the State Department could review the book for any adverse impact on national security. They did so. They were very, very helpful, as I note in the acknowledgments. They gave me an office over there at the department where I could keep the materials and have access to them.

Tom DeFrank and I, we did the work for the book in various places, most of it here in Washington, because that's where the source materials were. These highly classified documents were here on file in the State Department, but Tom came out as well to my ranch in Wyoming, and we spent ten days or two weeks out there at the very beginning where he just sort of picked my brain on various things. I would ramble and talk, and he'd take it down on a tape recorder and later type it up and write from that as background.

Tom [Thomas] Friedman [of *The New York Times*] had written *From Beirut to Jerusalem,* and he was very knowledgeable about the Middle East. And I would occasionally pick his brain, off the record, whenever I felt like it or he felt like it. I don't see anything wrong with that. I don't see where there's any breach of journalistic ethics or certainly not any breach of governmental ethics. I think a government policymaker ought to use whatever intelligence he can and whatever assets he can. I only acted—that I can recall—one time on Tom's advice, and that's when he had suggested to me that we ought not to go chasing after peace in the Middle East, chasing after the parties. We ought to let the parties know that we were not going to devote presidential and secretarial time and attention and resources to a useless pursuit and that if they were not serious about peace, then they could count us out. When they got serious, let us know.

BUT I'LL TELL YOU A FUNNY STORY—I'm not sure it's in the book. I bought this ranch in Wyoming because it's remote. I love remoteness and being out in the country. It's good for hunting, good wildlife, good fishing, and so forth. When I bought the ranch, I said, "Now, we're not going to have any television out here, and we're not going to have any telephone. This is going to be a place where we can retreat." This was in November of 1988.

Well, we lasted about one year with no telephones. What the State Department would do is bring in a secure communications satellite dish, and put it on the big boulder outside my cabin. And I would talk to whoever I needed to through that. But to do it for overseas calls, I would have to hit a satellite over the Indian Ocean, and there were occasions when we couldn't hit a satellite, couldn't make communications, for instance, with a Shevardnadze. Finally the State Department insisted on putting in a telephone line. They said, "We just can't continue to do business this way." And I acquiesced, provided I could pay some of the cost.

GEORGE BUSH AND I MET IN 1957 when I moved back to Houston from law school and when he moved to Houston from Midland, Texas, where he had been in the oil business. He's very, very competitive. He's dogged. He has great determination and great instincts. As I write in the book, he's a man that I have always looked up to, and he's always been there for me when I needed him. We did argue like crazy, and loudly, though. Quite frequently, too. I also say in the book that on more than one occasion I am the one person who tells him what I think, even when he doesn't want to hear it, and that's true. He has likened our relationship to a big brother/little brother relationship. I also say in the book that I consider that quite a compliment.

I gave some thought to [running for president] in 1996, but not as much, probably, as people supposed that I did. As I've told people since, I never really had the virus to the extent and degree that people thought I did. I guess they thought that because I had been chief of staff to two presidents, and treasury secretary, and secretary of state, and primarily because I had run these five presidential campaigns, everybody sort of assumed that I really wanted to be president. I was going to run for president in '96. [In the book,] I'm giving you the reasons why I didn't.

I had sworn that I would never write [a] political book, and I still think I probably won't, because such a book is, almost of necessity, a kiss-and-tell. And I think that people that come to Washington and write kiss-and-tell memoirs generally diminish themselves in the writing of those memoirs. It's hard to write a political book like that about the inner workings of the Bush and Reagan White Houses, for instance, that doesn't turn into a kiss-and-tell. This book, by contrast, is a serious rendition of the fundamental changes in the world from 1989 to 1992, but written in a readable and interesting way.

The publishers suggested at one point that I call the book *Whirlwind*, because what I was involved in was really a whirlwind. But that didn't sound like the right title as far as I was concerned. This title, *The Politics of Diplomacy*, really said it all, in terms of what I was writing and the ideas I was trying to convey.

Lani Guinier √

Lani Guinier, a law professor at the University of Pennsylvania and the author of The Tyranny of the Majority: Fundamental Fairness in a Representative Democracy, *appeared on the program on June 26, 1994. In April 1993, Ms. Guinier was nominated as assistant attorney general for civil rights in the Clinton administration. After controversy erupted over some of Ms. Guinier's writings about voting and race, the administration withdrew her name.*

*I*F SOMEBODY DOES PAY the $24.95 for the book, they get a collection of the essays that got me into trouble in the first place. I wrote an introduction that pulls the ideas together, and I also included an epilogue, which was the speech that I gave after my nomination was withdrawn. I decided to include that speech because one of my neighbors, a young girl in the sixth grade, was told by her teacher that she had to memorize the speech by an important person in the twentieth century and present it to her class. And she asked me for a copy of my speech because she wanted to present it to her class. So I was both flattered and honored that she was interested, and I thought, well, maybe there are other people who would also like to see the way somebody can experience a disappointment but still be committed to the dissemination of ideas.

Interestingly enough, the editor at the Free Press, Bruce Nichols, called me about two years ago and said he had read some of my work and was interested in talking to me about a book. And then after my nomination was pulled, based in part on the misinterpretation or the reaction to some of these essays, the Free Press contacted me again, as did several other publishers. I thought it made sense to go ahead and publish these essays because I felt that the same essays that had gotten me into trouble would get me out of trouble once people actually had a chance to read them.

The day after my nomination, *The Wall Street Journal* had an op-ed with the headline "Clinton's Quota Queen," and then for the next week *The Wall Street Journal* editorialized against the nomination. I knew there was something wrong when I wasn't allowed to respond, and no one else was responding.

When I go around to talk about the book or when I meet people on the street, the reaction is very different than the reaction right after my nomination was withdrawn. People are much more friendly and open. They feel that I was denied fundamental fairness on some level by not having a hearing, so they are certainly expressing their sympathy on that score. But they're also very intrigued. They want to know more. What were my ideas, and what was so crazy or radical about what I was saying? And then when I talk about them or when they read the book, many of them come up and say, "I really had you wrong. I misunderstood or misinterpreted you." In fact, I had a guy come up to me just last week and apologize. He said after he had read the press accounts, he had written to his senator and his congressman saying that I should not be confirmed, and then he read an excerpt from the book and he felt horrible that he had misjudged me.

MY PARENTS MET IN HAWAII, and that's the origin of my name. I was named after the woman who introduced them, although her name was Iwalani. When my parents met, my mother was in the Red Cross and my father was in the army. When they came back and I was born, I was named after Iwalani, but my mother was afraid that Americans would have trouble with the name, so she named me Carolani. Then when people would meet me they'd say, "Oh, Carolina" or "Caroluni," so she just dropped the "Carol." And then, of course, last year when my nomination was pending, there were all sorts of plays on my name, including "Loony Lani." So even though she thought she was getting away from that forty-three or forty-four years ago, it came back.

My father was an intellectual. He was always talking to me about ideas, about the importance of standing for something. He was serious. His hobby, when we would go to the beach, was to take a copy of *The New York Times* with us. We would go to the beach and he would sit under the umbrella and read *The New York Times*. That was a good day at the beach for him.

I HAVE A DIFFERENT STATUS NOW. I'm not simply a black woman; I am somebody who has been on television. Television is the great healer in that sense, and it gives everyone a sense of intimacy or a sense of familiarity, so that there is an ability for people to come and see me and not feel nervous or apprehensive because on some level they feel they already know me. In that sense, it has allowed me to move out of the status of simply being a minority. I think that's part of the problem for other members of a minority group—that they can't move out of the status of being a minority.

Robert Dole

Former Senator Robert Dole (R-KS)—the 1996 GOP presidential nominee— came to Booknotes *to discuss his* Historical Almanac of the United States Senate. *During the September 1990 interview, we asked him about his presidential ambitions.*

I DON'T THINK I WOULD RUN for president. I think probably age is a factor now. I feel young, but you have got to look at the calendar. But it would be a long, long shot, so I would say probably not. I've enjoyed running for the Senate, serving the Senate, serving in the House. We thought we had a pretty good shot in '88. Didn't work out. We did our best, so we'll move on to something else.

[THIS] IS A HISTORY BOOK, as I look at it. It's about senators; it's about things that have happened in and around the United States Senate. We put together [in 1987 and 1988] a series of about 312 different little one-minute speeches made on the Senate floor, and that, in essence, is the almanac. With the help of Senate Historian Dick Baker and his staff, we picked out points we thought might be of interest to readers.

The Senate started in 1789 on March third, and it's a strange thing. We [had] trouble getting enough people there to do business sometimes, so here when the United States started on March third, 1789, we couldn't get a quorum. There weren't enough senators there to do business. There were twenty senators eligible for the Senate. They could only muster, I think, eight. It was April the sixth before they finally got twelve senators to show up to do business. So nothing's changed.

I think my favorite excerpt is one by a senator—I should remember his name—who in 1806 said that speeches didn't have any impact on their colleagues and didn't change any votes. We keep trying to remind our colleagues of that today. But we still have a lot of speeches.

I remember suggesting a number of topics and how it would work. Dick Baker would give us some topics. We'd take a look at them, or I would suggest topics to him. He would take a look at them. I don't recall anybody lobbying me [to get into the book]. I think they may have said something to him. But we tried to get sort of a balance between Republicans, Democrats, Whigs, whatever—just a broad view of the history of the Senate over 200 years: what it meant; what it was like; how it changed. When you go back and take a look at—whether it's pay raises or members getting frustrated at each other, the length of the oratory, how we treated the press or the press treated us—you can go back and say, "Well, boy, nothing's changed in two hundred years."

I would say Robert Byrd from West Virginia [D-WV] is one of the most important senators in history. Senator Robert Byrd knows more about the United States Congress and the Senate, particularly, than any living person. In fact, he has written a multi-volume history of the Senate. Robert Byrd is pictured there [in the book]. He was very helpful in my effort in the *Almanac of the United States Senate.*

There's an old story—they say when you leave the House and go to the Senate, you improve the intelligence level of both bodies. They used to tell me that when I first left and went to the Senate in 1968. I was very proud of my House service, but there is a difference in the Senate. You have more opportunities. In the House, you're on a certain committee or maybe two committees, if you're there long enough, and you specialize in, say, agriculture or energy or education.

In the Senate, obviously, you have committee assignments, but you're pretty free to do whatever you want to do. And there aren't any rules anymore. You don't sit around for the first six years. You're acting the first day you're there. So the Senate, I think, has more freedom and more opportunities. I know a number of outstanding House members who don't get the credit they deserve for legislation because, I must confess, the media has a tendency to go to the Senate side. Senators are generally more well known, maybe not for any real reason, but many of my House colleagues who probably know much more about topics are rarely consulted.

Noa Ben Artzi-Pelossof ✓

Noa Ben Artzi-Pelossof, who at nineteen years old was the youngest person to appear on Booknotes, *is the granddaughter of assassinated Israeli Prime Minister Yitzhak Rabin. She came to the program on May 26, 1996, to discuss her book,* In the Name of Sorrow and Hope.

I DON'T THINK THAT ANY nineteen-year-old wakes up in the morning and says, "Today I'm going to write a book. I'm quite bored, so today's going to be the day that I'll write my book." No. Obviously, I got an offer to do so, and I needed some time to think about it because it's not that easy. You need a lot of courage to [make] this kind of decision, and you need a lot of support, which I had from my family. Then I decided to go for it.

I wanted to write a book about my grandfather in my, as they said, "special voice." What that means is that I tell, as I saw it, the story of my grandfather, the man, the human side, because there was a lot that has been said about Yitzhak Rabin, the politician, peacemaker, soldier, prime minister, and nothing has been said about the man, about my grandfather. And second, the publisher thought that it could be good to hear a young Israeli voice. My second thought was of the therapy—to deal with my emotions.

It wasn't easy. First of all, I had an editor from a French [publishing] company [named] Suzanne Alaya. We worked together to shape the book, in terms of chapters, and to measure what's going to be in what chapter. Then I sat down to write it, and I wrote it in Hebrew. Then it was translated, and I had to check the translation because this is a book that I'm signed on, and it's going to be something that will escort me for years. Although I did it quickly, it's not like I didn't think about it and I didn't pay attention to everything that was going in the book. So I had to check carefully the translation, and to check that nothing had been changed because of misunderstanding of language.

I do not want to write another book soon. It's difficult. It's difficult, and I'm too young to write another one. I still have a few years to decide if I want to do it or not. I enjoyed writing this book. It was good for me, I think. I was very difficult on the editing part, because I never let anyone change what I want to say. The editors would want to add some details which I thought were too romantic, which I didn't like, because I want this book to be authentic and not nostalgic, and I think I did it.

Colin Powell

*Retired general Colin Powell, former chairman of the Joint Chiefs of Staff,
appeared on* Booknotes *on January 7, 1996, to talk about his autobiography,*
My American Journey.

WRITING THE BOOK was perhaps one of the most difficult things I've
ever done in my life. And frankly, it all sort of worked; the book came
together. There were some days I wished I had never started it, there were
some days I tried to figure out how to get out of it, but most days were
pleasant. On balance, it was a good experience, something good for me to
do, to get what was in me out of me and onto paper. What worked was the
collaboration with a great writer by the name of Joseph Persico. I could not
have done this book without him.

I had signed the contract for the book in the summer of 1993, about two
months before I retired. For the rest of that summer period, July and
August, I was looking for a collaborator. I interviewed a number of people,
I looked at a lot of résumés. I read a lot of books and nothing really clicked
for one reason or another. And so I started to get nervous because it was
now toward the end of September; I'm getting ready to retire and in a few
weeks, I've got to start this book and I don't have a collaborator. And a day
or two before I retired, I got the call from my agent, [who] said, "Well,
there's this fellow named Persico and he wants to come down and see you.
And he's interesting. He's written a number of books as a biographer. He's
never done an autobiography as a collaborator, but he looks interesting."

So I glanced through a couple of his books rather quickly, and the day
before I retire, my secretary announces that "Mr. Persico is here." Into my
office walked this tall, gangly, white-haired gentleman who looked like, as I
say in the book in the acknowledgments, a rumpled professor with a
crushed, strange leather briefcase. He is neither impressive looking nor
impressed by me, but he is an impressive man. He just doesn't feel it necessary to show his impressive nature—he's a very at-ease fellow. He looked
around my office, and he took it all in, as a writer should, and then he
looked at me and didn't seem to be terribly impressed by me either. We sat

down and chatted for a few moments, and I knew that I had my collaborator. He could handle me.

He made it clear at the very beginning that if we were going to do a good book, I really had to go to the depth of my heart and soul and bring it all out. We could shape it later if I said some things or we wrote some things that I couldn't live with at the end of the day, but we had to get the whole story out. It took a while for me to get comfortable doing that. As a Washington person, as a general, as a military officer, you learn to control, you learn to show only what you have to [to] get the mission done. Never let all of your emotions flood out. You have to be in control, and that wouldn't work in a collaboration like this and in writing a book like this, and Joe taught me that I had to let it all come out. And some days it took some prodding, particularly in the Vietnam period.

I'm not entirely sure why I was holding back on Vietnam, except my two tours in Vietnam were difficult tours. I lost a lot of friends in Vietnam. It was an experience that was not the most pleasant . . . for the United States armed forces. We came out of that war with a large number of problems that we had to deal with. We dealt with those problems, but all of us are carrying around some Vietnam memories, and I had suppressed a lot of that and Joe helped me bring it all out.

I arrived in Vietnam on Christmas morning 1962, and I think there may have been about 12,000 advisers, give or take a couple of thousand. It was really the second wave of advisers going in. We were replacing the first batch, and were all bright-eyed and bushy-tailed captains and majors and lieutenant colonels. And we were there to save the world from communism, and if this is where it popped up, by gosh, here's where we're going to do it. We were going to help the freedom-loving people of South Vietnam from being overwhelmed by this red tide. It was more in that context [not that] we were getting ourselves involved in a war that was fundamentally a nationalist war [but that] it was part of the great contest with the evil empire. But we were ready to go, and we were all twenty-four, twenty-five years old, and this was the great adventure of our young military careers. We went over there with a lot of enthusiasm.

It was a few weeks after I arrived in Vietnam, and I went up to the northern part of the country, into the Ashow Valley, and on our first patrol out, I think a day or two in, they finally realized where we were moving. The Viet Cong realized the routes we were taking and were able to get in front of us. And suddenly, there was just a burst of fire, and then we returned fire and a lot of noise going back and forth, and for the first time in my life I heard bullets coming our way with that distinctive crack. And then it was all over in a few seconds. I went forward to see what had happened, and I heard screaming and shouting and the noise and confusion. And there in the creek bed lay this young Vietnamese soldier who was dead and a couple of others who'd been wounded, and that was my first experience seeing someone killed.

It was quite an emotional moment to be in combat for the first time and know that this is no longer a game. This is deadly serious. We knew it was deadly serious, but until you see somebody actually killed, it has a certain adventuristic aspect to it. But now this is what it's going to be like every day, because the enemy knows where we are and they can get in front of us every morning. We're going to face this every morning for as long as I'm out here in the jungle with these guys. So it was a bit of a shock and a bit of a downer. And we carried the wounded and the body with us for a while until we could get evacuation by a Vietnamese helicopter, and then we camped for the night on a hillside and it all sort of sunk in.

But then the next morning, when I woke up, there was this sense that, "Hey, I'm alive. It's a new day." There was this sense of exhilaration and also a sense of guilt that I think everybody in combat goes through. You have a certain sense of delight that somebody else is dead and you're not, and now you've got to try to get to the next day without getting killed and hopefully keeping your fellow soldiers from getting killed as well by doing your job as well as you could. And sure enough, the next day we were ambushed again.

I title one particular chapter "It'll Take a Half-Million Men to Succeed" because I remember telling somebody about the time [Robert] McNamara said, "Let's bring some of the advisers home early because we're doing so well," that *this* adviser knew that we were not doing well. We could hardly ever find the enemy. We did not control the ground we claimed to control, and it would take a half-million men to succeed, I thought, and it turned out that, six or seven years later, we had half a million men there and we still didn't succeed.

THE BOOK TOUR around the country has lasted five weeks. We have made twenty-five stops. We had a private airplane that took us around, or else we never would have been able to do it. We tried to keep it to no more than two signings a day. These are not little trivial events. These were events that went on for two, three, sometimes four hours, where I would sign 2,000 to 4,000 books at a sitting. So two of those a day, max, and then a number of radio interviews, television interviews, print interviews with the newspapers in each of the communities, and we tried not to have any dinners or lunches or receptions. We really had to fly out to the next city or get some rest so that my back and arm were up to the challenges of the next day; because of the size of the crowds that were coming out, we really had to keep it moving. So I was dedicating 2.9 seconds, roughly, per book, per person, and they would get a signature, they would get eye contact, and I almost always was able to say something to each person who went through the line, and we averaged roughly 700 to 900 people an hour depending on the setup, how fast people could pass books to me, and what mood I was in that morning or afternoon.

During the book signings, I used a big, fat Sharpie pen—principally because it gives you a nice bold signature. It's nice and round and soft with no edges and didn't cause me any calluses. I could hold it without having to grip too tightly, and it allowed me to have a smooth motion. Other people use a Bic or ballpoint pen, but I found the Sharpie to be useful. I would go through about ten or fifteen Sharpies in a sitting.

I had to make sure that it didn't become so mechanical that there wasn't a human contact between me and everybody who came up. So I was very sensitive to trying to make that eye contact, saying hello and thanking them, really, by my eye contact or saying hello, for having stood in line to get a book and to wait to have it signed. It was a very pleasant, moving experience to have so many people come out to see you and to get an autograph and to say hello.

I signed 60,001 signatures during the tour. We did the last one in an independent bookstore in Norfolk late on a Friday night at the end of week five, and I'll never forget when we did 60,000 they said, "One more. One more." I made 60,001 as a symbol in the book and then gave it to my publisher, Random House, which they spirited away somewhere. I'd better find out what they did with it. I mean, for all I know they're auctioning it off or something.

During the book tour, there were many moments. A lot of old friends showed up, people I'd served with over the years. A lot of my boyhood friends came out in the Bronx. One of the prominent figures in the book from my youth was a fellow by the name of Ronny Brooks, who was kind of my role model when I was a young kid in college. Ronny died a few years ago. But at the book signing in New York, suddenly there appeared in front of me this wonderful black lady who I hadn't seen in a number of years—frankly, since his funeral. It was his mother, who had said nothing, she just got there early and stood in line and waited to see if I would recognize her. Of course I did, and we all teared up and did some hugging and kissing. Some of the young soldiers who were in a helicopter crash with me in Vietnam—two of them showed up. One showed up with his whole family. It was very, very touching.

The audiotape for the book was hard to do. It's about a third of the book. That's about all you can get on an audiotape. It's certainly not the whole book, which surprised me. I thought I was going to have to do the whole book and was relieved when I discovered that it was only about a third of the book. But it was extracted down by professional people, so that you really are getting the essence of the book when you listen to the audiotape.

It took about four days to do, and it's done under the most exacting professional circumstances. They had to know what I had eaten that morning to make sure it wasn't syrupy so that when I started speaking I didn't have any sugar pieces in my mouth that would pop. I had to make sure that I didn't have anything for breakfast that would cause my stomach to rumble because they could hear it. And any time I made a mistake, the slightest mistake of pronunciation or stumbling, we had to stop and we had to do it all over again. It was essentially being like an actor going to the Academy Awards. So those four hours took about four days. We did it at a studio in Washington [D.C.]. I haven't listened to it. I've been afraid to listen to it.

I have read Robert McNamara's book. I have very, very mixed emotions about the book. I don't condemn Mr. McNamara, nor do I congratulate him. I think he has added to the body of knowledge that we have of Vietnam, but I can't help but think that if he felt that strongly about it at that time and he had such knowledge of the failed situation we were in back in '68 or '69, I think he had an obligation to speak up at that time. And he chose not to. He chose to wait a number of years until coming out with this book.

From the time I retired from the military until the time this book came out, [I] wasn't so much controlling my public image as [trying] to get off-stage. I was a private citizen and I was writing a book, and my publisher wanted to make sure that I was not giving away, for nothing, my story, which they had paid me to put in a book. And so, as part of my contract arrangements, I was not doing any interviews because we were waiting for my life story to be reflected in the book.

I wrote the last word, the last comma in the book on the night of the third of July of this year [1995]. That night I called my publisher and said, "Tomorrow is July Fourth. Come get this thing." And the next morning somebody came down on the shuttle from New York. I met her at the airport, handed over the manuscript and said, "Be gone." And I never touched the book again until it was printed and I saw it. That was it.

Bill Clinton

On December 15, 1996, President Bill Clinton was interviewed in the Map Room of the White House about his book Between Hope and History: Meeting America's Challenges for the 21st Century.

A GOOD WRITER IS SOMEONE who, I think, understands character, understands people, understands what makes people tick, understands their fears and their hopes and the drama of daily life, as well as the drama of whatever the theme of a book is, and that continuously fascinating interplay between people, and then can somehow communicate it all and can give large ideas and large emotions and large feelings—reality, in one life or the lives of the characters in the book. It's very, very hard work. It's a great gift.

When I was a young man I loved Thomas Wolfe and the late William Faulkner—the great southern writers. In my adult life I think the finest novel I've read is Gabriel García Márquez's *One Hundred Years of Solitude.* I read it when I was in law school, and I've gone back to it two or three times since then. It's a rhapsodic, mystical, marvelous work.

A lot of the fiction I read now is more for relief—I read a lot of mysteries and thrillers. I just read a mystery by Gerald Seymour, a British writer, about Bosnia and Croatia. I just read an interesting book by Thomas Gifford, who is a great mystery writer, called *Saints Rest;* and a kind of a fun read called *Jack and Jill* by a mystery writer named James Patterson. And I read everything that Sarah Paretsky or Sue Grafton write. I like Jonathan Kellerman, Walter Mosley, a lot of others. David Lindsey—he's a very good mystery writer from out of Texas, a very interesting man.

I read a great deal—magazines, books—all kinds of books: books about politics, books about history, mysteries. I love mysteries. I'm an addict. That's one of my little cheap thrills outlets—I'm always reading mysteries. Normally, I try to read at least thirty minutes a day, usually before I go to bed [but] sometimes in the middle of the day in my office, I have time if I can get away. Sometimes on weekends or a long plane ride I'll read for a couple of hours at a time. It's hard for me to read more than two hours at a time because I normally have to stop and do some work, even on the weekend or on a long plane ride.

The best book about politics I've read in 1996 I would say is E. J. Dionne's book *They Only Look Dead.* It had a good result. He predicted that the administration and the Democratic Party weren't dead. So I liked that, even though we looked dead. But I thought it was good, because it was an attempt to analyze what was going on in America today, in real people's lives in larger historical terms: the forces that are shaping America today, the parallels they have to the industrial revolution changes of a hundred years ago. And I thought it was a very, very good book.

THE TITLE OF MY BOOK comes from a poem by Seamus Heaney called *The Cure at Troy.* It's actually a play. I read it when I was in Ireland, and I quoted a section of it when I spoke in Derry last year [1994]. And Seamus Heaney, I guess, heard about the speech, or saw it, and when I got to Dublin he came and gave me a handwritten copy of those paragraphs of the play, [the section called] "With Hope and History." And there's a two-paragraph section from "With Hope and History" in the book, in the frontispiece.

What the title means is that there are moments in history when people's hopes are more likely to be fulfilled. It means that, if you read between the lines, there's a moment when hope and history rhyme, when there's a greater possibility than at other times where people's hopes can really be fulfilled. I think this is such a time. And that gives us a special opportunity, but it also imposes upon us special responsibilities.

At various times, poetry has played a big role in my life. I didn't read poetry very seriously when I was young. When I went to England, I started reading poetry a little bit. And then I went several years and didn't read any, and periodically I get back into it. I have actually been trying to read some more lately. Last year, when I was going through Ireland, I read a lot of Yeats, and especially the poems that were written around the time of the Irish civil war to try to get a feel for it, and also because it's wonderful poetry.

I did this book because I wanted to get a simple, straightforward, fairly brief account out to the American people in 1996, for anyone who wanted to read it, about what we had tried to do, what we were going to do if I got another term, and what the larger worldview behind it was—why I was trying to do the specific things I was doing. I wanted people to understand how I view America now and how I view the world, and where we are going.

I started thinking about doing it, oh, probably about a year ago, maybe just a little less. But, you know, since I knew what I wanted to do, and it essentially was a distillation of a lot of the things that I had been saying and doing for years, I knew it wouldn't take a long time to do what I wanted to do in this book. But we didn't finish it until last summer.

In the back of the book, I give credit to someone by the name of William E. Nothdurft. I couldn't have done the book without him, because I was in the middle of not only being president, but running for president. And he volunteered to help me on it. We met Bill [Nothdurft]—I and the vice president, people in our administration did—when he did some work in the drafting of one of the reinventing-government annual reports the vice president does. And I read it, and I was very impressed with it. He seemed to understand what it was we were about, what our administration was trying to do.

I asked him to help me on the project, and he was very, very helpful. We spent hours and hours and hours talking about this project, with me telling [him] what I wanted and where I wanted certain things that I had said and done or written before. Then he did a proposed outline for me, and I changed it and said this is the way I want it, and then he did some drafts, and I changed it. Then he did another draft, and then I took it off to Wyoming and essentially substantially rewrote it the way I wanted it to be. But he did a fabulous job. He really understood exactly what needed to be done after we talked. And I think it would have taken me probably two or three times as long to do it if he hadn't been involved in helping me write it.

Bill Nothdurft is a writer and a man who cares about public policy. He lives in the Pacific Northwest. He's been active on and off in public affairs through the Democratic Party for several years, but I never met him before he came to my attention for writing this reinventing-government report that the vice president puts out every year. And he did such a fine job with what some people think is a dry subject. He made it come alive to me.

THIS BOOK DIDN'T SELL WELL because I didn't promote it. First of all, I thought we probably should have made a paperback book and had fewer copies out. But I know how hard Hillary worked to sell her book. Books sell when people go around and go on book tours and talk about them and do interview shows; sit in bookstores and sign copies for hours. And I think I was in one bookstore when my book was out, and that's because I just happened to be in Chautauqua, New York, one day preparing for the debates, and there was a pretty bookstore there. I went in and shook hands with people and talked to them. And I think I signed twelve copies in ten minutes—or five minutes or something.

But you have to sell a book, and I think I feel bad for the publishers. I think they may be able to sell some more around Christmas, and perhaps around the inaugural. I'm proud of the book; I'm proud of what's in it, I'm proud of the work that I did on it. I am proud of the collaboration I had with Bill Nothdurft. I think he did a fine job. And it does give a feel for what this administration is about at greater length, but still a manageable length, than anything else has done.

In the book, I talk about a teacher who taught me Latin, Elizabeth Buck. She's now in Pennsylvania, but she taught me in Hot Springs, Arkansas, where I grew up. I had four years of Latin from her, and she was a remarkable, educated, cultivated, interesting woman. And I stayed in touch with her [for] many, many years. A large number of us took Latin, even though we knew it was a so-called dead language and we would never be speaking it on the street corner anywhere. And I'm very glad I did now. I have great memories of that class, and I understand a lot more, I think, about language and the structure of language than I would have ever otherwise.

IF I WASN'T THE PRESIDENT of the United States and I weren't in politics, it's hard to know what I would have done with my life. I might have been a teacher and a writer. When I was in my early twenties a friend of mine said I shouldn't go into public life because I wasn't mean enough to be a politician, but that I was a great writer and I should just keep writing. So I might have done that.

I READ DAVID BRODER ON A REGULAR BASIS, and I respect him. And once in a blue moon he says something that I think is just haywire, but I think he's an honest fellow that tries to call it like he sees it. I read [Robert] Samuelson in *The Washington Post*. Once in a while I think he says something that's just wildly partisan and way off the mark, but normally I think he's trying to give constructive criticism. And I read him from time to time. And there are others.

But, you know, it's interesting. I get my best constructive criticism from people that are very often quite sympathetic with me, because more moderate columnists, from moderate to liberal columnists, basically try to write balanced columns, by and large, whereas the people that are on the right, they normally stay right there. They have a political objective every day that they pursue, and I kind of admire them—they do it with great discipline. But you can't learn a lot from some of them.

I wouldn't mind doing a column, actually. I think I could do a good job of it, and I think I could offer observations without being hateful. I think I'd have a lot more empathy for the kinds of choices that people in public life face than many do who write. I've often wondered whether I can do a decent job if the shoe were on the other foot. I think it's very hard to write a column. I feel a great sympathy for these folks that have to produce three, four, five columns a week. I think that's really hard to do—and make every one of them interesting and new and substantive. I think it's a difficult thing.

IF ANYTHING, I AM LESS CYNICAL and more idealistic than I was the day I became president, because I look back over the last four years and I see what can be done and what a difference we'll make. I am able in this book to include the outlines of what has been done in the last four years, what the American people have done together, what the government's role in it was. And I did it with the hope [that] the people who read it would say, "Well, you know, these ideas matter. What government does or doesn't do matters. What I do or don't do—that matters too."

Robert McNamara

Former Defense Secretary Robert McNamara, whose role in Vietnam has been discussed in many Booknotes *programs, appeared on* Booknotes *himself on April 23, 1995, to discuss his book,* In Retrospect: The Tragedy and Lessons of Vietnam.

IN THE BOOK, there's a pictorial section. I was under contract to do sixteen pages of pictures. My wife always took care of photographs and things, and so when I began to work on the book—she died fourteen years ago, and I have absolutely zero order in my home with respect to pictures. So I took two or three days out to try to find pictures that I thought might be interesting. I wanted to start with a picture of me as an Eagle Scout. You may think that's absurd, but that's there for the reason that scouting began to set my values. We had to earn twenty-one merit badges. One of them was in civics. In earning the civics merit badge, I learned in a broad sense that it's the responsibility of every citizen to serve. So, I began to think of public service, in various forms, when I was twelve or thirteen years old.

Dean Rusk [secretary of state from 1961 to 1969] was one of the greatest patriots this nation's ever had. I'm so glad he died. Now, that sounds inhuman. He died December 20 [1994]. I'm so glad he died. I thought often after I sent the book to press—he died after it went to press—I thought, my God, I can't face Dean when he reads it. It's going to hurt him. To the day he died, he believed we were right. The subtitle of the book is *The Tragedy and Lessons of Vietnam.* He didn't believe it was a failure. He didn't believe it was a tragedy. He thought it was an essential step to defend this nation.

In the preface of the book, I mention that my wife, Marg, brought to my attention thirty-five or forty years ago four lines from T. S. Eliot. I think they're from his *Four Quartets,* "Little Gidding." It's in the preface [of *In Retrospect*]. I know the lines. I know what they say:

"We shall not cease from exploration
And the end of all our exploring

Will be to arrive where we started
And know the place for the first time."

Now, I haven't ceased from exploring, but I'm a little farther along than I was fifteen or thirty years ago, and I think I see a little more clearly—not as clearly as I will a few years hence or before I die—but I see events more clearly today than I saw five, ten, thirty years ago.

To tell you the truth, I didn't really see clearly enough to be confident in my judgment about the mistake we had made in Vietnam until two or three years ago. I thought I understood the lessons. I had understood and believed, long before then, that it was a failure, but I wasn't completely clear in my mind why it was; and, particularly, I wasn't clear what the lessons were. About two and a half or three years ago, I was in my office one day and I just felt compelled to try to write them down. I don't use a computer. I write longhand. And I just felt compelled to write down—off the top of my head, with no research, no documentation, no reference to books that had been written on it at all—just off the top of my head what I thought were the lessons. I wrote them down, and the last chapter, which includes the eleven mistakes—the statement of the eleven lessons—is almost verbatim what I wrote down at that time. Then having written that, I thought maybe I could go farther. People had been pressing me to go much farther. Coincidentally, at that time, a young man began to write a biography of me. I had never heard of him. He called and asked if I would be willing to talk to him about this biography. He said, "Of course, there'll be no opportunity to see what I write, no opportunity for you to censor it. If you're willing to do it on that basis, I'd like to talk to you."

So he came, and we talked once. He came again, and we talked twice. It turned out that he is a very, very young assistant professor at the [U.S.] Naval Academy, a professor of history. His name is Brian VanderMark. Moreover, he had written one book, one small book, on Vietnam, and he had assisted Clark Clifford and Dick [Richard] Holbrooke in writing Clark's book [*Counsel to the President*]. So VanderMark came in after these two or three interviews with reference to his biography, and he said, "You know, I'm a historian. I'm a professional historian." He said, "I've begun to understand that really the only person that can talk authoritatively about Vietnam is you. You say that you're never going to do it because you didn't take any papers out of the Defense Department excepting one little three-ring binder of very highly classified memos to Presidents Johnson and Kennedy. You didn't take any papers out. You didn't keep a diary. You don't have any access to classified materials. You say you can't, by yourself, develop the documentary base. You say you don't want to write off the top of your head. You don't want to write from memory. You don't trust your memory. It isn't, you say, that you would consciously distort, but you've told me, McNamara, that it's your experience that people writing about themselves and their own decisions look at that through glasses that are favorable to them. You say you don't want to do that and that's one of the reasons you haven't written [a book]. Well, I would be willing to do the research, and, moreover, I would be willing to review everything you write and adhere to the strictest standard of scholarship, and I'll call it if you ever deviate from the written record in any way, or if you appear to express judgments which you might not have had at the time, or if you appear to be writing in ways that put a favorable gloss on your position or your action," he said. "I will agree that I will check that and bring it to your attention." So I said, "Okay, we'll start."

I signed a contract to write an autobiography. After he'd said he'd work with me on an autobiography, I developed a written proposal covering my life—the early years, my education at [the University of California at] Berkeley and Harvard, my experience in World War II, my fifteen years at Ford Motor Company, my seven years in the Defense Department, and my thirteen years in the World Bank. I laid out, for each of those sections of my life, what I'll call the story line that I was going to use as a foundation for the autobiography. I hired an agent, Sterling Lord, a wonderful agent, and asked him to take this to the publishers. He did. A number were interested. Four put forward very substantial proposals, and out of that I chose one. I knew that I obviously had to cover Vietnam, and I knew that would be, or thought it'd be, the most difficult part of it. So I said to Brian, "I'm going to start there. I was secretary for seven years during that period when we went through a whole series of decisions on Vietnam. I'm going to break the seven years into nine periods, not equal in length, but nine periods related to the substantive decisions, the policy decisions of those periods. I'm going to give those calendar periods to you, and I want you to go to all the libraries, all the depositories of documents—Defense Department and the Library of Congress, the LBJ Library, the Kennedy Library, etc. For each one of these nine periods, I want you to bring me the piles of documents, and I'll draft the chapter based on that. Then you take my draft, and you go over it and compare it to the documents—and be damn sure that it's founded in documentation and in reality and not in my desire to make the decisions look wise today." And that's the way we worked.

I didn't have copies of the book until last Friday, and so I shipped them to my children. They haven't read it yet, but one of them was with me last night. Kay Graham, the former publisher of the *Post,* gave a book party here. I was embarrassed that she did, but it turned out to be a wonderful affair, and my daughter was there, the one that lives in Washington, and she was very excited about it. We were talking about protests. My children were of college age [during the Vietnam War]. My son, the youngest, who was nine years younger than the oldest, went to Stanford after I left the Department of Defense. But my oldest child was in Stanford while I was in the Department of Defense, and my middle child was in university as well while I was there. Of course, they were all exposed, in varying degrees, to protesters in some fashion. Last night at this book party, we got talking about protests. My middle child, Kathy, had a friend who organized thousands of young people to march against the president and against me on Vietnam. After one or two of these marches, she invited [that friend] to dinner, so he came and had dinner at our home several times. I recall one occasion [when], after dinner, we went in the library and we talked until about ten-thirty or so, and as he got up to leave, he said, very seriously, "Well, I guess nobody can be all bad who loves the mountains as much as you do." Now, the man's name is Sam Brown. He was nominated by President Clinton to be ambassador to the CSE, the Council on Security and Cooperation in Europe, about a year and a half ago. Senator [Jesse] Helms [R-NC] said, "Hell, no. That guy was a traitor. We're not going to confirm him." So Sam wrote me a note and said, "Bob, would you write Senator Helms and say whatever you want, but I hope you'll say I wasn't a traitor, that I believed in this nation, and I was trying to save the nation from what I considered to be mistakes. Maybe I was wrong, but that was my belief. I surely wasn't a traitor." So I wrote Senator Helms and told him that. It had no impact. They refused to confirm him. But [Brown is] dedicated to public service, too, so he is serving over there now as the U.S. representative to the Council on Security and Cooperation in Europe, but not as ambassador.

I've gone to the Wall [the Vietnam Veterans Memorial]. That's not an issue. But I don't want to confront the veterans. I want the veterans to be respected and admired by our people in ways that they haven't been. And I hope the book will contribute to that. It wasn't the veterans who caused this. They're the ones who did their duty, and we should respect and admire them. The greatest help we can give them is to ensure that their sacrifice isn't repeated in the future.

Hanan Ashrawi ✓

Hanan Ashrawi, author of This Side of Peace, *appeared on* Booknotes *on June 4, 1995. Ms. Ashrawi, a former professor, now commissioner general of the Palestinian Independent Commission for Citizens Rights, lives on the West Bank in Israel. Her father's struggle with Alzheimer's was one of the more emotional personal stories ever told on the program.*

MY FATHER HAD ALZHEIMER'S at the end of his life. He was a brilliant man. He was a man of keen intellect and yet gentle humanism, and so the last few years of his life he had Alzheimer's, and he couldn't remember names. He developed a new language and so on. But he kept his serenity, his gentleness. So one night he just walked out. He evaded his companion and walked out of the house. It was the stormiest part of the year. It was just before Christmas.

We lived in the same house, but different floors. It's the house my father built. You see, we have a tradition in Palestine where you build family homes. It's a sign of your history, your past, and your continuity, and you leave it to your children. So the family lived in this home. It's a big home, and he was living with my mother on the first floor, and I was on the floor below that. And he just walked out in the middle of a storm and disappeared for three days. That was in the middle of the *intifada*, the uprising. So we had to go out looking for him. We went to the police. The police wouldn't do anything, because at that time the Palestinian police had resigned and there were only Israeli police. They said, "You get the intifada kids to the intifada *shabāb*, to look for him." And we did. We went to the neighborhood committees, the popular committees, and for three days and three nights, through the worst storm in our history, we were looking for him. We finally found him. He had gone to the place where he used to go hunting and picnicking with his family when he was a child, and we found him in a pastoral setting. He was as if sleeping next to a little pond and a small waterfall, and it had been snowing, so there was a very light film of snow. We never knew where he was those three days, but it was a very mystical experience, so to speak. Some friends of ours wrote us and said he loved nature, and therefore he found the most appropriate place to die.

I didn't want to go see him, because I said if a person was lost for three days and found out there, you know, just the images were horrific in my mind of what could have happened to this man who didn't even remember his name. When my husband saw him, he said, "You've got to see him just to rest, you know, to have the proper image." When I went to see him, he was very peaceful, and he had a very relaxed smile on his face, and he looked very neat and still now. And we sent out messages. We asked everybody, "Who had sheltered him for those three days?" because he couldn't have been out there wandering in the wilds for three days. Nobody came forth. But obviously, he had had a very peaceful ending.

Hillary Rodham Clinton ✓

First Lady Hillary Rodham Clinton appeared on the program on March 3, 1996, to discuss her book It Takes A Village: And Other Lessons Children Can Teach Us.

I'VE THOUGHT ABOUT WRITING A BOOK for a long time, but I actually took it seriously when the publisher came to see me, Carolyn Reidy, who's the publisher and president of the trade division at Simon & Schuster, and Rebecca Salatan, the editor. They had published my mother-in-law's book, which is a marvelous book, *Leading with My Heart*. Becky Salatan had been the editor. They showed up and said, "Have you thought about writing a book?" And I said, "I've thought about it, but it's not anything I've taken seriously." And we began to talk a year ago January [1995].

Writing the book was something that I thought was going to be a lot easier than it turned out to be. The original plan was for me to just sit down and talk and have the conversations transcribed and then to have some research done and some help, sort of editing the transcriptions and basically for that to be the book. I found out that did not work for me. I'm just someone who has to sit down and think hard about what I want to say. It takes me many drafts. I had to do it in longhand because my computer skills were not up to the task that I'd undertaken. So it took about a year to do.

The book is filled was a lot of my views about how children and political decisions intersect, because I do think that all of us, in whatever role we're in, have a responsibility for children. And I don't just mean electoral politics. I mean, politics with a small *p*—how we organize ourselves in neighborhoods and communities and churches and businesses and schools.

There are eighteen chapters and at the beginning of each there is a quote—all the way from Lady Bird Johnson [to] John Silver to Booker T. Washington. I started with a collection of quotes that I've had for a long time, and I went through those, but I found I had to expand. One of my favorite times was sitting reading quote books, which I did for hours on end, looking for exactly the right quote to fit the meaning that I wanted to give it, to capture it.

There are a lot that are my favorite. Probably, the Verna Kelley quote at the beginning of "No Family Is an Island"—"Snowflakes are one of nature's most fragile things, but just look what they can do when they stick together." I just love that quote, and the book came out in January when we were in the midst of our great Blizzard of '96, so it seemed particularly apt.

The book size was suggested by the publisher, and I really like it because it's sort of a handy size to carry around. I learned a lot about publishing. For example, the number of pages in the book meant that if I had added one more page, they would have had to add, I think, sixteen more pages because of the way that books are put together. So the size really was perfect for what I wanted to convey.

My hardest part was cutting back. I had so many more examples that I wanted in and more stories that I had in. My editor was wonderful in helping me get it down to a manageable size. It could have been hundreds of more pages long if I had my way.

There is no index partly because it wasn't meant as a textbook. It was really meant more as a kind of meditation, if you will, about my work for the last twenty-five years, about children. And also I was running very late. The index would have meant that it would have been held up even longer. Since I was months over the deadline that I'd originally set, that was something we just didn't have time for.

Many human beings deserve credit for having worked on this book. That was my problem. I had so much help, both directly and indirectly. I had friends who read every word with great care and critiqued it. And I literally started making a list. I had sixty names, and I was nowhere near done. I just threw up my hands, and I said, "I can't do this," because I was afraid I would leave somebody out. It wasn't only the direct help, it was the indirect help. There were so many people in that book who talked to me on the telephone, whom I have yet to meet, others who have influenced me for more than twenty years. I thought it was the fairest way to basically thank everybody who had helped me. The writer paid by Simon & Schuster to spend time with me? Well, I thanked her for what she did for me. She worked for me for a number of months. She did not work [on] the entire project, and I was grateful for the assistance she gave me.

BOTH MY PARENTS WERE SO ENCOURAGING OF ME, telling me that I could do whatever I want. There were never any distinctions made between boys and girls. If my father was throwing pass patterns around our elm trees, I ran with the boys just as everybody else in the neighborhood did. But he was, I think, a much more demanding father for my brothers.

Actually, I've struggled to raise [my daughter] Chelsea in the same way, despite the difference in circumstances. We had a very middle-class normal upbringing, my brothers and I. We were lucky to live in a great suburb with great schools. We could come and go because it was a safe neighborhood. So it's not only the differences that all of us face today that make me sad because my child's life is not as free and independent as I was able to be, but certainly my husband being a governor and now president makes it quite different. I have to struggle all the time to make her life as normal— by my definition of normal, I fall back on my upbringing.

When Chelsea was about nine, and she and a little friend had been riding [bicycles] around the grounds of the governor's mansion, and they came running in and they wanted to ride their bikes down to the library, which was about ten blocks away. And I just got tears in my eyes because nearly every day in the summertime, I'd ride my bike to the library, to the pool, to play with my friends. My mother would say, "Be home in time for dinner," and nobody worried about me. And I had these two little girls, and I had to tell them no, I didn't feel comfortable. It wasn't because her daddy was the governor. It was because they were two little girls living in the downtown area of Little Rock, Arkansas, which is not as safe as it should be or [as] it used to be. That just made me very sad. It's one of those moments . . . that [as a mother] gave me a great deal of regret, that we have not taken care of our society in a way that would enable my daughter to be as free as I was.

At dinner one night, we told her that her daddy was going to be running for reelection as governor, and that in elections people said mean things about each other. We didn't want her to be surprised. And they sometimes told stories about each other. She was very upset at first, but we have continued to kind of work with her. We're always talking with her and asking her if she has any questions. So it's never easy, and it's always painful. It's hard not only on my daughter but on my mother, on other people who care about us. We do our best to reassure them and to let them know that unfortunately this is part of the process.

It was really hard to make the decision to put Chelsea in the book. This book is kind of a hybrid. It's not a memoir by any means, but it does rely on my personal experiences both as a daughter and a mother, as well as my work as an advocate and [with] the experts . . . [who are] trying to get their information out to the public. So I made the decision that I did have to include her. But I was very careful about how I talked about her. And I cleared everything with her. I didn't want her to feel that I was either breaching any confidence or giving her an uncomfortable moment as a teenager by talking about her.

It's been a real challenge raising her in the White House. But it's something that I probably spent more time on before we moved here than anything else. I had a great conversation—actually, two of them—with Jackie Kennedy Onassis about raising children in the public eye. I talked with other people. I read a lot of the press coverage of children who were in the White House. That led both Bill and me to make some decisions about how we would refer to her, even, how we would talk about her in public. And, really, we pled, and I think I'm very grateful that it was so positively received with the press, just to give her as much space and privacy as they could.

I think that there are a lot of people [in the press] who are around our age raising children, and I believe that they know what we go through. Because if you're a journalist who's on television or who's well known because of what you write, that gives you a taste of how your children can be drawn into your own career. And certainly it's much more dramatic where we live, but I think they have a certain sympathy and empathy with that.

I wrote the book because I really wanted to get these ideas out and to get them shared. It's been well received, and I'm grateful that people have been buying it. But I would like it to be part of a broader conversation about what we do for kids. I'd like it to be something that people talk about, not the book necessarily, but the ideas that are part of this conversation, about what people can do in their own homes and in their own neighborhoods and churches and everywhere else.

I really wish the message of this book would be that it's just not parents who have responsibility for children, it's all of us. My daughter's life will be affected by countless people she'll never meet who will make decisions about our economy, about the safety of our food, about all kinds of things that will determine how she lives in the future.

George Shultz

George Shultz, who served as secretary of state during the Reagan adminis-
tration, appeared on Booknotes *on June 27, 1993, to discuss his book* Turmoil and Triumph: My Years as Secretary of State.

I DEVELOPED AN APPROACH TO TRAVEL that helped me quite a lot. First
of all, don't eat too much for a day or two before you leave, and go easy—
if at all—on anything alcoholic. Drink a lot of water while you're traveling.
Don't drink anything alcoholic. Don't eat too heavily. Pasta is very good for
you. You can digest it relatively easily, and you can sleep. When you get
there, try not to have anything scheduled right away so you can go someplace and lie down. And maybe before you lie down, if there's a swimming
pool or a tennis court or something like that, get some exercise just to kind
of un-kink the muscles. Get a little bit of a rest, and then start in. I found
that while there's always jet lag and you can't get away from it, those tech-
niques helped me quite a bit.

When I was secretary of state, there was in my office a big globe. When
ambassadors who were newly going to their posts or in their posts and coming back to visit me, would get ready to leave, I would say to them, "Ambassador, you have one more test before you can go to your post. You have to go
over to the globe and prove to me that you can identify your country." So,
unerringly, they would go over and they'd spin the globe around and they'd
put their finger on the country they were going to, and pass the test.

So Mike Mansfield—a great elder statesman in America, former Senate
majority leader and ambassador to Japan for a while before I was there, and
a close friend of mine from back when I was in the Nixon administration—
was visiting, and he got ready to leave. I said, "Mike, I've got to give you
the same test I give everybody else. Before you can go back to Japan, you've
got to show me that you can go over to the globe and put your finger on
your country." So he went over and he spun this globe around, and he put
his hand on the United States and said, "That's my country."

I've told that story, subsequently, to all the ambassadors going out,
"Never forget, you're over there in that country, but your country is the

United States. You're there to represent us. Take care of our interests and never forget it, and you're representing the best country in the world."

FOR THE BOOK, I DID A LOT OF WORK. I wrote and wrote and wrote. I did some dictation. It wasn't tight enough, really. I could work from it to some extent. I did a lot of writing on a yellow pad. I had wonderful notes that were taken in my office, contemporaneous notes, that showed me everything as it took place so I didn't have to remember. My memory isn't that great. I had these notes, and I have a fellow named Charlie Hill, who is a very talented foreign service officer. He's the one who took the notes, and he would cull them out and get the notes on the various subjects, kind of archiving them, I'd say, and putting them into written form, and that was some raw material. The notes were the raw material. And I had a research assistant to get the public record material together. I had my own calendar—everybody I saw, every telephone call, in and out, to look at. I would go through all this on a given subject, and then I'd start to write. I had an outline, and the outline evolved. When you write, you realize what you need to learn more about to be sure you're right, and so on. It was that kind of a process.

RIGHT NOW, I LIVE on the Stanford University campus. It's a great place to live. I see lots of students, and of course I've been writing this book. It's been a huge effort, an interesting effort, but I've put an immense amount of time into it. I've done this at the Hoover Institution [on War, Revolution and Peace at Stanford], which is a wonderful place for writing, and had a wonderful editor, Cynthia Gunn, who worked with me on this book, and a wonderful archivist who kept track of my papers. It's a very good setup there and wonderful people to work with. I have some business interests and financial interests that I've been doing. Life is good.

Lewis B. Puller, Jr.

Lewis B. Puller, Jr., son of the famous marine "Chesty" Puller, suffered devastating injuries in the Vietnam War. He called his Pulitzer Prize–winning book Fortunate Son: The Autobiography of Lewis Puller, Jr. *He appeared on the program on May 24, 1992.*

WHEN I WAS YOUNG, everybody told me that I had the ability to write—all of my English teachers and everyone who ever read any of my papers. And so I thought that I could write, but I didn't think I had anything to say. Then I went to Vietnam and had this incredible experience, but didn't have the ability anymore. Then the two came together about eleven years ago, and I just knew that the story had to be told.

I was wounded twice. The first wound was very minor. The second wounding was, well, my legs—traumatic amputation of both legs, one at the hip; one six inches below the thigh. Fingers on both hands. I was burned on my right arm, from the wrist to the elbow—first-, second-, and third-degree burns. I had a punctured eardrum, a dislocated shoulder, numerous shrapnel wounds, perforated scrotum—it goes on and on. About the only thing that was spared was my face.

When I got back from Vietnam, I—like so many combat veterans coming back from that terrible period in our history—wasn't allowed to talk about what we'd done, what we'd gone through. It wasn't considered civilized. We got so many subliminal signs and overt signs that we just clammed up and didn't say anything to anybody, and I did that. I kept everything in and it finally had to come out. And that's not completely about Vietnam, of course. I think it's a bigger book than Vietnam, but the Vietnam part—even my wife had never heard anything about. She typed the first 150 pages of that book for me, and when she started typing it— we'd been married for eighteen years—we'd never talked about Vietnam. She said when she was typing, her hands were just shaking and she was just rushing through it, trying to get to the next page.

I went to see *An Officer and a Gentleman,* and when I came out of the movie, I said, "You know, that was pretty good, but I don't think that guy's got quite the material that I've got." And I went home and I got my Bic pen and my yellow pad and I started writing. After I got it to 125 pages or so I started looking for an editor and an agent. I found the agent first, of course, and he eventually found me the right editor and the result is what you see. I don't know what attracted [the agent] really, but he told me he picked it up in his office. It came, he said, in the five o'clock mail. He said he was about ready to go home, and he picked it up and started reading it, and he said he looked at his watch again and it was eight or nine o'clock. He'd just totally forgotten time. He called me and said, "I've got to be a part of this." He said, "I just want to see that this gets published, and whatever I can do, I want to do." And I said, "Go ahead and run with it." Three weeks later, he had it sold.

I wrote in my bedroom. I've got a little captain's desk in there, and I would come home from work, or work on it on weekends. I'd turn on an old sixties music station and sort of get back into that framework and listen to those songs and write the page or page-and-a-half that I tried to do every day. Some parts are difficult, some parts are easy. Amazingly enough, the Vietnam part is not very difficult for me. The problem was that I was just not given an outlet. I wasn't allowed to talk about Vietnam, so that was very easy. Once it started coming out, it almost gushed. The part about my father's declining health and death was very difficult to write and talk about.

After the book started tapering off—after it had been out for seven or eight months—my editor said, "Well, we'll put you in for the usual awards." I thought, "okay." Then the National Book Awards came out and I wasn't even a nominee and I thought, "Well, this one's just been overlooked," or "It's about Vietnam and it's a subject that Americans have not really come to terms with and there are a lot of people who have sort of left-wing leanings on book panels." I thought this is not the kind of book they're going to cotton to. So I didn't think any more about it. Then I came home from work a month ago, and my wife came running out to the garage mumbling something about *Good Morning America* and Pulitzer prizes and I started talking about the moon being made out of green cheese, and sure enough, it was true.

Before I got the prize, I got a letter from a young man. He said that when he goes down to the Vietnam Veterans Memorial, he thinks that anybody can visit that memorial and take something away from it—be they left-wing, right-wing, conservative, hawk, dove, radical, whatever. And he said reading my book is the same way. He said that anybody can read that book and take something sort of spiritual away from it. I think it's that sort of healing thing—not just my healing but sort of the healing of the country, and I think that's what appealed to the [Pulitzer] board.

Basically you've got on that book cover a legless man with a frown, sitting in front of a cemetery. People look at it, and they think it's going to be a downer. They think, "I'm looking for something to read." They're going on vacation, and they think, "Oh, my God, I'm not gonna read about something like this." They don't understand what it's like not to have legs. They don't realize that, really, this book is an affirmation. This book is certainly about some difficult things, but it's about some beautiful things, too. It's about the power of love and relationship between man and woman, and a man and his father, and a man and his son, and a man and his country, and a man and himself. Those are all love relationships, which are all resolved satisfactorily. For that reason, I don't think it's a downer book. I think it's a real affirmation of the human spirit, but you don't get that from the cover. I think maybe we'd have been better off if we'd put my wife and my children and my dog on the cover with me rather than something like this. I'm looking into the sun in that picture, and people look at that and they see a scowl and they think, "This is a terribly angry young man." And I'm not an angry man. I'm a very happy man today, but that's what happens when you have your picture taken at six o'clock in the morning and look into the sun.

Clark Clifford

Clark Clifford, author of Counsel to the President: A Memoir, *appeared on* Booknotes *on July 28, 1991. In his book, Mr. Clifford chronicles his rise from young lawyer to adviser to presidents Truman, Kennedy, Johnson, and, later, Clinton. To explore the nature of a coauthor relationship, Mr. Clifford was asked to explain how he had come to work with his coauthor Richard Holbrooke, who later served as President Clinton's State Department adviser on Bosnia.*

RICHARD HOLBROOKE [the coauthor] and I have been friends for twenty years. I got to know him particularly well during the Carter administration when he served as assistant secretary of state for Southeast Asian Affairs. I thought he did a superb job in that position. He left office then, after the Carter administration went out, and became a banker in New York, an investment banker. We would see each other from time to time. He started ten years ago to begin quietly and steadily and consistently to tell me I had to write a book. After a little while, he said, "I can persuade you to write a book. I will help you with the book." I said, "I'm still not ready for it." But as time went on, almost four years ago, I became ready. He said one time to me, in what was an understandable remark, "If you're going to write that book, you'd better write that book. One just doesn't know how much time you're going to have." I was eighty at the time, you see. So I took the advice. It was good advice, and we went to work on it together. We worked almost four years on it.

The first eight months we didn't put a word on paper. I dictated. He would come to Washington with four or five topics. I would have been told ahead of time, so I would be prepared. We had a tape machine on the table and he would ask me questions and then I would answer those questions. I would speak sometimes fifteen or twenty minutes at a time, maybe a half an hour. I would have gone back and refreshed my recollection. Then after the taping was over, I would have a young lady prepare a transcript of it. The pile of transcripts grew and grew and grew, and they must have ultimately been a foot high.

After about eight months of time had gone by, he said, "All right, the time has come to turn all this material into a book." That's the way it started. So it came right from within me, and yet he was invaluable in structuring the material into the various chapters of the book. He would come up with a plan and then we'd spend much time together reworking it, changing it the way we wanted.

We also had four separate presidential libraries upon which we could draw. . . . [There was] a plan started years ago, right after Truman. After a president has gone out of office, he sets up his library. He gets an oral history from the important figures in his administration and young people are sent out, trained, and they sit [with those figures]—I think I must have spent fourteen or fifteen hours with a young man, a representative of the Truman Library, when the whole administration was fresh in my memory. Then that gets placed into a transcript and goes into the library—much of it not to be read for twenty-five years. I did that for the Truman and Kennedy and Johnson and Carter [libraries]. That is a gold mine of material. With Truman, forty years had gone by before I decided to start the book, but we went back. We also had the services of a young man, a graduate of the University of Texas, who was getting his doctorate in American history. The fact is, he devoted it [his dissertation] to Vietnam. We employed him full time for two years in checking every fact that occurred in the book. It's been checked and rechecked. If there's anything that bothers me about a book, it's to read a review, and the review could be quite complimentary—even commendatory—and then it comes to the point where it says, "But it's too bad the book is marred by the following errors," and it will state three or four errors that would be in the book. We wanted very much to avoid that. I hope that we have. No one has yet written in and caught a mistake in the book—yet. I hope it doesn't happen.

I CAME TO THE BAR IN ST. LOUIS on the first of June 1928. It was a reasonably busy time. In the summer of '29, though, the work slackened off a good deal in the law firm. I was messenger and kept the books in order. That's about all I was at that particular stage. Another young man and I talked about the fact that things were so slack and we might get leave to go to Europe for a while that summer. It would probably be the only chance we'd ever get. The management of the law firm said, "Sure, that's all right. There's not going to be very much doing this summer." So we took off and planned a trip, just the two of us. His name was Louis McKuen, so we called our trip the "Louis and Clark Expedition." We were entirely on our own and on a very low budget. We stayed at pensions and paid twenty-five cents to get a bath and things like that. We planned one time in Germany to get up and get the eight o'clock boat and go up the Rhine—I think it's from Cologne to Mainz—and see the old German castles and all.

But the night before, we'd been out with a group of young German people at a beer garden, and my friend had looked at the wine while it was red, and I couldn't get him up at eight o'clock. But we got the nine o'clock boat. On the nine o'clock boat we got on, here was the prettiest group of girls I thought I had ever seen, about eight or nine of them, on a Wellesley [College] tour from the United States. We set off and watched them for a while, and then after a bit we went up and said, "You know, we haven't spoken English with anybody for so long, we hope you don't think we're rude if we come up and introduce ourselves." They said, "Of course not." By the end of the day, Lou had picked out a perfectly glorious redhead from Pittsburgh, and I'd picked up a tall, willowy blonde from Boston named Margery Pepperell Kimball. We'd really got to be good friends that day, so we got a copy of their itinerary. They had to be at certain places. From that time on, for the next five or six weeks, every place they showed up, by accident Lou and I showed up, and we would call, and the four of us would go out and have dinner together. We had the best time four young people ever had about in their life.

But at the time, Marnie—her nickname for Margery—told me on about the third date we had, "I must tell you ahead of time that back home I'm practically engaged to Alan" somebody or other—some dope back in Boston. I said, "Well, I must tell you, too, that there's a girl named Dorothy back in St. Louis, but at least we'll have a good time this summer." I go back to St. Louis. Something had changed after that three months abroad, and the arrangement with Dorothy began to drift off, you see. It began to deteriorate. But I wouldn't get in touch with Marnie because she said when we got back, it wouldn't be long before she'd be married.

A year goes by. I'm walking back from the courthouse to my office in St. Louis. I run into a friend of mine, and he said, "I was in Boston last week and I ran into a friend of yours." I said, "What's his name?" "It wasn't a him. It was a her." I said, "Well, what's her name?" He said, "Marnie Kimball." I said, "What's her married name?" He said, "She doesn't have any married name." I said, "Are you sure?" He said, "I'm sure." In five minutes, I'm on the telephone back in the office calling, but she wasn't in that afternoon. But the next morning, I got her on the phone. We had a talk. It was getting near Christmastime, and I said, "If you were to invite me, I'd come up and pay you a visit between Christmas and New Year because things slacken off in the law business then." She said, "Well, I invite you." I went. From the day I arrived, it started right up again where it had been. She had gone back and the same thing had happened to her with Alan that happened with Dorothy and me. We picked it right up, had one more visit up there and then agreed that we had postponed it much too long. Our parents both happened to be in New York at the same time, and they met and had dinner together and they liked each other. So on October 3, 1931, we were married.

Marnie and I, on October third of this year [1991], will have been married sixty years. Same wife for sixty years. All through my career, when I was a young lawyer, I was a trial lawyer and she used to be my standard juror. When I began to work for presidents, she was my ordinary member of the public. I'd try out speeches on her, and she'd say, "That one's not going to fly." I used her all through the years. So when we started on the book, she became the ordinary reader, read every word. She had good suggestions and was very frank—sometimes I thought maybe a little too frank. She proved to be really quite invaluable in the writing of the book.

George Ball

On May 23, 1993, George Ball, undersecretary of state during the Kennedy and Johnson administrations, joined us to discuss his book The Passionate Attachment: America's Involvement with Israel, 1947 to Present.

THE TITLE IS FROM George Washington's farewell address. It was delivered in 1796, when there was a serious threat of factionalism in the new fledgling republic. Washington was concerned that it would lead the country into trouble. There was a large group that was deeply attached to the French Revolution and to the revolutionary France that emerged from that. There were an equal number, or perhaps more, who favored Britain. And this factionalism led to internal fights that sometimes resulted in riots.

Washington was very concerned that France might lead the United States into a foreign war, which would be a disaster. Justice [John] Marshall was over there before he was on the Supreme Court. He was commissioned to talk to Talleyrand, who was the French foreign minister. Talleyrand treated him in a most arrogant and high-handed fashion and said to him, "Now you may think that you can, because you're a small, young country, that you can treat France in the way that you have, but we have great resources in your country as well as abroad. And you won't get away with it." Well, this angered Washington and also angered a great many people in the United States. They finally broke up [with France] because the French behaved so arrogantly that even their American friends turned against them.

So Washington said that "a passionate attachment to another country creates an illusion of a common interest when, in fact, there is no common interest." [When] one country [is favored] over the others, that country becomes a subject of jealousy on the part of all the other countries. He said that what the United States should do would be to exercise equal treatment of all and cultivate peace and security.

·   ·   ·

364 / George Ball

ISRAEL HAD WORRIED ME A LOT over the years, although when I was in the [State] Department, I didn't actually involve myself very much in Israeli affairs. But later, I got worried about the fact that it seemed, to me, to be a relationship which was not in the American interest and where we were far too complacent in our relations with Israel.

Israel is controversial because it's an inordinate drain on American resources without getting any real return. Because while Israel claims that it's an ally of the United States, it certainly doesn't behave like one. And while it claims that it's a strategic asset of the United States because it defends it from the encroachment of communism in the Middle East, that has obviously disappeared now with the dissolution of the Soviet empire. So they're looking for a new explanation in the form of a new common enemy. So they've invented one, which we're going to hear a great deal more about in the future, and that is Islamic fundamentalism, which they say is the great wave that's threatening the West.

I hope the book will convince a few people, I mean, shake a lot of people who I think are inclined to accept the conventional wisdom. And I think the conventional wisdom is just plain wrong, and I think at the moment, we are [bringing] hardship—not only to ourselves, but I think to the Israelis.

The reviews, by and large—from the respectable papers, I mean, other than the papers that are slanted or limited—have been uniformly bad. They've not been the kind of reviews that I hoped I would get, which would be reviews that would begin a discussion, the controversy. They've largely taken the form of trying to diminish me and my competence, which is not anything of wide public interest. They want to avoid any controversy because they want to see the book drop like a stone.

I'm toying with the idea of another book. I'm unwilling at the moment to commit myself to the kind of sustained, protracted effort that a book would take. So I do short articles and book reviews and that sort of thing.

William Rehnquist ✓

On July 5, 1992, Chief Justice William Rehnquist became the first Supreme Court Justice to be interviewed on Booknotes. *He was sworn in as the sixteenth Chief Justice of the United States in 1986. Previously, Chief Justice Rehnquist had written a book titled* The Supreme Court: How It Was and How It Is. *Television cameras in the Supreme Court building are a rarity; therefore, we were pleased to be able to interview him about his book* Grand Inquest *in the Supreme Court's East Conference Room.*

NOBODY EVER ASKED ME TO SPEAK at public meetings when I was a lawyer in Phoenix—except the Rotary Club or something like that. People weren't interested in my views particularly. When I was in the Justice Department, they got a little more interested because I was an assistant attorney general. And then, when I became a member of the [Supreme] Court, they became very interested. I'm sure it had nothing to do with the inner me or anything. It was just the position I occupied.

If I had lived back in the early 1800s, I certainly would have been a Federalist, I think, when the whole scheme started out. I think Hamilton's vision of the future of the country was more realistic in many ways than was that of the Jeffersonian Democrats or Jeffersonian Republicans. But the Federalist Party became ossified. It did not change with the times, and they had no idea of expanding the nation beyond the Appalachians. Jefferson had that sort of a vision—the forerunner of Manifest Destiny. And so the Federalist Party just withered because it didn't react to events. I'm sure sooner or later, just like many Federalists, I probably would have gone over to the Jeffersonian Republican Party, which gradually absorbed most of the Federalist Party. That was the era of good feelings, when everybody belonged to the same party.

I think Alexander Hamilton has received a little bit of short shrift from history, and I think Jefferson has been treated a little bit too generously. I admire them both, but I admire them both about equally. I think if you asked most people, they would say that Jefferson is kind of a star of the first magnitude, whereas Hamilton is a star of the second or third magnitude. I don't agree with that assessment.

The thing for which [Aaron] Burr challenged [Alexander] Hamilton to a duel in 1804 was that Hamilton said Burr was a dangerous man and shouldn't be trusted with the governorship of New York. Think how many duels we would have today if criticism of that sort were grounds for a duel.

THE CHIEF JUSTICE I admire most has to be John Marshall. I think every one of his successors had to admire him. If you could say of any one individual that the court, as an institution, is the length and shadow of that individual, surely it would be John Marshall. He was probably by no means the best educated of his colleagues and was not even thought of as an absolutely top-notch lawyer at the Virginia bar when he was appointed. As I understand, he was more engaged in politics. He had served as a captain of an artillery company with George Washington at Valley Forge in 1777 and fought in the battles of Brandywine and Monmouth. I've always had the feeling that he must have developed, in that more freewheeling atmosphere than the strictly scholarly one, kind of an ability to get along with other people and to persuade them. That stood him in very good stead when he was chief justice of the [Supreme] Court. He and all of his colleagues would live in the same boardinghouse here in Washington during the very short term of the court.

Perhaps, you could say, there should be mandatory retirement even of members of the court, members of the federal judiciary. I'm sure there can be questions about whether one does as good work when you get into your—you know, I'm sixty-seven. I'm sure that lots of things are inferior in me, physically, now than they were fifteen years ago. I'm sure at some times maybe your mental facilities begin to fail, and they say people don't realize it themselves. But the way the system has worked, in the time that both Marshall and [Roger Brooke] Taney served there was no provision for retirement. Taney held on until he was eighty-eight because he needed the monthly paycheck. There was no way to retire. Now there are retirement provisions, and I don't think you have quite that same tendency that, you know, you've got to just keep the wolf from the door, so to speak.

I WROTE THIS BOOK for a sense of personal satisfaction. Just like taking a good photograph or painting a picture or playing a good golf game or something, it's the thing in itself that justifies it.

Mikhail Gorbachev

Mikhail Gorbachev, former president of the Soviet Union, appeared on
Booknotes *on November 24, 1996, to discuss his book* Memoirs. *During the*
taping, we used Mr. Gorbachev's translator of many years, Mr. Pavel
Palazchenko, to perform simultaneous translation for both Mr. Gorbachev
and me.

O F COURSE, MY BOOK IS MORE ABOUT PAST EVENTS. But you cannot
divide the past and the present. And everyone is writing books now. I wrote
this book because I sometimes read books about perestroika and saw my
name in those books, but the rest was totally false, stupid, silly, a lot of
rumors, a lot of speculation. Some other books are quite serious, of course.
I don't want to overdramatize it. But anyway, I thought that I am the principal witness and the principal person who bears responsibility for what
happened, and I believed that it was important for me to explain my position about how I started reforms, why I came around to the view that
reforms were necessary; why did I decide and how that decision emerged
about reforms and how difficult the process was.

So I thought that it is important to write a book about the time of perestroika because perestroika had far-reaching consequences for my country
and for the world. I cannot accept it when people speak but Gorbachev is
silent. I had to speak out and I did that and I tried to avoid the temptation
of the writers of many memoirs to prettify myself, to show myself in a better light. I tried to keep within the facts. I have a lot of facts about various
events, about all that happened and about my relationship with various
people in domestic and international politics. I could say a lot. I tried to
write about the most important things. At first I dictated 10,000 pages of
material. Here, this book is equivalent to 1,000 pages of typewritten text.

There's a preface in my book by Martin McCullough of the University
of London. He only participated in the editing of the English edition, trying to make the book more concise. He contributed some ideas about the
structure of the book. But the book is mine. Many people helped me
because it took a lot of work to complete this book, but the main burden of

the work was mine. I had to decide eventually what kind of book it was going to be, what will be left out of the initial 10,000 pages, what will be left in the German edition, what will be in the English edition. This English edition was born after a good and friendly cooperation, but sometimes we had a lot of debate—a lot of sharp debate—because those people who know publishing, they said that I should produce a more concise edition for English and American readers. I eventually agreed, but I disagreed with some other suggestions. I am a democratically minded person, but eventually the decisions I make myself.

Reading is really our great hobby and, because of this, we [my wife and I] have an enormous library. We have been buying books all our life. We have in our library a lot of fiction, a lot of books about history and philosophy, because Mrs. Gorbachev has a Ph.D. in philosophy, a lot of material of a reference kind. So my library is of great help to me. It helps me out in difficult situations. We have the *Encyclopaedia Britannica* and we use it because our daughter speaks English and Mrs. Gorbachev can read a little English, so we use that as a source.

My hobby particularly is Russian fiction, but also European and American classics. I have read many of the books by your writers—Theodore Dreiser, Scott Fitzgerald, to say nothing of Mark Twain and Jack London—and I could go on and on. And I read them; I read more than one book by each author. If I started reading Jack London, I wanted to read all that he wrote. I also like European fiction. I read many books by European authors, fewer books by Asian authors. I would say I read some books on Eastern history and philosophy. I like books on history. I like historical fiction, memoirs. Recently, for example, I started to reread Dostoyevsky, particularly *The Possessed, The Brothers Karamazov*. There's a lot there that's extremely instructive. I am amazed at the magnitude of that writer, and he was able to render human sufferings and he really was on a quest to study the human soul. I think he is probably the best on that score. Tolstoy, Chekhov, too, are great writers. It's amazing what they can do.

And I also read detective stories, crime stories. I like them. James Hadley Chase, Georges Simenon and some of our writers, Agatha Christie. So I'm quite curious.

I continue to read a great deal. We used to be a closed society ideologically—a very closed, controlled society. And that meant that even well-educated people did not get a chance to read many of the books of Russian philosophers because our ideologues did not like those philosophers. But when we began perestroika, we very quickly published thirty volumes of all the philosophers of prerevolutionary Russia. And I have those thirty volumes, and I read a lot by them. They were great minds: Ilian, [Sergey] Solovyov, Perdiyev. They said a great deal of what today we are only rehashing. So sometimes we are reinventing the wheel. That is our problem. We reinvent the wheel. We sometimes think as though there were no thinkers before us, and that can be tragic. We really have to go back to those thinkers and writers.

Books should not be replaced by anything, by TV or any such thing, because books make it possible to think more deeply. Probably American audiences will say, "Well, Gorbachev knows that we're reading less than we used to." Well, I know that in all countries people are spending more time watching TV than reading. But still, I think that books will continue to exist. There will always be books. Television has a role, of course. Television has a role in terms of allowing people to spend time at leisure. But in terms of formative work for the individual, it's very important to read books.

I think that Alvin Toffler is right in many of his writings. I recently read the translation of *The Third Wave* by him and his wife, and Speaker Gingrich wrote a preface to that book. And it's extremely interesting, because they speak about human civilization, which is entering a new phase of its development. And we must find a way to adjust to it. We cannot stop the process of the evolution of our civilization. If we do not adjust, if we do not understand both the positive aspects and the dangers, if we do not change our behavior or our action, that could be very dangerous. We should understand how civilization is evolving. If we do so, then we will be able to take advantage of the positive aspects and to limit the negative aspects of those changes. I think he provides very interesting illustrations of that and I agree with him.

In America, I think it's wonderful that many books have been published that are extremely interesting. For example, some economists have published books that question the entire paradigm of the development of laissez-faire society and laissez-faire economics. Those are people who really think freely. They are freethinkers. They're not like cowboys. I don't want, of course, to offend cowboys. I like cowboys. But what I mean is that they are not cowboys, but they are putting things very starkly.

If I lived in America, and I had to choose whether to be a Democrat or a Republican—well, my God, you first have to sort out whether there is a real difference between the two parties. Frankly, I see no big difference between them. Perhaps now some difference is emerging. I think that I am a democratic person. My nature is democratic. My experience of working and interacting with Americans was working with two Republican presidents, and I must say that we were able to work together, to cooperate. We were able to go very far. And I will not recount all of that; you know very well that my opinion of President Reagan is very high, even though he is a Republican traditionalist and he represents the Republican Party's right wing. But it was this president, President Reagan, who really, I think, understood that he had to do something and even to buck the trend. And therefore, I can only say that I am committed to democracy, and within the old system that we had when I was in politics, this is something that people recognized. I was recognized as a person whose style and whose thinking are democratic from the start; from my very young years, I was like this.

So maybe that's my nature. I come from a peasant family. I come from the soil. From my young years, I saw a great deal; I've worked a great deal. I know what it is to earn one's bread, to earn one's salary. I know what it is to build a home; for a peasant, it's not simple. And I must say, I had a talk with Tom Brokaw here and we talked about land, because he comes from the heartland, from South Dakota. He worked on the combine, on the harvesting combine. And we started to discuss this and talked about our memories. And I said that I don't forget where I come from. To me, this is the most important moral test, and I have never forgotten that I come from among working people, from very simple people. And I recently heard from a friend of Speaker O'Neill. He was a very colorful politician who was one of the first American visitors whom I saw in Moscow when I became general secretary. His friends told me that Speaker O'Neill, when he spoke about people, he said, "I have a very important test. This man has not forgotten where he comes from. When a person doesn't forget where he comes from, that's very important." From that standpoint, I can say I don't forget where I come from, and that probably is the foundation of my democratic spirit. What I did, what Raisa did—we come from working families—we took advantage of the opportunities that existed in the Soviet period for such people. We were able to take advantage, and this is our life, despite all of the tribulations and problems inherent in that Soviet system.

You cannot just say, "Well, it was a bad system and, therefore people could do nothing and what people could do didn't matter." No. The first thing is that you have a life. You have a life and you have to live this life. You have to continue the human race. And this is what people do, even in the most difficult conditions, in the most difficult situations, under the harshest regimes. And we had a very harsh regime. So the lessons of those generations that lived under that old regime and that developed the country, that industrialized the country under that old regime, that created our science, our education system, that created opportunities and access to education for all, despite the incomes and status of those people. This is something that you cannot negate. You cannot throw out one word from a song, and you cannot negate what actually happened. But, by the way, that old system, by giving people those opportunities, created the prerequisites and the forces that eventually buried that system because we, people of my generation and people of the generations that followed, we had education, we had knowledge, but we could not realize our potential. The system was really fettering our potential. So the system in that way created preconditions for its own demise. And that is because it was in conflict with the culture and with the education and with the intellect of the people.

This is the first time in history that a former Russian leader has ever been able to write a book and travel the world and talk about life when they were head of Russia. Nikita Khrushchev was under house arrest, and he wrote his memoirs in secret and he was not able to publish them in the Soviet Union. And, of course, he was not able to leave the country or even to leave Moscow. I once joked that it is known that 128 groups of mountain climbers climbed Mount Everest; one-third died. But 40 percent of those who did, died during descent. I mounted and climbed Mount Everest, and then I descended from Mount Everest politically and I am still alive. In that sense, this too is a kind of revolution that is associated with Mikhail Gorbachev. Many people in Russia say that while Gorbachev is in Russia, despite all the problems that are being created for him, despite the information blackout to which he is subjected, if he is still here, if he is not leaving Russia, this is very important for all of us. This is an important reference point. So when people ask me, "Would you like to move, to go to live abroad? Why involve yourself in the struggles, in proving again to those reactionaries or to the current authorities, to the rulers of Russia, who don't deserve you? Why do that? Go abroad." No. I don't do that. Of course, I travel abroad, but I live in Russia. This is my country. This is my land. This is my fate. I will not go anywhere because this is my moral principle.

In terms of another book, a few days ago, I had a meeting with the officials from a Russian publishing house on my next book. And I and my colleagues, my associates for many years, Anatoly Chernayev and Vadim Zagladen, we wrote a book which I believe is a very necessary book for political leaders, for those who are interested in the problems. And that is called *The New Thinking: Yesterday, Today and Tomorrow.* I am convinced that we will not be able to break through the jungle of the stereotypes and the clichés that exist today if we do not sort things out in our minds. We need a revolution in our minds. And I believe that that can happen only on the basis of the new thinking based on the new situation, based on the understanding of the global challenges that mankind is facing. So this book is a very different book, but I'm looking forward to seeing it published. So I continue to write and I will continue to write. I have still a lot to say.

You have the Bible, and the Bible is not a very big book, but you have many volumes of commentary of the Bible. So this book is not that big, but there's a lot in that book that I could elaborate on. For example, the drama that happened in Reykjavik, it's a long story, but here it's just a few pages. In fact, it was a real drama. And there were many events here in this book which I described very concisely but which could be elaborated upon. And if you add here the human dimension, that is to say, my opinions and views of my counterparts, of my partners, of people with whom I worked, I would have a lot [more] to say. I don't know whether I will have the strength. I don't know how many years God will be giving me, what his plans are. But, of course, I spent my life in politics, I made political speeches. I did not write books in the past. Now I am more interested in sharing my views and emotions and my thoughts, and I will continue doing so.

Dan Quayle

Former Vice President Dan Quayle appeared on Booknotes *on July 24, 1994, to discuss his personal story of the 1992 campaign, which he told in his book* Standing Firm.

I GREW UP IN A NEWSPAPER FAMILY, and one of the surprising aspects about the media is, at the upper echelons, it is a very homogeneous crowd. They have similar ideologies—and now they have similar backgrounds: they don't have the blue-collar background that many of the working journalists used to have in the past. They've gone to the Ivy League schools. They've known each other. It's very much of a crowd. The one surprising element—it happened to me; it's happened to other people—is that when one reporter goes in a direction that looks like a good story, they all just follow. It's the same line, the same theme. Yet we have the First Amendment, we have a free press, and you'd think we might have a diversified press, but we really don't. I talk a lot about the media, and I wrote about it extensively in the book and that was my concluding shot.

Gene Pulliam was my grandfather. He was an independent publisher and a very intelligent, tough individual. He had a tremendous amount of influence on me, on my mother and my father, our whole family. He at one time was recognized by the Boys Clubs of America and presented [with] the Horatio Alger Award. He went from rags to riches, but he did it the old-fashioned way—he earned it. He was probably one of the last of his kind. As the publisher, he actually ran the newsroom. You couldn't do that today. He and Bill Loeb [former publisher] of *The Union Leader* [in Manchester, New Hampshire] were two of a kind. They literally would say what was going to be on those front pages, call up the reporters and say, "I think that this is a good angle for the story." It's unheard of today. He was a person that started out as a son of an itinerant Methodist minister in the plains of Kansas and worked his way up to being a very well-respected newspaper publisher. He was one of the people that made a real impact in the media and the newspaper business when he was around.

·   ·   ·

I WAS NOT ONLY A REPORTER; I started out delivering newspapers. I had a motor route when I was sixteen and seventeen years old. It was good income, a very good income, in those days. I was able to pay for my Ford that I drove in the afternoons. It's an afternoon and early Sunday morning paper. I also worked in the pressroom. I worked in the days when we had hot metal rather than the offset press that you have today, which is cold type. I also was a cub reporter. I used to cover the police beat; I covered the planning commissions. I was associate publisher of the Huntington newspaper, which is my father and mother's newspaper in Huntington, Indiana, circulation of 9,000, I believe. It might be 9,100 today. I wrote editorials, I did the whole ball of wax. I started out in the pressroom and ended up in the newsroom and writing editorials. So I've done it all.

IN THE ACKNOWLEDGMENTS for my book I thank a lot of people. I . . . wrote, "I'd also like to thank the press—well, some of them—specifically Bob Woodward, Michael Barone, David Broder, Britt Hume, Dan Rather, Mark Shields, and Len Downey. All of them sat down with me as I worked on this book, offering valuable reflections upon my unique experience with the fourth estate."

I would guess I had spent anywhere from an hour and a half to two and a half hours with each person [interviewed for this book]. It took place over a period of time of about two or three months. It was an opportunity for me to ask them some questions about themselves, about how they covered me, and about the media. I think I quote almost every one of them in the book. Each one offered a different insight and a different viewpoint, but there were also a lot of similarities.

The striking thing that came through, time and time again, was just these first impressions. I always asked them the question, "Look, you know me. You've seen me as vice president. You saw me as senator. What happened? How did this train get so far off the track?" It came back to those first few days in the 1988 campaign. It's an important lesson to learn and to appreciate: . . . the impact of how important first impressions really are. You know how it is when you meet someone and sort of size them up, and sometimes your first impressions are right and sometimes they are wrong? But in politics, and especially in a national campaign, first impressions are most important. Unfortunately for me, the first impression that many had, and certainly most Americans who saw it via the media, was very negative, and I write about it in the book. In 1988, it was a political victory for me: I was elected vice president of the United States. But, as I say, it was a personal defeat.

I did not tape-record these interviews. I took notes. I had a reporter's notebook for some of them, and at other times I had just a piece of paper. In most cases, I actually called them back and read what I was going to write about them in the book. I think they were surprised that I did that.

Clearly I had some very pointed questions to ask them. It was, in a way, not turning the tables on them, but it was my opportunity to ask the questions and let them do the talking, because in the past most of them, not all of them, had interviewed me. So it was sort of nice to sit back and to listen and take notes. There were a couple of points I wanted to get. I wanted to find out why, as I said, the train got off the track. I wanted to find out why the media really got this caricature. I wanted to find out why the media was unwilling to change this caricature. I wanted to focus on the Woodward-Broder articles, because the Woodward-Broder articles, to me, were not that flattering. As a matter of fact, I've gone back and read them recently, and I tell you, I will not recommend that to my friends nor to my family to read.

I am very critical of the media. I basically say that the caricature that was formed of me was not only untrue but it was unfair, that there was an ideological problem. There was a generational problem. There was this searing experience in Huntington, Indiana, when right after the convention, George Bush and I went back to my hometown where we had all the people from Indiana on my side against the media. I go into all these things in the concluding chapter I had about the media. To this day there has not been any response from the media, saying, "Oh, yes, we were right about Dan Quayle." They know that they weren't. Now we have to turn the page. This book had to be written. It had to be written for me to be able to set the record straight. Serious journalists will admit that that caricature was just totally out of bounds.

The book took me about sixteen months to write. It was time-consuming. I first sat down right after the election, in November of 1992, and wrote about a five-page outline and stuck to the outline. First impressions—that is what I wanted to write about, and that is what I did write about. I expanded the outline to fifteen or twenty pages. Then I sat down with another person, put in about one hundred hours on tape. That was then given to a transcriber, and that part was cleaned up and made grammatically correct and everything. That became the first draft.

On the last rewrite I spent six days in hotel rooms with my senior editor at HarperCollins, Rick Horigan—three days in New York, three days here in Washington. We spent eighteen-hour days: twenty minutes for breakfast, twenty minutes for lunch, twenty minutes for dinner. It was an exhaustive process. Once the book was completed it was just a sense of relief. But I will tell you, and my publishers will tell you, I had a very hard time letting go of it because I wanted to make sure that everything was just perfect. I didn't want any mistakes. I was very careful about the choice of words. It was a very difficult book to write. It was difficult to write about your friends and a difficult book to write about your colleagues and the people that you like and have worked with very closely. It's easy to write about your critics. You just sort of have at it. You don't really care that much. You care about the people that have been close to you. So it was a tough book to write.

By the end of this book tour, I will have done hundreds of interviews. We're going to thirty-six cities. Larry King [of CNN] told me, "By the time you conclude your book tour, you're going to want to talk about anything except your book." I'm enjoying talking about the book because, quite frankly, most of the interviews have been on politics rather than on the book.

People will show up and stand in line for hours. I was in Philadelphia recently, and I always ask the first couple of people in line how long they've been there. The signing in Philadelphia was at seven at night, and this young lady had been there since nine-thirty in the morning. That's almost ten hours. She said she got there at nine-thirty because she was trying to attend one of my book-signing ceremonies in New York and couldn't get in because there were so many people there, and she wanted to have her book signed. Now, I'm just totally amazed on how much and how long people will stand and wait to talk to me briefly and have a book signed. I hadn't anticipated that.

I will probably write another book. I would imagine on the next book I will not commit to a thirty-six-city tour. It's exhausting. The events are the same. I enjoy meeting the people, but it is very, very tiring. When you sign 2,000 books in one evening, you really have cramps in your hand and your forearm by the time you're leaving. It's a wonderful experience, and I'm thoroughly enjoying it, but I doubt if I'd do it as extensively the next time.

Betty Friedan

Betty Friedan is probably best known for her 1963 book, The Feminine Mystique. *She appeared on* Booknotes *on November 28, 1993, to talk about her new book,* The Fountain of Age, *which explores the myths surrounding the aging process.*

I WENT ON AN OUTWARD BOUND TRIP called "Going Beyond," a wilderness expedition program for people over fifty-five, when I was in my early sixties. I told myself that I was doing it to do research for the book, because of the kind of people I was looking for—women and men that would continue to develop and evolve and that didn't fit that deterioration and decline. I was already beginning to see that a strong element of aging was adventurousness, a willingness to risk, an ability to risk in ways you couldn't do when you were younger. And I figured I'd find them on this trip, but, secretly, it was something I'd always yearned to do myself, that wilderness exploration kind of thing. In my long married life and then in my hectic life since my divorce—all this women's movement and lecturing—I'd somehow never done this wilderness stuff. I really wanted to do it myself. Of course, what it became was a metaphor of the whole search for the fountain of age.

We didn't tell people our last names when we started this Outward Bound trip. I don't think we told people our ages, and I don't think we told people our professions. It was just what city we came from or something like that, but it was no real identifying thing. So I wasn't seen through my mask, as it were, my persona, you know, the great feminist. And we became great friends. It was great fun for me to just be on my own without having to wear my public mask. I loved it.

The interesting thing now is that with this book, men are telling me—men and some women, too, of course, but men are having the same sort of emotional reaction that women had to *The Feminine Mystique,* of saying, "It's made me think altogether differently about the rest of my life."

Originally, I wasn't interested in the subject of age. I had the same dreary view of age as anybody in America, the same absolute denial. It didn't apply to me. But once I began on this little path, that large path that led me to break through an even more pernicious, pervasive mystique—the mystique of age only as decline from youth. I guess all the thirty years of writing *The Feminine Mystique* and the women's movement gave me a way to—well, I can't say more quickly, because it took me ten years to write this book, but at least to be able to break through this other thing.

Then I actually started working on the book. I took a fellowship at Harvard at the Institute of Politics at the Kennedy School and I taught *The Second Stage,* which was a book that I just finished. I taught a seminar in that, but otherwise I could use the resources of the university. I figured I'd immerse myself in whatever research had been done on aging.

In that great university all I could find was information on medical schools, Alzheimer's, nursing homes, and books on ethical issues, such as when do you pull the plug. I'd go to these conferences and the gerontological meetings I was beginning to attend in these paneled halls with the young Turks, in their white coats, with research money for aging. They would talk about "them" [the aged] sort of with the same contemptuous compassion, and it reminded me of something. It reminded me of the way the male experts on women used to talk about the "woman problem," all those years ago. I would come out of that feeling so depressed. That didn't interest me at all, this Alzheimer's, nursing home stuff.

Then I began to interview women and men—and I was finding it much easier than I thought I would—who were clearly very vital in these years beyond sixty and beyond seventy, even beyond eighty. I remember one I interviewed in Cambridge [was] beyond ninety. They were continuing to grow and develop. So that would exhilarate me. Then I began to feel depression, exhilaration, and then a kind of a weird panic. I thought, "What is wrong with me? What was wrong with me?" I'd never had that kind of writing block before. Then I realized what was wrong with me—I had just had my own sixtieth birthday. And I was furious when my friends threw me a surprise party on my sixtieth birthday. I felt very hostile to them, and they were very hostile to me to have done that, because I was as much in denial as anyone else.

The last chapter of my book is on "generativity," the freedom to risk, age as adventure and generativity. I think what finally evolves is that there is a sense of the affirmation of your whole life as you've lived it and in the history, and then some great sense of the meaning of that life. Your life is a part of the continuum that will live after you—through your children, through your grandchildren, but also through your human generativity— that's not just biological.

This is what the research and my own interviews show: that if you continue to grow and develop through the years and in the new years of life that are open to you, you become more and more authentically yourself. You shed the masks, and that is enormously liberating. Finally, with all its pains, you affirm the life that you have lived, and you put it all together.

At this moment, my dear, I am so relieved to get this finished that I have no immediate plans for another book. Do you know that I shipped for seven years, back and forth across the country, twenty boxes of papers, of notes, of books for this project—every year when I'd leave New York for my spring-winter teaching at the University of Southern California. I just was drowning in all that research, and the fact that I finally finished that book is such a liberation. I don't know what's next. I don't want to do another heavy book like that. I'm going to do short stuff. Maybe I'll do a column. Maybe I'll do a program like yours. Maybe I'll do a detective story. Maybe I'll write science fiction or a novel, but no more heavy books.

Norman Schwarzkopf

Retired general Norman Schwarzkopf wrote It Doesn't Take a Hero, *with Peter Petre, recounting his experiences in Vietnam, Grenada, and, most notably, the Gulf War. He appeared on the program on November 22, 1992.*

I DEALT WITH THE PRESS on a different level in Vietnam than I did in Grenada and in the desert war. I will confess to you that I'm one of those people who came away very disappointed in the press coverage of Vietnam. I saw what I called "cooked" stories—plain and simply, military operations that were well planned and well executed and were real success stories but made very dull reading. So you throw in a few civilian atrocities, you throw in a few short rounds or something like that, and all of a sudden it becomes a sexy story that sells. I saw that happen to operations that I participated in. There were bold-faced lies. So I came away disappointed and, I will confess, somewhat prejudiced.

Having said that, by the time Grenada came around I had matured far beyond that. I had learned from my Vietnam experience, but I still believe very much in the American public's right to know. Believe it or not, in the Grenada thing, something that people find hard to believe, but on the Sunday preceding the Tuesday that we went into Grenada, I sat there in a meeting where the plan was to introduce the press onto the island at five o'clock Tuesday afternoon. It was planned.

PETER PETRE [THE BOOK'S COAUTHOR] is an editor with *Fortune* magazine who wrote *Father, Son and Company* with Tom Watson, the former CEO of IBM. Peter had been through the process of writing this kind of book, number one. Number two, he had no military background at all, so he wasn't going to bring any biases to this story that were his own. Peter and I worked for one solid year on the book. It started with us sitting down together and coming up with an outline of what the book was going to be about—how long is it going to be? how much of it's going to be devoted to the Gulf War? how much of it's going to be devoted to [my] early life?—

that sort of thing. We put it together that way, and then literally hundreds of hours of my narrating [went] onto tapes, being recorded. Peter would then go back and review those tapes, come back the next morning, ask me a lot of questions to clarify my narration and also to translate it into English—because when military people talk, we have our own acronyms and our own language. So Peter was very good about saying, "Say that in a different way so that the readers will understand what you're talking about." Then it was all transcribed. Peter would then take the narration and write the first chapter. He would give it to me. I, of course, extensively rewrote it. I would give it back to him. He then, of course, would extensively rewrite what I rewrote; he would give it back to me; I would rewrite it again; I would give it back to him; he would rewrite it again; he'd give it back to me and I would rewrite it—about six iterations of rewrite between the two of us went into certainly the first ten or twelve chapters. And then one chapter would be complete and we would submit it to the publisher, where it started all over again because then the editor would come back and say, "Can't you give us a little bit more here to clarify this?"; and then, of course, the fact checkers would come in; and then, of course, the legal review would come in; and then, of course, the copy editor would come in. So those first chapters had probably up to ten to eleven rewrites before they finally became the chapter.

Peter moved down to Florida, lived right in the same complex that I lived in, came into my house at eight-thirty in the morning. We would work many days until seven o'clock at night. We would work often three or three and a half weeks straight—no Saturdays [off], no Sundays [off], right through. That really is the way the first ten or more chapters were written. See, he was in the process of writing and at the same time transcribing— you know, writing the earlier chapters and transcribing for the later chapters. He really knocked himself out and did a tremendous job.

The Pentagon did not have to review [the book]. The law says that once I'm retired from active duty I don't have to submit it to the Pentagon for review unless I use classified sources of information to write the book, so I very, very stridently avoided using any classified information. An awful lot of stuff was declassified. Right after the war, an awful lot of stuff was a matter of public record in the newspapers and this sort of thing, so I had a great deal of material to draw on. But the best thing I had, the most important thing I had, was this: In any other war I've ever fought, most of the instructions are sent by message back and forth so you have a hard-copy record of every decision that was made. Because of where we are today, most of the orders and instructions were sent back and forth over secured telephone. I mean, it was all by word of mouth. It became apparent very quickly that we weren't going to have a record of an awful lot of the decisions that were made unless we kept the record ourselves, so every conversation, as the conversation was going on, I would write down what I was saying and what was being said to me, and I had an executive officer that also sat in there, and he wrote down every time I would make a decision. If I called a staff meeting and as a result of that staff meeting I'd make a decision, he would log it into a private journal that we kept of every decision that was happening during the war. I'll tell you what, if it hadn't been for that, the book wouldn't have been written.

I'm probably going to donate [the 3,000 pages of notes] to the Library of Congress, donate them to the National War College archives [in Washington, D.C.], Army War College archives [in Carlisle, Pennsylvania], or something like that. I would ask that they be placed there and embargoed for ten years or something like that, and at the end of ten years somebody is going to have a ball—go in there and get hold of them and write the next version of the book.

I've got hundreds of hours of tapes sitting at home. I'm going to put [the tapes and the notes] all in one package. A lot of people have come to me for my papers. I'm going to tell you something—five years ago I didn't have any papers. It's amazing. One of the collections I have at home is all the stuff I saved from Grenada—the map that I carried around with me in my pocket in Grenada, which became the planning map; the enemy map that we captured, that showed us where the enemy was, that became sort of our prime piece of intelligence; a lot of the briefing slides that I used right after Grenada to give pit talks about what happened in Grenada. I have all that stuff at home, and I've kind of kept that together, which was, of course, the principal source material I used for the chapter on Grenada in here. You find out you accumulate a whole bunch of stuff. You send messages to the general, back channels and that sort of thing, that when you finally leave you find some very efficient secretary has kept all of that and filed it, and she gives it to you. I had taken all that stuff and put it in boxes and put it out in the garage. One of these days I'm going to have to sort through this and throw it all away because when I'm paying for my own move it'll cost me a fortune to move this to my next house or something like that.

Now people want it. Now people say, "Hey, we'd love to have all this stuff that you've accumulated over the years." I don't know how they're going to make any sense out of some of it. First of all, I'm left-handed and my handwriting is atrocious, and an awful lot of it is my own handwriting. But there are people out there that would be just delighted to have it. They say they'd catalog it and arrange it and put it all together and make it into something.

What the book has got to show is that it is a tortuous process coming up with the decisions that involve the lives of hundreds of thousands of people. It's not simple. All the war movies make things look so easy. A guy comes in and says, "Well, let's go to war," and we go to war. That's not the way it happens. You agonize over your decisions. You agonize over your plans. You get input from everywhere. People up and down the line have to make very, very tough calls.

Ulysses S. Grant refused to write his memoirs for years and years and years. He was asked to write them, and he didn't write them. Finally Grant went bankrupt once again and also found out he was dying. It sort of happened simultaneously. He tells you right at the very front of his memoirs, "The only reason I'm writing these memoirs is because I've gone bankrupt again and I want to leave an estate behind for my family and they've offered me an awful lot of money for these, and so, therefore, I'm writing these memoirs now." He's right up front about it.

Melba Patillo Beals

On November 27, 1994, Melba Patillo Beals, author of Warriors Don't Cry: A Searing Memoir of the Battle to Integrate Little Rock's Central High, *appeared on* Booknotes. *Ms. Beals wrote of her experience in 1957 when, as a young girl, she helped integrate Central High School escorted by the National Guard.*

I ALWAYS KNEW I had to write a book that both my mother and my grandmother, if she was still alive, would approve of. The process of writing this book, as you see it, was almost as difficult as attending Central High School. The first publisher I had was kind of a caretaker, plantation-owner kind of guy, a former southerner, who wanted to take over the process and wanted to direct in accordance with his lens, or his vision of where it should go. And I said, "Always, it must be told through the eyes of the child; never through the eyes of an adult who then puts the layers of judgment over what happened." I just wanted the incidents to stand alone, uncommented upon: just "This is what happened."

It took me a long time to cough it up. It was very difficult to write. I always thought that one day someone would walk in and there'd just be this large brown puddle of tears, and it would be me, you know. It took therapy; it took focus; it took prayer to get it up, to talk about it, to remember it all, to be able to talk about it from a neutral pedestal. I did not want to write the book through any veil of hostility, but just to simply tell you my story and let you decide what you think about it.

I write things down incessantly. I mean, I would hear snatches of conversation on a bus or in a lobby. So I always have kept notes, scraps of paper, or, in this case, a diary. I actually have a little pink diary, with a little white girl on it with a ponytail, that locked, which was one of my diaries given to me by my grandmother because I used to talk too much. I used to say things like, "People are like clothes on a coat hanger—our souls are the coat hanger and the clothes can be interchanged. We're not our bodies; we're our souls." Grandmother would say, "Shh, darling. Write that down. Don't tell everything."

I was kind of psychic as a child, predicting, at one point, a cousin's death, saying, "Oh, I think Debra's going to drown soon." Grandmother would say, "Shh, don't talk about that. Write that down." That's how I started writing things down, because people thought I was a little strange. So she would say, "Write letters to God," or, "Write it down," because as early as five, I would say, "Wait a minute, now, what's going on here? Are the white folks going to be in charge forever, or is it that we're going to be in charge, come June to December? They're in charge now. I mean, how did this whole system get set up? You say everything's equal; you say God loves us all. Well, Grandma, what's going on?" And she'd say, "Shh, write a letter to God." Hence, the whole writing thing was an early thing in my life.

I got serious [about writing this book] two years after I left Central High. I was serious during the time I was there. I was taping notes, writing it down, because it was just too big for me to handle. I couldn't tell anybody everything that was happening. I couldn't tell my grandma, even, everything that was happening. I could only tell God about it. I have twelve drafts of it. I have boxes at home of that book. I wrote the first draft when I was nineteen. But before that, I had a kind of collection of loose pages of it.

The first time I sent this to an agent—I have a friend, Danielle Steel, who introduced me to her agent—her name is Phyllis. We called her "God." And she was very instrumental, Phyllis was, in helping me along this pathway, although she was not my agent ultimately, when it was published. That was Sandra Dykstra. The first time I wrote this book, it was 380 pages long and only 70 pages were about the actual incident. Phyllis said, "You're not really ready to spew this story yet. You must do some work." Indeed, I went back into therapy, dealt with it, prayed about it. I had to live with this. I had to get this up. It was like a concrete in my gut, a solid concrete bolt of pain in my gut, that I had to get up piece by piece.

So it was a long time and a lot of dealing with myself in it, a lot of going to school to learn how to write, to get the craft down. Although I have a master's in broadcast journalism, there was a difference in the languaging, and so this took a lot of my energy and a lot of my time.

The first manuscript was 700 pages long and weighed about eight pounds. It had to be cut back. Also, the editor thought that the extent of the violence would really turn the reader off, and so we cut some of it out.

I want people to understand the enormity of mistreating another human being—the enormity, the impact of that. No matter what the context of it, to assume that you ever have the right to mistreat another human being is wrong. You don't. You don't have a right to deflower that spirit, you see. So that's why I wanted to write this book, because I believe if I put it on paper, people would understand why it's wrong to do that.

Newt Gingrich

In July 1995, a year into the 104th Congress, Newt Gingrich, the first Republican Speaker of the House in forty years, appeared on Booknotes *to discuss his book* To Renew America.

I STARTED THE BOOK, in a real way, in December of '92. It just occurred to me that we had to go back to our roots, so I began reading about the American Revolution and the Founding Fathers and how we got to this. It was very much influenced by two books by Gordon Wood on the American Revolution, and this was all done in my spare time.

I took the laptop everywhere in order to write this book. It was on the airplane with me, it was in the car with me. I did most of it at home, though, in Georgia. We bought a house last September in East Cobb, and so I did most of it sitting out in the yard, just writing away. And then we used CompuServe to ship chapters back and forth, because [Bill] Tucker [the book's coauthor] and [Adrian] Zackheim [its editor] were both in New York City.

The $24 price was HarperCollins's decision. The 260 pages were a random accident. I wrote 140,000 words and they edited it down to 80,000. They could have gone to 290 or they could have gone to 240 pages. We had a much longer section on the "Contract [with America]" that I really liked, about taking over the House and all this. My wife read it and she said, "Throw this stuff out," she said, "because they don't need to see this." But she did say, "That's a different book. Write that some other time." That killed about, I would say, three good chapters—bam!—they were gone.

That was my wife's say-so. She said, "This won't work." It was all dialogue. You sit there, and you argue it out, and you say, "Do you want to keep this in? Do you want to take it out? How much detail do you really want?" And you try to think from the standpoint of a typical American who may not be passionately involved in the question of: how did you organize this particular subcommittee? And why did you pick this particular chairman? Or, why did this happen? It's stuff that would be wonderful in a Washington book but is not particularly helpful in a book about civilization.

If I had to give my book a grade, I think I'd give it probably between an A– and a B+. I think it's not polished enough to be an A. It would have taken another two or three months to have really polished it as well as you'd like for a book—[so] you could say, "Hey, this is right." But it captures so much of what I wanted to say and says it so directly and so readably—I think it's an easy book to read—that I think that it's pretty close to an A–. But I'll leave that up to you. I would survive with a B+.

In my book, I do include a lot of lists: "there are five reasons why you must do this," "there are four reasons," "there are six points." It's like cookbooks. People work better if they have very specific, step-by-step directions. I was trying to write, in part, an introduction to where we have to go. And the numbers aren't magic. What I would do is I'd sit and I'd say, "Gee, what do I think we have to do?" I'd list all of them, and then I'd take the number that list became, and that'd be the number that goes in that particular slot.

I will consider the book a success if enough people look at it and decide that its ideas are worthwhile. Every indication we have in the opening couple of days is that it's going to be very, very successful, so I'd rather just say I'm confident. I think we need an argument about whether or not there's an American civilization. And if there is an American civilization, what are the rules for its survival? I think this book helps launch that argument. And I'd rather measure the success that way. If we have a serious discussion in the next year and a half about renewing American civilization versus continuing down the road of the welfare-state bureaucracy, then I think the book's massively successful.

I LIKE [MICHAEL] CRICHTON'S BOOKS. Let me say up front that I thought *Jurassic Park* was fabulous. A lot of his books are very, very well done, and he's a very interesting guy, and I'd love to sit and talk to him sometime. But consistently [in Crichton's books], humans are the bad guys, and consistently it's sort of Frankenstein revisited over and over again. I don't think that's the history of the human race. Most technology, on balance, has improved things. I think that sitting in an air-conditioned room watching C-SPAN on a color television set beats being next to a primitive fireplace outside of a cave.

Madeline Cartwright ✓

Madeline Cartwright, a former principal of Blaine Elementary School in Philadelphia, is currently a consultant to that city's school system. She was our guest on Booknotes *on September 19, 1993, to talk about the experiences, chronicled in her book,* For the Children: Lessons from a Visionary Principal; How We Can Save Our Public Schools.

THE IDEA OF A BOOK came from a writer in Philadelphia, Vernon Loeb. He came out to Blaine [School], looked at it and said, "Now, this is really a nice story." He wrote it and put it in a newspaper, *The Philadelphia Inquirer.* Then Knight-Ridder bought it and it ran [throughout] the country. Vernon said to me, "Madeline, there is a story here to be told and somebody is going to tell it. You should tell it yourself." I said, "Well, you come and help me tell it." He said, "I don't have time, but you can do it. Just go and do it."

I started right then collecting my stories and writing them and putting them aside. Then I began to write the educational part of it, the educational program at that school. When I finished writing the educational program I gave it to a girlfriend and asked her if she would read the stories and sift them into the education.

Then another newspaper writer [Richard Louv] came to Philadelphia looking for a story on childhood in America. I said to him, "I'm writing, too. I'm writing my story. However, if you're going to write about the children, good. If you're going to write about me, I don't want to talk." He says, "No, I'm going to write about the children." We talked all day long, all day. He had a good time, and we like to share. Richard came and wrote this story, and then he went back and wrote a book. One chapter in that book was about the Blaine School and me. *The New York Times* bought that one chapter and put me on the front of *The New York Times Magazine.*

I was sitting on the bed—that's where I work, on the bed. Everybody said, "You're going to ruin your bed," but as I sat on the bed, my grandson would crawl on the bed, run round and put his arms around my neck. No mattress was worth that—I had to have that! I'm sitting here, working with my book; Jared is running around the floor, because I locked him in the room with me. The telephone rang, and a lady says to me, "Would you hold? A vice president from Doubleday wants to speak with you." I said, "This is a joke. I've been home from school one month." Sure enough, there was Martha Levin, a vice president of Doubleday, saying to me she heard I was writing a book and would like me to give them a chance of publishing my book.

I still think this is a joke, but I'll go along with the program. She says, "I'm going to send you some books that we have done, and you can look at them. Let us see your draft as soon as possible." I said, "All right." By now, I'm convinced! I started screaming, because that is how I am. I started screaming. My baby [grandson, Jared] started crying. My daughter came running. By this time, the kid looks up and sees that I'm laughing, and in the middle of his tears, he stopped and started laughing, too. She [my daughter] said, "What's going on?" I said, "Doubleday wants to publish my book!" It was real. And that's how we got published.

The most difficult [thing] from that moment forward was writing with the [ghost]writer. I said to the writer, "We need to sit down side by side and write this book." Because sometimes, changing a word can change my meaning. I wanted to make a book that did not put down our parents—because they weren't to be put down. They had worked hard. I wanted to make sure that this book said what I wanted it to say; it didn't change anything from what happened. From time to time I had to say to the writer, "What happened was dramatic enough. Don't embellish it. Just tell it like it was." He would say to me, "I'm a writer, and you're an educator." I'd say, "*We're* writing this book." But we got through it. He understood where I was coming from. I understood his responsibility and what he had to do.

I had a whole lot more. They edited the book down, which was all right, because I understood they were the professionals at this. They took out a lot that I would have put back in. Some of the stuff they took out, I did put back in. They allowed me to do that. We agreed that this is what we want.

This book changed my entire life in that many, many people started to come to the school. Many people called the school. I knew that I better get this book finished, and I really started working on it hard then. I took a sabbatical leave and worked on it full time.

Since this book came out, I have gone to celebrity status. Folks kind of treat me like I was a martyr, like I've done something special. I feel like I really haven't done so much special. I had kids when I came to North Philadelphia who slept on the filthiest mattresses.

I'm going to take that [celebrity status], I hope, and be able to consult with school districts. I can show them what we did to make it better. I know that when you involve parents and teachers, and principals, and children in your community in one team—all on one side of the team, going in one direction—then education can improve.

Linda Chavez √

On March 22, 1992, Linda Chavez appeared on the program to discuss her book Out of the Barrio: Toward a New Politics of Hispanic Assimilation. *In 1995, Ms. Chavez became president of the Center for Equality in Washington, D.C. She is also a syndicated columnist.*

I'M AN ASSIMILATIONIST. I believe in assimilation. I think that assimilation is the only model that works in a society as diverse as ours, that if each and every group keeps its primary attachment to the ethnic group or the racial group or the religious group that it's divisive. Having said that, though, one of the unique characteristics about American assimilation is that we do feel that we have some connection to the past. I mean, we eat different foods; we have different kinds of traditions in our homes and celebrations. I think that so long as the ethnic part is private, so long as public funds are not being used to promote it that there's nothing wrong with it and it, in fact, can make a richer nation and make a richer life. It's when the public gets involved and when we begin expending public money to promote attachment to ethnicity or race that I have a problem.

I was motivated to write this book, in part, because I thought the book needed to be written, and no one else would write it. I do a lot of public speaking, particularly on campuses. And I found a very strange thing when I would go out around the country, particularly speaking to audiences where there were young Mexican-American and other Hispanic students, that I was constantly hearing from the leadership in the community this notion that there'd been no progress, there'd been no change in twenty years—that if you look at the statistics about earnings or education or the other social and economic indicators and you compare today's figures to the figures twenty, thirty, forty years ago, they don't look very different.

Yet, it was very clear to me, having grown up in that period, that, in fact, a great deal has changed, an enormous amount of progress was taking place. It became almost an obsession with me. How can I figure out why the numbers don't reflect the reality of progress and change?

Actually, the first draft was longer and I cut it. I guess most of the writing that I've done in my career has been journalistic writing. I've written a syndicated column, and I've written lots of op-eds. In the book, I'm writing for a general audience, so I attempted to keep it free of as much jargon as I could. Initially, I had an appendix at the back with multiple-regression tables, explaining some of the statistics that I used. That got cut at the end. My attempt was really to write something that was accessible to people who know nothing whatsoever about Hispanics as well as accessible to people who consider themselves expert. It's for a very general audience.

You don't grow up in the Southwest in the 1950s without having encountered prejudice and discrimination. I certainly did as a child. I can remember lots of things. I can remember the little boy who lived across the alley from me in Denver, who played with me every day until one day, he told me his dad said he couldn't play with a Mexican. I remember being kicked off of playgrounds. I remember being snickered at and called names by girls, at high school, at the dances. I can remember being invited by a boy to a dance at the country club and being so shunned by the other people there that I felt very isolated and sort of withdrew into the ladies' room and stayed. I spent most of the night there. I mean, those things happen.

Cubans are unique in the Hispanic community in that they came here, first of all, not as immigrants, but as political refugees. They also came here expecting to go back. I think most of the Cubans who came here in the early 1960s expected that their stay here would not be for very long, that Castro would be overthrown and that they would return back to their homeland. They also were predominantly middle class. They were not struggling peasants who, you know, had lost their jobs in the sugar fields or something and came here looking for a better life. They tended to be small-business men, to be skilled workers, some of them professional, some of them wealthy. So their experience here reflects that difference in their background.

Puerto Ricans, on the other hand, many of them did migrate here because of changes in the economy of Puerto Rico. Many of them do come from very rural backgrounds [and had] very little education when they came, predominantly in the 1940s and early '50s. And so it's a very big difference between the two groups.

There's never really emerged any national Hispanic political leader in part, I think, because the communities are so different. Henry Cisneros, who was very well thought of when he was mayor of San Antonio, looked like he might be able to break into that kind of a prominence. Whether he would have been embraced and accepted by Cubans in Miami and Puerto

Ricans in New York is questionable. I think Mexican-Americans found him to be a prominent Hispanic figure. Whether or not he would have had that kind of broad reach, I don't know.

[The pronunciation of my name] became an issue during my race for the U.S. Senate. My consultants decided that people who were not Hispanic couldn't learn to say Chavez, that it sounded somehow strange to their ears and it wouldn't form on the tongue. So they persuaded me that, first of all, the announcer couldn't say Chavez and that it should be pronounced "Shavez." So I went around for about a year and a half saying it that way while I was running, saying "Shavez," Finally, I woke up and said, "Wait a second. That's not the way I've ever pronounced my name, and I'm going back to the original."

People tend to be wary of people who are different from them. It's something that I think we have done a better job in the United States fighting against than most people have in other parts of the world, but it's still there. It's very difficult to legislate an end to prejudice. We can legislate and have, in this country, an end to discrimination. We can make it illegal to act on the basis of our prejudices, but eliminating those prejudices is a much harder thing to do.

I DEDICATED THE BOOK TO MY FATHER, who died in 1978. My father had the most profound influence on my life of anyone. I guess my husband, maybe, comes a close second, but my father really had an enormous impact on my life. He was a very smart man. He was very well read. He introduced me to the world of books as a very little girl. I went to the library in Albuquerque when I was with him, when I was four or five years old. Books were always a very important part of my life. He did not have the advantage of an education. He had to drop out of school when he was still in high school, after ninth grade, to help support his brothers and sisters. And I think I always felt very bad that he was not able to continue that education, because he was a very smart man.

Margaret Thatcher

Former British Prime Minister Margaret Thatcher appeared on Booknotes *on December 5, 1993, to talk about the first volume of her memoir,* The Downing Street Years.

FIRST, I HAD TO DECIDE if I wanted to do the book in one volume or two. I had already thought that the first thing I must do is to tell the story of the years when I was in 10 Downing Street. They were exciting years. They were purposeful years. We changed the entire economy; we had the Falklands War to fight; we had the Libyan raid; we had the end of the Cold War; we had the [Persian] Gulf War—how should I do it? So I thought that instead of telling it in enormous detail, as some people do, almost a diary of every day, I would take the main themes and follow them through and try to put them in a time frame of the three elections which I fought. So the first thing I had to do was to get the whole structure of the chapters right, and then I sat down and wrote as much as I could remember about each, without, in fact, referring to documents. I made a note of what I needed to look up. And then, for accuracy, there were masses and masses of documents which must be consulted. Every meeting I had with a foreign statesman or with an internal minister was documented, and what was said in the interview and what was concluded. Also, we had to look up, where there was an archivist, some of the reporting in the newspapers when we had exciting "Question Times" in the House and the times when we had exciting debates. So the volume of paperwork was enormous.

Gradually, it came down to writing each and every chapter, partly dictated, partly written, and then assembled, and then rewritten and rewritten and rewritten to get it to flow. I was very lucky with some things because after the end of the Falklands—it had been such a deep, agonizing experience that the following Christmas I sat down and wrote it up while all the memories were very fresh in my mind. So that is perhaps particularly vivid. I wrote up some other special occasions, if we had a particularly difficult one, in negotiating finance with Europe; if I had a particularly difficult problem when someone resigned—all of these were written up.

But apart from that, I was on official records, the sort of thing that a biographer would have. I looked at all of these rather clinically, beautifully phrased and drafted minutes and cabinet minutes and conclusions, but no biographer could have gotten, really, any flavor, from that, of the sense of battle we had in some of the meetings, the sense of debate, the sense of argument. So I became an absolute convert to the person [myself], who had gone through all the experiences, writing the book. It's now in the one volume so it can be read without too much difficulty. It would be a little bit much to read in bed—a little bit heavy, perhaps—but otherwise it can be read as one volume.

My publisher did say, "Look, try to put personal recollections because that makes it human." But you don't need urging to do that, because so many of the things occur because you either get on very well with someone or you've had a breakthrough in negotiations or you've had a difficulty or a problem. This is the very stuff of politics. It's the very stuff of negotiations.

It is lonely being prime minister, and there are times when you are down in the dumps. There are times when things don't go right, particularly in politics, and you've just got to have your husband there, whose loyalty and affection are just unquestioned, and also can give you quite good advice— "Don't get things out of proportion," which is very, very important because sometimes a small thing can get completely out of proportion. At the end of the day, I might have returned from the House of Commons at about eleven o'clock, and Denis [Mr. Thatcher] perhaps would be up in the flat. There is a small flat at the top of Number 10—not a grand flat at all, nothing like the White House—small, in the rafters. We had no housekeeper, no cook; we just had daily help in the morning. So in the evening, I used to go and get supper ready if neither of us had it—a very light supper. And we'd just sit down and talk for an hour or so, to let one's hair down and perhaps to get an outside view. Denis was in the oil and chemical industry, in contact with all industries. He always kept off politics and spoke about what he knew. He never had an interview. He wouldn't. He never had a political secretary. He wrote, himself, between thirty and fifty replies every week to letters he'd had from the public. So, really, I was terribly lucky. He was always there.

Now I've been out of power for nearly three years. I think I'm treated the same way in the United Kingdom and the United States. I'm almost hailed as a heroine, as people look back and see what we did—how purposeful and exciting it was. A fantastic number of young people come to buy the book. They didn't always like what I did, but they knew that it had purpose and direction. I found this as I went on a book tour of the United Kingdom. Of course there are some people who are against one. The Socialist Workers Party will demonstrate against you. But by and large the appreciation is enormous, and I think the thing they say to me most often in Britain is, "Thank you for what you did for our country," and that matters to me a great deal.

Appendix

Readers can review an online appendix to Booknotes:
America's Finest Authors on Reading, Writing and the Power of Ideas
on the World Wide Web at:

http://www.booknotes.org

Available on the C-SPAN Web page are:
- *Complete transcripts of nearly five hundred* Booknotes *interviews.*
- *An interactive "cyber-photo gallery" where you can learn more about the writers in the book.*
- *Audio and video archives looking back at programs over the past nine years.*

Complete List of C-SPAN *Booknotes*
(1989–1997)

1. SEPTEMBER 14, 1988
Pre-BOOKNOTES Interview
with Neil Sheehan
*A Bright Shining Lie: John
Paul Vann and America in Viet-
nam*
Publisher: Random House

2. APRIL 2, 1989
*[official start of
BOOKNOTES]
Zbigniew Brzezinski
*Grand Failure: The Birth and
Death of Communism in the
Twentieth Century*
Publisher: Macmillan

3. APRIL 9, 1989
Judy Shelton
*The Coming Soviet Crash: Gor-
bachev's Desperate Pursuit of
Credit in Western Financial Mar-
kets*
Publisher: The Free Press

4. APRIL 16, 1989
Bruce Oudes
*From: The President—Richard
Nixon's Secret Files*
Publisher: HarperCollins

5. APRIL 23, 1989
Susan Moeller
*Shooting War: Photography and the
American Experience of Combat*
Publisher: Basic Books

6. APRIL 30, 1989
Henry Brandon
*Special Relationships: A Foreign
Correspondent's Memoirs*
Publisher: Atheneum

7. MAY 7, 1989
Colonel David Hackworth (with
Julie Sherman)
*About Face: The Odyssey of an
American Warrior*
Publisher: Simon & Schuster

8. MAY 14, 1989
James Fallows
*More Like Us: Making America
Great Again*
Publisher: Houghton Mifflin

9. MAY 21, 1989
Gregory Fossedal
*The Democratic Imperative:
Exporting the American Revolu-
tion*
Publisher: Basic Books

10. MAY 28, 1989
Stanley Karnow
*In Our Image: America's Empire
in the Philippines*
Publisher: Random House

11. JUNE 4, 1989
James McGregor Burns
The Crosswinds of Freedom
Publisher: Knopf

12. JUNE 11, 1989
Robert Christopher
*Crashing the Gates: The De-
WASPing of America's Power Elite*
Publisher: Simon & Schuster

13. JUNE 18, 1989
Senator Robert Byrd
The Senate: 1789–1989
Publisher: Government Printing
Office

14. JUNE 25, 1989
Elizabeth Colton
*The Jackson Phenomenon: The
Man, the Power, the Message*
Publisher: Doubleday

15. JULY 2, 1989
Nathaniel Branden
*Judgment Day: My Years with
Ayn Rand*
Publisher: Houghton Mifflin

16. JULY 9, 1989
Roger Kennedy
*Orders from France: The Ameri-
cans and the French in a Revolu-
tionary World (1780–1820)*
Publisher: Knopf

17. JULY 14, 1989
(BASTILLE DAY SPECIAL)
Simon Schama
*Citizens: A Chronicle of the
French Revolution*
Publisher: Knopf

18. JULY 16, 1989
George Wilson
*Mud Soldiers: Life Inside the New
American Army*
Publisher: Scribner

19. JULY 23, 1989
Jeanne Simon
*Codename: Scarlett—Life on the
Campaign Trail by the Wife of a
Presidential Candidate*
Publisher: The Continuum Pub-
lishing Company

20. JULY 30, 1989
Michael Kaufman
*Mad Dreams, Saving Graces—
Poland: A Nation in Conspiracy*
Publisher: Random House

21. AUGUST 6, 1989
Porter McKeever
*Adlai Stevenson: His Life and
Legacy*
Publisher: Morrow

22. AUGUST 13, 1989
(Gary Paul Gates and)
Bob Schieffer
The Acting President
Publisher: E. P. Dutton

23. AUGUST 20, 1989
Bruce Murray
*Journey Into Space—The First
Thirty Years of Space Exploration*
Publisher: Norton

24. AUGUST 27, 1989
Jack Germond and Jules
Witcover
*Whose Broad Stripes and Bright
Stars: The Trivial Pursuit of the
Presidency, 1988*
Publisher: Warner Books

25. SEPTEMBER 3, 1989
Walter Laquer
*The Long Road to Freedom:
Russia and Glasnost*
Publisher: Scribner

26. SEPTEMBER 10, 1989
Thomas Friedman
From Beirut to Jerusalem
Publisher: Farrar Straus Giroux

27. SEPTEMBER 17, 1989
General Ariel Sharon
Warrior: An Autobiography
Publisher: Simon & Schuster

28. SEPTEMBER 24, 1989
George Gilder
*Microcosm: The Quantum Revo-
lution in Economics and
Technology*
Publisher: Simon & Schuster

29. OCTOBER 1, 1989
Mort Rosenblum
*Back Home: A Foreign Correspon-
dent Rediscovers America*
Publisher: Morrow

30. OCTOBER 8, 1989
Barbara Ehrenreich
*Fear of Falling: The Inner Life of
the Middle Class*
Publisher: Pantheon

31. OCTOBER 15, 1989
Harrison Salisbury
*Tiananmen Diary: Thirteen Days
in June*
Publisher: Little, Brown

32. OCTOBER 22, 1989
Kenneth Adelman
*The Great Universal Embrace:
Arms Summitry—A Skeptic's
Account*
Publisher: Simon & Schuster

33. OCTOBER 29, 1989
Ralph David Abernathy
*And the Walls Came Tumbling
Down*
Publisher: Harper & Row

34. NOVEMBER 5, 1989
Vassily Aksyonov
Say Cheese: Soviets and the Media
Publisher: Random House

35. NOVEMBER 12, 1989
Felix Rodriguez
(and John Weisman)
*Shadow Warrior: The CIA Hero
of a Hundred Unknown Battles*
Publisher: Simon & Schuster

36. NOVEMBER 19, 1989
Robin Wright
*In the Name of God:
The Khomeini Decade*
Publisher: Simon & Schuster

37. NOVEMBER 26, 1989
Peter Hennessy
Whitehall
Publisher: The Free Press

38. DECEMBER 3, 1989
Clifford Stoll
*The Cuckoo's Egg: Tracking a Spy
Through the Maze of Computer
Espionage*
Publisher: Doubleday

39. DECEMBER 10, 1989
Arthur Grace
*Choose Me: Portraits of a Presi-
dential Race*
Publisher: University Press of
New England

40. DECEMBER 17, 1989
James Reston, Jr.
*The Lone Star: The Life of John
Connally*
Publisher: Harper & Row

41. DECEMBER 24, 1989
Richard Rhodes
*Farm: A Year in the Life of an
American Farmer*
Publisher: Simon & Schuster

42. DECEMBER 31, 1989
William Lutz
*Doublespeak: From "Revenue
Enhancement" to "Terminal Liv-
ing"—How Government, Busi-
ness, Advertisers and Others Use
Language to Deceive You*
Publisher: Harper & Row

43. JANUARY 7, 1990
Sig Mickelson
*From Whistle Stop to Sound Bite:
Four Decades of Politics and Tele-
vision*
Publisher: Praeger

44. JANUARY 14, 1990
John Barry
*The Ambition and the Power—
The Fall of Jim Wright: A True
Story of Washington*
Publisher: Viking

45. JANUARY 21, 1990
Fitzhugh Green
George Bush: An Intimate Portrait
Publisher: Hippocrene Books

46. JANUARY 28, 1990
Charles Fecher, editor
The Diary of H. L. Mencken
Publisher: Knopf

47. FEBRUARY 4, 1990
Jim Mann
*Beijing Jeep: The Short, Unhappy
Romance of American Business in
China*
Publisher: Simon & Schuster

48. FEBRUARY 11, 1990
David Burnham
*A Law Unto Itself: Power, Politics,
and the IRS*
Publisher: Random House

49. FEBRUARY 18, 1990
Peggy Noonan
*What I Saw at the Revolution: A
Political Life in the Reagan Era*
Publisher: Random House

50. FEBRUARY 25, 1990
Michael Fumento
The Myth of Heterosexual AIDS
Publisher: Basic Books

51. FEBRUARY 27, 1990
Hedley Donovan
Right Places, Right Times: Forty Years in Journalism Not Counting My Paper Route
Publisher: Henry Holt

52. MARCH 4, 1990
Richard Barnet
The Rockets' Red Glare: When America Goes to War—The Presidents and the People
Publisher: Simon & Schuster

53. MARCH 11, 1990
Frederick Kempe
Divorcing the Dictator: America's Bungled Affairs with Noriega
Publisher: Putnam

54. MARCH 18, 1990
(Neil Livingstone and)
David Halevy
Inside the PLO
Publisher: Morrow

55. MARCH 25, 1990
James Abourezk
Advise and Dissent: Memoirs of South Dakota and the U.S. Senate
Publisher: Lawrence Hill Books

56. APRIL 1, 1990
Fred Graham
Happy Talk: Confessions of a TV Newsman
Publisher: Norton

57. APRIL 8, 1990
Leonard Sussman
Power, the Press, & the Technology of Freedom: The Coming Age of ISDN
Publisher: Freedom House

58. APRIL 15, 1990
Helmut Schmidt
Men and Powers: A Political Retrospective
Publisher: Random House

59. APRIL 22, 1990
Michael Barone
Our Country: The Shaping of America from Roosevelt to Reagan
Publisher: The Free Press

60. APRIL 29, 1990
Robert Caro
Means of Ascent: The Years of Lyndon Johnson
Publisher: Knopf

61. MAY 6, 1990
Morley Safer
Flashbacks on Returning to Vietnam
Publisher: Random House

62. MAY 13, 1990
Steven Emerson and Brian Duffy
The Fall of Pan Am 103: Inside the Lockerbie Investigation
Publisher: Putnam

63. MAY 20, 1990
Allister Sparks
The Mind of South Africa
Publisher: Knopf

64. MAY 27, 1990
Bette Bao Lord
Legacies: A Chinese Mosaic
Publisher: Knopf

65. JUNE 3, 1990
Dusko Doder (and Louise Branson)
Gorbachev: Heretic in the Kremlin
Publisher: Viking

66. JUNE 10, 1990
Thomas Sowell
Preferential Policies: An International Perspective
Publisher: Morrow

67. JUNE 17, 1990
Judith Miller
One, by One, by One: Facing the Holocaust
Publisher: Simon & Schuster

68. JUNE 24, 1990
Kevin Phillips
The Politics of Rich and Poor: Wealth and the American Electorate in the Reagan Aftermath
Publisher: Random House

69. JULY 1, 1990
Chris Ogden
Maggie: An Intimate Portrait of a Woman in Power
Publisher: Simon & Schuster

70. JULY 8, 1990
Denton Watson
Lion in the Lobby: Clarence Mitchell, Jr.'s Struggle for the Passage of Civil Rights Laws
Publisher: Morrow

71. JULY 15, 1990
Caspar Weinberger
Fighting for Peace: Seven Critical Years in the Pentagon
Publisher: Warner Books

72. JULY 22, 1990
Teresa Odendahl
Charity Begins at Home: Generosity and Self-Interest Among the Philanthropic Elite
Publisher: Basic Books

73. JULY 29, 1990
Michael Shapiro
The Shadow in the Sun: A Korean Year of Love and Sorrow
Publisher: Atlantic Monthly Press

74. AUGUST 5, 1990
Dan Raviv and Yossi Melman
Every Spy a Prince: The Complete History of Israel's Intelligence Community
Publisher: Houghton Mifflin

75. AUGUST 12, 1990
Roger Kimball
Tenured Radicals: How Politics Has Corrupted Our Higher Education
Publisher: Harper & Row

76. AUGUST 19, 1990
Tad Szulc
Then and Now: How the World Has Changed Since World War II
Publisher: Morrow

77. AUGUST 26, 1990
Christopher Wren
The End of the Line: The Failure of Communism in the Soviet Union and China
Publisher: Simon & Schuster

78. SEPTEMBER 2, 1990
Lee Edwards
Missionary for Freedom: The Life and Times of Walter Judd
Publisher: Paragon House

79. SEPTEMBER 9, 1990
Robert Dole
Historical Almanac of the United States Senate
Publisher: Government Printing Office

80. SEPTEMBER 16, 1990
M. A. Farber, et al.
Outrage: The Story Behind the Tawana Brawley Hoax
Publisher: Bantam Books

81. SEPTEMBER 23, 1990
Janette Dates
Split Image: African Americans in the Mass Media
Publisher: Howard University Press

82. OCTOBER 14, 1990
Harold Stassen
Eisenhower: Turning the World Toward Peace
Publisher: Merrill Magnus

83. OCTOBER 21, 1990
Tim Weiner
Blank Check: The Pentagon's Black Budget
Publisher: Warner Books

84. OCTOBER 28, 1990
Pat Choate
Agents of Influence: How Japan's Lobbyists in the United States Manipulate America's Political and Economic System
Publisher: Knopf

85. NOVEMBER 4, 1990
Paul Taylor
See How They Run: Electing a President in the Age of Mediaocracy
Publisher: Knopf

86. NOVEMBER 11, 1990
Blaine Harden
Africa: Dispatches from a Fragile Continent
Publisher: Norton

87. NOVEMBER 18, 1990
Jean Edward Smith
Lucius D. Clay: An American Life
Publisher: Henry Holt

88. NOVEMBER 25, 1990
Martin Mayer
The Greatest-Ever Bank Robbery: The Collapse of the Savings and Loan Industry
Publisher: Scribner

89. DECEMBER 2, 1990
Carol Barkalow (with Andrea Raals)
In the Men's House: An Inside Account of Life in the Army by One of West Point's First Female Graduates
Publisher: Poseidon Press

90. DECEMBER 9, 1990
Sally Bedell Smith
In All His Glory: The Life of William S. Paley, The Legendary Tycoon and His Brilliant Circle
Publisher: Simon & Schuster

91. DECEMBER 16, 1990
Shen Tong (with Marianne Yen)
Almost a Revolution: The Story of a Chinese Student's Journey from Boyhood to Leadership in Tiananmen Square
Publisher: Houghton Mifflin

92. DECEMBER 23, 1990
Janet Wallach and John Wallach
Arafat: In the Eyes of the Beholder
Publisher: Lyle Stuart

93. DECEMBER 30, 1990
Garry Wills
Under God: Religion and American Politics
Publisher: Simon & Schuster

94. JANUARY 6, 1991
Ben Wattenberg
The First Universal Nation: Leading Indicators and Ideas About the Surge of America in the 1990s
Publisher: The Free Press

95. JANUARY 13, 1991
Daniel Roos
The Machine That Changed the World
Publisher: Macmillan

96. JANUARY 27, 1991
Daniel Yergin
The Prize: The Epic Quest for Oil, Money and Power
Publisher: Simon & Schuster

97. FEBRUARY 3, 1991
Carl Rowan

Breaking Barriers: A Memoir
Publisher: Little, Brown

98. FEBRUARY 10, 1991
Theodore Hesburgh
(with Jerry Reedy)
God, Country, Notre Dame: The Autobiography of Theodore M. Hesburgh
Publisher: Doubleday

99. FEBRUARY 17, 1991
Ronald Brownstein
The Power and the Glitter: The Hollywood-Washington Connection
Publisher: Pantheon

100. FEBRUARY 24, 1991
Robert Kuttner
The End of Laissez-Faire: National Purpose and the Global Economy After the Cold War
Publisher: Knopf

101. MARCH 3, 1991
Haynes Johnson
Sleepwalking Through History: America in the Reagan Years
Publisher: Norton

102. MARCH 10, 1991
Georgie Anne Geyer
Guerilla Prince: The Untold Story of Fidel Castro
Publisher: Little, Brown

103. MARCH 17, 1991
Leonard Goldenson (with Marvin Wolf)
Beating the Odds: The Untold Story Behind the Rise of ABC: The Stars, Struggles and Egos That Transformed Network Television
Publisher: Scribner

104. MARCH 24, 1991
Richard Brookhiser
The Way of the WASP: How It Made America and How It Can Save It . . . So to Speak
Publisher: The Free Press

105. MARCH 31, 1991
Dayton Duncan
Grass Roots: One Year in the Life of the New Hampshire Presidential Primary
Publisher: Penguin

106. APRIL 7, 1991
Tom Wicker

One of Us: Richard Nixon and The American Dream
Publisher: Random House

107. APRIL 14, 1991
William Strauss and Neil Howe
Generations: The History of America's Future, 1584–2069
Publisher: Morrow

108. APRIL 21, 1991
Robert Shogan
The Riddle of Power: Presidential Leadership from Truman to Bush
Publisher: Dutton

109. APRIL 28, 1991
Caroline Kennedy and Ellen Alderman
In Our Defense: The Bill of Rights in Action
Publisher: Morrow

110. MAY 5, 1991
Nick Lemann
The Promised Land: The Great Black Migration and How It Changed America
Publisher: Knopf

111. MAY 12, 1991 (PART ONE)
Lou Cannon
President Reagan: The Role of a Lifetime
Publisher: Simon & Schuster

112. MAY 19, 1991 (PART TWO)
Lou Cannon
Ronald Reagan: The Role of a Lifetime
Publisher: Simon & Schuster

113. MAY 26, 1991
Robert Reich
The Work of Nations: Preparing Ourselves for 21st Century Capitalism
Publisher: Knopf

114. JUNE 2, 1991
Robert Kaiser
Why Gorbachev Happened: His Triumphs and His Failure
Publisher: Simon & Schuster

115. JUNE 9, 1991
George Friedman and Merideth Lebard
The Coming War with Japan
Publisher: St. Martin's Press

116. JUNE 16, 1991
Dixy Lee Ray
Trashing the Planet: How Science Can Help Us Deal with Acid Rain, Depletion of the Ozone, and Nuclear Waste (Among Other Things)
Publisher: Regnery

117. JUNE 23, 1991
Bob Woodward
The Commanders
Publisher: Simon & Schuster

118. JUNE 30, 1991
Roger Gittines
Consequences: John G. Tower—A Personal and Political Memoir
Publisher: Little, Brown

119. JULY 7, 1991
Donald Ritchie
Press Gallery: Congress and the Washington Correspondents
Publisher: Harvard University Press

120. JULY 14, 1991
Michael Beschloss
The Crisis Years: Kennedy and Khrushchev, 1960–1963
Publisher: HarperCollins

121. JULY 21, 1991
Alan Ehrenhalt
The United States of Ambition: Politicians, Power, and the Pursuit of Office
Publisher: Random House

122. JULY 28, 1991
Clark Clifford and Richard Holbrooke
Counsel to the President: A Memoir
Publisher: Random House

123. AUGUST 4, 1991
Elaine Sciolino
The Outlaw State: Saddam Hussein's Quest for Power and the Gulf Crisis
Publisher: John Wiley & Sons

124. AUGUST 11, 1991
Len Colodny and Robert Gettlin
Silent Coup: The Removal of a President
Publisher: St. Martin's Press

125. AUGUST 18, 1991
Liz Trotta

Fighting for Air: In the Trenches with Television News
Publisher: Simon & Schuster

126. AUGUST 25, 1991
E. J. Dionne
Why Americans Hate Politics
Publisher: Simon & Schuster

127. SEPTEMBER 1, 1991
Andrew and Leslie Cockburn
Dangerous Liaisons: The Inside Story of the U.S.-Israeli Covert Relationship
Publisher: HarperCollins

128. SEPTEMBER 8, 1991
Liva Baker
The Justice From Beacon Hill: The Life and Times of Oliver Wendell Holmes
Publisher: HarperCollins

129. SEPTEMBER 15, 1991
Reuven Frank
Out of Thin Air: The Brief Wonderful Life of Network News
Publisher: Simon & Schuster

130. SEPTEMBER 22, 1991
Robert Dallek
Lone Star Rising: Lyndon Johnson and His Times 1908–1960
Publisher: Oxford University Press

131. SEPTEMBER 29, 1991
Stephen Carter
Reflections of an Affirmative Action Baby
Publisher: Basic Books

132. OCTOBER 6, 1991
Ken Auletta
Three Blind Mice: How the TV Networks Lost Their Way
Publisher: Random House

133. OCTOBER 20, 1991
Anthony Lewis
Make No Law: The Sullivan Case and the First Amendment
Publisher: Random House

134. OCTOBER 27, 1991
Don Oberdorfer
The Turn: From the Cold War to a New Era—The United States and the Soviet Union, 1983–1990
Publisher: Simon & Schuster

135. NOVEMBER 3, 1991
Larry Sabato
*Feeding Frenzy: How Attack
Journalism Has Transformed
American Politics*
Publisher: The Free Press

136. NOVEMBER 10, 1991
Tina Rosenberg
*Children of Cain: Violence and
the Violent in Latin America*
Publisher: Morrow

137. NOVEMBER 17, 1991
Suzanne Garment
*Scandal: The Culture of Mistrust
in American Politics*
Publisher: Times Books

138. NOVEMBER 24, 1991
James Stewart
Den of Thieves
Publisher: Simon & Schuster

139. DECEMBER 1, 1991
Gary Sick
*October Surprise: America's
Hostages in Iran and the Election
of Ronald Reagan*
Publisher: Times Books

140. DECEMBER 8, 1991
James "Scotty" Reston
Deadline: A Memoir
Publisher: Random House

141. DECEMBER 15, 1991
Thomas Byrne Edsall and Mary
Edsall
*Chain Reaction: The Impact of
Race, Rights, and Taxes on
American Politics*
Publisher: Norton

142. DECEMBER 22, 1991
Martin Gilbert
Churchill: A Life
Publisher: Henry Holt

143. DECEMBER 29, 1991
Jimmy Breslin
Damon Runyan: A Life
Publisher: Ticknor & Fields

144. JANUARY 5, 1992
Charles Hamilton
*Adam Clayton Powell, Jr.: The
Political Biography of an
American Dilemma*
Publisher: Atheneum

145. JANUARY 12, 1992
August Heckscher

Woodrow Wilson: A Biography
Publisher: Scribner

146. JANUARY 26, 1992
Frederick Downs
*No Longer Enemies, Not Yet
Friends: An American Soldier
Returns to Vietnam*
Publisher: Norton

147. FEBRUARY 2, 1992
Robert Cwiklik
*House Rules: A Freshman Con-
gressman's Initiation to the Back-
slapping, Backpedaling, and
Backstabbing Ways of Washington*
Publisher: Villard Books

148. FEBRUARY 9, 1992
Francis Fukuyama
*The End of History and the Last
Man*
Publisher: The Free Press

149. FEBRUARY 16, 1992
Al Gore
*Earth in the Balance: Ecology and
the Human Spirit*
Publisher: Houghton Mifflin

150. FEBRUARY 23, 1992 (PART
ONE)
Richard Nixon
*Seize the Moment: America's
Challenge in a One-Superpower
World*
Publisher: Simon & Schuster

151. MARCH 1, 1992 (PART
TWO)
Richard Nixon
*Seize the Moment: America's
Challenge in a One-Superpower
World*
Publisher: Simon & Schuster

152. MARCH 8, 1992
Robert Massie
*Dreadnought: Britain, Germany,
and the Coming of the Great War*
Publisher: Random House

153. MARCH 22, 1992
Linda Chavez
*Out of the Barrio: Toward a New
Politics of Hispanic Assimilation*
Publisher: Basic Books

154. MARCH 29, 1992
Nan Robertson
*The Girls in the Balcony: Women,
Men, and* The New York Times
Publisher: Random House

155. APRIL 5, 1992
Robert Remini
*Henry Clay: Statesman for the
Union*
Publisher: Norton

156. APRIL 12, 1992
Orlando Patterson
*Freedom in the Making of Western
Culture*
Publisher: Basic Books

157. APRIL 19, 1992
Paul Hollander
*Anti-Americanism: Critiques at
Home and Abroad, 1965–1990*
Publisher: Oxford University
Press

158. APRIL 26, 1992
Tinsley Yarbrough
*John Marshall Harlan: Great
Dissenter of the Warren Court*
Publisher: Oxford University
Press

159. MAY 3, 1992
Earl Black and Merle Black
*The Vital South: How Presidents
Are Elected*
Publisher: Harvard University
Press

160. MAY 10, 1992
David Moore
*The Superpollsters: How They
Measure and Manipulate Public
Opinion in America*
Publisher: Four Walls Eight
Windows

161. MAY 17, 1992
Robert Bartley
*The Seven Fat Years and How to
Do It Again*
Publisher: The Free Press

162. MAY 24, 1992
Lewis Puller, Jr.
*Fortunate Son: An Autobiography
of Lewis Puller, Jr.*
Publisher: Grove Weidenfeld

163. MAY 31, 1992
Lester Thurow
*Head to Head: The Coming
Economic Battle Among Japan,
Europe and America*
Publisher: Morrow

164. JUNE 7, 1992
R. Emmett Tyrell

The Conservative Crack-Up
Publisher: Simon & Schuster

165. JUNE 14, 1992
William Lee Miller
The Business of May Next: James Madison and the Founding
Publisher: The University Press of Virginia

166. JUNE 21, 1992
John Jackley
Hill Rat: Blowing the Lid Off Congress
Publisher: Regnery

167. JUNE 28, 1992
David Savage
Turning Right: The Making of the Rehnquist Supreme Court
Publisher: John Wiley & Sons

168. JULY 5, 1992
William Rehnquist
Grand Inquests: The Historic Impeachments of Justice Samuel Chase and President Andrew Johnson
Publisher: Morrow

169. JULY 12, 1992
Jeffrey Bell
Populism and Elitism: Politics in the Age of Equality
Publisher: Regnery

170. JULY 19, 1992
David McCullough
Truman: A Life and Times
Publisher: Simon & Schuster

171. JULY 26, 1992
Richard Ben Cramer
What It Takes: The Way to the White House
Publisher: Random House

172. AUGUST 2, 1992
Gilbert Fite
Richard B. Russell, Jr.: Senator From Georgia
Publisher: The University of North Carolina Press

173. AUGUST 9, 1992
Robert Donovan and Ray Scherer
Unsilent Revolution: Television News and American Public Life, 1948–1991
Publisher: Cambridge University Press

174. AUGUST 16, 1992
Martin Anderson
Imposters in the Temple: American Intellectuals Are Destroying Our Universities and Cheating Our Students of Their Future
Publisher: Simon & Schuster

175. AUGUST 23, 1992
Mickey Kaus
The End of Equality
Publisher: Basic Books

176. AUGUST 30, 1992
Neil Postman
Technopoly: The Surrender of Culture to Technology
Publisher: Knopf

177. SEPTEMBER 6, 1992
Terry Eastland
Energy in the Executive: The Case for the Strong Presidency
Publisher: The Free Press

178. SEPTEMBER 13, 1992
James Billington
Russia Transformed: Breakthrough to Hope
Publisher: The Free Press

179. SEPTEMBER 20, 1992
Paul Simon
Advice and Consent: Clarence Thomas, Robert Bork and the Intriguing History of the Supreme Court's Nomination Battles
Publisher: National Press Books

180. SEPTEMBER 27, 1992
Walter Isaacson
Kissinger: A Biography
Publisher: Simon & Schuster

181. OCTOBER 18, 1992
George Will
Restoration: Congress, Term Limits, and the Recovery of Deliberative Democracy
Publisher: The Free Press

182. OCTOBER 25, 1992
Susan Faludi
Backlash: The Undeclared War Against American Women
Publisher: Crown

183. NOVEMBER 8, 1992
Paul Brace and Barbara Hinkley
Follow the Leader: Opinion Polls and the Modern Presidents
Publisher: Basic Books

184. NOVEMBER 15, 1992
Derrick Bell
Faces at the Bottom of the Well: The Permanence of Racism
Publisher: Basic Books

185. NOVEMBER 22, 1992
General Norman Schwarzkopf
(with Peter Petre)
It Doesn't Take a Hero
Publisher: Bantam Books

186. NOVEMBER 29, 1992
Charles Sykes
A Nation of Victims: The Decay of the American Character
Publisher: St. Martin's Press

187. DECEMBER 6, 1992
Daniel Boorstin
The Creators: A History of Heroes of the Imagination
Publisher: Random House

188. DECEMBER 13, 1992
Brian Kelly
Adventures in Porkland: How Washington Wastes Your Money and Why They Won't Stop
Publisher: Villard Books

189. DECEMBER 20, 1992
Eric Alterman
Sound and Fury: The Washington Punditocracy and the Collapse of American Politics
Publisher: HarperCollins

190. DECEMBER 27, 1992
Michael Medved
Hollywood vs. America: Popular Culture and the War on Traditional Values
Publisher: HarperCollins

191. JANUARY 3, 1993
Hunter Clark and Michael Davis
Thurgood Marshall: Warrior at the Bar, Rebel on the Bench
Publisher: Carol Publishing Group

192. JANUARY 10, 1993
Jeffrey Birnbaum
The Lobbyists: How Influence Peddlers Get Their Way in Washington
Publisher: Times Books

193. JANUARY 17, 1993
P. F. Bentley
Clinton: Portrait of Victory
Publisher: Warner Books

194. JANUARY 24, 1993
Robert Gilbert
The Mortal Presidency: Illness and Anguish in the White House
Publisher: Basic Books

195. JANUARY 30, 1993
Benjamin Stein
A License to Steal: The Untold Story of Michael Milken and the Conspiracy to Bilk the Nation
Publisher: Simon & Schuster

196. FEBRUARY 7, 1993
Jack Nelson
Terror in the Night: The Klan's Campaign Against the Jews
Publisher: Simon & Schuster

197. FEBRUARY 14, 1993
Nathan Miller
Theodore Roosevelt: A Life
Publisher: Morrow

198. FEBRUARY 21, 1993
Richard Norton Smith
Patriarch: George Washington and the New American Nation
Publisher: Houghton Mifflin

199. FEBRUARY 28, 1993
Kay Mills
This Little Light of Mine: The Life of Fannie Lou Hamer
Publisher: Dutton

200. MARCH 6, 1993
Alex Dragnich
Serbs and Croats: The Struggle in Yugoslavia
Publisher: Harcourt Brace

201. MARCH 13, 1993
Paul Kennedy
Preparing for the Twenty-First Century
Publisher: Random House

202. MARCH 21, 1993
Deborah Shapley
Promise & Power: The Life and Times of Robert McNamara
Publisher: Little, Brown

203. MARCH 28, 1993
Michael Kelly
Martyrs' Day: Chronicle of a Small War
Publisher: Random House

204. APRIL 4, 1993
Nadine Cohodas
Strom Thurmond and the Politics of Southern Change
Publisher: Simon & Schuster

205. APRIL 11, 1993
Blanche Wiesen Cook
Eleanor Roosevelt: Volume 1, 1884–1933
Publisher: Viking

206. APRIL 18, 1993
Douglas Brinkley
The Majic Bus: An American Odyssey
Publisher: Harcourt Brace

207. APRIL 25, 1993
Lisa Belkin
First, Do No Harm: The Dramatic Story of Real Doctors and Patients Making Impossible Choices at a Big-City Hospital
Publisher: Simon & Schuster

208. MAY 2, 1993
Marshall DeBruhl
Sword of San Jacinto: A Life of Sam Houston
Publisher: Random House

209. MAY 9, 1993
Charles Adams
For Good and Evil: The Impact of Taxes on the Course of Civilization
Publisher: Madison Books

210. MAY 16, 1993
Anna Quindlen
Thinking Out Loud: On the Personal, the Political, the Public and the Private
Publisher: Random House

211. MAY 23, 1993
George Ball (and Douglas Ball)
The Passionate Attachment: America's Involvement with Israel, 1947 to the Present
Publisher: Norton

212. MAY 30, 1993
Douglas Davis
The Five Myths of Television Power: Or, Why the Medium is Not the Message
Publisher: Simon & Schuster

213. JUNE 6, 1993
J. Bowyer Bell
The Irish Troubles: A Generation of Violence, 1967–1992
Publisher: St. Martin's Press

214. JUNE 13, 1993
David Brock
The Real Anita Hill: The Untold Story
Publisher: The Free Press

215. JUNE 20, 1993
Howard Kurtz
Media Circus: The Trouble with America's Newspapers
Publisher: Times Books

216. JUNE 27, 1993
George Shultz
Turmoil and Triumph: My Years as Secretary of State
Publisher: Scribner

217. JULY 4, 1993
Joel Krieger
The Oxford Companion to Politics of the World
Publisher: Oxford University Press

218. JULY 11, 1993
David Halberstam
The Fifties
Publisher: Villard Books

219. JULY 18, 1993
Molly Moore
A Woman at War: Storming Kuwait with the U.S. Marines
Publisher: Scribner

220. JULY 25, 1993
David Remnick
Lenin's Tomb: The Last Days of the Soviet Empire
Publisher: Random House

221. AUGUST 1, 1993
Alexander Brook
The Hard Way: The Odyssey of a Weekly Newspaper Editor
Publisher: Bridge Works

222. AUGUST 8, 1993
Tom Rosenstiel
Strange Bedfellows: How Television and the Presidential Candidates Changed American Politics, 1992
Publisher: Hyperion

223. AUGUST 15, 1993
Lewis Lapham
The Wish for Kings: Democracy at Bay
Publisher: Grove Press

News Trade
Publisher: Putnam

255. APRIL 3, 1994
Andrew Young
A Way Out of No Way: The Spiritual Memoirs of Andrew Young
Publisher: Thomas Nelson Communications

256. APRIL 17, 1994
James Cannon
Time and Chance: Gerald Ford's Appointment with History
Publisher: HarperCollins

257. MAY 1, 1994
Howell Raines
Fly Fishing Through the Midlife Crisis
Publisher: Morrow

258. MAY 8, 1994
John Keegan
A History of Warfare
Publisher: Knopf

259. MAY 15, 1994
Forrest McDonald
The American Presidency: An Intellectual History
Publisher: University of Kansas Press

260. MAY 22, 1994
James McPherson
What They Fought For, 1861–1865
Publisher: Louisiana State University Press

261. MAY 29, 1994
Pete Hamill
A Drinking Life: A Memoir
Publisher: Little, Brown

262. JUNE 5, 1994
Stephen Ambrose
D-Day, June 6, 1944: The Climactic Battle of World War II
Publisher: Simon & Schuster

263. JUNE 12, 1994
Mark Neely
The Last Best Hope of Earth: Abraham Lincoln and the Promise of America
Publisher: Harvard University Press

264. JUNE 19, 1994
Sam Roberts
Who We Are: A Portrait of

America Based on the Latest U.S. Census
Publisher: Times Books

265. JUNE 26, 1994
Lani Guinier
The Tyranny of the Majority: Fundamental Fairness in a Representative Democracy
Publisher: The Free Press

266. JULY 3, 1994
Murray Kempton
Rebellions, Perversities, and Main Events
Publisher: Times Books

267. JULY 10, 1994
Cal Thomas
The Things That Matter Most
Publisher: HarperCollins

268. JULY 17, 1994
David Hackett Fischer
Paul Revere's Ride
Publisher: Oxford University Press

269. JULY 24, 1994
Dan Quayle
Standing Firm
Publisher: HarperCollins

270. JULY 31, 1994
Colman McCarthy
All of One Peace: Essays on Nonviolence
Publisher: Rutgers University Press

271. AUGUST 7, 1994
Peter Collier (with David Horowitz)
The Roosevelts: An American Saga
Publisher: Simon & Schuster

272. AUGUST 14, 1994
Merrill Peterson
Lincoln in American Memory
Publisher: Oxford University Press

273. AUGUST 21, 1994
Hugh Pearson
The Shadow of the Panther: Huey Newton and the Price of Black Power in America
Publisher: Addison-Wesley

274. AUGUST 28, 1994
John Leo
Two Steps Ahead of the Thought

Police
Publisher: Simon & Schuster

275. SEPTEMBER 4, 1994
Paul Weaver
News and the Culture of Lying: How Journalism Really Works
Publisher: The Free Press

276. SEPTEMBER 11, 1994
Shelby Foote
Stars in Their Courses: The Gettysburg Campaign
Publisher: Modern Library

277. SEPTEMBER 18, 1994
Irving Bartlett
John C. Calhoun: A Biography
Publisher: Norton

278. SEPTEMBER 25, 1994
Ben Yagoda
Will Rogers: A Biography
Publisher: Knopf

279. OCTOBER 2, 1994
Harry Jaffe and Tom Sherwood
Dream City: Race, Power, and the Decline of Washington, D.C.
Publisher: Simon & Schuster

280. OCTOBER 9, 1994
Henry Louis Gates, Jr.
Colored People: A Memoir
Publisher: Knopf

281. OCTOBER 16, 1994
Nicholas Kristoff and Cheryl Wudunn
China Wakes: The Struggle for the Soul of a Rising Power
Publisher: Times Books

282. OCTOBER 23, 1994
Liz Carpenter
Unplanned Parenthood: The Confessions of a Seventysomething Surrogate Mother
Publisher: Random House

283. OCTOBER 30, 1994
David Frum
Dead Right
Publisher: Basic Books

284. NOVEMBER 6, 1994
Bill Thomas
Club Fed: Power, Money, Sex, and Violence on Capitol Hill
Publisher: Scribner

285. NOVEMBER 13, 1994
John Kenneth Galbraith

This Side of Peace: A Personal Account
Publisher: Simon & Schuster

315. JUNE 11, 1995
Peter Brimelow
Alien Nation: Common Sense About America's Immigration Disaster
Publisher: Random House

316. JUNE 18, 1995
Yuri Shvets
Washington Station: My Life as a KGB Spy in America
Publisher: Simon & Schuster

317. JUNE 25, 1995
Norman Mailer
Oswald's Tale: An American Mystery
Publisher: Random House

318. JULY 2, 1995
Ari Hoogenboom
Rutherford B. Hayes: Warrior and President
Publisher: University of Kansas

319. JULY 9, 1995
DeWayne Wickham
Woodholme: A Black Man's Story of Growing Up Alone
Publisher: Farrar Straus Giroux

320. JULY 16, 1995
Armstrong Williams
Beyond Blame: How We Can Succeed by Breaking the Dependency Barrier
Publisher: The Free Press

321. JULY 23, 1995
Newt Gingrich
To Renew America
Publisher: HarperCollins

322. JULY 30, 1995
John Hockenberry
Moving Violations: A Memoir; War Zones, Wheelchairs, and Declarations of Independence
Publisher: Hyperion

323. AUGUST 6, 1995
Marc Fisher
After the Wall: Germany, the Germans, and the Burdens of History
Publisher: Simon & Schuster

324. AUGUST 13, 1995
Robert D. Richardson, Jr.

Emerson: The Mind on Fire
Publisher: University of California Press

325. AUGUST 20, 1995
Cartha DeLoach
Hoover's FBI: The Inside Story by Hoover's Trusted Lieutenant
Publisher: Regnery

326. AUGUST 27, 1995
Robert Timberg
The Nightingale's Song
Publisher: Simon & Schuster

327. SEPTEMBER 3, 1995
Robert Leckie
Okinawa: The Last Battle of World War II
Publisher: Viking

328. SEPTEMBER 10, 1995
Emory Thomas
Robert E. Lee: A Biography
Publisher: Norton

329. SEPTEMBER 17, 1995
Elsa Walsh
Divided Lives: The Public and Private Struggles of Three Accomplished Women
Publisher: Simon & Schuster

330. SEPTEMBER 24, 1995
Irving Kristol
Neoconservatism: The Autobiography of an Idea
Publisher: The Free Press

331. OCTOBER 1, 1995
Andrew Sullivan
Virtually Normal: An Argument About Homosexuality
Publisher: Knopf

332. OCTOBER 8, 1995
Susan Eisenhower
Breaking Free: A Memoir of Love and Revolution
Publisher: Farrar Straus Giroux

333. OCTOBER 15, 1995
Nicholas Basbanes
A Gentle Madness: Bibliophiles, Bibliomanes, and the Eternal Passion for Books
Publisher: Henry Holt

334. OCTOBER 22, 1995
David Fromkin
In the Time of Americans: The

Generation that Changed America's Role in the World
Publisher: Knopf

335. OCTOBER 29, 1995
Ben Bradlee
A Good Life: Newspapering and Other Adventures
Publisher: Simon & Schuster

336. NOVEMBER 5, 1995
Marlin Fitzwater
Call the Briefing! Reagan and Bush, Sam and Helen: A Decade with Presidents and the Press
Publisher: Times Books

337. NOVEMBER 12, 1995
Pierre Salinger
P.S., A Memoir
Publisher: St. Martin's Press

338. NOVEMBER 19, 1995
bell hooks
Killing Rage: Ending Racism
Publisher: Henry Holt

339. NOVEMBER 26, 1995
Sanford Ungar
Fresh Blood: The New American Immigrants
Publisher: Simon & Schuster

340. DECEMBER 3, 1995
James Baker (with Thomas DeFrank)
The Politics of Diplomacy: Revolution, War and Peace, 1989–1992
Publisher: Putnam

341. DECEMBER 10, 1995
David Brinkley
A Memoir
Publisher: Knopf

342. DECEMBER 17, 1995
Evan Thomas
The Very Best Men—Four Who Dared: The Early Years of the CIA
Publisher: Simon & Schuster

343. DECEMBER 24, 1995
David Herbert Donald
Lincoln
Publisher: Simon & Schuster

344. DECEMBER 31, 1995
Charles Kuralt
Charles Kuralt's America
Publisher: Putnam

345. JANUARY 7, 1996
Colin Powell (with Joseph
Persico)
My American Journey
Publisher: Random House

346. JANUARY 14, 1996
William Prochnau
*Once Upon a Distant War: Young
War Correspondents and the Early
Vietnam Battles*
Publisher: Times Books

347. JANUARY 21, 1996
Michael Kinsley
Big Babies
Publisher: Morrow

348. JANUARY 28, 1996
Carlo D'Este
Patton: A Genius for War
Publisher: HarperCollins

349. FEBRUARY 4, 1996
Dennis Prager
Think a Second Time
Publisher: HarperCollins

350. FEBRUARY 11, 1996
Lance Banning
*The Sacred Fire of Liberty: James
Madison and the Founding of the
Federal Republic*
Publisher: Cornell University
Press

351. FEBRUARY 18, 1996
Dan Balz (and Ronald
Brownstein)
*Storming the Gates: Protest
Politics and the Republican
Revival*
Publisher: Little, Brown

352. FEBRUARY 25, 1996
H. W. Brands
*The Reckless Decade: America in
the 1890s*
Publisher: St. Martin's Press

353. MARCH 3, 1996
Hillary Rodham Clinton
*It Takes a Village: And Other
Lessons Children Can Teach Us*
Publisher: Simon & Schuster

354. MARCH 10, 1996
Johanna Neuman
*Lights, Camera, War: Is Media
Technology Driving International
Politics?*
Publisher: St. Martin's Press

355. MARCH 17, 1996
Clarence Page
*Showing My Color: Impolite
Essays on Race and Identity*
Publisher: HarperCollins

356. MARCH 24, 1996
Robert Merry
*Taking On the World: Joseph and
Stewart Alsop—Guardians of the
American Century*
Publisher: Viking

357. MARCH 31, 1996
Fox Butterfield
*All God's Children: The Bosket
Family and the American
Tradition of Violence*
Publisher: Knopf

358. APRIL 7, 1996
Jean Baker
*The Stevensons: A Biography of an
American Family*
Publisher: Norton

359. APRIL 14, 1996
Wayne Fields
*Union of Words: A History of
Presidential Eloquence*
Publisher: The Free Press

360. APRIL 21, 1996
Robert Kaplan
*The Ends of the Earth: A Journey
at the Dawn of the 21st Century*
Publisher: Simon & Schuster

361. APRIL 28, 1996
David Reynolds
*Walt Whitman's America: A
Cultural Biography*
Publisher: Knopf

362. MAY 5, 1996
(Haynes Johnson and) David
Broder
*The System: The American Way of
Politics at the Breaking Point*
Publisher: Little, Brown

363. MAY 12, 1996
Stanley Crouch
*The All-American Skin Game, or
the Decoy of Race: The Long and
the Short of It, 1990–1994*
Publisher: Pantheon

364. MAY 19, 1996
Michael Sandel
*Democracy's Discontent: America
in Search of a Public Philosophy*

Publisher: Harvard University
Press

365. MAY 26, 1996
Noa Ben Artzi-Pelossof
In the Name of Sorrow and Hope
Publisher: Knopf

366. JUNE 2, 1996
James Thomas Flexner
*Maverick's Progress:
An Autobiography*
Publisher: Fordham University
Press

367. JUNE 9, 1996
Christopher Matthews
*Kennedy and Nixon: The Rivalry
That Shaped Postwar America*
Publisher: Simon & Schuster

368. JUNE 16, 1996
Albert Murray
*The Blue Devils of Nada: A
Contemporary American
Approach to Aesthetic Statement*
Publisher: Pantheon

369. JUNE 23, 1996
Seymour Martin Lipset
*American Exceptionalism: A
Double-Edged Sword*
Publisher: Norton

370. JUNE 30, 1996
Larry Sabato and Glenn Simpson
*Dirty Little Secrets: The Persis-
tence of Corruption in American
Politics*
Publisher: Times Books

371. JULY 7, 1996
Paul Greenberg
*No Surprises: Two Decades of
Clinton Watching*
Publisher: Brassey's

372. JULY 14, 1996
Theodore Sorensen
Why I Am a Democrat
Publisher: Henry Holt

373. JULY 21, 1996
Eleanor Randolph
*Waking the Tempests: Ordinary
Life in the New Russia*
Publisher: Simon & Schuster

374. JULY 28, 1996
James Lardner
*Crusader: The Hell-Raising Police
Career of Detective David Durk*
Publisher: Random House

A Biography
Publisher: Random House

402. MARCH 2, 1997
(PART TWO)
Sam Tanenhaus
Whittaker Chambers:
A Biography
Publisher: Random House

403. MARCH 9, 1997
Sarah Gordon
Passage to Union: How the
Railroads Transformed American
Life, 1829–1929
Publisher: Ivan R. Dee

404. MARCH 16, 1997
John Fialka
War by Other Means:
Economic Espionage in America
Publisher: Norton

405. MARCH 23, 1997
Jon Katz
Virtuous Reality: How America
Surrendered Discussion of
Moral Values to Opportunists,
Nitwits and Blockheads like
William Bennett
Publisher: Random House

406. MARCH 30, 1997
Claude Andrew Clegg III
An Original Man: The Life
and Times of Elijah
Muhammad
Publisher: St. Martin's Press

407. APRIL 6, 1997
Keith Richburg
Out of America:
A Black Man Confronts Africa
Publisher: Basic Books

408. APRIL 13, 1997
David Horowitz
Radical Son:
A Generational Odyssey
Publisher: The Free Press

409. APRIL 20, 1997
Leonard Garment
Crazy Rhythm: My Journey from
Brooklyn, Jazz, and Wall Street,
to Nixon's White House,
Watergate, and Beyond
Publisher: Times Books

410. APRIL 27, 1997
Stephen Oates
The Approaching Fury: Voices of

the Storm, 1820–1861
Publisher: HarperCollins

411. MAY 4, 1997
Christopher Buckley
Wry Martinis
Publisher: Random House

412. MAY 11, 1997
Richard Bernstein
(with Ross Munro)
The Coming Conflict with China
Publisher: Knopf

413. MAY 18, 1997
Anne Matthews
Bright College Years:
Inside the American
Campus Today
Publisher: Simon & Schuster

414. MAY 25, 1997
Jane Holtz Kay
Asphalt Nation: How the Auto-
mobile Took Over America, and
How We Can Take It Back
Publisher: Crown

415. JUNE 1, 1997
Jill Krementz
The Writer's Desk
Publisher: Random House

416. JUNE 8, 1997
Pavel Palazchenko
My Years with Gorbachev and
Shevardnadze: The Memoir of a
Soviet Interpreter
Publisher: Pennsylvania State
Press

417. JUNE 15, 1997
Walter McDougall
Promised Land, Crusader State:
The American Encounter with the
World Since 1776
Publisher: Houghton Mifflin

418. JUNE 22, 1997
James Humes
Confessions of a White House
Ghostwriter: Five Presidents and
Other Political Adventures
Publisher: Regnery

419. JUNE 29, 1997
Walter Cronkite
A Reporter's Life
Publisher: Knopf

420. JULY 6, 1997
Jack Rakove

Original Meanings:
Politics and Ideas in the Making
of the Constitution
Publisher: Knopf

421. JULY 13, 1997
Tom Clancy
(and Gen. Fred Franks [Ret.])
Into the Storm:
A Study in Command
Publisher: Putnam

422. JULY 20, 1997
Robert Hughes
American Visions: The Epic His-
tory of Art in America
Publisher: Knopf

423. JULY 27, 1997
Sylvia Jukes Morris
Rage for Fame: The Ascent of
Clare Boothe Luce
Publisher: Random House

424. AUGUST 3, 1997
LeAlan Jones
(and Loyd Newman)
Our America: Life and Death on
the South Side of Chicago
Publisher: Scribner

425. AUGUST 10, 1997
James Tobin
Ernie Pyle's War: America's Eye-
witness to World War II
Publisher: The Free Press

426. AUGUST 17, 1997
Pauline Maier
American Scripture:
Making the Declaration of
Independence
Publisher: Knopf

427. AUGUST 24, 1997
Peter Maas
Underboss: Sammy "The
Bull" Gravano's Story
of Life in the Mafia
Publisher: HarperCollins

428. AUGUST 31, 1997
Frank McCourt
Angela's Ashes: A Memoir
Publisher: Scribner

429. SEPTEMBER 7, 1997
Brian Burrell
The Words We Live By: The
Creeds, Mottoes, and Pledges That
Have Shaped America
Publisher: The Free Press

430. SEPTEMBER 14, 1997
John Toland
Captured by History: One Man's Vision of Our Tumultuous Century
Publisher: St. Martin's Press

431. SEPTEMBER 21, 1997
Peter Gomes
The Good Book: Reading the Bible with Mind and Heart
Publisher: Morrow

432. SEPTEMBER 28, 1997
John Berendt
Midnight in the Garden of Good and Evil: A Savannah Story
Publisher: Random House

433. OCTOBER 5, 1997
Howard Gardner
Extraordinary Minds: Portraits of Four Exceptional Individuals and an Examination of Our Own Extraordinariness
Publisher: Basic Books

434. OCTOBER 12, 1997
Geoffrey Perret
Ulysses S. Grant: Soldier and President
Publisher: Random House

435. OCTOBER 19, 1997
Nat Hentoff
Speaking Freely: A Memoir
Publisher: Knopf

436. OCTOBER 26, 1997
Alan Schom
Napoleon Bonaparte
Publisher: HarperCollins

437. NOVEMBER 2, 1997
Thomas West
Vindicating the Founders: Race, Sex, Class, and Justice in the Origins of America
Publisher: Rowman & Littlefield

438. NOVEMBER 9, 1997
Paul Nagel
John Quincy Adams: A Public Life, A Private Life
Publisher: Knopf

439. NOVEMBER 16, 1997
David Gelertner
Drawing Life: Surviving the Unabomber
Publisher: The Free Press

440. NOVEMBER 23, 1997
Anita Hill
Speaking Truth to Power
Publisher: Doubleday

441. NOVEMBER 30, 1997
Jeff Shesol
Mutual Contempt: Lyndon Johnson, Robert Kennedy, and the Feud That Defined a Decade
Publisher: Norton

442. DECEMBER 7, 1997
Tim Russert
Meet the Press: Fifty Years of History in the Making
Publisher: McGraw-Hill

443. DECEMBER 14, 1997
Susan Butler
East to the Dawn: The Life of Amelia Earhart
Publisher: Addison Wesley Longman

444. DECEMBER 21, 1997
Jim Hightower
There's Nothing in the Middle of the Road but Yellow Stripes and Dead Armadillos
Publisher: HarperCollins

445. DECEMBER 28, 1997
Sally Quinn
The Party: A Guide to Adventurous Entertaining
Publisher: Simon & Schuster

446. JANUARY 4, 1998
Paul Nagel
John Quincy Adams: A Public Life, a Private Life
Publisher: Knopf

447. JANUARY 11, 1998
Iris Chang
The Rape of Nanking: The Forgotten Holocaust of World War II
Publisher: Basic Books

448. JANUARY 18, 1998
Allan Metcalf (with David Barnhart)
America in So Many Words
Publisher: Houghton Mifflin

449. JANUARY 25, 1998
Daniel Pipes
Conspiracy: How the Paranoid Style Flourishes and Where It Comes From
Publisher: Free Press

450. FEBRUARY 1, 1998
Roger Simon
Show Time: The American Political Circus and the Race for the White House
Publisher: Times Books

451. FEBRUARY 8, 1998
Carol Reardon
Pickett's Charge in History and Memory
Publisher: The University of North Carolina Press

452. FEBRUARY 15, 1998
Joseph Hernon
Profiles in Character: Hubris and Heroism in the U.S. Senate, 1789–1990
Publisher: M.E. Sharpe, Inc.

453. FEBRUARY 22, 1998
William Gildea
Where the Game Matters Most
Publisher: Little, Brown

454. MARCH 1, 1998
John Lukacs
The Hitler of History
Publisher: Knopf

455. MARCH 8, 1998
John Marszalek
The Petticoat Affair: Manners, Mutiny and Sex in Andrew Jackson's White House
Publisher: The Free Press

456. MARCH 15, 1998
Randall Robinson
Defending the Spirit: A Black Life in America
Publisher: Dutton

457. MARCH 22, 1998
Ernest Lefever
The Irony of Virtue: Ethics and American Power
Publisher: Westview Press

458. MARCH 29, 1998
Douglas Wilson
Honor's Voice: The Transformation of Abraham Lincoln
Publisher: Knopf

459. APRIL 5, 1998
Paul Johnson
A History of the American People
Publisher: HarperCollins

460. APRIL 12, 1998
Taylor Branch

Pillar of Fire: America in the King Years 1963–65
Publisher: Simon & Schuster

461. APRIL 19, 1998
John S. D. Eisenhower
Agent of Destiny: The Life and Times of General Winfield Scott
Publisher: Free Press

462. APRIL 26, 1998
Molly Ivins
You Got to Dance with Them

What Brung You: Politics in the Clinton Years
Publisher: Random House

463. MAY 3, 1998
David Aikman
Great Souls: Six Who Changed the Century
Publisher: Word Publishing

464. MAY 10, 1998
Arthur J. Schlesinger, Jr.
The Disuniting of America
Publisher: Norton

465. MAY 17, 1998
Patrick Buchanan
The Great Betrayal: How American Sovereignty and Social Justice Are Being Sacrificed to the Gods of the Global Economy
Publisher: Little, Brown

466. MAY 24, 1998
Jill Ker Conway
When Memory Speaks: Reflections on Autobiography
Publisher: Knopf

Index